BHĀMATĪ AND VIVARAṆA SCHOOLS OF ADVAITA VEDĀNTA

A Critical Approach

अनिर्वाच्याविद्या-द्वितय-सचिवस्य प्रभवतो;
विवर्ता यस्यैते वियदनिलतेजोऽबवनयः।
यतश्चाभूद्विश्वं चरमचरमुच्चावचमिदं;
नमामस्तद्ब्रह्मापरिमित-सुखज्ञानममृतम्॥

—(*भामती* - *1.1.1.1*)

Anirvācyāvidyā-dvitaya-sacivasya prabhavato,
Vivartā yasyaite viyadanilatejo'bavanayaḥ;
Yataścābhūdviśvaṁ caramacaramuccāvacamidam;
Namāmastadbrahmāparimita-sukhajñānamamṛtam.

—(*Bhāmatī* - *1.1.1.1*)

पालने विमल-सत्त्व-वृत्तये।
जन्मकर्मणि रजोजुषे लये;
तामसाय जगतः पराकृत-
द्वैत-जाल-वपुषे नमः सते॥

—(*विवरण* - *1.1.1.1*)

Pālane vimala-sattva-vṛttaye
Janmakarmaṇi rajojuṣe laye;
Tāmasāya jagataḥ parākṛta-
Dvaita-jāla-vapuṣe namaḥ sate.

—(*Vivaraṇa* - *1.1.1.1*)

Bhāmatī and Vivaraṇa Schools of Advaita Vedānta

A Critical Approach

Pulasth Soobah Roodurmun

Foreword by

V.N. Jha

Edited by

Kanshi Ram

MOTILAL BANARSIDASS PUBLISHERS
PRIVATE LIMITED • DELHI

First Edition: 2002

ISBN: 81-208-1890-3

Also available at:

MOTILAL BANARSIDASS
41 U.A. Bungalow Road, Jawahar Nagar, Delhi 110 007
8 Mahalaxmi Chamber, 22 Bhulabhai Desai Road, Mumbai 400 026
120 Royapettah High Road, Mylapore, Chennai 600 004
236, 9th Main III Block, Jayanagar, Bangalore 560 011
Sanas Plaza, 1302 Baji Rao Road, Pune 411 002
8 Camac Street, Kolkata 700 017
Ashok Rajpath, Patna 800 004
Chowk, Varanasi 221 001

Printed in India
BY JAINENDRA PRAKASH JAIN AT SHRI JAINENDRA PRESS,
A-45 NARAINA, PHASE-I, NEW DELHI 110 028
AND PUBLISHED BY NARENDRA PRAKASH JAIN FOR
MOTILAL BANARSIDASS PUBLISHERS PRIVATE LIMITED,
BUNGALOW ROAD, DELHI 110 007

Dedicated to
My Revered Parents and Teachers,
and to
all *Seekers* of *Truth*

FOREWORD

It gives me great pleasure in writing a few words about the work of *Pulasth Soobah Roodurmun.* I have gone through the work and I am of the opinion that it is a work of a mature thinking.

The aim of this work has been to present in clear terms the distinct views of *Bhāmatī* and *Pañcapādikā-vivaraṇa* on various philosophical issues. These two great commentaries by two great philosophers, Vācaspati Miśra and Prakāśātman gave birth to the two schools of thought on Advaita Vedānta of Śaṅkara, popularly known as *Bhāmatī* school and *Vivaraṇa* school.

The present author has selected some important issues from the Advaita Philosophy like the theory of error, concepts of *Jīva, Jagat, Īśvara, Brahman,* and *Mokṣa* and has presented them with the views of both the schools in a very clear and cogent manner. He has been successful in highlighting both, the points of similarities and those of dissimilarities, between the views held by Vācaspati and Prakāśātman, and has left it to the readers to draw conclusions independently. All the conclusions of the author are authenticated by citing relevant texts from the respective commentaries. This has enhanced the authenticity of this work.

I am sure, this work will certainly help in understanding these two schools of Śāṅkara-Vedānta in particular and the Advaita Vedānta in general. I hope that the book is received with enthusiasm.

V.N. JHA

Director
C.A.S.S.
University of Pune
Pune-411 007

FOREWORD

PREFACE

While studying the Brahma-sūtra-bhāṣya of Śaṅkara at Post-Graduation level, I developed an interest in Advaita Vedānta thanks to the masterly treatment of the subject by scholars of the calibre of Dr. S.N. Nigam, Prof. B.R. Sharma, Prof. Raghunath Sharma and others. This interest was given a new fillip when I started studying the Bhāmatī from Dr. Kanshi Ram who, seeing my keen interest in the subject, suggested that I should do research in this very subject for my Ph.D. It was thus that the idea of undertaking an analytical study of the Bhāmatī and the Vivaraṇa was envisaged which has materialized in the form of this thesis.

I am, therefore, grateful to my Supervisor, Dr. Kanshi Ram, Reader, Department of Sanskrit, Hans Raj College, for having initiated me into the present study, and for the pains taken by him to meticulously go into each and every detail of the thesis, and for giving valuable suggestions for betterment all through. It goes without saying that this study would not have been accomplished in time but for his continuous and tireless support. I am also thankful to the Department of Sanskrit of the University of Delhi, in particular, Prof. S.P. Narang, Head of the Department, for his technical advice and support; Prof. P. Kumar, for his tacit support; Prof. B.R. Sharma, for his active interest and encouragement; Prof. A. Kumar, for taking personal interest with regard to the research project and for wider suggestions given by him from time to time; Prof. M.M. Agrawal, for all help, consideration and moral support. A word of thanks is also addressed to Prof. R.R. Pandey, Head of the Department of Philosophy, Banaras Hindu University, for his constructive suggestions.

I would fail in my duty if I were not to pay my respects to Dr. Ramashraya Sharma, my M. Phil Supervisor, who has been all along a source of inspiration for me. To him, therefore, I wish to express my deep gratitude.

Thanks are also due to the Librarian and Staff of the

Central Reference Library of the University of Delhi without whose co-operation this research work could not have been pursued successfully, and in the same breath, I want to convey a word of appreciation to the Principal and Staff of the Hans Raj College (University of Delhi) for all help and facilities extended to me.

The completion of this study was made possible by the financial and logistic support received from the Mahatma Gandhi Institute (Mauritius), the Tertiary Education Commission (Mauritius) and the University Grants Commission (Delhi). To all these institutions, and to Prof. Uttam Bissoondoyal, Director of the Mahatma Gandhi Institute in particular, I am therefore deeply indebted.

I would also like to express my gratitude to all the authors and Publishers whose works (as duly acknowledged) have contributed directly or indirectly to the writing of this thesis.

P.S. ROODURMUN

ABBREVIATIONS

APTR	:	Avidyā-A Problem of Truth and Reality (by E. Solomon)
AS	:	Advaita-Siddhi
ATIP	:	The Advaita Tradition In Indian Philosophy (by C.D. Sharma)
AVLBS	:	Advaita Vedānta Literature—A Bibliographical Survey (by R. Thangaswami)
Bṛh. Up	:	Bṛhadāraṇyaka Upaniṣad
BS	:	Brahma-Sūtra (of Bādarāyaṇa)
Ch. Up.	:	Chandogya Upaniṣad
EIP	:	The Encyclopedia of Indian Philosophies (by Karl H. Potter)
EOR	:	Encylopedia of Religion
fn	:	Foot-note
HEVP	:	A History of Early Vedānta Philosophy (by H. Nakamura)
HIP	:	A History of Indian Philosophy (by S.N. Dasgupta)
IS	:	Iṣṭa-Siddhi
Ka.Up.	:	Kaṭhopaniṣad
KK	:	Kāśikā (on ŚV)
LV	:	Lights on Vedānta (by V.P. Upādhyāya)
Mbh	:	Mahābhārata
MK	:	Mādhyamika Kārikā
MS	:	Mīmāṁsā-Sūtra (of Jaimini)
NR	:	Nyāyaratnākara (of Pārthasārathi)
NS	:	Nyāya-Sūtra (of Gautama)
PA	:	The Philosophy of Advaita (by T.M.P. Mahadevan)
PB	:	Praśastapādabhāṣya (on VS)
PD	:	Pañcadaśī
PP	:	Prakaraṇa-Pañcikā (of Śālikanātha)

PPD	:	Pañcapādikā of Padmapāda (by D.Venkataramiah)
ṚV	:	Ṛg Veda
ŚV	:	Śloka-Vārttika (on MS)
SB	:	Śāṅkara-bhāṣya
SD	:	Śāstradīpikā (of Pārthasārathi)
SPB	:	Sāṅkhya-Pravacana-bhāṣya (on SS)
SPS	:	Sāṅkhya-Pravacana-Sūtra
SS	:	Sāṅkhya-Sūtra (of Kapila)
SSV	:	Sāṅkhya-Sūtra-Vārttika (on SS)
Tai. Up.	:	Taittirīya Upaniṣad
TOV	:	The Tradition of Vedānta (by R. Balasubramanian)
TS	:	Tarka-Saṅgraha
UOM	:	University of Madras
Vāt. B.	:	Vātsyāyana-bhāṣya (on NS)
VB	:	Vyāsa-bhāṣya (on YS)
VPP	:	Vedānta-Prakriyā-Pratyabhijñā (by Sw. Satchidanandendra Saraswati)
VPS	:	Vivaraṇa-Prameya-Saṅgraha (by Vidyāraṇya)
VS	:	Vaiśeṣika-Sūtra (of Kaṇāda)
YD	:	Yuktidīpikā
YS	:	Yoga-Sūtra (of Patañjali)
YV	:	Yoga-Vārttika (on YS)

CONTENTS

CHAPTER I

INTRODUCTION

The *Bhāmatī*, as it is well known, is the name of the Commentary written by Vācaspati Miśra on the *Brahmasūtra-Śāṅkara-bhāṣya*, while the *Pañcapādikā-Vivaraṇa*, also known as the *Vivaraṇa*, is the Commentary written by Prakāśātman on the *Pañcapādikā* which itself is another Commentary on the *Brahmasūtra-Śāṅkara-bhāṣya* written by Padmapāda, a close disciple of Śaṅkara.

The *Bhāmatī* and the *Vivaraṇa* assumed so much importance in the realm of Advaita Vedānta that the very trend of Advaita philosophy was given a new direction with their advent. So influential were they that each one came to be known eventually as an independent school of thought. Hence the appellations *Bhāmatī-Prasthāna* and *Vivaraṇa-Prasthāna* by which they are respectively known today in philosophical circles. Vācaspati Miśra, it is believed[1], belonged to a tradition of Advaita Vedānta known as the *Prasaṅkhyānavāda* which believed in the "Theory of Continuous Meditation" or "Meditation Theory"[2]. According to this theory, contrary to what is propounded by the *Samuccayavādins*, the performance of *karma-s* does not contribute to the attainment of *Brahman*-knowledge. The aspirant, it claims, should indeed have renounced all *karma-s* before undertaking the practice of meditating on the meaning of the *mahāvākya*, *"Tat tvam asi"*. It also believes that even 'Right Knowledge' produced by Vedāntic teaching may be sublated by incorrect knowledge[3]. As a true follower of Maṇḍana Miśra, Vācaspati Miśra endorses the former's view that "no injunction is necessary for the practice of meditation, since there are instances in ordinary life of the repetition of knowledge giving rise to correct knowledge'[4]. Prakāśātman, who was on the other hand, a disciple of Ananyānubhava, is the most important successor of Padmapāda. Though Prakāśātman's philosophical theories emanate mostly from the *Pañcapādikā*, yet his contribution to Advaita Vedānta proved so significant that he outclassed even Padmapāda and took the lead of the

Advaita tradition from his no-less able predecessors. His famous work, the *Pañcapādikā-Vivaraṇa*, home to many innovative and revolutionary philosophical ideas, such as, Self-Realization resulting directly from Verbal authority, *Avidyā* being the cause of the false appearances as well as of their knowledge, 'reasoning' as an aid to the realization of Truth, etc., commanded so much authority and respect that contemporary Advaita Vedānta came to be identified with the *Vivaraṇa-Prasthāna*, "thus almost supplanting the *Pañcapādikā* and the *Iṣṭa-Siddhi*"[5].

It is indeed due to this indisputable importane of these two schools represented by the *Bhāmatī* and the *Vivaraṇa*, that the present study was initiated. This consists of a critical analysis of the *Bhāmatī* and the *Vivaraṇa*, bringing to light the main tenets of Advaita Vedānta as propounded by Vācaspati Miśra and Prakāśātman, showing thereby the points of agreement and disagreement between the two schools.

As per information gathered from different sources, it is clear that not much research work has been attempted till date in this area. Some light, it is true, has been thrown on the lives and works of Vācaspati Miśra and Prakāśātman and their philosophy, but a critical analysis of their philosophical schemes as proposed herein has not been hitherto attempted, as is evident from the account given below. Among the works available, the following are worth mentioning:

1. Dubey, Rajendra Prasad—Vācaspati Miśra—Jīvanī Aur Siddhānta, Capital Publishing House, Delhi, 1981. The book deals principally with the life and works of Vācaspati Miśra, including an account of his views on *Avidyā* and *Ātman*.
2. Dubey, Rajendra—Vācaspati Darśanam (in Sanskrit), Classical Publishing Company, Delhi, 1983. In this book the author has focussed on Vācaspati's concepts of *Brahman* and *Avidyā*.
3. Īśvara Singh, Dr.—Bhāmatī: Eka Adhyayana, Manthan Publications, Rohtak, 1983. This book throws some light on pre-Śaṅkara and post-Śaṅkara Vedānta, with emphasis on the contribution of Vācaspati Miśra to Indian Philosophy with special reference to the Bhāmatī.
4. Rao, V.N. Sheshgiri—Vacaspati's Contribution to Advaita Vedānta, Samvit Publishers, Mysore, 1984. This work surveys the life and thought of Vācaspati in the context of the Bhāmatī. It develops certain points discussed by S.S. Hasurkar

in his book, "Vācaspati Miśra on Advaita Vedānta". (Darbhanga, 1958).

On the *Vivaraṇa* as well, a few research works have been undertaken, specially on the *Vivaraṇa-prameya-saṅgraha* of Vidyāraṇya Muni. Among these, the following are noteworthy:

1. Dvivedi, Sudhakar—Vivaraṇa-Prameya-Saṅgraha Mein Avidyā Kā Svarūpa, M. Phil. dissertation, University of Delhi, 1984.
2. Gupta, Shashi — Vidyāraṇyakṛta Vivaraṇa-Prameya-Saṅgraha ke Antargata Ābhāsa-Prakaraṇa—Eka Adhyayana, Ph.D. thesis, University of Delhi, 1986.
3. Sengupta, Bratīndra Kumar—A Critique of the Vivaraṇa School, Calcutta, 1959.

Apart from these works, a few research articles have also been published both on the *Bhāmatī* and the *Vivaraṇa.* Here are a few of them :

1. (1963)—Rao, Sheshagiri—Vācaspati Miśra on Sādhana-catuṣṭaya, Tattvāloka.
2. (1964)—Cammann, Klaus—Reflections on the Validity of Knowledge in the Vivaraṇa, Journal of Oriental Research, Madras.
3. (1968)—Sengupta, Bratīndra Kumar—'Prakāśātman', Preceptors of Advaita.
4. (1969)—Mukherjee, J.C.—Vācaspati Miśra on Illusion, Indian Philosophy and Culture.
5. (1979)—Mukherjee, J.C.—Vācaspati Miśra on the Place of Karma in Sādhanā, Journal of Mysore University.
6. (1985)—Śaṅkaranārāyaṇa, S.—The Colophon in the Bhāmatī—A New Study, Brahmavidyā (Adyar Library Bulletin, Madras).
7. (1987)—Rao, Sheshagiri—The Distinctive Contribution of Vācaspati Miśra to Advaita, The Voice of Śaṅkara.
8. (1990)—Ranganath, S.—Vācaspati's Interpretation of the Sūtra *"Śāstrayonitvāt"*, The Voice of Śaṅkara.

It is clear from the account given above that none of the works available so far covers amply the study being proposed herein. It is, therefore, hoped that the present research work will be accepted as an attempt, however humble, to answer a long-felt need in this field. It needs to be pointed out here that the present study focuses on the *Bhāmatī* and the *Pañcapādikā-Vivaraṇa,* and not on the Bhāmatī School and the Vivaraṇa School as such. Attention needs also to be drawn to the fact that barring an English translation of the *Catuḥsūtrī* portion of the *Bhāmatī,* by S.S. Suryanarayana Sastri and C. Kunhan Raja, and an unpublished English translation of the first *Varṇaka* of the *Vivaraṇa* by S.S. Suryanarayana Sastri, no other translation of these works has come to light whether in India or elsewhere. From this point of view also the present study assumes special significance. The present study is based mainly as per necessity on the original texts of the *Bhāmatī* and the *Vivaraṇa,* contained in the following editions of the *Brahma-sūtra-Śāṅkara-bhāṣya* and of the *Pañcapādikā* respectively:

(a) Brahma-Sūtra-Śāṅkara-Bhāṣya with *Bhāmatī,* Kalpataru and Parimala, edited by K.L. Joshi and Published in 1982 by the Parimal Publications, Delhi.
(b) Brahma-Sūtra-Śāṅkara-Bhāṣya with *Bhāmatī,* Kalpataru and Parimal, edited by Anantakrishna Śāstrī and published in 1982 by the Chowkhamba Series Office, Varanasi.
(c) Pañcapādikā with Pañcapādikā-*Vivaraṇa,* edited by T. Chandrashekharan and published in 1958 by the Government Oriental Manuscripts Library, Madras.
(d) Pañcapādikā (with *Vivaraṇa*), edited by S.S. Subramaṇya Śāstrī and published in 1992 by Mahesha Research Institute, Varanasi.

The present thesis is divided into eight chapters inclusive of the Introduction and the Conclusion. As per requirement, the chapters have been subdivided into different sections dealing principally with the *Bhāmatī* and the *Vivaraṇa,* with a general introduction in the first section and a summary in the last. With a view to situating the Advaita Vedānta, in particular, the *Bhāmatī* and the *Vivaraṇa* in the context of Indian Philosophy, a survey of the Advaita tradition has been undertaken in the second chapter, tracing back its root to the Ṛg Veda where allusions are found to have been made to Advaita doctrines such as the concepts of *Māyā,* one Supreme Being, and *Vivarta,* etc. The same concepts were taken up subsequently by ancient Advaita teachers, such as Ātreya, Āśmarathya, Auḍulomi, etc., who developed these ideas further, paving thus the way for Bādarāyaṇa, Upavarṣa and Bhartṛhari, etc. The advent of Gauḍapāda saw the rejuvenation of the *Advaita* tradition, especially with the composition by him of the *Māṇḍūkya-kārikā*. But it was Śaṅkara who, following closely the footprints of the latter and his pupil Govindapāda, took the Advaita tradition to its zenith through the composition by him of the all-time philosophical master-piece, the *Śārīraka-bhāṣya* (or *Śāṅkara-bhāṣya*, as it came to be known) on the *Brahma-sūtra* (or *Vedānta-Sūtra*) of *Bādarāyaṇa*. The interpretation of Śaṅkara's *Bhāṣya* by Padmapāda, Sureśvara and Maṇḍana, all direct disciples of the former, gave rise to further deliberations on Śaṅkara's philosophy and led to the emergence of two distinct schools of thought within the fold of Advaita, viz., the *Bhāmatī* School and the *Vivaraṇa* School as a sequel to the writing of the *Bhāmatī* and the *Vivaraṇa* respectively.

The concept of Error, which in Śāṅkara Vedānta is alluded to as *Adhyāsa*, is taken up for a detailed discussion in chapters third and fourth, this being the basis on which the Advaitin-s declare that the world is a mere illusion while the *Jīva* is no other than *Brahman*. That the concept of *Adhyāsa* occupies a central place in Śaṅkara's philosophy becomes evident from the fact that Śaṅkara finds it imperative to first analyse this concept in its depth before starting his commentary on the *Brahma-sūtra*. This is so because it provides an irreproachable argument for the justification of the unity of Self as proclaimed in the Upaniṣads, which defies being explained in the face of the difficulties encountered in this context on the empirical plane. As a prelude to this discussion, therefore, the theories of Error propounded by the non-Advaita Schools have been critically analysed in the third chapter, in which have been reviewed successively the following theories of Error: *Anyathākhyāti*, *Sadasatkhyāti*, *Viparīta-khyāti* and (*Viveka*) *Akhyāti*, *Asatkhyāti*, *Ātmakhyāti* and *Satkhyāti*.

This chapter concludes with a discussion showing the inadequacy of the non-Advaita theories of Error in supplying a satisfactory explanation of the phenomenon of Illusion. Hence it is that in the fourth chapter, the theory of *Anirvacanīyakhyāti* propounded by the Advaitin-s as the only sound explanation of *Adhyāsa*, is discussed with special reference to the *Bhāmatī* and the

Vivaraṇa. This chapter analyses the Advaita claim that *Adhyāsa* is as beginningless and indeterminable a phenomenon as its cause, viz. *Māyā* or *Avidyā*, and that it can be sublated by Knowledge (of the true nature of *Brahman*) alone.

This discussion leads inevitably to an analysis in Chapter fifth, of the concepts of *Jīva, Īśvara* and *Jagat*, which lays bare the fundamental differences that separate the *Bhāmatī* and the *Vivaraṇa* from each other. These differences are noticed more specifically with regard to the problem of the locus of *Avidyā* related to which is the problem of the multiplicity of *Avidyā*. Linked to this is the question of *Māyā* and *Avidyā* being one and the same phenomenon, or separate phenomena. Also discussed herein are the theories of *Avacchedavāda* and *Bimba-pratibimba-vāda* that again point to the controversy existing between the two schools on the question of the nature of *Jīva-Brahman*-identity. The third view on this subject, viz., that of *Ābhāsavāda* is also roped in here along side the other two for the sake of comparison.

The Advaita doctrine that *Brahman* is the sole Reality, with *Jīva* as non-different from It, is discussed in depth in the sixth chapter. The views of the *Bhāmatī* and those of the *Vivaraṇa* that concern the nature of *Brahman* have been dealt with here together with the doctrine that *Sat, Cit, Ānanda* are but the very essence of *Brahman* and not Its attributes. Also analysed herein are the questions of omniscience and omnipotence attributed to *Brahman*. This discussion on *Brahman* touches also upon the doctrine that *Brahman* is both the efficient cause and the material cause of the world. The question of *Brahman* being the origin of the Veda-s, giving thus credence to their eternality and to the absoluteness of their authority concerning *Brahman*, is also dealt with in this chapter.

The discussion on the concept of *Mokṣa* that constitutes chapter seventh, reveals still further the divergence of views that exists between the *Bhāmatī* and the *Vivaraṇa*, with regard more specifically to the nature of *Mokṣa* and the means to its attainment. This chapter includes, therefore, an analysis of the question as to whether *śravaṇa, manana, nididhyāsana* are the objects of injunctions or not. It also looks at the problem of the efficacy of rites, rituals and purificatory acts in the process of the attainment of Knowledge. The other point of disagreement that is taken up here for discussion is whether or not Verbal Testimony leads, on its own, to *Brahman*-knowledge. The chapter concludes with an analysis of the concept of *Brahmāvagati* or final Release and its nature, and also of the attainment of *Jīvan-mukti* and the nature of the *Jīvan-mukta*.

Chapter eighth concludes the whole discussion and reviews the conclusions arrived at as a result of this study.

Notes

1. Vide, Sw. Satchidānandendra Saraswatī–"Naishkarmya-Siddhi", pp.17-18 (Adhyātma Prakāsha Kāryālaya, Holenarsipur, 1968).
2. Karl H. Potter, EOI, Vol. I.
3. Sw. Satchidānandendra Saraswatī, Op. Cit.
4. Ibid.
5. Vide, Vedānta-Prakriyā-Pratyabhijñā, pp.119-120.

CHAPTER II

HISTORICAL BACKGROUND OF ADVAITA VEDĀNTA

A. Pre-Śaṅkara Advaita

'Vedānta' is a general term used to denote the philosophy of the Upaniṣads, which are themselves philosophical discourses held by the Vedic Seers over a range of more than a thousand years. The *Vedānta* Philosophy, and for that matter the philosophy of *Advaita Vedānta,* therefore, cannot be anterior to the Vedic Scriptures as such. The fact is that *Advaita* Philosophy emerged, side by side with other *Vedāntic* traditions, with the emergence of Upaniṣadic Literature. In common parlance, *Advaita Vedānta* is mainly attributed to Śaṅkara, due especially to his '*expose*' on the "*Prasthāna-trayī*", i.e., the *Brahma-sūtra,* the ten *Upaniṣads,* and the *Bhagavad-gītā,* which together, form the very basis of *Advaita* Philosophy. Among these, the *Śārīraka-bhāṣya* of Śaṅkara on the *Brahma-sūtra,* also known as the *Śāṅkara-bhāṣya* for obvious reason, is considered to be the main pillar of *Advaita Vedānta.*

But *Advaita Vedānta per se* did not originate with the composition of the *Brahma-sūtra* nor with the advent of Śaṅkara. As a matter of fact, both Bādarāyaṇa, the author of the *Brahma-sūtra,* and Śaṅkara, the author of the *Śārīraka-bhāṣya* (commentary) on the *Brahma-sūtra,* have referred to some ancient teachers and schools belonging to the Advaita tradition in their respective work(s) at more than one place, as will be seen hereinafter. Bādarāyaṇa, for example, makes allusion (s) to teachers like, Āśmarathya, Auḍulomi and Kāśakṛtsna[1], etc., while Śaṅkara, referring to "his" "*Sampradāya*" (i.e. tradition), quotes certain old teachers "with the reverence appropriate to the elders of a tradition one accepts"[2]. The latter and his pupils make constant references to certain "*Vṛttikāra-s*" (authors of subcommentaries on the *Brahma-sūtra*), in their works, and specially to a "*Śārīrakamīmāṁsā-vṛtti*" (i.e., a sub-commentary on the *Brahma-sūtra*), whose author is named as Upavarṣa. Śaṅkara considers this commentator as a member of his own tradition, and refers to him in reverence as "*Bhagavān*". About ninety-nine such "*vṛtti-s*" are referred to in the *Śārīraka-bhāṣya* where Śaṅkara even refutes some of them. The references given above are so significant that it becomes imperative to survey the old Advaita tradition which may be called the "*mystic*" tradition, as in most cases not much is known about the teachers referred to above, apart from their names, and in some cases, their thoughts and works.

Advaita Vedānta lays great emphasis on proving both the immanence and the transcendence of *Brahman*, the Supreme Being, in this world which is seemingly plural and which is of an illusory nature. This notion of Absolutism forms the central teaching of the Upaniṣads. "The Absolute is called "*Brahman*" or "*Ātman*", the transcendental unity underlying the subject and the object. The word '*Ātman*' here does not mean the individual self (*Jīvātman*) which is an appearance, but the foundational Self, the self-luminous and the self-proved Real which is the innermost Being of each individual"[3]. The Upaniṣads describe this Supreme Soul as "Being, Consciousness and Infinitude"[4] or as "Consciousness and Bliss"[5]. It is beyond senses, thought and speech and can be indirectly indicated through negative predicates ("*neti-neti*")[6].... The three states of empirical consciousness viz. waking, dream and deep sleep, are analysed with respect to their individual and cosmic reference, and the Aboslute is declared to be the Fourth ("*Turīya*"), the Measureless ("*Amātra*"), the Ineffable foundational Self, which is immanent in all the three states and yet transcends them all"[7].

This concept of an Absolute *Brahman* reigning supreme over the world of sentient and insentient creatures, seems in all evidence to have been first propounded by Yājñavalkya, and to him therefore would go the credit of being the first exponent of Advaita Vedānta. In the Bṛhadāraṇyaka Upaniṣad, (III. 7), Yājñavalkya is found expounding first the immanent and the transcendent nature of *Brahman* separately, and then proceeding to show that "these two poises are not of two different Reals but of the same Supreme, whose essential nature as non-dual spiritual experience is not at all affected by the apparent change and multiplicity of the world". Yājñavalkya tells Uddālaka that *Brahman* is the **thread-self** ("*Sūtrātman*"), which runs through, binds and controls all from within, is the immanent innermost Self ("*Antaryāmin*") of all[8]. "All things form His body, He is the immanent inner controller of all things, He is the Self, the Immortal", Says Yājñavalkya[9]. The Advaita concept of *Māyā*, like that of *Brahman*, can also be traced back to the Ṛg Veda where reference has been made to the Supreme Being appearing in multiple forms through *Māyā*[10]. The concealing nature of *Avidyā* as propounded in Advaita Vedānta finds its origin in the Kaṭha Upaniṣad where people acting under the spell of *Avidyā* (Ignorance or Nescience) are compared to blind people". It is not difficult to infer from this that *Avidyā* is blinding in nature. It is this very notion that we find developed in Advaita Vedānta in the form of the "concealing potency (*āvaraṇa śakti*) of *Avidyā*[11]. The concept of the phenomenality of the world is also traceable to the Upaniṣadic Wisdom. The Chāndogya Upaniṣad, for example, says that in the beginning there was only *Sat*, without a second[12], and describes everything apart from the One Reality as mere "words", "modes" and "names"[13]. That the worldly creatures are veiled by falsity, as is discussed by Śaṅkara in the *Adhyāsabhāṣya*, is also revealed by the Upaniṣadic Seers who indicated also the way out of this sorrowful world[14]. The Advaitic influences in the Vedic Scriptures are so significant that the author of *Brahma-sūtra* finds it unavoidable to refer to a number of teachers as his predecessors, implying that Advaita Vedānta has had a long tradition in the sphere of philosophical deliberation in India. Consequently, it is found that, apart from the three teachers mentioned above, many others, such as Ātreya, Bādari, Jaimini, Kārṣṇājini, Upavarṣa, Bhartṛprapañca, Draviḍācārya, Ṭaṅka, etc., are referred to by both Bādarāyaṇa and Śaṅkara. Among these, Ātreya, who was a pupil of Vāmadeva according to the Mahābhārata[15], was a student of non-dualism. "According to Bādarāyaṇa, the teacher Ātreya believed that agentship in meditation belongs to the master (or lord of the ceremony).... Jaimini adds that....according to Ātreya this fruit is real and genuine....In all likelihood he upheld the view of gradual combination of "*Karma* and *Jñāna*" (for the attainment of "Mokṣa)[16]. Āśmarathya, another ancient teacher quoted by

Bādarāyaṇa[17], believed on his part that "Vaiśvānara, the First-Principle, is well established inside every person"[18]. He is of the opinion that *Brahman* 'manifests himself in the form of a body for the sake of worshippers'. Vide,

"Abhivyakterityāśmarathyaḥ" (BS. I.2.29)

Later mystics interpreted this as meaning the "manifestation of *Brahman* as an incarnation of God. It takes place in the heart of the devotee....This is the reason why mystics experience such supernatural objects as unstruck sound, contactless touch, non-objective smell, absolute taste and the like"[19]. The *Brahma-sūtra* quotes Āśmarathya as also interpreting the Vedic injunction "*draṣṭavya*" (*to be seen*), saying that it should be regarded as a 'sign indicative of the fulfilment of the declaration-"*when Ātman has been known, this all is known*"[20]. "From this Śaṅkara rightly understands that Āśmarathya's statement of identity is a qualified one and (what) he means (is) that there is some sort of causal relationship between the individual consciousness and the Supreme Consciousness. Thus the view of Āśmarathya is not Non-dualism....but..essential Identity-cum-difference. Thus according to Āśmarathya the individual consciousness is essentially identical to, and essentially different from, the Supreme Consciousness"[21].

Against the view of Ātreya quoted above, Auḍulomi, another teacher of ancient age, holds that the fruit of a sacrifice goes to the priest, and not to the master of the ceremony. This view of Auḍulomi was favoured by Śaṅkara, though the latter reconciled both the views and held that there is no harm in maintaining that the priest cannot be connected to the fruit of a sacrifice since he serves the purpose of another person. The fruit of the sacrifice goes partly to the master and partly to the priest. The master gets the fruit that is described in the Scriptures and the priest gets the fruit in the form of rewards and his own personal purification[22]. Auḍulomi's view with regard to the *Jīva-Brahman*-identity is of particular interest. He is of the opinion that the identity between the individual soul and *Brahman* is of the nature of becoming[23]. Commenting on Auḍulomi's view about the *Jīva-Brahman*-identity, Śaṅkara says that "according to Auḍulomi, both difference and non-difference become clearly discernible as bound up with the different states of the soul under bondage and freedom"[24]. On his part, commenting on Auḍulomi's view, Vācaspati says that, "in the stage of the world where there is difference between the individual soul and *Brahman* there is also an identity which is to be or to become". He says further that "there are two stages of this relation, the stage of the world and the stage of *Mokṣa.* In the state of *Mokṣa,* there is perfect identity between the individual soul and *Brahman,* while in the state of the world there is perfect difference between them"[25]. Auḍulomi says (further) that the liberated soul becomes established in Consciousness as Consciousness itself, that being its true nature"[26]. It can therefore be said that Auḍulomi believed in "The theory of double truths", viz., "empirical truth" and transcendental truth". It appears also that he believed in the efficacy of meditation and made a synthesis of meditation (*Upāsanā*) and knowledge (*Jñāna*) for the realization of *Brahman*[27].

But Bādari, of the same tradition, seems to be closer to *Śāṅkara Advaita* than the other ancient teachers referred to so far. He is quoted in the *Brahma-sūtra* as being of the opinion that, "when *Brahman* is said to have assumed some form in the heart of the seeker this description is only for the sake of remembering *Brahman*"[28]. Bādari believed also that when a person realizes *Brahman* and attains *Mokṣa,* the body together with the sense-organs gets dissolved and does not continue to exist any further. There exists neither body nor sense-organs in the liberated individual self"[29]. Bādari, quite in line with Advaita Metaphysics, says also that when movement or motion is ascribed to *Brahman,* it is the lower *Brahman* that is meant, not the higher *Brahman*[30].

It is believed that apart from the *Brahman-sūtra* compiled by Bādarāyaṇa, there was yet at least one other *Brahma-sūtra* known to the old Advaita tradition, and which is believed to have been composed by Jaimini, the author of the *Mīmāṁsā-sūtra.* This is probably the reason why Bādarāyaṇa quotes Jamini at as many as eleven places in his own work. Though Jamini's *Brahma-sūtra* is now considered to have been lost, yet he is believed to have been a Vedāntist of the old tradition, apart from being a *Mīmāṁsaka*[31]. This may explain also the reason for which he was given such importance in the extant *Brahma-sūtra.* Jaimini's views were so prominent among the

Vedāntists that even Śaṅkara is seen approving these views in his *Śārīraka-bhāṣya*. An instance of this is the view that "when Vaiśvānara is said to be merely one span long (*"prādeśamātra"*), it is merely in a figurative sense that this is said"[32]. Jaimini believed also that Vaiśvānara is the Supreme Being in the real sense of the term. No meditation is required for the realization of *Vaiśvānara-Brahman*-identity according to Jaimini[33]. Jaimini is also quoted by Śaṅkara as upholding the view that the passages occurring in the Upaniṣads with regard to the nature of the individual soul have the explanation of the concept of *Brahman* as their real purpose[34]. According to Jaimini, once a *seeker* reaches a higher stage in spiritual pursuit, there is no coming down for him (to a lower stage)[35]. As though clearing the way for Śaṅkara, Jaimini says in addition that "the Self is free from sin, and is Truthful, All-knower, All-ruler etc. These are the real and natural characters of the Self"[36].

In the backdrop of such a long tradition of Advaita Vedānta appeared *Bādarāyaṇa* and his *Brahma-sūtra*. Bādarāyaṇa, also known as Bādarāyaṇa Vyāsa, or simply Vyāsa, whose time is generally agreed[37] to be C. 300BCE, is said to have "resuscitated the *Brāhmaṇic* way of life and thought by reorganising, systematising, simplifying, and popularising it"[38]. As the Upaniṣadic teachings were often "sheer flashes of spiritual radiance" and not a coherent system of Philosophy, it became necessary in due course, to systematise them and present them in a harmonious form so that they may prove to be more" reasonably meaningful". This herculean and yet revolutionary task was undertaken by Bādarāyaṇa which culminated in the composition of the philosophical master-piece of all time, the "*Brahma-sūtra*", also known under various names, such as the '*Vedānta-sūtra*', the '*Śārīraka-sūtra*', the '*Uttara-mīmāṁsā-sūtra*' etc. This momentous work consists of 555 *Sūtra-s* (aphorisms) divided into four chapters under the headings '*Samanvaya*', '*Avirodha*', '*Sādhanā*' and '*Phala*' respectively, which are further sub-divided into four '*pāda-s*' each, consisting of a number of "*adhikaraṇa-s*" dealing with specific topics.

In the first chapter Bādarāyaṇa treats the problem of the world and its origin, showing *Brahman* to be its unique source, and proving at the same time that there is harmony among all the Upaniṣads in this context. The second chapter establishes the Vedāntic doctrines by repudiating the doctrines of other schools, such as Sāṅkhya, Nyāya and Buddhist. In the third chapter the nature of the individual soul ("*Jīva*") has been discussed, showing how it is related to *Brahman*. It also deals with the concept of 'Knowledge' as the way to Liberation. The last chapter of the *Brahma-sūtra* discusses the "fruits" of meditation and the nature of Liberation in this life and thereafter.

The '*Brahma-sūtra*' very soon assumed such importance that all subsequent philosophical speculations came to be centered around it, so much so that along with the Upaniṣads and the Bhagavad-gītā, it became established as the pivotal point in Vedānta Philosophy, and claimed a place among the "*Prasthāna-trayī*" along with the Upaniṣads and the Bhagavad-gītā.

On the other hand, it is remarked that though "the literary form of the "*Brahma-sūtra*" undoubtedly eminently suited its original purpose, yet in the course of time, it inevitably rendered the '*Sūtras*' multi-vocal, (for) by themselves they could hardly be made to yield any cogent philosophical teaching."[39] The result was that a series of commentaries saw the day, each claiming to unravel the real meaning of the '*Brahma-sūtra*'. But in practice it would seem to be more convenient to say that each Philosopher-cum-Commentator used the already popular "*Vedānta-sūtra*" as a means to propagate his own philosophy.

Foremost among the above was Śaṅkara, who, toeing the line of Gauḍapāda and Govindapāda, his predecessors, wrote his famous "*Śārīraka-bhāṣya*" on the "*Brahma-sūtra*', giving thereby a new turn to the Advaita School of Vedānta. After him came Rāmānuja, who, through his "*Srībhāṣya*", laid the foundation for his own school of Vedānta, that of Viśiṣṭādvaita. A few centuries later came Nimbārkācārya with his philosophy of Dvaitādvaita and added to the commentaries on the "*Brahma-sūtra*" his own, viz., the "*Vedānta-pārijāta-saurabha*". Following him came Vallabha (1479 - 1531 A.D.) who wrote yet another commentary, the "*Aṇubhāṣya*" (on BS. I.1.1 to BS III. 2.34 only) for the propagation of his new doctrine of "Śuddhādvaita" Vedānta. Madhvācārya (1238-1317 A.D.) is also said to have written a commentary on the "*Brahma-sūtra*" on the basis of which he propounded his philosophy of Dvaita Vedānta.

But the first Ācārya to be 'credited with the earliest commentary on the *Brahma-sūtra* is Upavarṣa"[40] Śaṅkara refers to a discussion by Upavarṣa on the nature of the self in *Brahma-sūtra* III.3.53, indicating that the same discussion could have been undertaken by the latter in his commentary on the *Mīmāṁsā-sūtra* I.1.5, implying by this that Upavarṣa had written commentaries on both the "*Pūrva*" and "*Uttara*" *Mīmāṁsā*[41]. "Śaṅkara suggests in the same connection that his commentary on the *Brahma-sūtra* was called *Śārīraka-mīmāṁsā-vṛtti*....Śaṅkara took the name *Śārīraka* from Upavarṣa and called it (i.e. his commentary) *Śārīraka-mīmāṁsā-sūtra*"[42]. Śaṅkara refers to Upavarṣa as the propounder of the theory of "*Varṇavāda*" (in contrast with the theory of "*Sphoṭavāda*" propounded by Bhartṛhari), according to which phonemes (*varṇa-s*) alone are the real constituents of a word, and that there is nothing else in a word (apart from phonemes)[43]. Elaborating on this theory, Śaṅkara says that it is not proper to bring in the concept of "*Sphoṭa*" in deciding upon the meaning of a word when this can be known from the letters themselves that constitute the word[44]. Upavarṣa is reported to have held the view that "*Brahman* is the source, the ground and the goal of the whole universe", which view is supported by both Śaṅkara and Padmapāda[45]. He is also quoted as explaining the compound-word, "*Brahmajijñāsā*" as *Brahmaṇe jijñāsā* so as to give it the meaning 'inquiry for *Brahman*'. It is observed in this connection that 'when the Vṛttikāra (Upavarṣa) says that (the) inquiry is for *Brahman*, he is ...right, for, the knowledge of *Brahman* is the fruit of this inquiry'[46].

Padmapāda says that Upavarṣa explained the word "*atha*" as meaning that, 'after the enquiry into the antecedent condition' the enquiry into *Brahman* follows; while the word '*ataḥ*' is interpreted by him as stating that what has already been indicated is the reason in regard to *Brahmajijñāsā*[47]. As for the proof about the existence of *Ātman'*, Upavarṣa holds the view that *'Ātman'* is known by perception as it is the object of.... "*I*"[48].

Making evident the indebtedness of both Śabara and Śaṅkara to Upavarṣa, it is observed that, "as Śabara has mostly drawn upon Upavarṣa for his commentary on the *Mīmāṁsā-sūtra*, so *Śaṅkara* too has drawn upon Upavarṣa's *Vṛtti* on the *Brahma-sūtra*. A comparative study of the *Śārīraka-bhāṣya* and the *Śābara-bhāṣya* may give a number of explanations that can be attributed to Upavarṣa. For example, the objection to *Dharma* raised in the *Śābara-bhāṣya* on (MS) I.1.1, as to whether *Dharma* is well-known or unknown is exactly the same as the objection raised (with regard) to the nature of *Brahman* in the *Śārīraka-bhāṣya* as to whether *Brahman* is known or unknown. (Now) these objections and their solutions can be attributed to Upavarṣa and it can be said that both Śabara and Śaṅkara have faithfully reproduced the explanations of Upavarṣa in their works"[49].

A commentary under the name '*Vārttika*' is said to have been written by Sundarapāṇḍya, another ancient teacher, on Upavarṣa's *Śārīraka-mīmāṁsā-vṛtti*. In his *Vārttika*, Sundarapāṇḍya is said to have formulated two more means of knowledge in addition to the six mentioned by Upavarṣa in his *Vṛtti*, viz., Perception (*Pratyakṣa*), Inference (*Anumāna*), Śāstra (*Śabda*), Analogy (*Upamāna*), Presumption (*Arthāpatti*), and Non-apprehension (*Abhāva*)[50]. The *Vārttika-kāra* believes that these six means of knowledge are valid only until the Self is ascertained, but thereafter the Self cannot be known through these means. He therefore makes a difference between "relative knowledge ("*Śeṣajñāna*") and Absolute Knowledge ("*aśeṣa jñāna*")", and also between their means[51]. He believes that Absolute Knowledge is attainable only through the method of "*adhyāropa*" and "*apavāda*"[52]. (It is said in this context that the line, "*adhyāropāpavādābhyāṁ niṣprapañcaṁ prapañcyate*", is verily from the abovementioned *Vārttika*)[53]. Sundarapāṇḍya says that "the characterless *Brahman* can be described by the method of *superimposition* and consequent *sublation*. The Absolute Knowledge is neither the process of superimposition nor that of negation. It is a dialectical relation of these two processes. *Jñāna* is more akin to a process than to a reality.... The method of '*adhyāropa*' and '*apavāda*' ultimately culminates in the realization of the Supreme Self and of the unreal character of the world"[54]. Sundarapāṇḍya is also held to have deliberated on the concept of *Māyā*, and on the doctrine of Pure *Brahman* devoid of *Māyā*[55]. It is evident from these facts how much Śaṅkara owes to both Upavarṣa and Sundarapāṇḍya for his theories about the world and *Brahman*.

Another doctrine of Advaita Vedānta, namely, that of *Vivartavāda*, finds expression in the work of yet another ancient teacher of the Advaita tradition, viz., Brahmānandin. This teacher is known as "*Vākyakāra*", following his commentary in the form of 'brief statements" on the Chāndogya Upaniṣad, which (brief-statements) are also referred to as "*Sūtra-s*" by Madhusūdana

Sarasvatī, they being similar to the *Vedānta-sūtra-s.* In the opinion of Brahmānandin, the process of creation is not amenable to any form of explanation, it being neither real nor unreal, anticipating thus, the doctrine of "*anirvacanīyatā*" of Śāṅkara Advaita. He maintains that all worldly objects are empirically real, but absolutely unreal, they being mere appearances. He therefore advances the view that all created objects are apparent transformation, and not real transformation, throwing thus his weight behind the doctrine of *Vivartavāda* in preference to that of *Pariṇāmavāda.* He views that '*Pariṇāmavāda*' is the 'initial stage' of *Vivartavāda*[56].

The *Chāndogya-vākya-s* of Brahmānandin have been commented upon by Draviḍācārya, who is believed to have written a commentary on the Bṛhadāraṇyaka Upaniṣad, and also a separate *Vedānta-sūtra.* It is claimed that Draviḍācārya illustrated the identity between the individual soul and the highest Self through the famous story of '*the huntsman and the prince*', which illustration was subsequently taken up by Śaṅkara, Sureśvara, Ānandagiri and Madhvācārya[57]. "The story very aptly describes how the individual soul is in reality the Highest Soul, how it forgets what it is and assumes a different character, how it is awakened by some enlightened teacher, and finally how it forsakes its assumed character and realizes its real identity with the Highest Self. It has become a classical illustration of the teaching of "That Thou Art", ("*Tat tvam asi*") and the consequent realization of "I am He" ("*So 'ham*") in the later Advaita Literature"[58].

Draviḍācārya is also said to have propounded the view that 'every instance of negation is due to an affirmation of a positive reality', as is taught by the Upaniṣadic texts, "*etad vai tat*" and "*neti neti*". Throwing light on the relation between these two *texts,* he says that 'the negation of duality is the cause and the realization of identity is the effect'. In other words, the cancellation of the world is prior to Self-realization. The cancellation itself establishes Self-realization'[59].

Another doctrine of Śāṅkara Advaita, namely that of *Avidyā* as the cause of apparent empirical plurality finds also its way back in the philosophy of an ancient teacher, in the person of Bhartṛprapañca. This Advaita teacher is believed to have written a commentary on the *Mādhyandin* recension of the Bṛhadāraṇyaka Upaniṣad, while in contrast, Śaṅkara wrote his commentary on the *Kāṇva* recension of this Upaniṣad[60]. It is argued that Bhartṛprapañca admitted of both multiplicity and unity of *Brahman*, It being One as well as many. The reason for this is that he believed in the theory of a *Lower Brahman* and *Higher Brahman*, respectively alluded to as *Para-Brahman* and *Apara-Brahman*. According to the theory, *Lower Brahman* is a real aspect of *Higher Brahman*. As a matter of fact, both *Lower Brahman* and *Higher Brahman* are real and their relation too is real. The two are inseparable from each other[61]. On the basis of the different ways of interpretation of this relation, four schools of the Vedānta of Bhartṛprapañca had developed in the course of time[62].

Bhartṛprapañca considers *Avidyā* to be the cause of the *finitude* of the *Jīva* and of the delimitation of one *Jīva* from another. He says that there can be no liberation without the removal of *Avidyā*[63]. This is a clear hint at the doctrine of liberation through true Knowledge advocated by Śāṅkara Advaita. Interestingly, this ancient teacher propounded the doctrine of eight phases of Reality, viz., *Antaryāmin, Sākṣī, Avyākṛta, Sūtra, Virāṭ, Devatā, Jāti* and *Piṇḍa*. He maintains that these are all phases of (lower) *Brahman*. "The doctrine of eight phases of *Brahman* indicates that as a matter of fact everything is *Brahman* which is thus the whole and Sole Reality"[64]. Advocating the doctrine of gradual Liberation through the eradication of *Avidyā* by True Knowledge and action, which doctrine is called *Samuccayavāda*, Bhartṛprapañca rejects the concept of *Jīvanmukti*. According to him there is nothing like instantaneous Liberation (*Sadyomukti*). Liberation is possible only after the dissolution of the present body, says he[65].

The *Brahma-sūtra* is believed to have been commented upon also by a successor of Bhartṛprapañca, namely by Bhartṛmitra. The views of Bhartṛmitra, especially those he held in connection with Advaita epistemology, are rather radical. He in fact denied the validity of *Śruti* as a proof for the existence of the Self. He says that, "if the existence of the Self is established by any *pramāṇa* other than *Śruti*, then the *Śruti* merely reiterates it and is superfluous. Again, if the existence of the Self is not established by any *pramāṇa*, then the *Śrūti* is uninformative as it can throw little light on the relation that it bears with the Self. Now the existence of the Self is either established or not established by any *pramāṇa* other than the *Śruti.* Therefore, the *Śruti* is either superfluous *per se* or uninformative *per se.* In either case it is not a *pramāṇa* at all"[66]. Bhartṛmitra also believed that the enquiry into the nature of *Brahman* is as a matter of fact an enquiry into the nature of the embodied self.

The Advaitic doctrine of *Māyā* is said to have been advocated also by Brahmadatta, who is also one among the teachers of the ancient Advaita tradition. According to him, action aims at the annihilation of desire, ultimately contributing to the attainment of Knowledge. He thus believed in the combination of action and knowledge as means to Liberation. He also believed in the doctrine of "*Dhyānaniyoga*", according to which Upaniṣadic passages such as "Self should be meditated upon", are *Apūrva-vidhi-s,* enjoining meditation which brings about the realization of the identity between the individual soul and the Supreme Soul[67].

In much the same way as the philosophers and teachers of the old Advaita schools discussed so far, or perhaps to a higher degree, Bhartṛhari, who is said to have written another commentary on the *Brahma-sūtra,* has also had his share in the development of Advaitic theories as taught by Śaṅkara. Though Bhartṛhari did not derive his philosophical ideals from any of the Vedāntic *Prasthānas,* yet he is considered to be an Advaitin whose doctrines could have been "substantially influential" in the formulation of Śaṅkara's Advaita and of later philosophers of the same school. Indeed, his conception of the world may be taken to be a "precursor of Śaṅkara's theory of *Vivarta*"[68]. Apart from the '*Vākyapadīya*', Bhartṛhari is believed to have authored several other books including the "*Mahābhāṣyaṭīkā* also known as *Dīpikā,* and the *Śabdadhātusamīkṣā.* His "*Vākyapadīya*" is considered to be of the same status as the "*Brahma-sūtra*" as far as Advaita Philosophy is concerned. This book is divided into three *Kāṇḍa-s* - the *Brahma* or *Āgama Kāṇḍa,* the *Vākya Kāṇḍa,* and the *Pada* or *Prakīrṇa Kāṇḍa.* It is believed that in the "*Vṛtti*" he had himself written on the first two *Kāṇḍa-s,* the Advaitic concepts of *Avidyā, Vivarta,* etc. have been dealt with[69].

As he believed that there is only one Eternal Principle, viz., the *Śabdabrahman,* Bhartṛhari's philosophy came to be known as "*Śabadādvaitavāda*". According to this school of thought, '*Śabda*' or "Word" is the Ultimate Reality. It has neither beginning nor end, and can be known only through the Scriptures, i.e., Veda and the Smṛtis, which Bhartṛhari considers to have been "revealed". The *Śabda-Brahman,* which is the "Word Principle", creates all objects and phenomena in the form of *Word,* and in the end, they all merge back into their cause, the *Śabda-brahman.* This world, says Bhartṛhari, is a "transfiguration" (*Vivarta*) of *Śabda-brahman.* In reality, being transcendental, it does not create the world *per se,* but does so through its "*Śabda-śakti*" called *Māyā,* which is also called "*Kālaśakti*" Brahman is itself beyond Space and Time according to Bhartṛhari, who believes that *Śabda-brahman* can be known only through Self-realization, at which level time ceases to exist, as it is itself the first result of *Avidyā.* Bhartṛhari, who does not believe in the existence of *Īśvara,* propounds the theory that though the Ultimate Reality is One, "It manifests itself as many in the form of the *experiencer,* the *object of experience,* and *experience* itself, due to Its infinite powers"[70]. The affinity of Bhartṛhari's "*Śabdādvaita*" to Śaṅkara's *Advaita* can be gauged from the fact that both propound the theory of One Absolute Reality and of the world as existing in the form of *Vivarta.*

There are still a few other ancient teachers of the Advaita tradition referred to by Bādarāyaṇa or Śaṅkara about whom very little if not nothing substantial is known. These include Kāśakṛtsna, Kārṣṇājini, Aṣṭāvakra, Ādiśeṣa, Dattātreya, Sanatsujātīya, Śukrācārya, and Vālmīki. The latter's *Yogavāśiṣṭha* is regarded as one of the most important texts on Advaita Vedānta[71].

B. The Advent of Gauḍapāda and His Māṇḍūkya-kārikā

Gauḍapāda, whose advent in the world of Advaita Vedānta may be rightfully considered to be a milestone, is generally taken to have flourished around 500 A.D. He is believed to have been the disciple of the sage Śuka, as per Advaita tradition. He also is reported to have been the teacher of Govindapāda, also known as Govindayati, who in turn was the teacher of the celebrated Śaṅkara. This is why Gauḍapādācārya is known as the "*Parama-guru*" (teacher's teacher) of Śaṅkara[72]. Gauḍapādācārya is believed to have spent the final part of his life in the Badarīkāśrama where he devoted his time to meditation. It is here that he composed the *Māṇḍūkyakārikā* "after obtaining an insight into the quintessence of Upaniṣadic Wisdom" through direct 'revelation'[73]. Commenting on the magnitude of this work, Śaṅkara is reported to have remarked that this "*Āgamaśāstra*" represents a revival of the philosophy of Non-dualism through its recovery from the Vedic Scriptures in the face of the assaults of Dualism perpetrated by the Sāṅkhya teachers"[74]. Gauḍapāda tried to give a new dimension to Vedic interpretation by his "*Ekatvapratijñā*" (i.e., establishment of Non-dualism or Monism), and "*Nānātvanindā*" (i.e., rejection of plurality). The Orthodox Vedāntic thought was caught in the assertions of the "*Sat*" and the "*asat*" in the beginning, and the philosophical thought seemed to have got stuck between the "*Sat-kāryavāda*" and the "*Asat-kāryavāda*". Gauḍapāda tried to destroy this very notion of causation by establishing the concept of "*Ajātivāda*" (i.e. non-origination). This indeed, it will be found, paved the way for Śaṅkara in the establishment of his philosophy of Non-dualism[75].

"Gauḍapāda clearly foreshadows the celebrated *Māyā* doctrine of Śaṅkarācārya, for he refers to the oft-quoted expression, "*Indro māyābhiḥ pururūpa īyate*", and clearly observes, "*Na iha nānā iti ajāyamāno bahudhā māyayā jāyate tu saḥ*" (III.24)[76] (The meaning of this is, "From the sacred text (*Śruti*) "there is no plurality here" and also from the text "Indra through *Māyā-s* etc." (it is to be known that) it is through illusion that He is variously born, though in fact He does not take birth)[77]. This, remarks Mainkar, is "perhaps the only logical reconciliatory of the two assertions of the Upaniṣads, "*Bahu syām prajāyeya*" and "*na iha nānātvaṁ vidyate*"[78]. Elaborating on the doctrine of 'illusion', Gauḍapāda uses the analogies of "*ākāśa*" and "*ghaṭākāśa*" (III.3), "*svapnamāyā*", "*gandharva-nagara*" (II.31) etc.[79]. Gauḍapāda's *Māṇḍūkyakārikā* is divided into four "*Prakaraṇas*" (Chapters) on the basis of the subject-matter discussed therein. In the first, i.e., the *Āgama Prakaraṇa*, Gauḍapāda discusses the meaning of the *Mantras* of the Māṇḍūkya Upaniṣad; in the second, the *Vaitathya Prakaraṇa*, is established the untrue nature of the Universe; in the third, the *Advaita Prakaraṇa*, which is the heart of Gauḍapāda's work, is established the doctrine of Non-dualism, wherein the dualist doctrine of the Sāṅkhya and the pluralist doctrine of the Nyāya school are refuted. Gauḍapāda establishes here the doctrine of non-origination, called "*Ajātivāda*", by proving the unintelligibility of the causation or origination of new things. Opposing the views of Sāṅkhya about the identity of cause and effect, to those of the Nyāya philosophers about the creation of the effect by the cause, Gauḍapāda refutes both of them, concluding by establishing that nothing can originate as such, and whatever appears to be created is but an illusion. There is in reality no plurality or diversity, for "the Ultimate Reality is a non-differential unity"[80].

Commenting on the "*Alātaśānti Prakaraṇa*" or the "Quietus of the Fire-Wheel", as he calls it, Belvalkar observes that "...if "*Mokṣa*" or emancipation were an event in time, possessing a definite beginning, it can never become endless, permanent, or immortal (IV.30); and what is true of "*Mokṣa*" must needs hold in the case of bondage. If bondage be real, its reality must be of the same grade and nature as the reality of *"Mokṣa"*. Reality as such is one and unique. If bondage be non-existent from the ultimate point of view, then *"jāti"* or birth—the cause of bondage must also be unreal from the ultimate point of view: thus the concept of "*Ajātivāda*" (IV.45). Gauḍapāda elucidates this concept of "*Ajātivāda*" by referring to the famous illustration of whirling fire-brand (IV.49-50)". "All that is "born"is "born through illusion. Therefore nothing eternal exists as a matter of fact. From the ultimate point of view everything is unborn, and hence nothing is ever destroyed (IV.57)[81]. In many ways the *"Kārikā"* of Gauḍapāda can be said to be a typical product of the age to which it belongs and it marks a definite stage in the endeavours of the Hindu Orthodoxy to stem the tide of encroaching Buddhism, and to assert its own age-worn superiority". "....It became increasingly obvious to discerning minds of the day that, after the rehabilitation of the old Vedic Religion in its *Purāṇic* garb,....Buddhism was able to maintain its own only by an increasing adoption of the cult and pantheon of Hinduism....". "If a system were to be put forth that could elude the four-edged rhetoric of the *Prāsaṅgika* School, and that could at the same time range itself on the side of Hindu Orthodoxy, as being based.... on some ancient scriptures like the Upaniṣads, its triumph was assured. Such a system was the Advaita Vedānta.... (which) professed to build upon the unshakable foundations of the mystic experience which was induced by arduous Yogic discipline.....". "It was this part of the programme that Gauḍapāda may be said to have carried out. He proved in effect that at the root and core of all self-destructive negations there ought to be something real and positive which is the cosmic counterpart of the psychic self and which not even the most thorough-going sceptic can succeed in gainsaying. "You can doubt everything, but cannot doubt the Doubter". "....It was now left for the great Śaṅkarācārya... to blaze a path which nobody need to be so weak or humble as to altogether despair of attaining and following to the limits of his own power and ability."[82]

Apart from the Māṇḍūkyakārikā, the other works ascribed to Gauḍapāda are[83]:

1. *Uttaragītāvyākhyā*
2. *Pañcīkaraṇa-vārttika*
3. *Nṛsiṁhatāpanīya-bhāṣya*
4. *Anugītā-bhāṣya*
5. *Srī-vidyāratna-sūtra*
6. *Durgā-saptaśatī-vyākhyā*
7. *Subhagodaya*

C. Śaṅkara's Guru—Govindapāda:

According to Advaita tradition, Govindapāda, also known as Govindayati and Govindabhagavatpāda, was the disciple of Gauḍapādācārya, and later on, the Guru of Śaṅkarācārya. Śaṅkara has himself referred to Govindapāda as his teacher at many places. For example, in *Viveka-Cūḍāmaṇi*, Śaṅkara paying his repect to his teacher, says,

"Govindaṁ Paramānandaṁ madguruṁ praṇato' smyaham"

i.e.'I bow to Govinda, my Guru, (who is) the abode of Bliss.'

This is the reason for which Śaṅkara refers to Gauḍapāda as his "*Prācārya*" or "*Parama-guru*" (i.e. teacher's teacher)[84].

According to the "*Vṛddhatraya*" written by Haladhara, Govindapāda was a great "*yogi*" who believed in "*Sanātana Dharma*" and who advocated the Advaita tradition[85]. He is said to have been taught the "*Mahābhāṣya*" and Advaitic doctrines by Gauḍapāda[86]. He in turn revealed these doctrines to Śaṅkara when the latter became his disciple. It is also believed that it was he who directed Śaṅkara, at the end of his internship, to write a commentary on the *Brahma-sūtra*[87].

Govindapāda is believed to have four works to his credit[88], namely,

1. *Yoga-tārāvalī*
2. *Advaitānubhūti*
3. *Brahmāmṛtavarṣiṇī*
4. *Rasahṛdayam*

Equipped with such a rich inheritance of Advaitic values Śaṅkara, therefore, set forth to conquer the heart of one and all.

D. Śaṅkara and his doctrine of Non-Dualism

Born in Kāladi in C. 788 A.D., Śaṅkara was a "child-prodigy". Son of Śivaguru and Āryāmbā (or Satī Mādhavīyā or Viśiṣṭā)[89], Śaṅkara not only performed miracles in his early age[90], but even used his charisma to influence his mother to allow him to take sudden renunciation i.e., *āpat-saṁnyāsa*', at the early age of six or seven[91], to become a pupil of Govindapāda. This early phase of his life culminated in the composition by him (at the age of twelve)[92] of his famous commentary on the *Brahma-Sūtra,* the *Śārīraka-bhāṣya* or *Brahma-sūtra-bhāṣya,* which continues till date to pose a challenge even to the most articulate among the intellectuals of the world over.

As already stated above, Śaṅkara studied various *Śāstras* and the Advaita doctrines at the feet of his Guru Govindabhagavatpāda till the age of eleven. Prior to this, Śaṅkara is reported to have "mastered the Vedas along with the six *Aṅgas* in two years (till the age of seven). Although he himself belonged to the tradition specializing in (the) *Yajurveda* of the *Taittirīya-śākhā,* he is also said to have acquired proficiency in all the orthodox systems[93] of philosophy". "In the eighth year he retired to his home and spent sometime studying the *Vedas* and performing Vedic ritual"[94]. "Even while at *Gurukula,* Śaṅkara is said to have instructed pupils on his own, and the fame of his precocious learning is said to have spread far and wide"[95].

It is remarked further[96] that Śaṅkara, the child, composed the '*Saundaryalaharī*' as a sequel to the family-deity condescending to his supplication to partake of his offering. In like manner, the '*Kanaka-dhārā-stotra*' is said to have been composed by Śaṅkara while still a student of the *Gurukula,* out of compassion when he was offered an *āmalaka* fruit by a poor woman in response to his begging for alms as part of his daily duties. It is said that he was so touched that he prayed for her prosperity, as a result of which her house was "filled with gold".[97] Śaṅkara is also said to have caused the river *Cūrṇi* to change its course for the benefit of his frail mother[98].

At the end of his formal spiritual training, Śaṅkara proceeded to Kāśī at the behest of his Guru. "In Kāśī Śaṅkara is said to have stayed near the "*Maṇikarṇikā Ghāṭa*", worshipped "*Śiva*" and instructed a growing band of disciples which included the celebrated Sanandana (later Padmapāda) who had come from the banks of Kāverī...."[99]. It is here (in Kāśī) that *Śiva* is believed to have appeared before Śaṅkara in the form of a *Cāṇḍāla* and "directed him towards Badari where he was to write the commentary on the *Brahma-sūtra*"[100]. 'While at Badari he also composed his other commentaries, namely, those on the Upaniṣads and the Bhagavad-gītā, as well as independent treatises such as the Upadeśasāhasrī'[101].

It is believed that Śaṅkara's authorship of the following works goes undisputed : the *Śārīraka-bhāṣya*, the *Bhagavadgītā Bhāṣya*, and the *Bhāṣya-s* (commentaries) on the following Upaniṣads: Īśa, kena (verse), Kaṭha, Praśna, Muṇḍaka, Taittirīya, (Mahā)-Aitareya, Chāndogya and Bṛhadāraṇyaka[102]. Furthermore, it is still a matter of debate among scholars whether or not Śaṅkara composed the following works: the Hastāmalaka-stotra-bhāṣya, and the *Bhāṣya-s* (commentaries) on the following Upaniṣads-Māṇḍūkya, Śvetāśvatara, Nṛsiṁhapūrvatāpanīya, Kena (prose), Kauṣītaki and (Mahā) Nārāyaṇa-Upaniṣad[103]. Belvalkar supplies also a list of 31 works ascribed 'spuriously' to Saṅkara[104]. Apart from the above, Śaṅkara is believed to have composed about 220 *Stotra-s*[105], out of which the first one- "the *Devī-bhujaṅga-stava* of 28 verses - he composed while he was hardly five"[106]. "The greatness of Śaṅkara", says Mainkar," is very well reflected in the fact of his having become almost a mythical personality in so short a time[107]. Taking over the torch (of enlightenment) from his predecessors, specially Gauḍapādācārya, Śaṅkarabhagavatpāda moved about in all directions, spreading and establishing the '*absolutist*' doctrine of the '*Upaniṣads*' and the '*Brahma-sūtra*' through his unprecedented commentaries on the Vedantic texts (namely, the '*Brahma-sutra*', the *Bhagavadgītā* and the

Upaniṣads) and his passionate debate with the contemporary 'pundits' of all sides. Says Śaṅkara, "It is to refute all those who were opposed to the right doctrine of perceiving everything as the unity of Self ("*ātmaikatva*") that this "*Sārīraka*" commentary of mine is being attempted"[108]. "Reason with Śaṅkara never occupied the premier position; its value was considered only secondary, only so far as it helped one to the right understanding of the revealed Scriptures, the Upaniṣads. The *Ultimate Truth* cannot be known by reason alone. What one debator shows to be reasonable a more expert debator shows to be false, and what he shows to be right is again proved to be false by another debator. So there is no final certainty at which we can arrive by logic and argument alone. The *Ultimate Truth* can thus only be found in the Upaniṣads; reason, discrimination and judgement are all to be used only with a view to discovering the real purport of the Upaniṣads"[109]. Śaṅkara begins his "*Śārīraka-bhāṣya*" with the assertion that everything in this world operates in the backdrop of "an error which identifies the self with the body, the senses or with the objects of the senses (and vice-versa)"[110]. This being accepted, the world as it appears could not be real. It must be a mere magic show of illusion or *māyā*. Śaṅkara advocates the view that *Brahman* is the ultimate cause (the origin, sustenance and dissolution of) the whole world of "names and forms". "*Brahman* according to Śaṅkara, is the identity of Pure Intelligence, Pure Being, and Pure Blessedness. *Brahman* is the Self of us all. So long as we are in our ordinary waking life, we are identifying the self with thousands of illusory things, with all that we call "I" or 'mine', but when in dreamless sleep we are absolutely without any touch of these phenomenal notions, the nature of our true state as Pure Blessedness is partially realized. The individual self as it appears is but an appearance only, while the Real Truth is the True Self which is One for all, as Pure Intelligence, Pure Blessedness, and Pure Being"[111]. Śaṅkara declares that 'while other systems try to determine the objective truth of things or our attitude towards them through different means of knowledge, Vedānta seeks to reach beneath the surface of appearances, and enquire after the final Truth underlying the microcosm and the macrocosm, the subject and the object. The famous instruction of Śvetaketu, the most important Vedānta text, (*mahāvākya*) says, "*That art thou, O Śvetaketu*". This comprehension of the self as the Ultimate Truth is the Highest Knowledge, for when this Knowledge is once produced, our cognition of world-appearances automatically ceases. Unless the mind is chastened and purged of all passions and desires, the soul cannot comprehend this truth, but when this is once done, and the soul is anxious for salvation, by a knowledge of the Highest Truth, the Preceptor instructs him, "*That art thou.....*". "At once.....all ordinary notions and cognitions of diversity and of the many cease; there is no duality, no notion of mine and thine; the vast illusion of this world process is extinct in him, and he shines forth as the One, the Truth, the *Brahman*"[112].

According to Śaṅkara, "the sole means of achieving Liberation is Right Knowledge (Jñāna) leading to instantaneous spiritual illumination that somehow dissolves all except the residual effects of past-deeds (*Prārabdha-karman*)" "After death, Liberation is complete and final". The alternative paths of devotion ("*Bhakti*") and moral-cum-religious works ("*Karman*") may lead to a better rebirth either in this world or in the world of the gods, but they are of no use whatsoever for the Illumination that is Absolute Liberation. For this the sole pre-requisites are non-attachment to the things of this world, mental and emotional restraint and tranquility, a suitable Guru and the study, under his supervision, 'of the knowledge portion ("*Brahma-kāṇḍa*") or *Jñāna-kāṇḍa* of the Vedas, especially the Upaniṣads"[113].

Quite a good number of sub-commentaries have been written on the Śāṅkara Bhāṣya[114]. These are as follows:

1. Brahmavidyābharaṇa by Advaitānanda
2. Pradīpa by Ananta Krishna Śāstri
3. Śārīraka-nyāya-maṇi-mālā by Ananyānubhava
4. Prakaṭārtha-vivaraṇa by Anubhūtisvarūpācārya.
5. Nyāya-nirṇaya by Ānanda Giri
6. Bhāṣya-siddhānta-saṅgraha by Upaniṣad-brahmendra
7. Ānuguṇya-siddhi by Kṛṣṇa-Śāstri
8. Ratna-prabhā by Rāmānanda
9. Bhāṣya-bhāva-prakāśikā by Citsukhācārya
10. Vidyā-śrī by Jñānottama
11. Bhāṣyānuprabhā (or Bhāṣya-bhānu-prabhā), by Tryambaka Śāstri
12. Bhāṣya-vārttika by Nārāyaṇa-Sarasvatī

13. *Pañcapādikā* by Padmapāda
14. Bhāṣya-vārttika by Bālakṛṣṇānanda
15. Bhāṣyārtha-saṅgraha by Brahmānanda Yati
16. *Bhāmatī* by Vācaspati Miśra
17. Subodhinī by Śivanārāyaṇa
18. Bhāṣya-siddhānta-saṅgraha by Kṛṣṇānubhūti
19. Bhāṣya-nyāya-saṅgraha by Prakāśātman

E. Sureśvara and his Naiṣkarmya-siddhi

The Advaitic doctrines thus propounded by Śaṅkara were further elaborated by his disciples, among whom Sureśvara may be said to have led the way. Sureśvara is one of the most controversial personalities in the context of Indian Philosophy. This is so not only because of the fact that his very existence *per se* stands challenged, but also because to the other extreme, he is made out to have incarnated as many as four different personalities, viz. Sureśvara, Maṇḍana (Miśra), Viśvarūpa and Umveka (Umbeka)[115]. While G.A. Jacob in his introduction to the *"Naiṣkarmya-siddhi"* identifies Sureśvara with Maṇḍana Miśra, who, before meeting Śaṅkara, is said to have been a disciple of Kumārila Bhaṭṭa, and therefore a Mīmāṁsaka, others including Prof. M. Hiriyanna, P.V.Kaṇe, D.C. Bhattacharya, S. Kuppuswami Śāstrī, etc.[116], of more recent time, advocate the classification of the above-mentioned four-fold personalities into (i) Maṇḍana Miśra, the disciple of Kumārila Bhaṭṭa, defeated together with his wife by Śaṅkara in a debate, to become ultimately a follower of the latter, and (ii) Sureśvara alias Viśvarūpa, disciple of Śaṅkara, to whom the latter had at first given the responsibility to write a sub-commentary on his "*Śārīraka-bhāṣya*", but had to revise his decision ultimately in the face of opposition from the other disciples, on the ground that the latter was a 'crypto-Mīmāṁsaka'. But after a close study of "*Naiṣkarmyasiddhi*" and the "*Bṛhadāraṇyaka Upaniṣad-bhāṣya-vārttika*", admittedly written by Sureśvara, and the "*Brahmasiddhi*" written by Maṇḍana Miśra, Prof. S.N. Das Gupta, Śri Saccidānandendra Sarasvatī, etc., say that[117] "we are here in the presence of two separate individuals, though related both to Śaṅkara as his disciples, who have made an attempt, through their works to explain Śaṅkara on the basis of their individual convictions". Pending the final settlement of this issue, it would be a better course to toe the line of modern scholars and ascribe to Sureśvara an identity of his own.

Sureśvara, (who is believed to have flourished between 800 A.D. and 900 A.D.)[118], and his pupil Sarvajñātma Muni, are said to have been responsible for the origin of one of the three pre-Śaṅkara branches of the Advaita School. Sureśvara *et al* held "*Māyā*" to be only an instrument[119] ("*dvāra*") through which "*Brahman*" appears as many. Sureśvara holds "Māyā" to be positive, though it has "*Brahman*" for both its object and its support[120]. The real cause of all appearances is Pure "*Brahman*", while "*Māyā*" only hangs on it like a veil of illusion which makes this *one thing* appear as many unreal appearances'[121]. In his "*Naiṣkarmya-siddhi*", Sureśvara declares that Emancipation has nothing to do with the performance of actions. Vedic actions, says he, may have as fruit simply the purification of the mind, but not Salvation at any cost. He believes that the mere knowledge of the *Jīva-Brahman* - identity is not enough to remove ignorance, but added to it, "long and continuous meditation on the same"[122] is required, while performance of all obligatory duties should also continue. Cessation of action, believes Sureśvara, represents "transgression of one's duties", and, therefore, results in the accrual of sin, and hence in further bondage. In opposition to Śaṅkara, thus, Sureśvara preaches the philosophy of 'knowledge-cum-action' ("*Jñāna-karma-Samuccaya*") as a means to Salvation[123]. The experience of the ego which, according to Sureśvara, is a "changeful and extraneous element, and hence outside the element of Pure Consciousness, "vanishes with the dawn of True Self-Knowledge of unity"[124]. With True Knowledge, the individuality of the self vanishes, and so does this world of appearance. The Pure Self is not disturbed by the imposition on it of "*ajñāna*" (ignorance), leading to illusory appearances. Sureśvara believes also that the non-Self cannot be its own support and object, being itself a product of "*ajñāna*" (Nescience). "The ignorance of the self", says Sureśvara, "is also in regard to *itself*, since there is no other object regarding which ignorance is possible, and still further, since the entire field of objective appearance is regarded as the product of ignorance itself." It is the ignorance of the real nature of the self, believes Sureśvara, that transforms itself into all that is subjective and objective, the intellect and its objects.

He, therefore, contrary to Maṇḍana and Vācaspati Miśra, considers *Brahman* to be the locus of *Avidyā* (Nescience) rather than the individual self[125].

Apart from the *Naiṣkarmyasiddhi* and the Bṛhadāraṇyaka-Upaniṣad-bhāṣya-vārttika referred to above, Sureśvara has to his credit the following works as well[126]:

1. Taittirīya-Upaniṣad-vārttika
2. Praṇavārtha-kārikā
3. Mānasollāsa
4. Vedānta-sāra-vārttika-rāja-saṅgraha
5. Laghuvārttika
6. Mokṣanirṇaya
7. Pañcīkaraṇa-vārttika

F. Maṇḍana Miśra and his Brahma-siddhi

After Sureśvara, Maṇḍana Miśra came to the fore of Advaita Vedānta, taking a seemingly different path from his predecessor. According to Advaita tradition, Maṇḍana Miśra is believed to have been defeated together with his wife, by Śaṅkara in a debate consequent upon which he became a follower of the latter, discarding in so doing, his former garb of *Mīmāṁsaka* and adopting the Advaitic mantle of his new-found spiritual master. Till then Maṇḍana had been the disciple of Kumarila Bhaṭṭa, the great *Mīmāṁsaka*. Due to this background, Maṇḍana Miśra has to his credit more works on Mīmāṁsā, and also on Grammar, than on Advaita Vedānta, on which he has written the famous "*Brahma-siddhi*", which some say, "set forth a non-Śaṅkaran brand of Advaita"[127]. The "*Vibhrama-viveka*" written by him on the 'theory of error', is believed to reflect the *Anyathākhyāti* theory of the Mīmāṁsaka-s, and might have been written therefore by Maṇḍana, the "*Mīmāṁsaka*", rather than by Maṇḍana, the "Advaitin". Apart from the above, Maṇḍana is said to have written the following texts: *Bhāvanā-viveka, Vidhi-viveka, Sphoṭa-siddhi, Mīmāṁsā-sūtrānukramaṇī*[128].

The Brahma-siddhi

As indicated above, the "*Brahma-siddhi*" represents the only work on Advaita Vedānta by Maṇḍana Miśra, and yet, it can be said to be the most important among all his works. In

Advaita circles, the significance of this work is reckoned from the fact that the theory of "*Anirvacanīya-khyāti*" mentioned by Maṇḍana in this work "later became the stock term for an Advaita Theory of Error"[129]. This work is divided into four chapters under the following headings: (i) "*Brahma-kāṇḍa*", (ii) *Tarka-kāṇḍa,* (iii) "*Niyoga-kāṇḍa*", and (iv) "*Siddhi-kāṇḍa*". (It is interesting to note that the names of the chapters start with '*Brahma*' and end with '*Siddhi*'). Maṇḍana starts by a discussion on the nature of "*Brahman*" in the first-chapter and explains why the difference between the Self and the non-Self cannot be perceived through the empirical means of knowledge. He also embarks on a discussion as to why the *Upaniṣads* should not be interpreted on dualistic lines, and shows how perception reveals differences, (and as such cannot be a means to the establishment of unity or non-dualism)[130]. The "*Niyoga-kāṇḍa*" is of special significance for the students of philosophy in as much as we see in it an old Mīmāṁsaka refuting his old bretheren, the orthodox *Mīmāṁsaka-s.* The fact is that Maṇḍana having been himself a staunch protagonist of Mīmāṁsā, knows the very essence of that school of thought, and who would do better in dismantling the Mīmāṁsā theories? First and foremost, Maṇḍana refutes the Mīmāṁsā age-long claim that "*all Vedic texts command us to engage in some kind of action or to refrain from performing other actions*"[131], saying that the Upaniṣadic texts need not be interpreted according to this principle of interpretation. In the "*Siddhi-kāṇḍa,* Maṇḍana points out that the Upaniṣads, inter-alia, teach that the world of plurality and of appearance has no real existence. It has only an apparent existence which is due to the "*Avidyā*" of the *Jīva-s.* The "*Brahma-siddhi*" reveals also Maṇḍana's thought on the Vedāntic concept of subject-object-analysis ("*draṣṭṛ-dṛśya-viveka*"). He explains that it is only by abolishing the apparent duality of subject and object that the fact of experience can be explained. For, says he, "If there were to be any real duality of subject and object, that duality could not be bridged over and no relation between the two could be established; if, on the other hand, there is only the subject, then all things that are perceived can best be explained as being illusory creations imposed on (the)Self, the only reality"[132].

Maṇḍana believes that "*Avidyā*" is neither a characteristic (*sva-bhāva*) of *Brahman,* nor different from it, and is therefore neither existent nor non-existent. It is because of this peculiarity that it is said to be "*Māyā*" i.e. false appearance. And this "*Avidyā*", Maṇḍana believes, *pertains to the individual souls* (Jīva-s), *and not to Brahman.* And this being so, it leads to an inconsistency, in the manner that the *Jīva-s,* though essentially identical with *Brahman,* appear diverse as a result of imagination ("*kalpanā*"). But this imagination cannot have *Brahman* as its substratum since it is devoid of imagination. It cannot as well have the *Jīva-s* themselves as its substrata since they are themselves the products of imagination. Thus the inconsistency. Moreover, it is through this "*Avidyā*" that the *Jīva-s* came to be 'separated' from *Brahman.* Therefore it is through its destruction that they can attain *Brahma*-hood, their original identity[133]. The moment knowledge is obtained this "*Māyā*" or "*Avidyā*" stands destroyed. Knowledge, says Maṇḍana, is obtained "through listening to Vedantic texts, right-thinking, meditation, etc."[134] "One who has realised his identity with *Brahman* as a result of Vedic teaching, can no more be subject to the ills of worldly life, and one who is subject to these, has not evidently realised his identity with *Brahman*"[135].

"Owing to impressions of wrong knowledge.... the soul may continue to be swayed by the influence of false appearances of duality, to blot out which the repeated practice of Right Knowledge is necessary. Simultaneous practice of sacrifice, gift and austerity as laid down in the *Śruti-s,* precipitates the strengthening of his right impression." "Knowledge obtained through *Śruti* is only indirect and therefore cannot remove the actual experience of differences; meditation ("*nididhyāsana*") or continued repetition of Scriptural knowledge is needed to bring on the direct realization of *Ātman*", says Maṇḍana Miśra[136].

"*Avidyā*", according to Maṇḍana, which is located in the *Jīva-s,* and not in *Brahman* as pointed out above, is destroyed by mere Knowledge. Though "*Avidyā*" is natural and beginningless, it can be destroyed by "*Vidyā*"....The *knower* (then) attains release immediately after casting off the body. And the departure from the body is subject to the Law of *Karma*"[137].

So influential was Maṇḍana after Śaṅkara that it is said that "for several centuries following Śaṅkara's and Maṇḍana's lifetimes it was Maṇḍana who was viewed by other schools as the major figure in Advaita. Vācaspati Miśra is said to have continued Maṇḍana's brand of Advaita in a commentary, now lost, on the "*Brahma-siddhi*", and in his "*Bhāmatī*" on Śaṅkara's "*Brahma-sūtra-bhāṣya*"[138].

Among the commentaries on the "*Brahma-siddhi*", the following four are of greater importance[139]:

1. *Brahmatattva-samīkṣā* by Vācaspati Miśra
2. *Abhiprāya-prakāśikā* by Citsukhācārya
3. *Bhāvaśuddhi* by Ānandapūrṇa Vidyāsāgara
4. *Brahma-siddhi-ṭīkā* by Śaṅkhapāṇi

G. Vācaspati Miśra and his Bhāmatī

Taking over the torch of Advaita from Maṇḍana and following the same path paved by the latter, as indicated above, Vācaspati Miśra carried Śāṅkara Vedānta to a yet higher peak. It is believed that Vācaspati Miśra lived between A.D. 800 and 900 in either Bihar or Bengal, where it is said there exists a city called Bhāmā corresponding to ancient Mithilā[140]. A tank of the same name is also supposed to have been found there. According to Advaita tradition, Śaṅkara himself is believed to have incarnated as Vācaspati Miśra "to popularise the Advaita System through his Bhāmatī[141]. What is noteworthy of Vācaspati Miśra is that he had devoted the whole of his life to the cause of philosophy, and therefore of knowledge, composing on all *Śāstra-s* commentaries like the Bhāmatī composed by him on the *Śāṅkara-bhāṣya*. "He is considered to be one of the greatest literary geniuses that India has ever produced and one of those rare scholars who have written authoritative commentaries on the standard works in all the six *Āstika darśanas....*"[142]. His name is ever associated with the honorific title "*Sarvatantra-svatantra*" which is a rare honour conferred only upon literary prodigies. His literary productions bear ample testimony to the honour and dignity that are always associated with that title"[143]. His authoritative commentary on the "*Nyāya-vārttika*", viz. the "*Nyāya-vārttika-tātparya-ṭīkā*", is believed to have saved the *Nyāya-sūtras* from "sinking into oblivion". His contribution to this school is so significant that it has earned him the name "*Tātparya-ṭīkācārya*". On the Śāṅkhya and Yoga systems he has produced two famous commentaries: (i) The "*Sāṅkhya-tattva-kaumudī*", and (ii) the "(*Yogabhāṣya*) *Tattva-vaiśāradī*", respectively. The "*Nyāya-kaṇikā*" and the "*Tattvabindu*" are Vācaspati's works on Mīmāṁsā. The former is an authoritative treatise in which he discusses many important philosophical doctrines such as the '*Satkāryavāda*', the '*Asatkāryavāda*, the '*khyātis*' and the "*Kṣaṇabhaṅgavāda*", etc. The second is a short treatise dealing with the important question as to what actually constitutes the '*karaṇa*' (*internal instrument*) in verbal cognition. On Vedānta also Vācaspati Miśra has to his credit two works—(i) the "*Brahmatattva-samīkṣā*" on the "*Brahma-siddhi*" of Maṇḍana Miśra and (ii) the "*Bhāmatī*" on the "*Śāṅkara-bhāṣya*". The former, which is considered to have been lost now, was an authoritative commentary on the "*Brahma-siddhi*", while the latter has indeed proved to be a milestone in the evolution of Advaita Vedānta tradition, as will become evident from the ensuing discussion.

That Vācaspati Miśra was inspired mainly by Maṇḍana Miśra is now taken for granted by scholars, so much so that this has earned him the epithet "*Maṇḍana-pṛṣṭha-sevī* ("the faithful follower of Maṇḍana")[144]. His views on Vedānta are said to be based mostly on the "*Brahma-siddhi*". This borrowing from Maṇḍana is so significant that it is remarked that "the thoughts that.... are traced to Maṇḍana would have remained little known and barren but for Vācaspati Miśra's linking them up with Śaṅkara's teaching"[145]. Just as the views of Padmapāda came to be known as the '*Vivaraṇa-prasthāna*' on their being re-evaluated by Prakāśātman in his "*Pañcapādikā-vivaraṇa*" in like manner the views of Maṇḍana as reflected in the "*Brahma-siddhi*" came to be known as the "*Bhāmatī-prasthāna*" on their being embodied by Vācaspati Miśra in his "*Bhāmatī*". 'For the distinctive aspects of his teaching, he owes much to Maṇḍana; where he differs from Maṇḍana, he elects to follow Śaṅkara....'[146]

"Vācaspati Miśra incorporates Maṇḍana's modified "*Prasaṅkhyāna*" theory in his system, but rejects the latter's "*Jñāna-karma-samuccaya-vāda*" or "doctrine of combination of both knowledge and actions" as being too palpably against Śaṅkara's un-compromising position"[147]. Vācaspati further believes that 'at the time of the absolute dissolution ('*mahāpralaya*') the mind and other phenomena are dissolved in their cause and abide there in a subtle potential form along with the impressions of *Avidyā* which are the tendencies conducive to the projection of actions.... "He elaborates that theory by an additional doctrine that there are as many "*Avidyā-s*" as there are individual selves"[148]. Continuing on the same line, Vācaspati observes that the "*Avidyā*" of only that '*Jīva*' is destroyed who has realized his true nature, establishing thereby that the 'release' of one 'soul' does not engender the release of the rest'[149]. He believes in two kinds of "*Ajñāna*" - (a) psychological *Ajñāna* forming the mental cause of the mind, and (b) inner psychical nature of man - the material world outside. Vācaspati says that all appearances originate from *Brahman* in association with, or with the accessory cause of the two "*Avidyā-s*"[150]. According to him, each individual soul "confuses and misapprehends his physical frame and mental experiences as intelligent in themselves, and it is by such an illusory confusion that these psychical states attain any meaning as appearances, for otherwise these appearances could not have been expressed at all"[151]. Vācaspati believes that the unreality of world-appearances consists in their being ultimately negated and contradicted. But still they cannot be said to be absolutely non-existent, for had it been the case, they could not have been experienced at all. Inspite of their being made out of "*Avidyā*", the appearnaces have.... "*Brahman*" as their underlying ground, and it is for this reason that "*Brahman*" is to be regarded as the Ultimate Cause of the world[152]. As soon as "*Brahman*" is realised, says Vācaspati, the appearances vanish, for the root of all appearances is their illusory confusion with Reality, i.e., "*Brahman*"[153].

Commentaries on the Bhāmatī

The Bhāmatī has been commented and re-commented upon by a number of scholars in consonance with its prominent place in Advaita circles. The following can therefore be said to have been the literary products of the Bhāmatī school of thought[154]:

A. (i) The *Ṛjuprakāśikā*, also known as the *Bhāmatī-vyākhyā* by Akhaṇḍānanda;
(ii) The *Bhāva-dīpikā* by Acyutakṛṣṇānanda;
(iii) The *Bhāmatī-tilaka* by Allala Sūri;
(iv) The *Bhāmatī-vilāsa* by unknown author;
(v) The *Vedānta-kalpataru* by Amalānanda.

B. The *Vedānta-kalpataru* has been further commented upon by three scholars as follows:

(i) The *Vedānta-kalpataru-mañjarī* by Vaidyanātha Pāyaguṇḍe

(ii) The *Vedānta-kalpataru-parimala* by Appaya Dīkṣita

(iii) The *Ābhoga* by Lakṣmīnṛsiṁha

C. The *Vedānta-kalpataru-parimala* has a further gloss, the *Parimala-saṅgraha*

Main Tenets of the Bhāmatī School:[155]

The main tenets of the Bhāmatī school, as discussed earlier, may be summed up as follows:

1. *Karma-s* are useful for giving rise to the desire to know the Self:
2. The realisation of *Brahman* arises through the instrument of the mind.
3. There is no injunction in the Vedic text "*Ātman* should be realised; (and) for that purpose, It should be heard, reflected and meditated upon". ("*Ātmā vā are draṣṭavyaḥ śrotavyaḥ mantavyaḥ nididhyāsitavyaḥ*").
4. Meditation is the principal factor, and Vedantic study and reflection are its subsidiary factors.
5. '*Jīva*' is Consciousness limited by '*ajñāna*' and '*Īśvara*' is Consciousness transcending the limiting adjunct.
6. The locus and content of '*ajñāna*' are different.
7. The primal Nescience is manifold.
8. It is only *Brahman* that is conditioned by the '*vṛtti*' that is the content of the direct knowledge of *Brahman*.
9. The first factor in the four-fold aid is the discrimination between what is Real and non-Real.
10. The injunctive-text ("*Svādhyāyo' dhyetavyaḥ*") 'One's own recension of the Veda must be studied', has for its fruit the knowledge of the meaning of the Veda.
11. The world-creation is explained by adopting the theory of triplication.
12. The Omniscience of *Brahman* is derived from the essential nature of *Brahman*.
13. The mind is a sense-organ.
14. '*Avidyā*' is located in '*Jīva*'
15. The nature of *Jīva* and *Īśvara* is explained by the theory of "*avacchedavāda*".

H. Padmapāda and his Pañcapādikā

The doctrines enumerated above propounded by the Bhāmatī school were countered by the Vivaraṇa School which has its origin in the *Pañcapādikā*, the commentary on the *Śārīraka-bhāṣya*, written by Padmapāda, one of the direct disciples of Śaṅkara. Padmapāda, whose date is generally fixed at c. 800 A.D., is said to have been known as Sanandana prior to his becoming the disciple of Śaṅkara[156]. As per a legend that has found credence among the followers of the Advaita School of Vedānta, on being beckoned by Śaṅkara from the opposite bank of a river, Sanandana spontaneously stepped into the water and sped towards his new-found spiritual master, unmindful of the depth of the water. As he walked through, lotus flowers sprang up from beneath as support to his feet. Impressed by his devotion, Śaṅkara accepted him as his pupil on the spot and addressed him as 'Padmapāda'[157]. It is further said that Padmapāda is the only one among the disciples who stood by Śaṅkara till the end. It is in due recognition of his unadulterated devotion that Śaṅkara subsequently entrusted to him the charge of the Purī Monastery, but which he declined. One more feature in the life of Padmapāda that distinguishes him from the rest, is the fact of his having saved the life of Śaṅkara from the grip of one Abhinava Gupta[158]. Later on at Śaṅkara's instance, Padmapāda wrote his commentary on the "*Śāṅkara-bhāṣya*", the "*Pañcapādikā*".

It is traditionally believed that Padmapāda had commented upon the whole of the "*Śārīraka-bhāṣya*", but that was destroyed in a fire subsequent to which it was partially restituted by Śaṅkara on the basis of memory, earning it thus the name "*Pañcapādikā*", which is indicative of the fact that in its restituted form the commentary constituted of five '*Pādas*', the four of Book I and the first of Book II. But why should the extant "*Pañcapādikā*" consist of the commentary on only the first four *Sūtra-s*, ending abruply as it does with the commentary on *Sūtra* 1.1.4., is still a mind-boggling issue.

Inspite of the allegedly incomplete form in which it is now available, the "*Pañcapādikā*" represents one of the most important works on Advaita Vedānta. Apart from this, Padmapāda is believed to have written the following books[159]:

1. Vijñānadīpikā
2. Ātmabodhavyākhyā
3. Kaṭhopaniṣad-bhāṣya
4. Karma-nirṇaya
5. Tattvamasi-pañcakam
6. Prapañcasāra-vyākhyā
7. Svarūpānubhava

The Pañcapādikā-prasthāna

The Pañcapādikā, says the *Vedānta-prakriyā-pratyabhijñā*, is glaringly divergent from Śaṅkara's system in its description of '*Avidyā*"[160]. 'Padmapāda' was the first to have called '*Prakṛti*' by the name '*Avidyā*' or '*Ajñāna*', proclaiming it to be the material cause of "*Adhyāsa*"[161]. He defends the theory of '*Anirvacanīya-khyāti*', and equates the following terms to "avidyā": '*māyā*', '*avyākṛta*', '*prakṛti*', '*agrahaṇa*, '*avyakta*', '*tamas*', '*kāraṇa*', '*laya*', '*śakti*, '*mahāsupti*', '*nidrā*', '*kṣara*', *ākāśa*'. This "*avidyā*" stands as a screen reflecting ignorance, actions and past impressions of knowledge and produces the individual selves[162]. "This entity called '*avidyā*' obstructs the pure and self-luminous nature of *brahman*". Padmapāda says that "*avidyā*" functions as the 'doer of all activities and the enjoyer of all fruits of actions as it operates in the dual capacity of knowledge and activity. As a result of these activities the transformations that *avidyā* undergoes while having *Brahman* as its support, are variously referred to as '*antaḥkaraṇa*', '*manas*', '*buddhi*' or "*ahaṁpratyayin*", i.e. the 'ego' or 'ego-feeler', and in its 'bio-motor-functions', this same '*avidyā*' having *Brahman* as its support, is called '*prāṇa*' due to its vibratory activity[163]. Due to these apparent limitations ('*avaccheda-s*') caused by the functioning of beginningless "*avidyā*", *Brahman* is considered to be the cause of the appearance of plurality of souls.

Padmapāda claims that "*avidyā*" has a two-fold characteristic: one is its material nature (*jaḍātmikā*), and the other is its nature of power ('*avidyā-śakti*')[164]. It is the material nature of '*avidyā*' that is the material cause of the world-appearance. According to Padmapāda, knowledge which can be both mediate and immediate, is the manifestation of the object ('*artha-prakāśa*') as a result of the connection of the ego with the underlying Consciousness, which connection takes place following the preceding cognitive activity of the ego, connecting it with the object of perception[165].

The Pañcapādikā of Padmapāda has been quite an important source book for Advaita Vedānta during the post-Śaṅkara period. Its popularity is to be judged from the number of commentaries written on it, the list of which follows hereunder[166].

1. The *Prabodha-pariśodhinī* by Ātmasarvajña
2. The *Pañcapādikā-vyākhyā* by Ānandapūrṇa Vidyāsāgara
3. The *Vaktavya-prakāśikā* by Uttamajña Yatī
4. The *Vedāntaratna-kośa* by Nṛsiṁhāśramī
5. The *Pañcapādikā-vivaraṇa* by Prakāśātman
6. The *Pañcapādikā-vyākhyā* by Dharmarājādhvarīndra
7. The *Tātparya-dyotinī* by Vijñānātma
8. Other commentaries by unknown authors

I. Prakāśātman and his Pañcapādikā-vivaraṇa

Among the successors of Padmapāda the most prominent was Prakāśātman alias Prakāśātma-yati alias Svayam-prakāśānubhava, pupil of Ananyānubhava[167]. His date is fixed at 1200-1300 A.D.[168]

In his Pañcapādikā-vivaraṇa, the epoch-making commentary on the Pañcapādikā of Padmapāda, Prakāśātman has consolidated all that had been said before him i.c.w. objective '*avidyā*'. His contribution to the field of Advaita Vedānta was so significant and authoritative that his line of thought came to be known as the "*Vivaraṇa*" school which, supplanting even the "*Pañcapādikā*" and the "*Iṣṭasiddhi*" schools of his time, became the leitmotif of all subsequent developments in the evolution of the Advaita tradition. Prakāśātman's notes on Padmapāda's comments on the first four topics (*Adhikaraṇa-s*) are so extensive that the basic teachings (of the whole of "*Śāṅkara-bhāṣya*") have been preserved in them. As a matter of fact, the followers of Padmapāda are called the followers of the school of "*Vivaraṇa*", rather than the school of "*Pañcapādikā*"....'...."Though not a direct disciple of Padmapāda, Prakāśātaman is considered to be the spiritual heir to the great master. He is an inexhaustible fount of inspiration and ideas and is viewed as such by the later masters"[169].

Prakāśātman has expounded in his works all the tenets of

Advaita on the line of Śaṅkara. He is considered as being the first to have propounded the theory of "*mūlāvidyā*" or "*māyā*" as being of "positive beginningless nature" wielded by *Brahman*. His second major contribution is the clear enunciation of the theory that no knowledge occurs without an object. Prakāśātman believes that even in the case of illusion an indescribable object is produced from the ignorance of the substratum. This object serves the purpose of producing the objective knowledge and may even give rise to activity....". "Merely because it is eventually metaphysically cancelled, its momentary apparent existence and fruitfulness cannot be denied", says he[170]. Prakāśātman further declares that, contrary to the claims by the "*Pañcapādikā*" and the "*Bhāmatī*", the texts dealing with "*śravaṇa*", "*manana*" and *nididhyāsana*" are only "*arthavāda*" (i.e., eulogies), "*śravaṇa*" (study of the Scriptures) is enjoined as a means to be practised for the realization of *Brahman*, and that the very first *sūtra* of Bādarāyaṇa is meant to discuss the nature and implications of this injunction"[171].

'*Avidyā*, says Prakāśātman, is distinct from non-apprehension or misapprehension, and is in contact with *Brahman* in the same way as the blue colour is superimposed on the sky.[172] According to him, the false appearance and its knowledge are due to *Anirvacanīya Avidyā*, which operates in the form of three different *Cidābhāsa-s* in the three different states of consciousness (viz. *jāgrat, svapna and suṣupti*) giving rise to three different grades of being, characterized by three different thinking conditions[173]. The author of the "*Vivaraṇa*" was the first to lay down the "twin illusions of knowledge and objects" ("*jñānādhyāsa*", and "*arthādhyāsa*") as a corrollary of Śaṅkara's view about the dual illusion of the Self and the non-Self as "*anyo' nyādhyāsa*". According to him the superimposed is[174] not unreal, for, says he, the unreal cannot appear to be present at any time. He postulates that until the dawn of Knowledge, Nescience is not unreal, but it does get obliterated on the dawn of Knowledge, confirming thus, that at the Absolute level Nescience is unreal[175].

Deliberating on the concept of knowledge, Prakāśātman observes that "the compound of the mind and "*Ātman*" takes the form of any knowledge, which is, as such, changeless in itself. The particular mode of the mind associated with the object becomes the adjunct of "*Ātman*" that appears as knowledge, of an object. The object produces the knowledge, while the contact of the object with the senses gives rise to the paticular mental mode in which the knowledge is reflected. This direct reflection has as its base knowledge itself. In the absence of this mode of the mind knowledge remains indirect"[176]. 'The mind, says Prakāśātman, gives us knowledge of *Brahman*, however defective, which no other object can give, just as even a faulty mirror is the only object that can give, however blurred, and yet true knowledge of ourselves[177]. According to Prakāśātman, "both the soul and God are empirically real, and the identity is really real, but is manifested when Nescience is uprooted. And Nescience, says he, can be uprooted only with the Vedic sentence. Arguments, illustrations, rational explanations, etc. may help in understanding, but they cannot give the certitude. They may corroborate the knowledge gained by some definite means of knowledge. But here (i.c.w.*Brahman*), the Scripture is the supreme, and the only, means of knowledge"[178].

Commentaries on the Pañcapādikā-vivaraṇa:

Prakāśātman's "*Vivaraṇa*" has known a wide range of commentaries over the years, giving testimony to the special place it occupies in Advaita Philosophy. Given hereunder, therefore, is the list of these commentaries[179]:

1. *Tattvadīpana* by Akhaṇḍānanda Muni
2. *Vivaraṇa-darpaṇa* by Amalānanda
3. *Bhāvadyotinī* by Citsukhācārya
4. *Ṭīkāratna* by Ānandapūrṇa
5. *Ṛjuvivaraṇa* by Viṣṇubhaṭṭopādhyāya
6. *Vivaraṇa-prameya-saṅgraha* by Vidyāraṇya
7. *Bhāvaprakāśikā* by Nṛsiṁhāśrama
8. *Vivaraṇopanyāsa* by Rāmānanda Sarasvatī
9. *Vivaraṇojjīvanī* by Yajñeśvara Dīkṣita
10. *Bhāvaprakāśikā* by Parivrājaka
11. *Vyākhyā* by Rāmatīrtha
12. *Vyākhyā* by Kṛṣṇa

Apart from the "*Pañcapādikā-vivaraṇa*", Prakāśātman has also written the following books[180]:

1. *Śabdanirṇaya*

2. *Laukikanyāya-saṅgraha*
3. A metrical summary of *Śāṅkara-bhāṣya*

Main Tenets of the Vivaraṇa School

The main tenets of the *"Vivaraṇa"* School as propounded by Prakāśātman in the *"Pañcapādikā-vivaraṇa"* may be summed up as follows[180]:

1. *Karma* is responsible for the rise of the knowledge of the Self.
2. The direct knowledge of *Brahman* arises from major texts of the Upaniṣads.
3. In the text *"Ātman should be realised"*, etc. there is restrictive injunction.
4. Vedāntic study is the principal factor, and reflection and meditation are the subsidiary features (in Knowledge).
5. *"Jīva"* is the reflected image of *Brahman* in *"Avidyā"*.
6. The locus and content of *"avidyā"* is the same.
7. The Primal Nescience is one only.
8. The content of the direct knowledge of *Brahman* is pure *Brahman.*
9. The first factor in the four-fold aid is the discrimination between what is Eternal and what is non-Eternal.
10. The injunctive text *"One's own section of the Veda must be studied"* has for its fruit the learning of the Veda by rote.
11. The world-creation is explained on the basis of the theory of *quintuplication.*
12. The Omniscience of *Brahman* is based on the modes of *"avidyā"*
13. The 'mind' is not a sense-organ.
14. *"Avidyā"* is located in Pure Consciousness.
15. The nature of *Jīva* and *Īśvara* is explained by the theory of *Pratibimbavāda.*

NOTES

1. The Encyclopedia of Indian Philosophies (EIP). Vol. III, p.10.
2. Ibid, p.9.
3. C.D. Sharma, The Advaita Tradition in Indian Philosophy, (ATIP) P.121.
4. ("सत्यं ज्ञानम् अनन्तं ब्रह्म")। - Bṛh. UP. (III. 9.28).

5. ("विज्ञानम् आनन्दं ब्रह्म") । Bṛh. UP. (IV. 2.4)
6. C.D. Sharma, Loc. Cit., pp.121-122.
7. Ibid, p.122
8. Ibid.
9. "यः सर्वाणि भूतानि अन्तरो यमयति एष ते आत्मा अन्तर्यामी अमृतः।" Bṛh. UP. (III.7.15)
10. Ṛ. V. (VI. 47. 18)
11. "अविद्यायामन्तरे वर्तमानाः स्वयं धीराः पंडितंमन्यमानाः। दंद्रम्यमाणाः परियन्ति मूढा अंधेनैव नीयमाना यथान्धाः॥" Ka. UP. (II. 5)
12. "सदेव सोम्येदमग्र आसीदेकमेवाद्वितीयम्"। (Ch. UP. VI. 2.1)
13. "यथा सोम्यैकेन मृत्पिण्डेन सर्वं मृन्मयं विज्ञातं स्याद्वाचारम्भणं विकारो नामधेयं मृत्तिकेत्येव सत्यम्"। (Ibid. VI. 1.4)
14. "अथ ये चास्येह जीवा ये च प्रेता यच्चान्यदिच्छन्न लभते सर्वं तदत्र गत्वा विन्दतेऽत्र ह्यस्यैते सत्याः कामा अनृतापिधानास्तद्यथापि हिरण्यनिधिं विहितमक्षेत्रज्ञा उपर्युपरि संचरन्तो न विन्देयुरेवमेवेमाः सर्वाःप्रजा अहरहर्गच्छन्त्य एतं ब्रह्मलोकं न विन्दन्त्यनृतेन हि प्रत्यूढाः।" (Ch. UP. VIII. 3.2)
15. Vide, Mbh; Vana Parva, 192, 45-46 - quoted by S. L. Pandey, Loc. Cit., p.118.
16. S.L. Pandey, Loc. Cit., pp. 118-119.
17. Vide, Brahma Sūtra (BS), 1.2.29, 1.4.20
18. "वैश्वानरं पुरुषं पुरुषे अन्तःप्रतिष्ठितं वेद"। Quoted by S.L. Pandey, Loc. Cit., p.119.
19. Ibid.
20. Swami Gambhirananda, Brahmasūtra-Bhāṣya of Śaṅkarācārya, p.284. See also, "प्रतिज्ञासिद्धेर्लिङ्गमाश्मरथ्यः ।" (BS. I.4.20)
21. S.L. Pandey, Loc. Cit., p.120.
22. "आर्त्विज्यमित्यौडुलोमिस्तस्मै हि परिक्रीयते।" (BS. III. 4.45)
23. "उत्क्रमिष्यत एवंभवादित्यौडुलोमिः"। (BS. I.4.21)
24. Swami Gambhirànanda, Loc. Cit., p.287. See also, "औडुलोमिपक्षे पुनः स्पष्टमेवावस्थान्तरापेक्षौ भेदाभेदौ गम्येते।" (SB. on BS. 1.4.22)
25. S.L. Pandey, Loc. Cit., p.122. See also, "जीवो हि परमात्मनोऽत्यन्तं भिन्न एव सन् देहेन्द्रियमनोबुद्ध्युपधानसंपर्कात्सर्वदा कलुषः, तस्य च ज्ञानध्यानादिसाधनानुष्ठानात् संप्रसन्नस्य देहेन्द्रियादि-संघातादुत्क्रमिष्यतः परमात्मनैक्यो-पपत्तेरिदमभेदेनोपक्रमणम्।.... भविष्यन्तमभेदमुपादाय भेदकाले ऽप्यभेद उक्तः। (Bhāmatī on BS. I.4.21)
26. Swami Gambhirananda, Loc. Cit, p.900. See also, "चिति तन्मात्रेण तदात्मकत्वादित्यौडुलोमिः।" (BS. IV. 4.6)
27. S.L. Pandey, Loc. Cit., p.123.
28. Ibid, p.124; see also, "अनुस्मृतेर्बादरिः।" (BS. I.2.30)
29. Hajime Nakamura, A History of Early Vedānta Philosophy, (HEVP), Part-I, p.389. See also, "अभावं बादरिराह ह्येवम्"। (BS. IV. 4.11)
30. "कार्यं बादरिरस्य गत्युपपत्तेः"। (BS. IV. 3.7)
31. Vide, S.L. Pandey, Loc. Cit, p.125.

32. "संपत्तिनिमित्तां प्रादेशमात्रश्रुतिं युक्ततरां जैमिनिराचार्यो मन्यते"। (SB. on BS. I. 2.31)
33. "साक्षादप्यविरोधं जैमिनि:"। (BS. I. 2.28)
34. "जीवप्रधानं वेदं वाक्यं स्याद् ब्रह्मप्रधानं वेति। यतोऽन्यार्थं जीवपरामर्शं ब्रह्मप्रतिपत्यर्थमस्मिन्वाक्ये जैमिनिराचार्यो मन्यते"। (SB. on BS. I. 4. 18)
35. "तद्भूतस्य तु नातद्भावो जैमिनेरपि नियमातद्रूपाभावेभ्य:"। (BS. III. 4.40)
36. S.L. Pandey, Loc. Cit., p.128. See also, "स्वमस्य रूपं ब्राह्ममपहतपाप्मत्वादिसत्यसंकल्पत्वावसानं तथा सर्वज्ञत्वं सर्वेश्वरत्वं च, तेन स्वरूपेणाभिनिष्पद्यत इति जैमिनिराचार्यो मन्यते"। (SB. on BS. IV. 4.5)
37. Vide, Encyclopedia of Religion, (EOR), Vol. 15, p.209
38. Ibid.
39. Ibid.
40. S.L. Pandey, Loc. Cit., p.171.
41. Ibid, p.164.
42. Ibid.
43. Ibid, p.165. See also, 'तस्मान्नित्याच्छब्दात्स्फोटरूपादभिधायकात् क्रियाकारकफललक्षणं जगदभिधेयरूपं प्रभवति। वर्णा एव तु शब्द: इति भगवानुपवर्ष:"। (SB. on BS. I. 3.28)
44. "वर्णेभ्यश्चार्थप्रतीते: सम्भवात् स्फोटकल्पना अनर्थिका।" (SB. on BS. I. 3.28)
45. S.L. Pandey, Loc. Cit., p.174.
46. Ibid.
47. Ibid, p.175 See also, "अन्यैरपि स्ववृत्तौ वर्णितम्। तत्र अथात:शब्दौ प्रथमे एव अध्याये प्रथमसूत्रे वर्णितौ—अथेति पूर्वप्रकृतां धर्मजिज्ञासामपेक्ष्य अनन्तरं ब्रह्मजिज्ञासाप्रारम्भार्थ: ।" (Pañcapādikā, UOM., p.239)
48. S.L. Pandey, Loc. Cit., p.176.
49. Ibid, p.177.
50. Vide, S.L. Pandey, Loc. Cit., p.172.
51. Ibid, pp.200-201.
52. Ibid, p.200.
53. Ibid, p.201.
54. Ibid, p.202.
55. Ibid.
56. Ibid, pp.203-205.
57. Ibid, pp.205-206.
58. Ibid.
59. Ibid, p.207.
60. Prof. M.Hiriyanna, Fragments of Bhartṛprapañca, quoted by S.L. Pandey, Loc. Cit., p.211.
61. Ibid, p.214.
62. Ibid, pp.212, 214.
63. Ibid, p.217.
64. Ibid, pp.218-220.
65. Ibid, pp.225.
66. Ibid, pp.234-235.
67. Ibid, pp.238-241.
68. Vide, Encyclopedia of Religion, (EOR), Op. Cit., Vol.15, p.212.
69. S.L. Pandey, Loc. Cit., p.330.
70. Ibid, p.335.

71. Vide, R.Thangaswami, Advaita Vedanta Literature—A Bibliographical Survey, (AVLBS) pp.196-203
72. Vide, EOR, Op. Cit.
73. Ibid.
74. Ibid.
75. Vide, Mainkar, T.G., The Making of the Vedānta, pp.99-100.
76. Ibid.
77. Vide, Vidhuśekhara Bhattacharya, The Āgamaśāstra of Gauḍapāda, PP. 62-63.
78. Ibid.
79. T.G. Mainkar, Loc. Cit.
80. Vide, EOR, Op. Cit.
81. Vide, Belvalkar, Vedānta Philosophy, pp.204-205.
82. Ibid, pp.206-207.
83. Vide, AVLBS, Op. Cit., p.208.
84. Vide, Belvalkar, Loc. Cit., p.212.
85. Vide, AVLBS, Op. Cit., pp.211-212.
86. G.C. Pandey, Life and Thought of Śaṅkarācārya, pp.96-97.
87. S.N. Dasgupta, A History of Indian Philosophy, Vol. I. p.432.
88. AVLBS, Op. Cit.
89. G.C. Pandey, Loc. Cit.
90. Ibid.
91. Vide, EOR, Op. Cit., pp.64-65.
92. Ibid.
93. G.C. Pandey, Loc. Cit., p.80.
94. Ibid.
95. Ibid.
96. Ibid, p.81.
97. Ibid.
98. Ibid.
99. Ibid, p.87
100. Ibid.
101. Vide, EOR, Op. Cit.
102. Vide, Belvalkar, Loc. Cit., p.218.
103. Ibid.
104. Ibid, p.219.
105. Ibid, p.220.
106. G.C. Pandey, Loc. Cit., p.99.
107. T.G. Mainkar, Loc. Cit., p.114.
108. S.N. Dasgupta, Loc. Cit., p.433.
109. Ibid, p.434.
110. Ibid, p. 435.
111. Ibid, p.438.
112. Ibid, pp.439-440.
113. Vide, EOR, Op. Cit., pp.64-65.
114. Vide, AVLBS, Op. Cit., p.222.
115. S.N. Dasgupta, Loc. Cit., p.82.
116. Vide, EIP, Op. Cit., p.347.
117. Vide, Vedānta-prakriyā-pratyabhijñā, (VPP) pp.100-105.
118. Vide, AVLBS, Op. Cit., p.229.
119. S.N. Dasgupta, Loc. Cit., p.47.

120. Ibid.
121. Ibid.
122. Ibid, pp.98-102.
123. Ibid.
124. Ibid.
125. Ibid.
126. Vide, AVLBS, Op. Cit., pp.229-230.
127. Vide, EIP, Op. Cit., p.347.
128. Vide, AVLBS, Op. Cit., pp.228-229.
129. Vide, EIP, Op. Cit., p.347.
130. S.N. Dasgupta, Loc. Cit., p.88.
131. Ibid. Vide, "आम्नायस्य क्रियार्थत्वात् आनर्थक्यम् अतदर्थानाम्।" MS-I.2.1.
132. Ibid.
133. Ibid, pp.89-90.
134. Ibid.
135. Vide, VPP., Op. Cit., p.93.
136. Ibid, pp.93-94.
137. Ibid, p.98.
138. Vide, EIP, Op. Cit., p.17.
139. Vide, AVLBS, Op. Cit., p.209.
140. V.A.Ramaswami Śāstri, Pūrva Mīmāṁsā Śāstra, Introduction.
141. Ibid.
142. Ibid.
143. Ibid.
144. Vide, AVLBS, Op. Cit., p.234.
145. V.A. Ramaswami Śāstri, Loc. Cit.
146. Ibid.
147. Vide, VPP, OP. Cit., p.113.
148. Ibid, p.114.
149. Ibid.
150. S.N. Dasgupta, Loc. Cit., p.108.
151. Ibid, pp.109-110.
152. Ibid, p.111.
153. Ibid.
154. Vide, AVLBS, Op.Cit., p.235.
155. Ibid, Introduction.
156. Ibid, p.228.
157. Ibid.
158. Ibid.
159. Ibid.
160. Swami Satchidānandendra Saraswati, Loc. Cit., p.105.
161. Ibid.
162. S.N. Dasgupta, Loc. Cit., pp.102-106.
163. Ibid.
164. Ibid.
165. Ibid.
166. Vide, AVLBS, Op. Cit., p.228.
167. Ibid, p.237.
168. S.N.Dasgupta, Loc. Cit., p.103.
169. Pañcapādikā - (Maheshānanda Ed.), Introduction.

170. Ibid.
171. Sw. Satchidānandendra Saraswatī, Loc. Cit., p.120.
172. Ibid.
173. Ibid, p.121.
174. Vide, Pañcapādikā, Op. Cit.
175. Ibid.
176. Ibid.
177. Ibid.
178. Ibid.
179. Vide, AVLBS, Op. Cit., pp.237-238.
180. Ibid.
181. Ibid. Introduction

CHAPTER III

THEORY OF ERROR

Section I

NON-ADVAITA SCHOOLS

In their attempts to understand and explain the world-phenomenon with all its complexities and with Man at its centre, philosophers from time immemorial have formulated various theories with respect to the concept of Reality or Truth and the possible means of knowing It. As a sequel to the above there has been a proliferation of Theories of Reality (or Truth), of Perception and of Error, each claiming to hold the perfect key to the above-mentioned ontological and epistemological problems. Thus, the different schools of Indian Philosophy, viz. Nyāya-Vaiśeṣika, Sāṅkhya, Yoga, Mīmāṁsā and Vedānta, apart from Cāravaka, Jainism and Buddhism, have postulated their own Theories of Reality, Perception and Error, which subsequently got further multiplied as a consequence of the divergent currents of opinion within these Schools. All the three problems referred to above being intertwined, the discussion of one of them entails of necessity a discussion of the other two. In the ensuing discussion therefore, though the focal point will be the Theory of Error, light will be thrown, *en passant*, on the Theories of Reality and Perception as well, postulated by the different Schools of thought, starting with Nyāya and culminating evidently in Advaita Vedānta.

The concept of Error, which may as well be termed "wrong knowledge" or "Ignorance" or "wrong perception", or "Nescience", can be traced back to the Vedas where we find the Seer inquisitively suggesting that in the "beginning" there was neither "naught" nor "existence"[1]. The same Hymn ends with a note of doubt as to whether the gods are themselves aware of the "Truth". Doubt contains the seed of error. It has ignorance or absence of knowledge of the Truth or Reality as substratum. As most of the theories of Reality, Perception and Error of the Indian Systems of Philosophy emanate from the Veda-s, it may be justifiably said that the above Hymn and other Hymns of Creation represent the fountainhead of Indian speculation about Truth and Reality of which an echo is to be found in the Upaniṣads and allied Scriptures.

A. Theory of Error of Nyāya-Vaiśeṣika

According to Nyāya the world is constituted of twelve objects, viz. the self, body, sense-organs, sense-objects, judgement or apprehension, mind or internal organ, activity, defect, rebirth, (or fruition), pain and release[2]. These therefore represent the *Prameya-s* of the Naiyāyika-s, i.e., they are the *Knowable-s* or objects to be known or perceived—with a view to knowing the Reality. According to Vātsyāyana, the true knowledge of these twelve objects leads to release (from pain) and the wrong knowledge or wrong apprehension of them leads to bondage.

"....*asya tu tattva-jñānād apavargaḥ; mithyā-jñānāt saṁsāraḥ*...."[3]

It is interesting to note here that Gautama and Kaṇāda consider Ātman to be an object of perception or cognition. This gives rise to a fundamental question as to who is the cognizer (*pramātā*) when the *Ātman* itself is made an object of cognition (*prameya*)? At the very outset, the Nyāya-Vaiśeṣika School seems to be treading on a contradictory path when, on the one hand, it declares *Ātman* to be a *prameya* (object of knowledge), and on the other, describes *Ātman* as the substratum of knowledge itself (which is enumerated among the qualities, referred to as *Guṇa*)—

"*Jñānādhikaraṇam ātmā*"[4]

Among the four means of knowledge that Nyāya acknowledges for the right cognition of the above - mentioned *Prameya-s*, viz. *Pratyakṣa* (perception), *Anumāna* (Inference), *Upamāna* (Comparison) and *Śabda* (Verbal Testimony), Perception is considered to be the most important "because it alone is self-sufficient to allay doubt"[5]. "When a thing has been apprehended by Perception (i.e., has been directly perceived), there is no further desire on the part of the cognizer (to have any other or further cognition of that thing)", says Vātsyāyana[6]. According to Gautama "sense-perception is that cognition which is produced by the contact of the sense-organs with the object (of perception). Such a cognition is one that is not expressible by words, that is not erroneous and that is well-defined"[7]. For perception to be possible, notes Vātsyāyana, there is first a contact between *Ātman* and the Mind, then the Mind comes into contact with the sense-organ, which ultimately comes into contact with the object (in front), and thus the latter is perceived sensually.

A cognition cannot be "errorless" unless it is free from *doṣa-s* (defects), the implication being that an 'erroneous' cognition falls into the category of '*mithyā-jñāna*', i.e. false-knowledge. Nyāya classifies erroneous knowledge (*viparyaya*) as *apramā,* i.e. invalid knowledge, along with doubt (*saṁśaya*) and hypothetical reasoning (*tarka*). It is noteworthy that in Vaiśeṣika too *viparyaya* is classified as *Avidyā* (incorrect cognition) along with *saṁśaya* (doubt), *anadhyavasāya* (indecision) and *svapna* (dream). The root cause of error is wrong-knowledge (*mithyājñāna*), since by its elimination are eliminated defects (*doṣa-s*), along with activity (*pravṛtti*), birth (*janma*) and pain (*duḥkha*)[8]. Elucidating the concept of *mithyā-jñāna,* Vātsyāyana says that it is the "wrong-apprehension of the non-Self as Self..... It is delusion, egoism, in the form of mistaking the non-Self to be the Self", i.e., identifying the non-Self with the Self—

> "*kim punaḥ tan-mithyā-jñānam-anātmanyātmagrahaḥ ahamasmīti moho' haṁkāra iti*"[9].

Vātsyāyana says that *mithyā-jñāna* is not a negation of true knowledge, but rather a "positive wrong-knowledge"—

> "*mithyā-jñānaṁ vai khalu moho na tattva-jñānasyānutpatti-mātram*"[10].

The Vaiśeṣika describes wrong-cognition as that "which is brought about by defective sense-organs and vitiated predisposition", while true-knowledge is one not so 'defiled'[11]—

> "*indriya-doṣāt saṁskāra-doṣācca avidyā tad-duṣṭājñānam; aduṣṭam vidyā*"[12].

According to the Nyāya-Vaiśeṣika school *viparyaya* is that erroneous cognition which occurs when 'due to a defect in the sense-organs, the trace of a previously perceived thing produces contact between the internal organ (Mind) and Self, which in combination with '*adharma*' (demerit), produces an erroneous idea, e.g. of "horse" with regard to "cow". Such errors arise, says Praśastapāda, both with respect to perception and otherwise. For example, we often mistake steam for smoke, and thus infer fire. Likewise people ....think the body is the Self., etc."[13]—

"*atasmiṁstad iti pratyayo viparyayaḥ. yathā gavi eva aśvaḥ iti*"[14]

According to Jayanta Bhaṭṭa, a mistake or error consists in misinterpreting a thing; e.g., "when one cannot 'read' an object in the right context he wrongly places it and commits a mistake"[15]. He (Bhaṭṭa) further avers that a knowledge, whether true or false, is necessarily a judgement, implying that even if a judgement is wrong it does refer to a real object[16]. Nyāya believes that truth or falsehood applies only to a judgement—the object cognized cannot be unreal[17].

Commenting on the theory of error in his *Nyāya-vārttika-tātparya-ṭīkā*, Vācaspati Miśra observes that "when a piece of shell is cognized as silver, there is nothing wrong with the object itself. There is also no error in the '*nirvikalpa pratyakṣa*' (undifferentiated perception) of the object in which brightness, etc. are cognized in an undifferentiated manner. But on account of certain defects in the sense-organ and the influence of memory, etc., the shell is cognized as silver in the '*savikalpa pratyakṣa*' (differentiated perception)"[18].

Nyāya believes that in the case of right cognition there is established a sense-organ-object contact; but in the case of erroneous cognition "a cognitional-contact (*jñāna-lakṣaṇa-sannikarṣa*) is established between the sense-organ and the other objects, like *silver*, etc. And this leads to the actual perception of those objects. "This perceived object is then referred to the locus "*this*", the "something" (viz. *shell*) which is (seen) in front and is perceived by the sense-organs". So far, says Nyāya, there is perception of "*this*" and of "*silver*" in two different ways, and there is nothing wrong in this. But error starts when the silver that is perceived elsewhere is predicated of the "*this*" (*shell*). The error lies not in the presentations involved in the perception but in the determination of one perception by another one, brought about by association, memory, etc. This determination results in the cognition of an object as something other than what it is and hence the term *"anyathā-khyāti"* by which it is called"[19]. "Error is thus a false apprehension of the real", says Nyāya. The difference between valid and invalid knowledge is that "while valid knowledge (*pramā*) is objective in the sense that it is grounded in the object itself (*artha-janya*), error (*apramā*) is subjective in so far as it is due to the introduction of a certain foreign character into the object by the knowing subject, i.e. the cognizer."[20]

Nyāya believes that knowledge, not being itself self-luminous, is the manifestation of objects, and in this character "it is neutral to validity or invalidity"[21]. "The validity or invalidity of cognition is brought about (*utpadyate*) by extraneous conditions such as healthy sense-organs, nearness of the object (of perception), etc. and defective sense-organs, distance, etc. respectively in the case of perceptual cognition.... Validity and invalidity of knowledge are thus extrinsic – "*parataḥ-prāmāṇya* and *parataḥ-aprāmāṇya*" respectively"[22]. Vide,

"*doṣo'pramāyā(ḥ) janakaḥ, pramāyāstu guṇo bhavet*"[23]

"Gaṅgeśa and his followers are guided by the principle that no cognition can be about the unreal. According to them even in the case of illusion not only the *viśeṣya* and the *prakāra* but also the *saṁsarga* are to be regarded as real"[24]. "If error means a false cognition, in which something appears *as* something *else*, it follows that for a cognition to be valid it is essential for it to be of the nature of "cognition of something *as* something, i.e., of something as having characteristics.... For it is only when perceiving (or cognizing) is seen as perceiving-*as*, that perceiving something as something *else* becomes a possibility in the first instance"[25]. The failure of an illiusory cognition to grasp the object in its true character does not make it cease to be perceiving *as*, i.e., it does not compromise its title as "qualificative cognition" (*savikalpa-jñāna*)[26]. "To see shell as silver, is to deal with, and connect two different objects which bear no such unity in the real world. When, in a situation where there is a direct contact with shell, we, instead of cognizing it in the form "this is shell", cognize it mistakenly as "this is silver", we connect the "*this*" which refers to the "shell" actually present to us, with "*silver*" which we had seen earlier, and which therefore exists elsewhere, and is not present at the moment, and thus set up a relation where it does not exist: the silver-character is attributed to "*this*" where it does not in fact belong[27]. Putting the same thing differently, Gaṅgeśa says, "A cognition is false if the qualifier does not occur in or is not contained in, the qualificand".

'Side by side with *asambandha-agraha*' (i.e., non-apprehension of the absence of relation) between what is being perceived and what is being remembered is present also in an erroneous cognition an element of '*sambandha-graha*' (i.e., apprehension of relation or connection) between what is being perceived and what is being remembered. Both the *asambandha-agraha* and the *sambandha-graha* result in the perceptual superimposition of the qualities of the remembered object on the object being perceived, giving rise to the *invalid cognition* called *error*. All such erroneous cognitions, says Vācaspati, are due to such similarities of qualities and characteristics—resulting in each case in superimposition of the above nature[28].

Jayanta Bhaṭṭa, postulates three possible *ālambana-s* (cognition-support for the perceptual error) in the case of the illusion of water:

1. the sun-rays,
2. water remembered, and
3. the sun-rays with the appearance in them of some characteristics foreign to them, viz. water *here*.

Therefore, Nyāya does not consider the object in front to be the *ālambana* of the illusory cognition, but rather the interferring external element "with its own characteristics hidden", thus helping in the superimposition of other qualities on it[29].

According to Jayanta Bhaṭṭa therefore, the *ālambana* is that which gives rise to the wrong cognition, without being itself the agent thereof. In any false cognition normally the *ālambana* is a support that is distinguishable from the appearance (*pratibhāsa*) of which it is a foundation. The "*shell*" then should normally be the *ālambana* for the "*silver*", and the "*rope*" for the "*snake*". But Jayanta Bhaṭṭa seems to suggest in the example cited above that it is "water" and not the object in front that is the *ālambana*.

For Nyāya, the illusory cognition is not non-perceptual or non-sensual in character, as both the subject and the object of the invalid cognition are real. The illusory cognition is however called *anyathā-khyāti* because the *"shell"* appears invested with a different character. Nyāya further states that "all our perceivings-*as* bear the mark of previous experience. In like manner our present illusions too can be traced back to our misapprehensions of the same". Furthermore, a thing like skyflower cannot be a subject of valid or invalid cognition as it cannot be perceived—whether at present or in the past. "It follows therefore that only a real object can be cognized—whether correctly or incorrectly"[30]. Therefore the so-called appearances are also part of reality, says Nyāya. The illusory object cannot be but real.

B. Theory of Error of Sāṁkhya-Yoga

Though the Sāṁkhya-Yoga does not elaborate explicitly on the nature of knowledge of *Prāmāṇya* (i.e., validity of knowledge), it can be said as belonging to the school of "*Svataḥ-prāmāṇya*" and "*Svataḥ-aprāmāṇya*", on the basis of the fact that it advocates the theory that everything is inherent in its cause. The Sāṁkhya-Yoga believes that knowledge does not depend on the external factor for its validity. This theory of intrinsic truth and error is based on the theory that an effect pre-exists in its cause-*(Satkāryavāda)*, as is mentioned in the Sarva-darśana-saṅgraha—

"*pramāṇatvāpramāṇatve svataḥ sāṁkhyāḥ samāśritāḥ*"[31]

Similarly, "Truth and Error, says Sāṁkhya, are inherent in knowledge; they cannot be brought about by any extraneous means. They both depend on the same causes which produce knowledge, and not on any other additional factor—they are revealed by knowledge itself. One need not go beyond knowledge for the ascertainment or its truth or falsehood"[32]. This is substantiated by the Yuktidīpikā also[33].

Knowledge, whether true or false, says Yoga, is the result of the fluctuations or modifications of the mind-stuff or "*buddhi*". These fluctuations of the mind-stuff or "*vṛtti-s*" are enumerated in the Yoga-Sūtra as (i) Sources of valid knowledge or real cognition, (ii) sources of invalid knowledge or wrong-cognition, or misconception; (iii) imagination (iv) sleep and (v) memory[34].

Viparyaya or error is described by Patañjali as "false knowledge of a thing which does not correspond to its real form"[35].

Commenting on this Sūtra, Vyāsa says that it is not true knowledge because it is contradicted by a source of true knowledge, since a source of true knowledge has an existent object as its content. In such instances (as *viparyaya*) it is seen that a false knowledge is contradicted by a source of true knowledge. Thus, for instance, the appearance of two moons is contradicted by the perception of the actually existent one moon[36].

Vijñānabhikṣu, commenting on the Sūtra, makes the following observations—"The description of false is, "not-resting on (the true form of) the object", viz., distinguished by an object which does not have a similar form. In misapprehension there is a superimposition of knowledge on the object. ...In this Nescience of Yoga, the theory of erroneous knowledge is "*Anyathākhyāti*" and not only non-discrimination ("*aviveka*"), as in the *Sāṁkhya system*"[137].

Vāscaspati Miśra on his part has this much to say on the Sūtra in question, "Unreal cognition is the *knowing of the unreal*, possessed of a form not its own.... It means that it has a form which shines out as if it were real knowledge. The words "possessed of a form not its own", are equivalent to "not possessed of the form which is its own"[38].

According to K.C. Bhattacharya, *"viparyaya"* or error as a *"vṛtti"* refers to an unreal content and may be generated by a form of words but the content is not verbally expressible (except as a contradiction) when it is known to be unreal. The content was meant by the generative verbal expression as a real object, and not as a "possible object plus its reality", so that now that the reality is negated, it is not reduced to possible object only. Of the erroneous content as such we can say that it appeared to be presented, but never that it is presented.... *Viparyaya* or error is to Yoga a "*vṛtti*" that has not the form of the object that it purports to refer to. It is then possible to refer to an object without a presentation having its form. That a contradiction is committed but not presented is just what is implied by the theory of *Anyathākhyāti*"[39].

Patañjali sub-divides "*viparyaya*" into five kinds, calling them "*kleśa-s*" or afflictions or hindrances, viz., "Nescience, Egoism, Attachment, Aversion and Love of Life"[40]. Elaborating the term "*Avidyā*" (Nescience), Patañjali says that, "Nescience is the taking of the non-eternal, the impure, the painful and the not-Self to be the eternal, the pure, the pleasurable and the Self"[41]. Commenting on this Sūtra, Vyāsa says that "the taking of the non-eternal to be eternal is the possession of such notions as that the earth is permanent, the firmament with the moon and the stars is permanent, the gods are immortal, etc. Similarly, the seeing of purity in the body, which is impure and highly disgusting, and... the cognition of the Self in the not-Self and of pleasure under these circumstances, is Nescience"[42].

Discussing further the concept of illusion, Vijñānabhikṣu says that "since the knowledge of the world has the appearance of *reality in unreality,* this illusion also is said to be like the knowledge of 'silver' in "mother-of pearl"[43]. Continuing on the same line, Vijñānabhikṣu observes that....the world is an effect of "*Avidyā*", because it is only due to the idea of doership, like, "I am the doer", etc., which, through giving rise to "*dharma*" (merit) and "*adharma*"(de-merit) is the cause of the entire world. He further adds that the term "*Avidyā*" should not be taken to mean "other than *Vidyā*", or "absence of *Vidyā*", (on the basis of the six meanings referred to in the famous couplet)[44], but rather "wrong knowledge".... The essence of "*Avidyā*" should be known as some existing thing and not (as) non-existence or absence"[45]. Vyāsa remarks that *Avidyā* is neither right knowledge nor a negation of right knowledge, but rather a different knowledge opposite of true knowledge[46].

Drawing the line of demarcation between *Avidyā* and *Viparyaya,* K.C. Bhattacharya notes that "to understand Empirical Error (*Viparyaya*), Yoga has to refer to *raw* "*Avidyā*", i.e. to *Avidyā* beyond "*asmitā*" or (to the) transcendental Principle of Error, which is conceived in Yoga as a function". The Empirical Error, says he, unlike other "*vṛttis*" referring to the object explicitly, embodies *Avidyā,* the transcendental "Principle of Error"[47]. *Avidyā,* continues K. C. Bhattacharya, is *essentially* the wrong viewing of the object as the Self, and *derivatively,* in cognitive, moral and hedonistic reference to the object of experience, the viewing of it as though it were as real, as clean or sacred, as doer or enjoyable as one's own self"[48].

In the 'Sāṁkhya-sūtra-vṛtti', Aniruddha says that the Sāṁkhya Theory of Error is known as "*Sadasat-khyāti*" as it acknowledges "the apprehension of both what is existent and non-existent" in an illusory cognition[49]. An error, according to this School, involves both "*this*", which in fact "*is*", and "*that*", which in fact, "*is not*"[50]. To some extent, says Sāṁkhya, there is a true perception when anyone mistakes one thing for another i.e., something is actually perceived that cannot be denied. The mistake lies in believing the thing perceived to be something else. "To this extent therefore, something, in fact, is perceived as what it is not"[51].

According to Sāṁkhya, Consciousness in its pure form cannot be the revealer of any external object. 'It reveals only its own true form'. It is on account of non-discrimination that the Self is wrongly perceived as the knower, the doer, etc. Vijñānabhikṣu says that this (erroneous cognition) is due to the fact that "the Pure intellect reflects the consciousness of *Puruṣa* and becomes intelligized – resulting in the false appropriation of the inherent "*ahaṁkāra*" of "*buddhi*" by the self. "*Vivekāgraha*" (non-discrimination) is therefore the root cause of all illusory cognitions[52]. This "*agrahaṇa*", says Sāṁkhya, is of "*svarūpa-bheda*", i.e., it involves the failure to discriminate between two "*vṛtti-s*" (or cognition)—one of true knowledge and the other of false knowledge.

The *Sāṁkhya-pravacana-sūtra* describing the doctrine of *Sadasatkhyāti*, mentions that in an illusory knowledge, something real (*sat*) is apprehended as well as something unreal (*asat*), because of its being uncontradicted and contradicted (affterwards)[53]. In the illusion '*this is silver*', '*this*' is existent because it is not contradicted and '*silver*' is non-existent because it is contradicted. The sublating cognition 'this is not silver' sublates the cognition '*silver*'[54]. This '*silver*' though "*sat*" as existing elsewhere, is '*asat*' when it is supposed to be present in "*this*" '*shell*'[55]. "At the transcendental level all things are real and are not cancelled or contradicted in respect of their very nature as they are eternal. But they are contradicted if they are wrongly known as identical with "*Caitanya*" or Pure Consciousness"[56].

C. Theories of Error of Mīmāṁsā

'*Dharma*', as propounded in the Veda, being the subject *par excellence* of the Mīmāṁsā School of Philosophy, it becomes imperative for that School to establish the infallibility of the

Veda so as to give weight to its concept of '*Dharma*' and its fruit—'*Niḥśreyasa*', i.e. Liberation (to be attained through the performance of Vedic actions). For doing so, Jaimini and his followers postulated their own epistemological theories, among which the Theory of Perception , in which is impregnated their Theory of Error, occupies a place of great significance.

All knowledge, claims the Mīmāṁsā, is *ipso facto* true. Indeed, "the unique epistemological theory of this school is that all cognitions are valid"[57]. The central concern of Mīmāṁsā therefore, is not so much "to prove the truth of a cognition (for, that is taken for granted) as to prove the falsity of cognition"[58] (or the absence thereof), with a view to establishing the 'unchallengeable validity of the Veda".

At the very heart of the Mīmāṁsa Philosophy is to be found the doctrine of "*Svataḥ-prāmāṇya-vāda*", i.e. the doctrine of 'self-validity of knowledge', according to which, all knowledge, except that emanating from memory (*smṛti*), is valid in itself–"for it itself certifies its own truth, and neither depends on any other extraneous condition nor on any other knowledge for its validity"[59]. Knowledge does not arise from any objective fact, says Mīmāṁsā, since all objective facts are themselves dependent upon it (i.e. knowledge) for their cognition. The objects get revealed to the perceiver as soon as knowledge arises in the person. And in this process, there is no intermediacy of any link whatsoever dependent on which knowledge reveals the external objects. Therefore be it in its own production or in its action (of object-illumination), knowledge is totally independent—

"*svakāryakāraṇe svataḥ prāmāṇyam jñānasya*"[60].

As a general rule, all knowledge is thus taken to be valid on its own strength, unless invalidated by contradictory knowledge. Knowledge may be invalidated either on account of subsequent contradictory experience referred to as "*bādhaka-jñāna*", or when the sense-organs and/or factors relating to them are proved afterwards to be faulty or defective. In this context, it is to be noted that memory (*smṛti*) is not considered to be valid knowledge as it is itself dependent upon previous congnitions or upon existing impressions. And so is dream also.

Kumārila Bhaṭṭa defines valid knowledge as "a firm or assured cognition of objects, which does not stand in need of confirmation by other cognitions"[61]; Vide,

"tasmāt dṛḍhaṁ yad utpannam nāpi saṃvādam ṛcchati;
jñānāntareṇa vijñānam tat pramāṇam pratīyatām" (Ś.V.II.80)

Pārthasārthi says that "valid knowledge is the apprehension of a previously unapprehended object, which is devoid of defects in its source and is not contradicted by subsequent experience"[62]; Vide,

"kāraṇa-doṣa-bādhakajñāna-rahitam agṛhītagrāhi-jñānaṁ pramāṇam"[63].

According to Pārthasārthi, therefore, for knowledge to be valid, it needs to be (i) novel, (ii) free from doubt, and (iii) true; and if any of the above three is absent, it loses its validity"[64]. To kumārila thus, the characteristic "*agṛhīta-grāhitva*", i.e., "the character of not having been cognized already, is indispensable for a cognition to be valid"[65]. According to him, "a knowledge which does not add something to our present stock of information cannot be valid. Validity consists in discovering new objects or new features of known objects..."[66] Differentiated perception (*savikalpa-jñāna*) is also considered as valid knowledge as "it adds much to the undifferentiated perception (*avikalpa-jñāna*)"[67].

Cognition once generated (through sense-object contact) 'proceeds independently in its task of ascertaining the true nature of things'—

"svataḥ sarva-pramāṇānāṁ prāmāṇyam iti gamyatām;
na hi svato' satī śaktiḥ kartumanyena śakyate;
ātmalābhe ca bhāvānāṁ kāraṇāpekṣatā bhavet;
labdhātmanāṁ svakāryeṣu pravṛttiḥ svayameva tu.

—Ś.V.II. 47/48

In his *Bhāṣya* on the Mīmāṁsā-sūtra I.1.2., Śabara says that the cognition which is followed by a cancelling cognition in the form "this is not as I have cognized it", should be considered as being erroneous or wrong—

"yo hi janitvā pradhvaṁsate, naitadevam-iti, sa mithyā pratyayaḥ"[68]

According to the Bhāṭṭa School of Mīmāṁsā, a cognition is said to be wrong when:

1. the mind is affected by some sort of derangement; or
2. the sense-organ is beset with some disability; or
3. The object itself has such drawbacks, as being too small for perception, etc.[69]. 'That cognition is wrong, says the Mīmāṁsā, whose means are defective or in respect of which there is a cancelling cognition'. It follows, therefore, that whereas validity of knowledge is intrinsic, invalidity of knowledge is extrinsic, being due to vitiating (external) conditions—

"*jñānasya prāmāṇyam svataḥ aprāmāṇyam parataḥ*"[70]

There are three kinds of invalid knowledge, says Kumārila Bhaṭṭa—viz.

1. "*Mithyājñāna*" (error or illusion);
2. Ajñāna (Non-cognition, or non-apprehension, or ignorance); and
3. Saṁśaya (doubt)—

"*aprāmāṇyam tridhā bhinnam mithyātvājñānasaṃśayaiḥ*
vastutvād dvividhasyātra sambhavo duṣṭakāraṇāt"[71]
—*Ś.V.II.54*

Illusion or Error represents an object in a form different from what it actually is—

"*anyathā-santam-ākāram anyathā gṛhṇāti*"[72]

In the classical example of illusion, says Kumārila, the eye, is in fact in contact with the "*shell*" or "*rope*" in front, which is represented by "*this*", while the '*silver*' or '*snake*' is represented by "*that*". Both the "*this*" and the "*that*" are real—only their mutual identity is false. The falsity here consists in perceiving the silver "here" and "now", while it actually exists elsewhere. The cause of the illusion, the Bhāṭṭa school believes, is the similarity between the "*shell*" and the "*silver*", and the defects in the eye contact. The (false) cognition of 'silver' is superimposed on the perceived "*this*"[73]. In the illusion of mirage, water is falsely perceived as a result of the eye coming into contact with the sand heated by sun-rays. Here, too, the sun-rays (and its substratum, the sand), and the water are both real, says the Bhāṭṭa school; only their connection is unreal[74]. Śālikanātha observes that in the cognition of hot water also there is erroneous cognition, as the heat experienced really belongs to particles of fire and not to water. But yet the cognition is valid and non-erroneous as both water and heat are perceived; only the identity of heat with water, which is due to superimposition, is wrong. In like manner, the cognition of "yellow-shell" in lieu of white conch-shell is also valid knowledge as there are cognitions of both the shell and yellowness. But as this cognition stands contradicted by a later cognition, it is erroneous; vide,

> "*yatra tu vyavahāra-visaṁvādo nāsti tatra bhrāntirapi na vyapadiśyate yathoṣṇajala-jñāne/tatrāpi hi na jalagatam-auṣṇyam anubhūyate kintu vahnyavayavagatameva; tasmāt pītaśaṁkhādi-jñānam pramāṇam eva bhrāntaṁ cetyanavadyam*"[75].

The Bhāṭṭa theory of illusion is known as *"Viparītakhyātivāda"*—as according to it, in an illusion, a real object is projected in the form of a different object, which too is real; vide,

> —"*tatra śuktikā-rajatādi-jñānaṁ śuktikākhyam bhāvaṁ śuktikārūpeṇa sadrūpaṁ bhāvāntarasya rajatasya yat sadrūpaṁ rajatarūpam tena rūpeṇa grahaṇād abhrāntaṁ bhavati*"[76].

In all cases of illusory perception it is only the relation between the subject and the predicate element which is unreal though appearing as real. But the 'relata' are always real—

> —"*sarvatra saṁsarga-mātram-asadevāvabhāsate saṁsargiṇastu santa eva; seyam viparīta-khyātirityucyate mīmāṁsakaiḥ*"[77]

"An illusion is therefore a positive mis-apprehension in which the mistake consists in identifying two *unrelated real* objects under the influence of some vicious subjective and objective conditions"[78].

Though the Bhāṭṭa Mīmāṁsaka-s agree with the Nyāya theory of Error, yet they reject the hypothesis that illusion is the result of extra-normal sense-contact (*alaukika sannikarṣa*). They argue that if distant objects could be perceived through such a contact, then there would be the possibility of everybody becoming omniscient—

> "*evaṁ hi na kaścidasarvajño bhavet*"[79]

According to the Bhāṭṭa theory of Viparītakhyāti, "an absent object has the power of producing its cognition, though it has no power to inspire other fruitful practical activities in relation to it. In an illusion, due to defective sense-functioning, an absent object appears to be present through the impression left in the mind by its past experience. A past object (e.g. silver) is not capable of producing its present cognition directly; it does so indirectly through its impressions residing in the soul. It could not have the said causal potency if it were absolutely non-existent. In the original experience the object "*silver*" was the direct cause of its impression produced in the soul. Thus, the cognition-producing power of the object was indirectly transferred to the soul, which now gives rise to the cognition of "*silver*"[80].

Prabhākara on his side reduces all error and doubt to simply an absence of knowledge. According to him "an illusion is not a unitary cognition, but a composite of two cognitions whose distinction is not apprehended. He believes that whatever is manifested in a cognition must be regarded as its object. Therefore, in the cognition "This is silver" where the actual object in front is the *shell*, since '*silver*' is manifested it must be regarded as the object of this cognition"[81]. He says further that "the cancelling cognition, "This is not silver but shell" does not render invalid the previous cognition, but merely points out the distinction between the elements of presentation and representation —i.e. between perception and memory, in the cognition, (which distinction, when not apprehended, leads to the erroneous cognition). The shell is thus not cognised at all. The silver is remembered but is not remembered as "*that*"— i.e. as something perceived in the past, but rather as "*this*". This failure to distinguish between "*that*" and "*this*" leads to the illusory cognition resulting from the superimposition of a wanting object on the one present. "The judgement thus partakes of the dual character of remembrance (*smaraṇa*) and direct apprehension (*anubhava*), and as such differs from a valid cognition wherein there is no room for remembrance. "The cognition, "This is silver" is of the form of an illusion or error inasmuch as a cognition of silver, which is in the form of memory, is passed on as presentation of silver, and this is found to be inconsistent and is contradicted in actual experience"[82]; vide, *"na hi anyasamprayukte cakṣuṣyanālambanasya jñānasyotpattis sambhavati, andhasyānutpādāt ityuktam, ata evedam ucyate-nānyākāraṁ ālambanam-anyākārasya jñānasyotpatti-hetur iti"*[83].

The failure to distinguish between memory and perception is due to some weakness of the mind and is the source of the erroneous judgement.

"kathaṁ tarhi viparyayaḥ? agrahaṇādeva iti vadāmaḥ ...yuktam ca duṣṭatāyāḥ kāryākṣamatvaṁ na punaḥ kāryāntara sāmarthyam; tasmād grahaṇanibandhanā eva viparyayāḥ"[84].

The cause of the non-discrimination referred to above is the lapse of memory *(smṛtipramoṣa)*, says Prabhākara. "When the memory is 'stripped' of *"that"*-ness (*pramuṣṭa-tattāka*) it becomes obscured. The illusory "silver", says Prabhākara, cannot be said to have been "perceived" as there was no eye-contact with it. It cannot be said to have been "inferred" also as there was no mark (*liṅga*) of its presence. Therefore by elimination it is established that the 'silver' was "remembered"[85]. Similarly, in the illusion of a yellow conch-shell there are two cognitions—

1. Apprehension of the "yellowness" of the bile present in the eye without apprehending the substance, i.e., the bile; and
2. Apprehension of the substance of the conch-shell without apprehending its whiteness. There, as a substance (conch) and quality stand in mutual expectancy (*ākāṅkṣā*), the two apprehensions cannot remain unrelated, and consequently the manifestation appears as similar to the manifestation of a real yellow conch"[86].

Śālikanātha observes that non-discrimination in an illusory cognition is due to defects which can only affect the normal functioning of the cause, but cannot give rise to a different effect. The defects of the sense-organs produce either an incomplete cognition (say, of "nacre") or no cognition at all, but they cannot produce an entirely different object (say, of "*silver*")[87].

"A sublating cognition (*bādhakajñāna*) does not contradict an illusion, says Prabhākara; it simply distinguishes the presentative element (shell) and the representative element (silver) from each other. The representative element does not appear in consciousness as representation owing to lapse of memory (*smṛtipramoṣa*)"[88]. Owing to lapse of memory representation appears to be perception.

> "*grahaṇasya viśeṣo hi gṛhīta-grahaṇam smṛtiḥ. gṛhītāṁśa-moṣeṇa gṛhītiriti tiṣṭhati*"[89]

Illusion is therefore nothing but an absence of discrimination (*vivekāgraha*); hence the appellation "*Vivekākhyāti*" by which Prabhākara's Theory of Error is known.

D. Theory of Error of the Mādhyamika School

Error, according to the Mādhyamika school, is the cognition of a totally non-existent object as existent. Illusion is to that school the apprehension of an unreal object as real. Error, they say, cannot be error if it reveals reality even partially. In other words, none of the contents revealed in an error is existent or real. Error is erroneous only because it presents the unreal as real[90]. In the illusion of shell-silver, there is the apprehension of non-existent silver as real. Though silver in this cognition does not exist, it is perceived as an existing object[91]. According to the Asatkhyātivādin-s, says Prabhācandra, "neither external things nor internal cognitions are ontologically real, and consequently, there is variety neither in external things nor in cognitions"[92]. The sublating cognition "This is not silver" proves that error reveals nothing". The sublating cognition though, is itself veridical, otherwise it would not correct error. Though the object presented in the illusory cognition manifests itself as real to consciousness, it is proved to be unreal by philosophical speculation[93]. The Mādhyamika 'Nihilist advocates thus the voidness (*śūnyatā*) of all existence. "Error is but the apprehension of non-being (*asat*)". According to Pārthasārthi, the Asatkhyātivadin-s negate both the relata and the relation in one erroneous cognition. In the illusion 'this is silver', for example, "*this*", "*silver*" as well as their relation—all three are unreal[94]. The erroneous cognition claims that something is (in existence) when (in reality) it is not. In the rope-snake cognition, for example, all that the cognition shows is that something is (in existence) and that (thing) is a snake. The consequent sublating or correcting cognition, 'It is not a snake' proves the voidness of the content "it". The Asatkhyātivādin-s therefore hold that "neither in error nor in the cancelling cognition does the cognizer cognize anything as real, for the erroneous cognition has an unreal as its object[95]. The Asatkhyātivādin-s argue that no part of the erroneous cognition can be taken as real, for if it were so, error could not be corrected or negated. As an illusory cognition claims its content to be real, if the content turns out to be real in effect then the erroneous cognition would cease to be so and there would be nothing to be corrected[96]. And if on the other hand, it is maintained that error has a real object as its content (and being an error it has to be subjected to correction), then a veridical cognition too will have to be subjected to correction, it having a real object as its content like an erroneous cognition. Thus, to maintain a distinction between error and veridical cognition it will have to be admitted that error has no real object as its content[97].

The correcting cognition too cannot be about something real. For in that case any (valid) cognition about a real content would have to be considered likewise as being corrective of some earlier cognition and *ad infinitum*. Hence the Asatkhyātivādin declares that the correcting cognition cannot be taken to be about a real object[98]. The Śūnyavādin-s argue further that if illusion were to have a real object as content, then that content (say, "silver"), should be taken as real up to the moment of the said error being corrected by the sublating cognition. And since the content of such erroneous cognition ceases to exist as soon as it is reported to be non-existent by the correcting cognition, it would follow then that the latter cognition destroys the real content of error. But this is untenable as this would imply that the negating cognition has the power not only to reveal its object, but also to destroy it. And as this is not the case, the content of an erroneous cognition cannot be held to be real[99]. "The correcting cognition does not substantiate, but rather refutes the claim of error that there is something real, and it can do so only when it is not about anything real"[100].

The Asatkhyātivādin-s say further that if the correcting cognition 'this is not silver' were to imply something real, then the '*not*' of that (correcting) cognition would be without any significance[101]. Furthermore, if the negating cognition instead of correcting the error asserts the existence of the content of erroneous cognition, then it would cease to be a correcting cognition, corroborating as it would, the erroneous cognition, and thus no correction as such would take place. It is therefore concluded, say the Asatkhyātivādin-s, that the content of error is unreal[102].

E. Theory of Error of the Vijñānavādin-s

According to the Vijñānavādin-s, consciousness (or cognition) is the only metaphysical reality and nothing external has any absolute reality. "The Yogācāra consistently with his subjective idealism, explains error or illusion as the externalisation or objectification of a subjective idea. In the nacre-silver illusion the subjective silver-form of cognition appears as the form of an external object. The silver is not absolutely unreal. It is real as a form of the internal cognition, but the mistake consists in taking it to be the form of an external object.... The Yogācāra does not recognize any cognizer other than the momentary idea (which itself is consciousness). So, according to him, in illusion a momentary idea cognizes itself as external"[103]. The Vijñānavādin-s belive that the mind (*citta*) and mental states (*caitta*) are produced by four types of causes, viz. (i) the co-operating cause (*sahakāripratyaya*), (ii) the dominant cause (*adhipati-pratyaya*), (iii) the immediate cause (*samanantara-pratyaya*), and (iv) the objective datum (*ālambana-pratyaya*)[104]. But according to the Yogācāra doctrine of Ātmakhyāti, none of these causes can be held responsible for the illusory cognition. They believe that in the illusory cognition "this is silver", the object of consciousness (silver)" appears as an extra mental object owing to the potency of erroneous cognitions—arising out of beginningless nescience. The beginningless series of various subconscious impressions are gradually awakened. On account of this, various cognitions arise, which cognize their own forms. There are no external objects corresponding to these cognitions"[105].

Vidyāraṇya says that, as per Yogācāra doctrine, the illusory cognition of silver is produced by a subconscious impression (*vāsanā*) of silver which arose some time or the other in the beginningless series of nescience (*avidyā*)[106]. The Vijñānavādin-s therefore consider as illusion the external appearance of an internal cognition[107]. The Yogācāra view of illusion is summed-up thus by Vidyāraṇya—Just as sense-object-relation is not required to perceive the cognizing mind, in the same manner the shell-silver also does not require the sense-object relation for its apprehension, being of the form of (mental) idea—It is therefore nothing but a mental-idea or cognition[108].

In support of their doctrine, the Vijñānavādin-s cite the example of dream-experience to show that there can be a cognition even without a corresponding external object, as is reported in the Bhāmatī[109]. They also cite the case of simultaneous cognition ("*sahopalambha*") of cognition and its content to support their own view[110]. The Vijñānavādin-s therefore claim that "an object is cognized invariably along with its cognition, and in the absence of cognition an object is never cognized"[111]. Consequently, the Ātmakhyātivādin-s conclude that since cognition and its object are apprehended simultaneously, "the object is not separate from the cognition"[112].

As regards the sublating cognition "this is not silver", the Vijñānavādin-s say that what is sublated is only the "*this-ness*" (*idaṁtā*) which characterizes the silver and not the silver itself. Hence the falsity of the "externality" of the silver[113]. If it be said, argue the Ātmakhyātivādin-s, that the sublating cognition negates 'silver', it would be tantamount to the outright denial of both the attribute and its substrate, following the rule that when an object (*dharmin*) is sublated its attribute (*dharma*) also stands sublated. For the sake of simplicity therefore, the negation of "this-ness" alone is to be preferred to the negation of 'silver'[114].

This being so, the fact that the sublating cognition denies the 'externality' of silver (i.e. "this-ness"), "shows by implication, that silver is internal[115], as is explained by Vācaspati Miśra—"There is the general rule that whatever is apprehended in a particular form should be accepted in that form, since it being other than that results (only) from a cognition of greater force which sublates it. When the sublating cognition 'this is not silver' is intelligible even as sublating the 'this' element alone, it is not meet to take it to extend to the 'silver' element. For, if the substrate 'silver' were sublated, then both the silver and its attribute of "this-ness" would be sublated. It would be better to take it that the attribute "this-ness" alone is sublated, not the substrate 'silver' as well. Hence it follows that silver which is sublated in respect of externality is by presumption confined to knowledge within us. Thus follows the imposition outside of what is of the form of cognition"[116].

Thus, the theory of error given by the Vijñānavādin-s is called Ātmakhyāti because they believe (in the theory) that error consists in the apprehension of the internal cognition, which is the Self, in the form of an external object, such as silver.

F. Theory of Error of Viśiṣṭādvaita

Rāmānūjācārya has worked out his theory of error, known as *Sat-khyāti* or *"Yathārtha-khyāti"*, on the basis of certain epistemological criteria, viz.,

1. that (object) alone is congnizable which is in existence; therefore a false cognition is inconceivable, for there can be no cognition in the absence of a real cognitum"[117];
2. every cognition reveals an object as it is, i.e., the object cognized exists in the very form as it is manifested[118];
3. there is no exception to the above rule[119];
4. only that cognition whose object is practically useful will be accepted as valid-knowledge (*pramā*)[120];
5. a cognition whose object cannot be put to (practical) use will be treated as erroneous, notwithstanding the fact that it reveals what is real[121];
6. all things contain other things (in small proportions), on the basis of the doctrine of "triplication" (*"trivṛtkaraṇa"*) or quintuplication (*"pañcīkaraṇa"*) of the elements[122]. As per this doctrine, "each gross element contains an admixture of the other elements"[123]. The gross element "earth" (*pṛthvī*); for example, contains apart from the "earth" element, smaller proportions of the other elements also. Viśiṣṭādvaita claims that just as one element is present in the other gross elements, every object is (present) in everything else (albeit in negligible proportions)[124].

Following the above, Rāmānuja says that the similarity between two objects is due to the same elements constituting both of them. An object appears different from other objects, not because of absolute difference, but because of the predominance of one element. "Even though there is *"silver"* in *"shell"*, the *"silver"* components are (so) negligible in it, and the *"shell"* components (so) predominant that only the "shell" aspect is perceived while the "*silver*" aspect remains unperceived. The object perceived as-such, therefore, owes its name to the predominant elements it is constituted of. "Thus, in what is called "*silver*" the *shell*-components are negligible, while the '*silver*' components are preponderant"[125]. Rāmānuja explains all illusory cognitions on the basis of the above-mentioned principles. According to him, when "*silver*" is apprehended in "*shell*", the "*silver*" thus apprehended is neither non-existent nor a '*real silver*' existing somewhere else. The '*silver*' very much exists within the "*shell*". Under normal conditions, the "*shell*" would have been perceived as "*shell*", but due to some defects in the eyes only the "*silver*" components of the "*shell*", though negligible, are perceived, while the "*shell*"-components which are indeed preponderant, are not perceived. This cognition of the "*shell-silver*", say the Viśiṣṭādvaitin-s, is erroneous, not on the ground of the cognition being unreal (which is inconceivable) but on the ground that the object apprehended, viz., 'silver', is not of any practical use. "So while the object of a valid cognition is serviceable in life, that of error is not"[126]. On the removal of the defects referred to above, the "*shell*" is perceived in its real form due to the apprehension of its preponderant *shell*-elements. And hence also the sublating cognition "this is not silver', which, as a matter of fact, does not sublate the *silver* as such but only makes manifest the predominant elements of the '*shell*'. "Thus, according to Viśiṣṭādvaita, in error, (a) what is real (*Sat*) in front is perceived; (b) the perception of the object (e.g., *shell-silver*) accounts for the volitional activity; and (c) the role of the sublating cognition can be explained in terms of the perception of the preponderant aspect—the sublating cognition does not negate the object cognized, but only arrests the volitional activity"[127].

One of the followers of Rāmāṇuja, Śrīnivāsa Dāsa, sayts that the illusory cognition 'this is silver' is due to the "absence of apprehension of the relation of the *nacre* to a large part of it"[128]. He further claims that the object of an illusion is real, but since such illusions cannot produce successful actions they are invalid[129].

Other cases of error, viz., the cognitions of yellow-conch-shell, dreams, two-moons, red-crystal, etc., are also explained by Rāmānuja in the light of the doctrines of triplication and quintuplication of elements discussed above. Accordingly, "when a person suffering from jaundice sees a white conch as yellow, the yellowness of the bilious matter in the eye gets actually transferred to the conch through visual rays. So the yellow colour of the conch seen by him is real"[130]. In like manner, the object seen in dreams also are real, claims Rāmānuja, for "dream-objects are creations of God for the private experience of the dreamer during the time of dream experience"[131]. Rāmānuja claims also that the water seen in a mirage is real as it exists in both the earth particles (i.e., sand), and in heat (i.e., sun-rays). Due to defects in the eyes, the heat and the earth-particles are not perceived, resulting in the apprehension of only the water-elements[132].

As for the 'red-crystal', Rāmānuja says that this cognition is due to the overpowering of the natural colour of the crystal by the redness of the 'China-rose' due to the latter's proximity with the former. Here, too, the non-apprehension of the natural colour of the crystal is due to defects in the eyes, as claims the Śrībhāṣya[133].

In the illusory cognition of two moons, the Viśiṣṭādvaitin-s claim that owing to the insertion of the fingers in the eyes, or owing to cataract, etc., the "opthạlmic rays" get bifurcated resulting in the apprehension of the object in front in duplicate. It is to be noted here that Rāmānuja does not claim the reality of the two-moons perceived, but rather of the "apprehension of two moons" and of its cause, the bifurcated "opthalmic rays"[134]. Therefore, in all cases of error, the objects cognized are real, even though they may exist only for a short while, as in the case of dreams, or for all the time, as in the case of *silver-in-shell*. But in all cases of erroneous cognition, the objects apprehended though real, as claimed by the *Satkhyātivādin-s, are of no parctical use*[135].

Section II

INADEQUACY OF THE NON-ADVAITA THEORIES OF ERROR

1. Anyathākhyāti

The theory of Anyathākhyāti or Viparītakhyāti claims that in an illusion the object in front is cognized as "this" through the normal process of perception (viz. *Laukika Sannikarṣa*), while the silverness of silver (present elsewhere) is associated with "this" in front through extra-normal-sense-relation (i.e., *Alaukika Sannikarṣa*). The Naiyāyikas and the Bhāṭṭas thus maintain that both the shell and the silver of the illusory cognition "*This is sliver*" are real, as the Nyāyaratnakāra puts it:

"Both the subject and the predicated of the erroneous cognition, "This is silver" are existent (i.e., *sat*). What is false (i.e., *asat*), is the relation between the "this and the silver", i.e., between the subject and the predicate"[136].

The Advaitins consider this theory as untenable. The Anyathākhyāti-vādin's explanation as to how an object existing elsewhere could be seen as though present in front is not satisfactory. The theory of extra-normal-sense-relation (i.e., *Jñāna-lakṣaṇā pratyāsatti*) fails to explain this phenomenon satisfactorily. If it were possible to thus cognize objects existing elsewhere as (though they were) present in front, then, says Sucaritamiśra, "everyone would become omniscient[137].

The claim that the content of the illusory cognition "This is silver" is real, is falsified by the sublating cognition "*This is not silver*". Since the sublating cognition does not show that silver is connected with some other place and time, as claimed by the Anyathākhyātivādin-s, it is wrong to say that "silver existing elsewhere at some other time is seen here and now"[138].

"The sublating cognition merely sublates silver-connected with some particular time and space; it does not exhibit silver as related to another time and space; for silver is not perceived to be so related"[139], just as the cognition "this is not a snake" merely denies the existence of snake; it does not prove the existence of the snake somewhere else[140].

Rejecting the theory of Anyathākhyāti, Prakāśātman queries

the propounders of that theory as to what is the nature of the "*anyathātva*" (i.e., "otherwise-ness"), of the erroneous cognition. Giving three possible answers to this query, the Vivaraṇakāra rejects them all [proving thus that the theory in question is untenable]. Analysing this theory, Prakāśātman "raises the following objections," "to what does the *anyathātva* of the illusory cognition belong? Does it belong to the act of cognizing, or to the resultant cognition, or still to the object of the resultant cognition?[141]. Elaborating on this, Vidyāraṇya says, "The otherwise-ness cannot belong to the act of cognizing; for, if the act of cognizing a 'nacre' should take the form of 'silver', then the nacre cannot be called the objective substrate of the illusory cognition of silver, for an object can impart its form to that cognition by which it is apprehended, and consequently, a 'nacre' cannot impart its form to a silver-apprehending cognition. As for the second alternative, that too is not possible, for the "otherwise-ness" cannot belong to the resultant cognition, i. e., to the manifestation in consciousness, since cognition, whether valid or invalid, does not differ as far as manifestation is concerned. The third alternative is also not tenable, since in that case, it would mean that either the nacre identifies itself with silver, or it gets 'modified' into silver. In the first conjecture, either the nacre is absolutely different from silver, or there is identity-cum-difference between the two. The first alternative does not stand the test, for there can be no identity between two things absolutely different from each other. As for the second alternative, that too does not stand the test, for in that eventuality, the perceptual judgment "the cow is short - horned", will also be treated as illusory knowledge. In the case of the nacre getting 'modified into silver', the very proposition is self-defeating, since in such an event, the silver being cognized would not be illusory. It would be the cognition of a real silver, and hence would not be sublated. And if it be claimed, says Vidyāraṇya, that the nacre gets modified into silver only so long as the illusion lasts, that too cannot be accepted, since in that case the illusory silver (being a real modification) would be perceived not only by one with defective vision, but also by those with sound vision. And since this is not so in actual practice, the theory of Anyathākhyāti or Viparītakhyāti is untenable'[142].

Vācaspati Miśra on his part says that in the illusory cognition, "This is silver", the contention of the Anyathākhyātivādin-s to the effect that the silver existing elsewhere is apprehended as present in "this", is self-contradictory. For, there cannot be activity in respect of the substrate "this-ness" unless one desires it. But in the case under consideration, there is contradiction between "desire" and activity in that one desires 'silver' present elsewhere and yet 'walks' towards "this" to pick it up. If it be said on this, observes the Bhāmatīkāra, that desire and activity in the present case are due to the substrate of the 'this-ness' not being apprehended as not of the nature of silver, then the question arises as to why one is not indifferent to it. Thus, says Vācaspati Miśra, the person desirous of silver is pulled in opposite directions. The bare memory of silver is not enough to cause activity, as on its own it does not lead to the knowledge that silver-ness resides in "this". Perception of subject and probans in the same place is indeed the cause of inference, notices our commentator, not perception in different places, as per the rule that, "Inference follows from perception of probans and subject in the same place by one who knows the relation (*Vyāpti*)"[143].

The Advaitins reject also the Anyathākhyātivādin's claim that it is the relation between the subject and the predicate which is false. and not the object of the illusory cognition. That this relation is real (*sat*) or unreal (*asat*), is not revealed by the sublating cognition as the latter is not at all concerned with that relation[144].

In the eyes, therefore, of the Advaitins, the Anyathākhyāti theory of error fails to explain illusion satisfactorily.

2. Akhyāti

According to Prabhākara's theory of Akhyāti, all knowledge is valid[145]. Even the illusory cognition of silver-in-shell is considered to be valid. This experience, says Prabhākara, consists of two cognitions, one being of the nature of memory and the other of the nature of direct apprehension. The theory thus rests on the propositions that (i) erroneous knowledge is a "composite" knowledge; (ii) "memory, although essentially an apprehension of the previously apprehended object, presents itself as bare apprehension because the element of reference to previous experience is lost through some defect; (iii) there is non-apprehension of the difference between memory (of the silver) and the apprehension (of the object in front) in respect of both their nature and their contents[146].

Showing the inadequacy of the Akhyāti theory in explaining erroneous Cognitions, Citsukha queries Prabhākara as to whether he accepts (the existence) of illusory knowledge or not. If yes, then his own doctrine is contradicted, and if he does not, then his theory suffers from the fallacy of "āśrayāsiddha"[147].

Reacting to Prabhakara's claim that "(in memory), the element of reference.... is lost....", Padmapāda says that there cannot be 'memory' without reference to the past, "for memory without past reference is a contradiction in terms, for such a reference constitutes the essence and differentia of memory-experience"[148]. Padmapāda says further that the illusory cognition contains no indication whatsoever that the illusory object had been the object of a previous apprehension[149]. Then non-presence of a memory-element in error having been rejected, the fact of its being a composite of two cognitions loses ground. Rejecting also Prabhākara's claim that the above-mentioned composite cognition is responsible for the percipient's act of picking up silver, Padmapāda says that the very fact that the erroneous perception (of silver) moves the percipient to a single action in a particular direction proves the unitariness of the illusory experience[150]. As to the contention that activity of the nature described above is caused by the non-apprehension of difference between perception and memory, this is rejected by Vācaspati Miśra, who contends that the non-apprehension of difference referred to above cannot be the cause of the activity of an intelligent being as such activity is a function of positive knowledge[151].

Vācaspati further adds that there connot be any activity without desire, and there cannot be desire without the assurance of the existence of its object. Thus, without the assurance that 'silver' is the substrate of "this-ness", one cannot desire it[152]. Vācaspati says that it would be futile to argue that desire arises because the "this" is not known to be different from the nature of 'silver', for, says he, "it is equally reasonable that the "this" should be discarded bacause it is not known to be of the nature of "silver"[153].

The Advaitin-s reject the Akhyāti theory on the ground also

that, should the cognition "this is a snake" be taken to be true on the premise that "all cognitions have a real object as their cognitum", then even on the dawning of the cognition "this is not a snake" the illusory snake would not be sublated, and this would be against actual experience[154]. It is again argued that, if the cognition "this is a false knowledge" be considered to be a true cognition, then it should have a "false knowledge" as its substrate. This, however, will incur the defect of "*anaikāntika hetu*" owing to the rise of the "true cognition" even in the absence of the cause[155].

It is thus that the inadequacy of Prabhākara's theory of Akhyāti leads to its outright rejection by the Advaita Vedāntin-s.

3. Asatkhyāti

The Mādhyamika-s contend that in an erroneous cognition, neither the object cognized nor its substrate is real. In the shell-silver illusion, for example, the Asatkhyātivādin-s claim that both the 'silver' cognized and its substrate, the shell in front, are non-existent. Denying the reality of both the relata and the relation subsisting between them, the Śūnyavādin-s advance the theory that illusion has *Avidyā* as its cause, which with the help of the latent impressions (*vāsanā-s*) of the previous or preceding cognition, has the power to manifest a totally non-existent object. Had the content of the illusory cognition been real, argue the *Asatkhyātivādin-s*, it would not have been denied by the sublating cognition. But since the object is denied, it cannot be existent, for whatever is existent cannot be denied.

Rejecting the Mādhyamika's contention referred to above that *Avidyā* has the power to reveal something unreal, Vācaspati Miśra argues that if *Avidyā* is the *śakti* (power) in the manifestation of an illusory object, wherein the cognition is the *śakta* (agent), then the object revealed through this cognition is the *śakya* (product). But this cannot be accepted, as the relation between the *Avidyāśakti* and its *śakya* cannot be satisfactorily explained[156]. Says Vācaspati,

"Nor is it admissible that, though the objects of experience are wholly devoid of any capacity to appear, the respective cognitions through the capacity residing in them as cognition can of themselves give rise to the appearance of the unreal, as a product of a unique nature, and that this capacity of the cognitions to make the unreal appear is Nescience"[157]. Vācaspati argues that the unreal cannot be the term of a causal relation. To say that the unreal is the effect of something is illogical, for an effect can never be unreal. Says Vācaspati, "What is this faculty of cognition whereby it makes the unreal appear? What is it that it is capable of? If it is the unreal, is it effected or only made known by it ? It cannot be effected since that is unintelligible in the case of the unreal"[158]. "If, furthermore, it is held that the *Avidyāśakti* of cognition gets realized in giving rise to an effect, it will be difficult to maintain that it is a power of presenting a wrong view. For, it is the nature of a cognition that it reveals an object. To say that cognition utilizes its power of *Avidyā* not in revealing something (real), but in giving rise to the unreal, is surely a bad epistemological explanation"[159]. The unreal object (so manifested) cannot be what is made known, for *Avidyā* "cannot appropriate to itself the epistemic function of revelation which really belongs to cognition.... The cognition which possesses *Avidyā* cannot be said to be produced by its *Avidyāśakti.* For, the agent or the *śakta* is always different from the *śakya* or that which is brought about by the power or *śakti* that belongs to the former. The (Mādhyamika) Buddhists will have, therefore, to say that the cognition which is produced by *Avidyāśakti,* and which reveals the unreal, is different from the cognition which is the seat of '*Avidyāśakti*'. However, there is no experiential evidence for two such cognitions"[160]. Vācaspati argues further that no other cognition can be accepted as revealing the unreal, on the ground also that this would lead to the falacy of infinite regress. For, says he, that cognition too "cannot be said to reveal the unreal directly, but.... through the actualisation of its own *Avidyāśakti* in a third cognition", and so, *ad infinitum*[161]. Vācaspati says that the cognition in question cannot also be said to reveal the unreal, for in that case too the relation subsisting between the real (i.e., the object) and the unreal, cannot be established. And this is so, says Vācaspati, because what is unreal, and (thus) devoid of being and efficacy, cannot be the support or determinant of anything (real)[162].

"If it be said, observes Vācaspati, that the cognition is not controlled by the unreal, but that it is of the very nature of cognition not to appear apart from the unreal[163], this too cannot be accepted, for in that case the cognition would be invariably linked to the unreal, without originating from it or being of its nature." The relation between cognition and the unreal which it reveals cannot be said to be one of identity—because cognition which is real and is revealing is different from its object which is unreal and is revealed. Nor can it be said that it is a causal relation. For, causal relation does not obtain between the.... real and the unreal; the unreal, therefore, cannot be a term of such a relation. The relation between cognition and the unreal then cannot even be one of invariable concomitance.... There can be thus no cognition about the '*asat*' (unreal), and therefore, the theory of 'Asatkhyāti' is untenable"[164].

Citsukha on the other hand, rejects the Asatkhyāti theory arguing that the object of an illusory cognition cannot be non-existent (*asat*), for a totally non-existent object cannot be the percept of even an apparent cognition. There would also not be any activity prompted by the desire of obtaining it[165]. Citsukha says further that the Asatkhyātivādin-s cannot also argue that in a particular case of unreality ("*asadviśeṣa*") there might occur apparent cognition (*pratibhāsa*) and the tendency to appropriate the unreal object, for, says the Tattvapradīpikākāra, that would not be logically convincing. The fact is that, in a non-existent thing there cannot be a particular or a universal. Should that thing contain any such property, it would cease to be non-existent, for a non-existent thing is devoid of any natural characteristics[166]. The Asatkhyāti theory stands, therefore, rejected.

4. Ātmakhyāti

The Vijñānavādin-s claim that the object of error is real (*sat*), being a mere reflection of the subject, i.e., consciousness or cognizer. While the content of illusion is real, the fact of its being cognized as existing externally is erroneous, since the externality of the object cognized is unreal. This is proved by the negating cognition, which merely negates the externality of the content of the illusory cognition, and not the content altogether. In the erroneous cognition, "This is Silver", what the cancelling cognition "This is not Silver", denies, is not the 'silver' *per se*, but merely the 'thisness' of the cognition[167].

Vācaspati Miśra takes exception to this claim. He argues that if the sublating cognition denies the proximity or the presence in front, of silver, this would imply that the silver is far away from the cognizer; for, what is not in proximity is far away. It does not follow from this (denial of the object as existing in front), that what is not proximate to the cognizer is extremely proximate to him. Thus, the mere fact that the object does not exist in front (or externally), does not prove that it exists internally, as claimed by the propounders of the theory of *Ātmakhyāti*[168]. The Bhāmatīkāra further argues that if the silver in the illusory cognition, "This is silver", is nothing but the cognition which is internal, as claimed by the Ātmakhyātivādin-s, then it should be the object as existing internally. And since, as per the theory under discussion, the subject and the object are different forms of the same cognition, the cognition in question should then be in the form, "I am silver". But since this is not the case, the Vijñānavādins'claim that the object cognized in error is of the nature of cognition and that, as such it exists internally is not valid. In defence of their claim, they cannot also say that the fact that the sublating cognition denies the existence of silver in front, supports their theory; for, the latter cognition simply distinguishes the "this", (i.e. the object in front), from silver. It does not show in any way that the 'silver' thus cognized, is of the nature of cognition[169].

Commenting on the nature of the sublating cognition in the case mentioned above, Vācaspati says that this cognition denies neither the silver nor the "this-ness. It simply denies the empirical usage of silver occasioned by the non-apprehension of distinctness[170]. Vācaspati adds also that the mere cognition of silver does not occasion its apearance in nacre; for, "the presentation of silver cannot have nacre as its basis, that being opposed to experience"[171].

Prakāśātman also rejecting the Ātmakhyātivādins' version of illusion, queries them as to the real nature and origin of the illusory silver they claim to be real. The Vivaraṇakāra asks, "is that silver born or unborn? If it is not born, then being formless, as the sky, it would not be apprehensible. And if it be said that it is born, then also it cannot be taken to be born of material object (existing externally), for the very existence of such external objects is denied by the Ātmakhyātivādin-s. If the silver is then said to be born of pure cognition, that too cannot be granted, as that would lead to the fallacy of infinite regress (there being no specific cognition as its cause). On the other hand, if it be said that the silver is born of immaterial cause, then will arise the contingency of the silver being invested with external existence, (much to the detriment of the theory in question). The theory is therefore untenable[172].

Elaborating on this, Vidyāraṇya observes that the claim by the Ātmakhyātivādin-s to the effect that the appearance of silver in the illusory cognition, 'This is silver', is due to beginningless '*Vāsanā*, raises many questions. Is the silver unborn owing to its being of non-material nature, or is it born as material silver? It cannot be the first, says Vidyāraṇya, as in that case it would not be the object of an apprehending cognition. If the second, then the question arises as to whether it is born of external object or out of consciousness? It cannot be said to be born out of external object, as the Vijñānavādin-s themselves do not subscribe to the view of external existence of any object. And in the second alternative, if the cause be taken to be Pure Consciousness, that too cannot be accepted, as Pure Consciousness is nothing but Emancipation (*Nirvāṇa*). Then, by elimination, it has to be accepted that the illusory silver is born out of impure Consciousness. This also cannot be granted, as in this case the silver being subjected to *arthakriyākāritā*, would very much be characterized by external existence, (contrary to what the theory claims). And in case of silver not being born at all, then the theory of Ātmakhyāti will fall (through) being deprived of its very essence—the silver under dispute. This theory is thus untenable[173].

5. Satkhyāti

The Viśiṣṭādvaitin-s claim that everything exists in everything else on the basis of the doctrines of 'triplication' (*"trivṛtkaraṇa"*) and quintuplication (*pañcīkaraṇa*). They hold that the content of all cognitions is real, and that it is inconceivable that there should be cognition whithout a real cognitum. In the illusory cognition, '*This is silver*', therefore, '*silver*' is real.

The theory of Satkhyāti suffers from many a fallacy, say the Advaitavādin-s. The doctrines of *Trivṛtkaraṇa* and *Pañcīkaraṇa* on the basis of which Rāmānuja claims the existence of everything in everything else are applicable to the gross elements, and not to the objects which are themselves products of gross elements subjected to the process of triplication or quintuplication[174]. If Rāmānuja's contention that everything contains everything else, is true, then not only *silver* should be seen in *shell,* but such things as gold, carbon, etc. should also be seen. The Advaitin-s observe further that "a *nacre* is similar to a piece of *silver* because it is endowed with brightness, etc., which are the common qualities of both and not because it contains a part of *silver.* If the ornaments of Caitra are similar to those of Maitra because the former contain a part of the latter, then Caitra will mistake Maitra's ornaments for his own"[175]. "The Śaṅkarite-s also hold that the illusory cognition of *silver* has only apparent or illusory existence (*prātibhāsika-sattā*), while according to Rāmānuja, it has real or ontological existence (*pāramārthika-sattā*)"[176].

Vācaspati Miśra, on his part, queries the Satkhyātivādin-s as to how water could be perceived in a desert if the object of an illusion were to have real existence? For, says Vācaspati, "it is not that manifestation alone constitutes reality, in which case, bodies, organs, etc., by the very fact of manifestation, would be real. It is not as if ropes, etc. do not appear as snakes etc., or crystals, etc., as endowed with red colour and so on; nor, as thus appearing, do they really become those objects or endowed with those qualities. If that were so, one would conclude in the case of a mirage that it is the *Mandākinī* (river) which has come down close by, with her garlands of constantly agitated waves high and low, and proceeding thereto, should be able to quench one's thirst by drinking of that water. Hence, of what is superimposed, even though manifest, absolute reality cannot be admitted, even though this conclusion be not desired"[177].

Citsukha also rejects the theory of Satkhyāti, saying that "the object of illusory cognition is not even existent (*sat*); it is sublated as "this is not silver" in (the case of) the illusion *silver-in-shell.* In defence of the existence of *silver* as real, it is not proper to say that it exists somewhere else, and not in the *nacre* where it is sublated, for this is against experience. Moreover, the experience of contradiction too does not prove its existence elsewhere"[178]. The impossibility of illusory cognition otherwise cannot also prove that the *silver* exists elsewhere, for though the illusion would not occur without (the cognition of) *silver*, it can occur even if *silver* does not exist in that particular place[179]. The cancelling cognition cannot also be said to prove the existence of silver elsewhere, for it removes simply what is being experienced there and then, presupposing the existence of the object only at the place where it contradicts it, and not elsewhere[180]. Moreover, says Citsukha, it would be wrong to contend that had the object not been existent somewhere, it would have been stultified, and hence it has to be taken as existing elsewhere, for there is no cancellation since the object does not come into question and the conclusion of its existence is hence not possible[181].

Citsukha says further that it cannot also be said that in the contradiction "this is not silver" with regard to what is in front, the knowledge of negation of identification leads to the ascertainment of its existence elsewhere, by elimination, because, should it be so, even after knowing, in the perception of identity of two separate trees from a distance, that they are actually separate from each other, the cognition of identity would persist[182].

NOTES

1. Ṛg Veda - X. 129
2. Vide, "आत्मशरीरेन्द्रियार्थबुद्धिर्मनःप्रवृत्तिदोषप्रेत्यभावफलदुःखापवर्गास्तु प्रमेयम्।"—Nyāya-sūtra (NS) I.1.9
3. Vātsyāyana-bhāṣya (Vāt. B) on NS. I. 1.2
4. Tarka-saṅgraha (TS) - 17
5. Vide, EIP, Op. Cit., Vol.II - p.241
6. Vāt. B on NṢ. I.1.3—Tr. Ganganāth Jhā, p.110. Vide, ".....प्रत्यक्षतो दिदृक्षते प्रत्यक्षत उपलब्धेऽर्थे जिज्ञासा निवर्तते।" (Ibid)
7. Ibid, p.111, on NS. I.1.4; Vide, "इन्द्रियस्यार्थेन सन्निकर्षादुत्पद्यते यज्ज्ञानं तत् प्रत्यक्षम्।...तस्मादशाब्दमर्थज्ञानमिन्द्रियार्थसन्निकर्षोत्पन्नम्।... तदव्यभिचारि।" (Ibid).
8. Vide, EIP, Op. Cit., p.222
9. Vāt.B on NS. IV. 2.1 (Introduction).
10. Ibid.
11. Vide, E. Solomon, Avidyā—A Problem of Truth and Reality (APTR), p.395.
12. Vaiśeṣika-sūtra (VS), IX.2. 10 - 12.
13. EIP, Op. Cit, p.293.
14. Praśastapāda-bhāṣya (PB)-Viparyaya - Prakaraṇa.

15. Vide, Bhattacharya J.V., Nyāya-mañjarī, Vol. I - Introduction, p.XXXIV.
16. Ibid.
17. Ibid.
18. Nyāya-vārttika-tātparya-ṭīkā, quoted in APTR, Op.Cit., p.403.
19. Ibid, p.405.
20. S.C. Chatterjee - The Nyāya Theory of Knowledge, quoted in APTR, Op. Cit., p.405.
21. APTR, Op. Cit.
22. Ibid, pp.405-406.
23. Ibid, quoting from Bhāṣā-pariccheda.
24. Sukharanjan Saha, Advaita Theory of Illusion, p.48.
25. Ramesh Kumar Sharma in "Studies in Humanities and Social Sciences", Vol. III, No.2, 1996.
26. Ibid, p.203.
27. Ibid.
28. Ibid.
29. Ibid.
30. Ibid.
31. G.P. Bhaṭṭ, The Basic Ways of Knowing, p.110.
32. Kāśikā (KK), on Śloka-vārttika (Ś.V.) - II. 34, quoted by G.P. Bhaṭṭ, Loc. Cit., p.110.
33. Yuktidīpikā (YD), Ed. R.C. Pandey, MLBD, 1967, p.48.
    ''नाऽविद्यमानस्य महदादेर्विकारस्य प्रधानादाविर्भाव इति प्रतिजानीमहे। तस्मात् काक-विषाणात् शशविषाण-सिद्धिवदयुक्तं सन्निवेश-विशेषमात्राभ्युपगमात् सत्कार्यसिद्धिरिति॥
    —(Y.D. on S.K.9)
34. प्रमाणविपर्ययविकल्पनिद्रास्मृतय: ॥—(YS-I.6)
35. ''विपर्ययो मिथ्याज्ञानमतद्‌रूपप्रतिष्ठम्''। —(YS-I.8)
36. T.S. Rukmini, Yoga-Vārttika of Vijñānabhikṣu, Vol. I; p.71; Vide,
    ''स कस्मान्न प्रमाणम्? यत: प्रमाणेन बाध्यते। भूतार्थविषयत्वात्प्रमाणस्य। तत्र प्रमाणेन बाधनमप्रमाणस्य दृष्टम्। तद्यथा द्विचन्द्रदर्शनं सद्विषयेणैकचन्द्रदर्शनेन बाध्यते इति।
    —Vyāsa-bhāṣya on YS-I.8
37. Ibid. pp.71-72; Vide,
    ''मिथ्येत्यस्य विवरणमतद्रूपप्रतिष्ठमिति! न तद्रूपो न स्वसमानाकारो यो विषयस्तत्प्रतिष्ठं तद्विशेष्यकमित्यर्थ:। भ्रमस्थले ज्ञानाकारस्यैव विषये समारोप इति भाव:। .... अत्र च शास्त्रेऽन्यथाख्याति: सिद्धान्तो न तु सांख्यवदविवेकमात्रम्।...।'' —Yogavārttika on YS-I.8
38. Rama Prasada, Patañjali's Yoga Sūtras, Munshiram Manoharlal, 1982: p.19.
39. Vide, Studies in Philosophy, MLBD, pp.262-267.
40. Rama Prasada, Loc. Cit., p.91; Vide,
    अविद्यास्मितारागद्वेषाभिनिवेशा: क्लेशा:। —(YS-II.3)
41. Ibid, p.95; Vide,
    ''अनित्याशुचिदुखानात्मसु नित्यशुचिसुखात्मख्यातिरविद्या॥'' —(YS-II.5)
42. Ibid, p.96.
43. T.S. Rukmini, Loc. Cit., Vol. II., p.21, Vide,
    ''तथा प्रपञ्चज्ञानस्यासति सदाकारकत्वात् भ्रमत्वमपि शुक्तिरजतादिज्ञानवद् गीयते इति''।

—(Vārttika on YS-II.5)

44. Vide, —Quoted by T.S. Rukmini, Loc. Cit., Vol. II. p.25, "तत्सादृश्यमभावश्च तदन्यत्वं तदल्पता। अप्राशस्त्यं विरोधश्च नञर्थाः षट् प्रकीर्तिताः॥"
45. Ibid, p.25, Vide, "तस्याश्चाविद्यायाः सतत्त्वं तत्त्वं वस्त्वेव विज्ञेयं न त्वभावोऽमित्रागोष्पदादिशब्दवदित्यर्थः।" —YV on YS - II.5
46. Vide, —Vyāsa-bhāṣya (VB) on YS - II.5 "एवमविद्या न प्रमाणं न प्रमाणाभावः किंतु विद्याविपरीतं ज्ञानान्तरम्।" —(VB on YS-II.5)
47. Vide, Studies in Philosophy, Op. Cit., p.268.
48. Ibid, p.269.
49. Quoted by Karl H. Potter, EOI, Vol. IV, p.361.
50. Ibid.
51. Ibid.
52. Anima Sen Gupta, Classical Sāṅkhya : A Critical Study : Lucknow, 1969 -pp.12-13.
53. "सदसत्ख्यातिर्बाधाबाधात्"। —(SPS-V.56) Quoted by Jadunath Sinha in Indian Psychology, Vol. III, Epistemology of Perception, p.87.
54. Ibid, p.88
55. "इदं रजतमिति पुरोवर्ति विषयतया सत् अबाधात्-रजतविषयतया त्वसत् बाधात्।"— (SSV-V.56)
56. E.Solomon, Loc. Cit., p.415, Vide, "......तत्र स्वरूपेणाबाधः सर्ववस्तूनां नित्यत्वात्। संसर्गतस्तु बाधः सर्वस्तूनां चैतन्ये अस्ति यथा शुक्त्यादौ बुद्धिस्थरजतादेः स्फटिकादिषु वा लौहित्यादेः तद्वत्॥"—(SPB on SS-V.56)
57. Vide, "A Source Book in Indian Philosophy", (Ed.) S. Radhakrishnan & C.A. Moore - p.486.
58. Ibid.
59. S. N. Dasgupta-Loc. Cit., p.372.
60. Ibid. p.374.
61. G.P.Bhaṭṭ : The Basic Ways of Knowing – p.73.
62. Ibid.
63. S.D. - quoted by G.P.Bhaṭṭ—Op. Cit.
64. Ibid.
65. E.Solomon-Loc. Cit., p.427.
66. G.P.Bhaṭṭ-Loc. Cit., p.74.
67. E.Solomon —Op. Cit.
68. Jaiminīya-Mīmāṁsā-Bhāṣya, Yudhiṣṭhira Mīmāṁsaka - 1977 - p.12.
69. Vide, E. Solomon - Loc. Cit., p.424.
70. Quoted by S.N. Dasgupta - Loc. Cit., p.375.
71. Ślokavārttikam, Ed. Ganga Sagara Rai- 1993 - p.46.
72. N.R. on Ś.V., Nirālambana, 118 - quoted by G.P.Bhaṭṭ - Loc. Cit., p.93.
73. Kāśikā of Sucaritamiśra on Ś.V. II.85 quoted by G.P. Bhaṭṭ-Op. Cit. "यादृशं हि ज्ञानस्य स्वरूपं तादृशमेवार्थेऽध्यारोपयतीति यावत्।"
74. Ibid p.94.
75. E. Solomon-Loc. Cit., p.429 : quoting - pp.43-44.
76. NR on ŚV, Nirālambana, 117-quoted by G.P. Bhaṭṭ - Loc. Cit., p.96
77. SD-p.58 - quoted by a G.P. Bhaṭṭ - Op. Cit., p.96.
78. G.P.Bhaṭṭ -Op. Cit., p.96.

79. KK - Op. Cit., on Ś.V. - V. 114, quoted by G.P.Bhaṭṭ—Loc. Cit.
80. Ibid.
81. E.Solomon - Loc. Cit., p.435.
82. Ibid.
83. Bṛhatī of Prabhākara Miśra - Ed. S.K.Ramnath Śāstrī - 1934 - pp.64-65.
84. Ibid - pp.66-67.
85. Vide, G.P. Bhaṭṭ - Loc. Cit., p.104.
86. Ibid.
87. Ibid - quoting pp. - III.21.
88. Vide, Jadunath Sinha : Indian Psychology III, 1985 - p.93 - referring to p.44.
89. Vide, p.45 quoted by Jadunath Sinha - Loc. Cit.
90. "असत्येव सद्धीर्भ्रान्तिरितीष्यताम्।" - Iṣṭa-siddhi (IS) Oriental Institute, Baroda, 1933; p.155.
91. "बौद्धास्तु असदेव रजतं ख्यायते इत्यसत्ख्यातिमाहुः।" - Prakaraṇa-pañcikā, quoted by Jadunath Sinha, Loc. Cit., Vol. III, p.83.
92. Ibid, p.84.
93. "प्रतिभासमानोऽर्थः सद्रूपो विचार्यमाणो नास्तीत्यसत्ख्यातिरेवासौ।" - Prameya-kamala-mārtaṇḍa, quoted by Jadunath Sinha, Loc. Cit., p.84.
94. "असत्ख्यातिवादिनस्तु संसर्गिणोऽपि अपलपन्ति इति विशेषः।" - Śāstra-dīpikā (SD), quoted by G.P. Bhaṭṭ, Loc. Ciṭ, p.99.
95. Ibid.
96. न स्याद्भ्रान्तिस्तया सच्चेद्बोध्यते काऽत्र बाध्यता। ततो बाधादसत्येव सद्धीर्भ्रान्तिरितीष्यताम्॥ —IS, Op. Cit., p.155.
97. Sukharanjan Saha, Loc. Cit., pp.2-3.
98. "नापि सद्धीर्बाधते सद्धियमसद्धियं वा सत्यरूप्यादिबुद्धिवत् अन्यथा अतिप्रसंगात् च। —IS, Op. Cit., p.155.
99. Sukharanjan Saha, Loc. Cit., p.3, Vide, "न च बाधो वस्तु नाशयति, तत्त्वनिवेदकत्वात् ज्ञानस्य। बाधकज्ञाने हि सति रूप्यं न भाति नास्ति च। यदि सत् रूप्यं तत् किं न भवेन्न भाति वा।" —IS, Op. Cit., p.154.
100. Ibid, p.3.
101. "ननु तुच्छं तुच्छत्वादेव न ख्यातिः, अतो रूप्यस्य तुच्छतां बाधो बोधयतीत्ययुक्तमुक्तमिति चेत्-एतद्वचनं नेदं रजतमित्यनयैव तुच्छख्यात्या विरुध्यते। न हि नेदं रजतमिति रूप्यसत्त्वं बोध्यते, नञो वैफल्यात्पूर्वज्ञानवदबाधकत्वप्रसंगाच्च।" —IS, Op. Cit., p.156.
102. "अतस्सद्धियोर्बाध्यबाधकत्वायोगात्तद्दर्शनाच्च असत एव सद्रूपेण ख्यातिर्भ्रान्तिः। तस्य चासत्त्वबोधनं बाध इत्युपेयम्।" —Ibid, p.155.
103. G.P. Bhaṭṭ, Loc. Cit., p.100; Vide, "बुद्धेरेव रजताकारो न बुद्धिरिति कुतः? संप्रयोगव्यतिरेकेणापरोक्षत्वाद् बुद्धिवत्।" —Pañcapādikā, Op. Cit, p.92.
104. Jadunath Sinha, Indian Psychology, Vol.I, Cognition, pp.287-288, Vide, "ननु चतुर्विधान् हेतून् प्रतीत्य चित्तचैत्या उत्पद्यन्त इति हि सौगतानां मतम्। (वि.प्र.सं.I.1) —Vivaraṇaprameya-saṅgraha (VPS), Ed. R. Tailaṅga, Varanasi, 1990, p.34.
105. Jadunath Sinha, Loc. Cit.
106. 'ततः कथं विज्ञानस्य रजताकार इति चेत्? संस्कारसामर्थ्यादिति ब्रूमः।......अनादिसिद्धज्ञानसन्ततौ यदा कदाचित्पूर्वं रजतज्ञानमुत्पन्नं तदेव संस्कार इत्यंगीकारात्।......यथा व्रीहिबीजमने-

काङ्कुरादिकार्यव्यवधानेन पुनः सजातीयबीजान्तरमुत्पादयति तद्वत्। अतः न पूर्वबीजादुत्तरबीजोत्पत्तिः किंतु पूर्वबीजजन्याङ्कुरादिसन्तानवदिति पूर्वरजतज्ञानजन्य ज्ञानसन्तान एवं संस्कारोऽस्तु। एवं पूर्वरजतज्ञानमपि पूर्वरजतज्ञानादुत्पद्यते। ततोऽनादिवासनाप्रापितं रजतबुद्धिरूपमेव सद् भ्रान्त्या बहिर्वदवभासत इति" —VPS, Op. Cit., p.34.

107. "ज्ञानाकारस्यैव बहिरवभासो विभ्रम इत्याहु:।" —Nyāya-makaranda, quoted by J.N. Sinha, Loc. Cit.

108. "विमतं रजतं बुद्धिरूपं संप्रयोगमन्तरेणापरोक्षत्वाद् बुद्धिवत्।" —VPS, Op. Cit.

109. "यो यः प्रत्ययः सर्वो बाह्यानालम्बनः, यथा स्वप्नमायादिप्रत्ययः तथा चैषः विवादाध्यासितः प्रत्यय इति स्वभावहेतुः। बाह्यानालम्बनता हि प्रत्ययत्वमात्रानुबन्धिनी वृक्षतैव शिंशपात्वमात्रानुबन्धिनीति तन्मात्रानुबन्धिनि निरालम्बनत्वे साध्ये भवति प्रत्ययत्वं स्वभावहेतुः।" —Brahma-Sūtra-Śāṅkara-Bhāṣya, Parimal Ed., Bhāmatī, p.544.

110. "सहोपलम्भनियमादभेदो विषयविज्ञानयोरापतति।" —Ibid.

111. R.Balasubramanian, Loc.Cit., p.83.

112. Ibid.

113. Ibid.

114. "अस्तु तर्हि बुद्धौ, स्वरूपेणासतो गगनारविन्दादिवदप्रतिभासात्, नेदं रजतमिति बाधस्येदंतामात्रगोचरत्वात्, द्वयोर्बाधकल्पनायां कल्पनागौरवात्, नेदं रजतमिति च रजते बाधादर्शनात्।" Tattvapradīpikā, Op.Cit., pp.126-127.

115. R.Balasubramanian, Loc.Cit.

116. The Bhāmatī of Vācaspati, Adyar Library, Madras, 1933, p.24; Vide, "यद्यादृशमनुभवसिद्धं रूपं तत्तादृशमेवाभ्युपेतव्यमित्युत्सर्गः, अन्यथात्वं पुनरस्य बलवद् बाधकप्रत्ययवशात्। नेदं रजतमिति च बाधस्येदन्तामात्रबाधेनोपपत्तौ न रजतगोचरतोचिता। रजतस्य धर्मिणो बाधे हि रजतं च तस्य च धर्मो बाध्यतां न पुना रजतमपि धर्मि। तथाच रजतं बहिर्बाधितमर्थादान्तरे ज्ञाने व्यवतिष्ठत इति ज्ञानाकारस्य बहिरध्यासः सिद्ध्यति।" —Bhāmatī on ŚB - I.1.1.

117. Vide, R. Balasubramanian-Advaita Vedānta-University of Madras, 1976, p.72.

118. "यथार्थं सर्वविज्ञानमिति वेदविदां मतम्। श्रुतिस्मृतिभ्यः सर्वस्य सर्वात्मत्वप्रतीतिः॥" (श्रीभाष्यम्- 1.1.) —Śrībhāṣyam - Vol. I - The Academy of Sanskrit Research, Melkote- 1987 - p.195.

119. Vide, R. Balasubramanian, Op Cit.

120. Ibid, Vide, "यथावस्थित-व्यवहारानुगुण-ज्ञानं प्रमा।" (यतीन्द्रमतदीपिका, I.7)

121. Ibid, p.73.

122. Vide, Jadunath Sinha, Loc.Cit., p.89

123. Vide, R. Balasubramanian, Op.Cit.,

124. Śrībhāsya, Op. Cit., Vide,
1. "बहुस्यामिति संकल्पपूर्वसृष्ट्याद्युपक्रमे। तासां त्रिवृतमेकैकामिति श्रुत्यैव चोदितम्॥
2. त्रिवृत्करणमेवं हि प्रत्यक्षेणोपलभ्यते। यदग्ने रोहितं रूपं तेजसस्तदपामपि॥
3. शुक्लं कृष्णं पृथिव्याश्चेदग्नावेव त्रिरूपता। श्रुत्यैव दर्शिता तस्मात् सर्वे सर्वत्र संगताः॥

125. R.Balasubramanian, Op.Cit., Vide, "तदेव सदृशं तस्य यत् तद्द्रव्यैकदेशभाक्। शुक्त्यादौ रजतादेश्च भावः श्रुत्यैव बोधितः॥

126. Vide R. Balasubramanian, Op.Cit., p.74.

127. Ibid, Vide,
"कदाचिच्चक्षुरादेस्तु दोषात् शुक्त्यंशवर्जितः॥ रजतांशो गृहीतोऽतो रजतार्थी प्रवर्तते॥ दोषहानौ तु शुक्त्यंशे गृहीते तन्निवर्तते। अतो यथार्थं रूप्यादिविज्ञानं शुक्तिकादिषु॥ बाध्य-बाधकभावोऽपि भूयस्त्वेनोपपद्यते। शुक्तिभूयस्त्ववैकल्यसाकल्यग्रहरूपतः॥ नाऽतो मिथ्यार्थ-सत्यार्थविषयत्वनिबन्धनः। एवं सर्वस्य सर्वत्वे व्यवहारव्यवस्थितिः॥ —(Śrībhāṣya - I.1.1) Op.Cit., pp.196-197.
128. Vide, Jadunath Sinha, Op.Cit., p.90.
129. "भ्रमादि प्रत्यक्ष-ज्ञानं यथार्थमेव। विषय-व्यवहार-बाधात् भ्रमत्वम्॥" —Quoted by Jadunath Sinha, Loc.Cit.
130. R. Bālasubramanian, Op.Cit., Vide,
"पीतशंखादौ तु नयनवर्तिपित्तद्रव्यसंभिन्नाः नायनरश्मयः शंखादिभिः संयुज्यन्ते। तत्र पित्तगतपीतिमाभिभूतः शङ्खगतशुक्लिमा न गृह्यते। अतः सुवर्णानुलिप्तशंखवत् "पीतः शंखः" इति प्रतीयते। —(Śrībhāṣya - 1.1.1)
131. Ibid, Vide,
"स्वप्ने च प्राणिनां पुण्य-पापानुगुणम् भगवतैव तत्तत्पुरुषमात्रानुभाव्याः तत्तत्कालावसानाः तथाभूताश्च अर्थाः सृज्यन्ते।" —(Śrībhāṣya - 1.1.1)-Op. Cit, pp.197-198.
132. "मरीचिकाजलज्ञानेऽपि तेजःपृथिव्योरपि अम्बुनो विद्यमानत्वात् इन्द्रियदोषेण तेजःपृथिव्योः अग्रहणात् अदृष्टवशात् च अम्बुनः ग्रहणात् यथार्थत्वम्।" - Ibid, p.201.
133. "जपाकुसुमसमीपवर्तिस्फटिकमणिरपि तत्प्रभाभिभूततया रक्तः इति गृह्यते। जपाकुसुमप्रभा विततऽपि स्वच्छद्रव्यसंयुक्तया स्फुटतरम् उपलभ्यते।" —Ibid, p.200.
134. "द्विचन्द्रज्ञानादावपि अंगुल्यवष्टम्भतिमिरादिभिः नायनतेजोगतिभेदेन सामग्रीभेदात् सामग्रीद्वयम् अन्योन्यनिरपेक्षचन्द्रग्रहणद्वयहेतुर्भवति। तत्र एका सामग्री स्वदेशविशिष्टं चन्द्रं गृह्णाति। द्वितीया तु किंचिद् वक्रगतिः चन्द्रसमीपदेशग्रहणपूर्वकं चन्द्रं स्वदेशवियुक्तं गृह्णाति। अतः सामग्रीद्वयेन युगपत् देशद्वयविशिष्टचन्द्रग्रहणे ग्रहणभेदेन ग्राह्याकारभेदात् एकत्वग्रहणाभावाच्च द्वौ चन्द्रौ इति भवति प्रतीतिविशेषः। ... तत्र सामग्रीद्वित्वं पारमार्थिकम्। तेन देशद्वयविशिष्टचन्द्रग्रहणद्वयं च पारमार्थिकम्। ग्रहणद्वित्वेन चन्द्रस्यैव ग्राह्याकारद्वित्वं च पारमार्थिकम्" —Ibid, p.202.
135. Vide, R. Bālasubramanian, Op. Cit.
136. B. Bālasubramanian, Loc. Cit., p.58; Vide,
"तत्र शुक्तिकारजतादिज्ञानं शुक्तिकाख्यं भावं शुक्तिकारूपेण सद्रूपं भावान्तरस्य यद् सद्रूपं रजतरूपं तेन रूपेण गृह्णद् भ्रान्तं भवति"। —Nyāyaratnamalā on Ś.V., Nirālambana, 117.
137. R. Bālasubramanian, Loc. Cit., p.60; Vide,
"एवं हि न कश्चिदसर्वज्ञो भवेत्।" —Kāśikā on Ś.V., V.2.14.
138. "तथा च बाधकज्ञानं नेदं रजतमिति विशिष्टदेशकालसम्बद्धं रजतं विलोपयदेवोदेति, न देशान्तरसम्बन्धमापादयति तथाऽनवगमात्।" —Pañcapādikā and Pañcapādikā-Vivaraṇam, UoM, 1958, pp.122-123.
139. N.K. Devaraja, An Introduction to Śaṅkara's Theory of Knowledge, MLBD, 1962, p.124.
140. "तथा च दूरवर्तिनीं रज्जुं सर्पं मन्यमानः तन्निकटवर्तिना आप्तेन "नायं सर्पः" इत्युक्ते सर्पाभावमात्रं प्रतिपद्यते न तस्य देशान्तरवर्तित्वम्। तत्प्रतिपत्तावसामार्थ्यात् वाक्यस्य"।— Vivaraṇa, Loc. Cit; p.67.
141. Jadunath Sinha, Loc. Cit., Vol-III, p.100; Vide,
"केयमन्यथाख्यातिः? अन्याकारं ज्ञानमन्यालम्बनं वा, वस्तुनो वस्त्वन्तरात्मनावभासो वा,

अन्यथा परिणते वस्तुनि ज्ञानं वा?।" —Pancapādikā, Loc. Cit; p.144.

142. Jadunath Sinha, Ibid, Vide,
"किं ज्ञानेऽन्यथात्वं किं वा फले उत वस्तुनि? नाद्यः। रजताकारज्ञानं शुक्तिमालम्बत नाम किं ज्ञानं प्रति स्वाकारसमर्पकत्वम् उत ज्ञानप्रयुक्तव्यवहारविषयत्वम् ? नाद्यः। रजताकारग्रस्तं ज्ञानं प्रति शुक्त्याकारसमर्पणासम्भवात्। न द्वितीयः। व्याघ्रादिदर्शनप्रयुक्त-व्यवहारविषयस्य खड्गकुन्तधनुरादेर्व्याघ्रादिज्ञानालम्बनत्वप्रसंगात्। नापि फलेऽन्यथात्वम्। फलस्य स्फुरणस्य भ्रान्तौ सम्यग्ज्ञाने वा स्वरूपतो वैषम्यादर्शनात्। वस्तुन्यपि.... अत्यन्तभिन्नयोर्वास्तवतादाम्यसंभवात्।.... भेदाभेदपक्षे तु खण्डो गौरितिवदभ्रान्तिः स्यात्।.... परिणामपक्षेऽपि बाधो न स्याद् विमतं रजतज्ञानमबाध्यं परिणामज्ञानत्वात् क्षीरपरिणामदधिज्ञानवत्। ततः क्षीरवदेव शुक्तिः पुनर्न दृश्येत। (न च).... रजतपरिणामहेतोर्दोषस्यापगमे पुनः शुक्तिभावोऽस्तु (इति वक्तव्यम्)।.... निर्दोषस्यापि रजतप्रतीतिप्रसंगात्। न ह्येकमेव क्षीरं दधिरूपेण कंचित्पुरूषं प्रति परिणतमन्यं प्रति नेति दृष्टचरम्।" —Vivaraṇa-prameya-saṅgraha (VPS), Kishore Vidya Niketana, Varanasi, 1990; p.23.

143. The Bhāmatī of Vācaspati, Op. Cit; pp.30-31; Vide,
"इदंकारास्पदाभिमुखी खलु रजतार्थिनां प्रवृत्तिरित्यविवादम्। कथं चायमिदंकारास्पदे प्रवर्तेत यदि तु न तदिच्छेत्? अन्यदिच्छत्यन्यत्करोतीति व्याहतम्। न चेदिदंकारास्पदं रजतमिति जानीयात् कथं रजतार्थी तदिच्छेत्? यदि अतथात्वेनाग्रहणात् इति ब्रूयात्, स च प्रतिवक्तव्यः, अथ तथात्वेनाग्रहणात् कस्मान्नोपेतेति। सोऽयमुपादानोपेक्षाभ्यामुभयत आकृष्यमाणश्चेतनः अव्यवस्थितः.... न च तटस्थरजतस्मृतिः इदंकारास्पदस्योपकारहेतुभावमनुमापयितुमर्हति, रजतत्वस्य हेतोरपक्षधर्मत्वात्। एकदेशदर्शनं खल्वनुमापकं न त्वनेकदेशदर्शनम्। यदाहुः-" ज्ञातसंबन्धस्यैकदेशदर्शनात् इति।" —Bhāmatī, Ibid.

144. R. Balasubramanian, Loc. Cit; p-61; Vide,
"नापि तयोरैक्यं बाध्यम्, ऐक्यं नास्तीति ज्ञानाभावात्। नेदं रजतमिति तु ज्ञानम्: तच्च सत्त्वान्न बाध्यमित्युक्तम्।.... न चैक्यं नास्तीति ज्ञानाभावो दोषाय, भ्रमानुसारित्वाद् बाधस्य। न ह्यनयोरैक्यमस्तीति ज्ञातभेदयोर्व्यधिकरणतया भ्रमः किंत्विदं रजतमिति सामानाधिकरण्येनैवाज्ञातभेदयोः। अतो नेदं रजतमित्येव बाधो न्याय्यः, न पुनरैक्यं नास्तीति-तदनुरूपभ्रमाभावात्।.... तस्मादिदं रजतमित्यैक्यभ्रमस्य नेदं रजतमित्येव बाधो युक्तः"। —IS, Op. Cit; p.107

145. Tattavapradīpikā.... Ṣaḍdarśana-Pratiṣṭhāna-Vārāṇasī: 1974 p.103.

146. N.K. Devaraja : An Introduction to Śaṅkara's Theory of Knowledge: Motilal Banarsidass, 1962: p.106.

147. "स्वीकारे विभ्रमाणां स्यात्स्वीयसिद्धान्तबाधता। अनभ्युपगमे तेषामाश्रयासिद्धिरुद्धता।" —Citsukhī - I. 11.

148. N.K. Devaraja, Op. Cit; Vide,
"स्मृतेः प्रमोषो न सम्भवति।.... तथा च तन्त्रान्तरीया आहुः अनुभूतविषयाऽसंप्रमोषा स्मृतिरिति।" (Pañcapādikā on B.S. I.1.1.)-(Pañcapādikā, Mahesha Anusandhāna Sansthāna, Vārāṇasī, 1972 : p.94).

149. Ibid, p.89. Vide,
"न चेह पूर्वप्रमाणविषयावभासित्वमस्ति। पुरोऽवस्थितार्थप्रतिभासनाद् इत्युक्तम्।" । (Pañcapādikā, Op. Cit.).

150. Ibid, p.95. Vide,
"सा चैकमेव ज्ञानम् एकफलं जनयति।" (Pañcapadikā, Op.Cit).

151. The Brahma-Sūtra- Śāṅkara- Bhāṣya, Parimala Publications, Delhi, 1981, p.28;

"वयं तु पश्यामः चेतनव्यवहारस्याज्ञानपूर्वकत्वानुपपत्तेः, आरोपज्ञानोत्पादक्रमेणैवेति।"
—Bhāmatī on ŚB. I.1.1).

152. "न चेदिदंकारास्पदं रजतमिति जानीयात् कथं रजतार्थी तदिच्छेत् - Ibid.

153. N.K. Devaraja, Op. Cit; p.127; Vide,
—"यदि अतथात्वेनाग्रहणादिति ब्रूयात् स च प्रतिवक्तव्यः अथ तथात्वेनाग्रहणात् कस्मान्नोपेक्षतेति।"
—Bhāmatī, Ibid.

154. "यथार्थशब्देन च सदर्थविवक्षायां नायं सर्पः इत्यादिबाधविरोधात् तुच्छव्यावृत्तार्थविवक्षायां चास्मान्प्रति सिद्धसाधानत्वात्।" —Tattvapradīpikā, Op. Cit; p.107.

155. Ibid.
"किं चायथार्थप्रत्ययोऽस्तीत्यस्य प्रत्ययस्य यथार्थत्वे तस्य सालम्बनत्वाय कश्चिदप्ययथार्थप्रत्ययोऽभ्युपेयः, तथा सति तत्रैव हेतोरनैकान्तिकता।" (Tattvapradīpikā).

156. Sukharanjan Saha, Loc. Cit; p.26.

157. The Bhāmatī of Vācaspati, Adyar Library, p.20; Vide,
"न च विषयस्य समस्तसामर्थ्याद् दृष्टान्तसिद्धस्वभावः भेदमुपजातमसतः प्रकाशनम्, तस्मादसत्प्रकाशन-शक्तिरेवास्याविद्येति सांप्रतम्।" —Bhāmatī on Adhyāsabhāṣya.

158. Ibid; Vide,
"यतो येयमसत्प्रकाशनशक्तिर्विज्ञानस्य किं पुनरस्याः शक्यम्? असदिति चेत्, किमेतत्कार्यम् आहोस्विदस्या ज्ञाप्यम्? न तावत् कार्यम् असतस्तत्त्वानुपपत्तेः।" -Bhāmatī on Adhyāsabhāṣya.

159. Sukharanjan Saha, Loc. Cit; pp.27-28; Vide,
"असतो प्रकाशनशक्तिव्याघाताच्च": - "असतो जन्यत्वे तज्जननशक्तिरेव विज्ञानस्य स्यात् न प्रकाशनशक्तिरित्यर्थः।" —Citsukha, quoted by Sukharanjan Saha.

160. Ibid; Vide,
"नापि ज्ञाप्यम्, ज्ञानान्तरानुपलब्धेः। —Bhāmatī, Ibid.

161. "अनवस्थापाताच्च।" —Ibid.

162. "विज्ञानस्वरूपमेव असतः प्रकाश इति चेत् कः पुनरेष सदसतोः संबन्धः? असदधीन-निरूपणत्वं सतो ज्ञानस्य असता संबन्ध इति चेत्, अहो बत.... असत्यपि निरूपणमायतते। न च प्रत्ययस्तत्राधत्ते किंचित् असत आधारत्वायोगात्।" —Ibid.

163. Bhāmatī of Vācaspati, Op. Cit, p.21.

164. Sukharanjan Saha, Loc. Cit. pp.31-32; Vide,
"असदन्तरेण प्रत्ययो न प्रथम इति प्रत्ययस्यैवैष स्वभावः न त्वसदधीनमस्य किंचिदिति चेत् अहो बत....अतदुत्पत्तिः अतदात्मा च तदविनाभावनियतः प्रत्यय इति। तस्मादत्यन्तासन्त.... नानुभवविषया भवितुमर्हन्तीति"। —Bhāmatī on Adhyāsa-bhāṣya.

165. "....विभ्रमालम्बनं तु किमसत्? .... न तावदसत्। असतोऽपरोक्षावाभासानर्हत्वात् तदादित्सया प्रवृत्त्यनुपपत्तेश्च।" —Citsukhī, (Tattvapradīpikā), Ṣaḍdarśanaprakāśana-pratiṣṭhāna, Kāśī, 1985, p.119.

166. —"क्वचिदसद्विशेषेऽपि प्रतिभासप्रवृत्ती किं न स्यातामिति चेत्, न, विशेषाधिकरणत्वे तुच्छत्वानुपपत्तेस्तस्य निःस्वभावत्वात्। —Ibid.

167. R. Bālasubramanian, Loc. Cit; p.87.

168. "स किं पुरोवर्ति द्रव्यं रजताद्विवेचयति आहो ज्ञानाकारतामप्यस्य दर्शयति? तत्र ज्ञानाकारतोपदर्शनव्यापारं बाधकप्रत्ययस्य ब्रुवाणः श्लाघनीयप्रज्ञो देवानां प्रियः। पुरोवर्तित्वप्रतिषेधादर्थाद् अस्य ज्ञानाकारतेति चेत्, न। असंनिधानाग्रहनिषेधादसंनिहितो भवति। प्रतिपत्तुरत्यन्तसंनिधानं त्वस्य प्रतिपत्रात्मकं कुतस्सत्यम्?" —Bhāmatī, Op. Cit; p.25.

169. R. Bālasubramanian, Loc. Cit; pp.86-87, Vide,

"न तावद्रजतानुभवः। स हि इदंकारास्पदं रजतमावेदयति न त्वान्तरम्। "अहम्" इति हि तदा स्यात्, प्रतिपत्तुः प्रत्ययादव्यतिरेकात्। —Bhāmatī, Op. Cit.

170. The Bhāmatī of Vācaspati, Op. Cit, p.25, Vide,
"न चैष रजतस्य निषेधः, न च इदंतायाः किंतु विवेकाग्रह प्रसञ्जितं रजतज्ञानेन।"—Ibid.

171. The Bhāmatī of Vācaspati, Op. Cit., p.25, Vide,
"न च रजतमेव शुक्तिकायां प्रसञ्जितं रजतज्ञानेन। न हि रजतनिर्भासस्य शुक्तिकालम्बनं युक्तम्, अनुभवविरोधात्।" —Bhāmatī, Ibid.

172. "स (आत्मख्यातिवादी) वक्तव्यः। किं रजतं जायते न वेति। न चेत् जायमानस्वरूपं न स्यादाकाशवत्। जायते चेत् नार्थात् अर्थान्तराभावात्।.... अथ पुनः.... प्रतीतेरेव रजतोत्पाद इति।.... तद्विषयत्वे सर्वप्रतीतिविषयत्वप्रसंगात् रजतजन्यतया तदालम्बनत्वे रजतस्यार्थक्रियावत्तया सत्त्वप्रसंगात्.....।" —Vivaraṇa, Loc. Cit; pp.93-94.

173. "किं तद्रजतलौकिकत्वाज्जन्मरहितम् उत लौकिकरजतवदेव जायते। आद्ये जायमानज्ञानस्वरूपं न स्यात्। द्वितीयेऽपि किं बाह्यार्थाज्जायते उत ज्ञानात्। नाद्यः। त्वया बाह्यार्थस्यानंगीकारात्। ज्ञानमपि विशुद्धं तावन्न जनकम्। विशुद्धज्ञानस्य मोक्षस्वरूपत्वात्। अथ दुष्टकारणजन्यज्ञानाद्रजतोत्पादः। दुष्टकारणजन्याऽपि यदि रजतजन्या तदा रजतस्यार्थक्रियाकारित्वेन सत्त्वे सति बाह्योऽर्थोङ्गीकार्यः स्यात्। रजताजन्यत्वे तु न रजतं तद्विषयः स्यात्। .... तस्मादात्मख्यातिपक्षे रजतमेव न प्रतीयेत"। —VPS, Op. Cit; pp.34-35.

174. R. Balasubramanian, Loc. Cit; p.75; Vide,
"भूतानामेव पंचीकृतत्वात् भौतिकानां तु तदभावात्।" —Saṅkṣepa-śārīraka-bhāṣya, I.20.

175. Jadunath Singha, Loc. Cit, Vol. III, p.91.

176. Ibid, Vol. I, p.396.

177. The Bhāmatī of Vācaspati, Op. Cit., p.19, Vide,
"न प्रकाशमानतामात्रं सत्त्वम् येन देहेन्द्रियादेः प्रकाशमानतया सद्भावो भवेत्। न हि सर्पादिभावेन रज्ज्वादयो वा स्फटिकादयो वा रक्तादिगुणयोगिनो न प्रतिभासन्ते, प्रतिभासमाना वा भवन्ति तदात्मानस्तद्धर्माणो वा। तथा सति मरुषु मरीचिकानिचयम् "उच्चावचमुच्चलत्तुङ्गतरङ्गभङ्गमालेयमभ्यर्णमवतीर्णा मन्दाकिनी" इत्यभिसंधाय प्रवृत्तः तत्तोयमापीय पिपासामुपशमयेत्। तस्मादकामेनापि प्रकाशमानस्याप्यारोपितस्य न वस्तुसत्त्वमभ्युपगमनीयम्।" —Bhāmatī on Adhyāsabhāṣya.

178. "नापि सत्; नेदं रजतमित्यादिबाधविरोधात्। यत्र बाध्यते ततोऽन्यत्रास्तीति चेत्, न। तत्र प्रमाणानिरूपणात्। भ्रान्त्यनुभवस्तत्र .... न .... प्रमाणम्। तस्य पुरोवर्तिरजतसत्तामात्रगोचरतयाऽसंनिहिततत्सत्तायामौदासीन्यात्।" —Citsukhī, Op. Cit., p.123.

179. "भ्रमानुपपत्तिः... न (तत्र)... प्रमाणम्। रजतावभासस्य यथाप्रतीतपुरोवर्तिरजतसत्तां विनानुपपत्तावपि देशान्तरे तदीयसत्तामन्तरेणानुपपत्त्यभावात्।" - Ibid.

180. "बाधानुभवस्यापि पुरोवर्तिन्यारोपिताभावविषयस्य देशान्तरतत्सत्तानावेदकत्वात्.... न बाधानुभवः.... (तत्र) प्रमाणम्।" - Ibid.

181. "न च वाच्यमन्यत्रापि तस्यासत्त्वे तत्रापि कुतो न तस्य बाधः स्यादिति। तत्र तस्याप्रसक्तेरेव बाधाभावोपपत्तौ तत्सत्ताध्यवसायायोगात्।" —Citsukhī, Op. Cit., p.123.

182. "नेदं रजतमिति पुरोवर्तिनि रजततादात्म्य-निषेधात्मबाधानुभवो रजतमर्थात् क्वापि परिशिनष्टीति चेत् न। तथा सति वनस्पत्योरिव विविक्तयोर्द्वयोरप्यत्रैवानन्तरं प्रतीतिप्रसक्तेः।" —Ibid.

CHAPTER IV

THE ADVAITA THEORY OF ERROR

1. The Bhāmati Prasthāna

In the foregoing discussion an attempt has been made to assess the position of various systems of philosophy with regard to the conception of the world and its relation with the Absolute Reality, with special reference to the Theories of Error. It will be seen from the ensuing discussion that as a sequel to the failure of all the above-mentioned systems to give a plausible explanation of the World-Phenomenon, especially of the problem of Illusion, the Advaita Vedānta has come forward with a novel theory, namely, the Theory of *Anirvacanīyakhyāti*, establishing thereby, once for all, the supremacy of *Brahman* on the one hand, and the illusoriness of the world on the other. This new Theory of Error propounded by Śaṅkara was so revolutionary and thought-provoking in its essence that it did not only generate a passionate debate in the non-Advaitic camp, but even within the Advaita camp, leading to the birth of two distinct schools of Advaitic thought, namely the *Bhāmatī Prasthāna* and the *Vivaraṇa Prasthāna* originating from the *Bhāmatī* (Commentary) of Vācaspati Miśra and the *Pañcapādikā-Vivaraṇa* (Commentary) of Prakāśātman on the *Śārīrakabhāṣya* of Śaṅkara and the *Pañcapādikā* of Padmapāda respectively.

Error in Advaita consists in the superimposition of one thing or the characteristic (s) of one thing on another. This superimposition in Śaṅkara's Philosophy, is known as '*Adhyāsa*', as is reported in the *Śārīrakabhāṣya.*

"But what have we to understand by the term 'Superimposition'? —The apparent presentation, in the form of remembrance, to Consciousness of something previously observed, in some other thing"[1]. Commenting on the meaning of the term "*avabhāsa*" used by Śaṅkara in the definition given above, Vācaspatī says that "*Avabhāsa*" is that appearance which is terminated or depreciated. This termination or depreciation is nothing but sublation by another cognition. Hence it (*avabhāsa*) is said to be an illusory cognition[2]. Deliberating on the nature of the superimposition referred to above, Śaṅkara says that, 'It is a matter not requiring any proof that the object and the subject whose respective spheres are the notion of the Thou' (the non-Ego) and the 'Ego', and which are opposed to each other as much as darkness and light are, cannot be identified. All the less can their respective attributes be identified. Hence it follows that it is wrong to superimpose upon the subject-whose Self is intelligence and which has of its sphere the notion of the Ego - the object whose sphere is the notion of the non-Ego, and the attributes of the object, and vice-versa, to superimpose the subject and the attributes of the subject on the object. In spite of this it is on the part of man a natural procedure - which has its cause in wrong knowledge - not to distinguish the two entities (object and subject) and their respective attributes, although they are absolutely distinct, but to superimpose upon each the characteristic nature and the attributes of the other, and thus, coupling the Real and the Unreal, to make use of expressions such as "That am I", "That is mine"[3]. Explaining the concept of superimposition as enunciated by Śaṅkara, Vācaspati Miśra says that in order to indicate the absolute difference between the Self and the not-Self the words 'I' and 'Thou' are used in the place of "I" and 'this', because the "countercorrelate of the word 'I' is not the word 'this', so much as the word 'thou'[4]. This is illustrated by the fact that in everyday experience one comes across expressions such as, "We are this, we are that", which are examples of the superimposition of the Self on the not-Self. In other words, this means the superimposition of the subject, which is of the nature of intelligence, on the object of cognition, such as the intellect, the organs, the body and the material objects, which are all non-intelligent[5]. Vācaspati observes that superimposition as described by Śaṅkara, means the indentity of one thing with another. And this erroneous identification of one thing with another thing, if not so evident in the case of substrates, is more evident in the case of their attributes as when the inert and non-eternal body is identified with the intelligent and eternal Self. This cross-identification of attributes, says the

Bhāmatīkāra, takes place even in instances where the substrates are visibly distinct from each other, as for example, in the illusory cognition of 'red crystal'. Here, though the crystal is distinguishable from the red hibiscus flower, yet due to their proximity, and owing also to the transparency of the crystal, the 'redness' of the flower is superimposed on the crystal giving rise to the erroneous cognition of red-crystal[6].

Reacting to the Bhāṭṭa Mīmāṁsaka's contention that the Intelligent Self cannot take on the reflection or attributes of other objects, being Itself the colourless subject, Vācaspati says that superimposition is pervaded by non-apprehension of difference[7]. And in the experience of the Self also there is non-apprehension of difference, for the true nature of the Self is not manifest in the experience of the "I". No superimposition would have occurred had there been apprehension of difference between the Self and the not-Self. The true nature of the Self, says Vācaspati, is not apprehended. As it is described in the Scriptures, the Self is "undefined by any limiting conditions, is endless Bliss and Intelligence, is indifferent and is One without a second"[8]. Furthermore, argues Vācaspati, the experience of the "I" exhibits the Self as "Finite and as confounded by a multitude of griefs and sorrows", and as such it having the true nature of the Self for its sphere is not evident. It cannot, therefore, be said of the "I" that it is not an undeluded experience[9].

Developing further the concept of superimposition, Vācaspati says that it would not be admissible to attribute the experienced 'finiteness' to the body, and not to the self, in the judgement "I am in this very abode, (but) cognizing", wherein the omnipresent Self is apprehended as finite. Should it be so, the experience would not be of the form "I (am)", nor even of the form "cognizing" (since the body, being inert, cannot 'be', and therefore cannot 'cognize'). The reason is that, the primary denotation of the word 'I' (in the example cited above), is not indeed experienced as determinately and specifically other than the body, etc. in which case alone that word would have the secondary sense of the body, etc.[10]. Referring to the example of *'taila'*, to illustrate his theory of erroneous cognition, Vācaspati argues that just as *'taila'* is used in the primary sense in the case of mustard oil despite the fact of *"taila"* being cognized as having a secondary sense, in like manner, in the case of superimposition of the Self on the not-Self, and vice-versa, the 'I' is identified with the 'body' and vice-versa, despite the cognition of the difference between the two. Vācaspati concludes that the secondary usage is therefore pervaded by the cognition of the difference between the primary and the secondary by those who know both"[11]. There, the pervader, viz. cognition of difference, eliminating itself eliminates also the secondary usage, thus giving rise to the illusory cognition[12].

Eventhough there is the experience of the difference in the bodies of youth and old age as in the cognition, "I am he", it cannot be said that the self is cognized as different from the body, etc. For, says Vācaspati, such a difference is perceptible only by the thoughtful man, not by the common man. And as far as practical life is concerned, no distinction is noted between the former and the latter, as Śaṅkara himself puts it, "And because there is no distinction from beast, etc." By the process of elimination, it is therefore fit to hold that in the example "I am in this very abode, etc.", quoted above, finitude applies to the self, and not to the body, just as ether is cognized as being subject to limitation by pot, ewer, etc[13].

Deliberating further on the nature of superimposition, Vācaspati observes that 'even if cognition be taken to be the substrate, the illusoriness of the concept "I" continues to be experienced as a permanent substance, despite the fleeting nature of cognitions. Therefore, cognitions themselves cannot be the substrate of the concept "I". As for the expressions such as, "I am fat, I am blind, I go" etc. these can be accounted for only with regard to superimposition[14].

Having established the illusoriness of the concept "I", Vācaspati proceeds by describing the nature of this concept, which is well-known from all trust-worthy Scriptures, traditional codes, epics and Purāṇas[15]. The "I" illusion, says the Commentator, takes the form of reciprocal superimposition of the natures of the two substrates - the body and the self, resulting in the identification of the body, etc. with the self. Hence, the experience "I am this body". This identification of the self with "this" is a matter of fact, says Vācaspati, and not a matter of knowledge. In like manner, the empirical usage "I am this" is symbolical of the association of the self with worldly experience, in the form of acceptance, rejection, etc., of what are apprehended as beneficial or injurious to the body, etc.[16]

Apart from the superimposition of one substrate on the other, the "I" illusion takes the form of superimposition of the attributes of one substrate on the other. For example, there is to be seen in the world, the imposition of the bodily attributes of birth, old age, diseases, etc. on the self, on whom bodies, etc. stand superimposed. In the same way, says Vācaspati, the attributes of the self, such as intelligence, etc. are superimposed on the body, etc., on which self-ness stands superimposed. The result of this type of superimposition is the empirical usage like, "Mine is this" -old-age, death, son, cow, ownership, etc.[17]

After elaborating on the nature of superimposition and on its relevance in empirical activities, Vācaspati defines the relation between superimposition and empirical usages. Following Śaṅkara, he says that superimposition is the cause of empirical usage, since the latter is a direct function of superimposition. This means that there can be empirical activities only under the influence of superimposition. It follows from this that should there be no superimposition there would be cessation of all worldly activities; so much so that the very existence of the external world is dependent on the existence of superimposition[18].

Having thus established the cause and effect relation between superimposition and empirical experience, Vācaspati Miśra discusses the very cause of the phenomenon of superimposition. Elucidating Śaṅkara's declaration in this context, viz., that it is 'through non-discrimination of each from the other', that superimposition occurs, Vācaspati says that what is meant is the "non-apprehension of distinctness" between the Self and the not-Self. And distinctness here, says he, means, from the absolute point of view, "the non-identity as far as substrates are concerned, and the absence of confusion as far as the attributes are concerned"[19].

It is interesting to note here that, like Prabhākara, Vācaspati also advocates non-apprehension of difference as the cause of illusory cognition. This is made more evident by the latter's explanation of the shell-silver illusion. He says that it is because of the non-apprehension of the differences existing between them, that there is the delusion of the identity of silver and nacre[20].

Making clear the difference between the Self and the not-Self, Śaṅkara refers to them as the true (*satya*) and the untrue (*anṛta*) respectively. And Vācaspati, commenting on this, says that, the true is the intelligent Self and the untrue are the intellect, the organs, the body etc.[21]

Vācaspati observes in this connection, that there being no possibility of real coupling between the phenomenal (i.e., the untrue) and the absolutely real (i.e., the true), the suffix '*cvi*' has been used by Śaṅkara to describe the essence of superimposition[22]. Amalānanda, commenting on the use here of the prefix '*cvi*', which signifies "what is not that becoming that as it were", says that the 'coupling' referred to above is also false[23]. The empirical activities thus generated by superimposition and by the coupling of the true with the untrue, says Śaṅkara, are natural ("*naisargika*"). Explaining this, Vācaspati says that 'natural' here means "beginningless". "Through the beginninglessness of the usage, there is declared the beginninglessness ot its cause i.e. superimposition"[24].

It follows from the above that an illusory cognition has a previous cognition as its cause. Hence, the description by Śaṅkara of an appearance, as being dependent on "what was seen before". Commenting on this, Vācaspati says that there cannot be any illusory apearance without the coupling of the superimposed object with the (real) object in front. And in this context, what is superimposed, and therefore untrue, is indicated by "what was seen before". By the use of the qualificative "seen" here, says Vācaspati, the phenomenality of the superimposed object is emphasised, making it clear thereby that such an object cannot be absolutely real[25]. Continuing in the same breath, Vācaspati observes that what is seen in the present cannot be superimposed, and conversely, what is superimposed is apt to have been seen before. And an object of superimposition though real (at the time of previous cognition), is yet as an appearance an indeterminable object, and therefore, unreal. The locus of superimposition, on the other hand is real, and is indicated by the word "elsewhere" in the definition, "*paratra pūrvadṛṣṭāvabhāsaḥ*". By elsewhere is therefore to be understood, 'in nacre', in the illusory cognition of nacre-silver[26].

Making clear the difference between an illusory cognition and a valid cognition, Vācaspati Miśra, referring to the definition of illusory knowledge, viz., "of a nature like that of recollection", given by Śaṅkara, says that recollection has as essence the non-presence of the object cognized (and superimposed), while recognition, being valid, has as substrate an object in front[27]. Illustrating the process of the superimposition of a previous cognition in the apprehension of an object in front, Vācaspati describes how a white-shell is wrongly apprehended as a yellow shell. Says he, "The yellow(ness), which resides in the bile that is in contact with the exceedingly pure rays going forth from the eye, is experienced in dissociation from the bile; the shell too is experienced ((but) with the whiteness concealed by a defect in the sense organ; the non-relation of the yellow colour to the shell is not experienced; because of similarity in respect of non-relationship, the appositional relation previously seen in experience like "yellow mass of gold, yellow "*bilva*" fruit", is imposed on yellow-ness and shell-ness, and one speaks of the yellow shell. In this way too, may be explained the apprehension "sugar is bitter"[28].

In the same way, Vācaspati gives a detailed description of the process of superimposition of the image in the mirror. Says he, "Rays of light from the organ of sight come in contact with the pure mirror or sheet of water facing the cognizer, but they are reflected therefrom by the stronger rays of the sun's light, and coming into contact with the face, apprehend the face; because of a defect, however, they do not apprehend the face as where it really is, i.e, not facing oneself, but impose on it the property of facing oneself that belongs to the formerly seen mirror or sheet of water. Thus, the definition (of illusory cognition given above) applies to the delusion of refletion too. In the same way may be suitably explained delusions like the perception of two moons, loss of sense of direction, the fiery circle, the "*gandharvanagara*", the snake seen in the bamboo, etc."[29]

With a view to strengthening the notion of indeterminability of the object cognized in an illusion, Vācaspati probes deeper into the illusory water appearing in a mirage. In this context, he asks whether the cognition of water appearing in the rays of the sun is of a real nature? If it be so, then being a valid cognition, it would not be sublated, it being non-delusive. Nor can it be said that the illusory object (here, water) is something different (from what is apprehended). For, if it were so , it should be either the rays or the water flowing (e.g.) in the Ganges. It cannot be the first, for in that case the cognition would be that of 'rays' and not that of 'water'. It cannot also be the second, for there too, the cognition would take the form "water in the Ganges", instead of "water here". And if the 'water' cognized is in dissociation from the particular location, then the cognition would be simply of the form "water", rather than of 'water here'. It cannot also be said of the cognized water that it is absolutely unreal, devoid of existence, for in that conjecture, the water would not remain within the sphere of experience. Hence, says Vācaspati concludingly, it has to be accepted that the water superimposed on the rays is neither real nor unreal, nor still real-cum-unreal' (-this being contradictory). The idea is that the illusory water is simply indeterminable (*asat* or unreal). Its reality cannot be denied straightaway, because it is like absolutely real water, similar to what was apprehended earlier (and therefore, within the scope of experience). It is not also absolutely real, nor exactly what was seen earlier, being subject to sublation (and not being in the scope of experience). It is thus untrue and indeterminable[30].

In the same manner, Vācaspati describes the indeterminability of the empirical world of experience. Just as the silver in the illusory cognition of silver-in-shell is indeterminable as real or unreal, in the same way, according to Vācaspati, the universe of bodies, organs, etc. is also indescribable as real or unreal. Though the empirical world of objects is experienced as novel, (it being in perpetual mutation), yet that too is a superimposition on some thing else, namely the self, and hence, it is also sublatable. As in the case of the illusory object, which has been shown to be real on its own ground, (and not in relation to the substrate), the empirical world also is real on its own ground, but in relation to the self, it is indeterminable as absolutely real or unreal. The absoluteness of the Self has as proof scriptural tradition and reasoning not in conflict with the latter, while the unabsoluteness of the empirical world is evident from practical experience backed by Scriptures and uncontradictory reasoning. Vācaspati, therefore, agreeing with Śaṅkara, projects the world of empirical experience as illusory in juxtaposition to the Self, the Absolute Reality[31]. To Vācaspati Miśra, the cause of all "evil" is therefore the superimposition of the not-Self on the inner-Self; for that alone is the cause of illusory cognitions, and hence of suffering. Superimposition itself is then the beginningless Nescience, the root - cause of the empirical world. Clarifying the manner in which Nescience or *Avidyā*, in the form of superimposition is the ultimate cause of all evil, Vācaspati says that owing to it, the non-suffering inner-Self is seemingly made to suffer through the imposition on it of the adverse internal organ (*'antaḥkaraṇa'*), etc. together with the sensation of appetite, etc., though the Self is essentially free from any such sensation. This fact is supported by the Scriptures, traditional codes, epics, Purāṇas, etc. where it is expressly declared that "Nescience is the seed of all evil"[32]. This Nescience, according to Vācaspati, is difficult to remove, due to its association with beginningless deep-rooted dense impressions. Under its spell, the ordinary man is unable to apprehend the difference between the not-Self and the Self on which the nature and attributes of the intellect, etc., are superimposed. This Nescience, says Vācaspati, is sublatable by the cognition of difference through knowledge which itself is of the[33] nature of the Intelligent Self. Vācaspati observes that the superimposition of the nature of the substrate, in the form of "I" ness, cannot on its own be the cause of evil. For this, the superimposition of the attributes, in the form of "mine"-ness, is also required. This latter superimposition is therefore solely responsible for the evil in the empirical world, in the form of migration. The erroneous identification of the body and its attributes with the Self results in the empirical usage such as belongingness of wife, son, etc. to one-self and...., "I am myself unsound or sound," etc. In the same manner, there is the superimposition on the self of the attributes of the senses which are more intimate than the body, and also those of the internal organ, which is still more intimate. And in all these cases there is the reciprocal superimposition of the nature of the self on the body, the senses, and the internal organ respectively[34]. This Nescience, in the form of Superimposition, is indeed indeterminable, says Vācaspati conclusively[35].

II. The Vivaraṇa Prasthāna

In his commentary on the *Śāṅkara-bhāṣya* Padmapāda describes illusory cognition as "the manifestation of the nature of something in another (thing) which is not of that nature."[36]. That manifestation, is "false" says he. According to him the word 'false' (*mithyā*) as used by Śaṅkara, has double signification. Firstly, it signifies 'negation', and secondly, it denotes "inexpressibility". To Padmapāda, 'false' here means 'negation". And following from this, Śaṅkara's statement, "*mithyeti bhavitum yuktam*", is to be interpreted as meaning that it is reasonable to ascribe non-existence alone to superimposition[37].

Prakāśātman on his part, says that the manifestation of something as something else is Nescience. According to him the erroneous association of the evils of doership and enjoyership with the self constitutes Nescience, in the form of superimposition. The imposition of enjoyership on the self is a sequel to the imposition of doership (on the self), since there cannot be enjoyership in the absence of an active entity. And doership in turn, issues from the superimposition of the concepts of likes and dislikes, for in the absence of these there is no doership. In the same manner, from enjoyership develops association with evil. Thus, says Prakāśātman, owing to the beginninglessness of this chain of causes, as in the case of sprout and seed, superimposition, is described (by Śaṅkara) as 'natural' (*naisargika*), i.e., as coming down to us in an uninterrupted succession of cause and effect[38]. Śaṅkara says that superimposition is "the wrong notion which is the cause of all evil", and adds that 'freedom' from this "wrong" leads to the knowledge of the absolute unity of the Self[39]. Commenting upon this, the author of the Pañcapādikā says that, the knowledge of *Brahman* as the solvent of the root-cause of the ills of life (*anartha*) is suggested in the *sūtra*, and '*anartha*' is constituted by the notion that the *Jīva* is an agent and an enjoyer, which again presupposes the belief that the *Jīva* is a cognizer. If that *anartha* be genuinely real, it cannot be annihilated by "*jñāna*" (Knowledge), for '*jñāna*' can remove only '*ajñāna*' (Nescience). If on the other hand, agency and enjoyership are grounded in Nescience, then..... knowledge of *Brahman* is (appropriately proclaimed to be) 'the solvent of the cause of *anartha*[40].

Elaborating on this, Prakāśātman proclaims that an injunction for meditation is prescribed here ("*vicāravidhi*") for those desirous of obtaining knowledge that leads to Liberation, through the removal of Nescience, the cause of evil (*anartha*)[41]. Agreeing with Padmapāda on the fact that superimposition (*anartha*) is not absolutely real, but false, it being grounded in Nescience, Prakāśātman supplies the following clarification: Just as the (right) knowledge of a colourful object removes only the wrong knowledge about it, and not (also) its attributes or even opposing qualities (residing elsewhere), in like manner the knowledge of (the true nature of) the self removes only the ignorance thereof (and the non-apprehension of difference), and not the relation '*per se*' existing between the Self and the not-Self[42].

Having thus elucidated the significance of Right knowledge (i.e., knowledge of the true nature of the self), in the elimination of Nescience, and all evils associated therewith, Prakāśātman pursues the discussion on superimposition by an analysis of its nature, on the same line as Padmapāda. Hinting at the very nature of superimposition and at the necessity of its removal for obtaining the Right Knowledge, Padmapāda, interpreting Śaṅkara, says that, the purport of the whole of Vedānta is to show that the "ultimate nature" of the individual soul, allegedly transmigratory in nature, is one uniform bliss, the very essence of existence, non-mutable and consciousness entire[43]. And consequently, that the empirical experiences, such as, "I am the doer", "I am happy", and "I am miserable", are in contradiction to the true nature of the soul, as referred to above, and are seemingly ceaseless. It is therefore imperative that the notion of the individuality of the soul be shown to be the creation of Nescience (*Avidyā*)[44].

Justifying the position taken by Padmapāda as shown above, Prakāśātman explains that the purport of the whole of Vedānta having been declared by *Śaṅkara* and Padmapāda to be the (establishment of the) unity or oneness of "*Jīva*" and "*Brahman*", i.e., of the individual soul and the Supreme Being, it is but logical that in the first place, owing to the dependence of the establishment of this identification on the ascertainment of the notion of superimposition, a detailed discussion on the illusoriness of empirical experiences, such as, "I am the doer, I am happy, I am miserable,"etc., is necessary[45].

Throwing further light on the phenomenon of superimposition, Padmapāda says that in the cognition "I" am "this", the "Pure Consciousness" is denoted by '*not-this*' in the experience of "I-ness". And with the Pure Consciousness there is the (false) identity of the not-Self denoted by the notion of Thou-ness. This is illustrated in the empirical usage, 'I am a man' wherein the object (*viṣaya*) "Thou", (here, "man") is identified with Pure Consciousness, (here, "I"). This (wrong) identification (of the not-Self with the Self, and vice versa), says padmapāda, is superimposition[46].

Explaining the manner in which the "Thou"-ness identified (erroneously) with I-ness, as indicated above by Padmapāda, Prakāśātman says that, owing to it being subject to illumination by the Pure-Consciousness cognized here as the subject "I", the Ego etc. (*Ahaṁkāra*) are reflected as "thou"due to their proximity (with the Self), even though there is absence of the sense of "thou"-ness as such. And though one, as the Pure Consciousness, they (the Ego, etc.) are reflected as many, as a result of the modes of the internal organ (*antaḥkaraṇa-vṛtti*)[47].

Śaṅkara describes superimposition as having false cognition (*mithyājñāna*) as its cause. Elaborating on this, Padmapāda says that which is erroneous and nescience at the same time is *mithyājñāna*. For him, the term *mithyā* denotes indescribability (or inexpressibility), while the word '*ajñāna*' refers to the potency of nescience (*avidyā*) which is of the nature of insentience and is the negation of true knowledge (*jñāna*). "*Tannimitta*", means "having that (i.e., *mithyājñāna*) as the material cause"[48]. Prakāśātman clarifies further the causality of erroneous knowledge vis-a-vis superimposition, by pointing to the fact that neither does the word '*ajñāna*' here mean 'absence of knowledge', nor does the word '*mithyā*' referred to above mean 'doubtful knowledge[49]. The causality of '*mithyājñāna*' with regard to superimposition lies in the fact that the latter (superimposition) arises on its (*mithyājñāna*) being there, and not arising on its not being there. Prakāśātman observes that though defects in the object being perceived and in sense-organs, etc. are also the causes of superimposition, there is yet this difference: That while these account for the efficient cause thereof, erroneous cognition (*mithyājñāna*) is the material cause[50].

It is interesting to note here that Prakāśātman attributes to *mithyājñāna* material causality following the logic that everything (in the empirical world) has a material cause, being a real effect, such as pot, etc. It may be inferred from this that the Vivaraṇakāra considers erroneous cognition (and therefore *Avidyā*) to be positive (at least at the empirical level)[51]. Padmapāda says that there is no contradiction in maintaining that superimposition is beginningless and yet an effect (or product) of *mithyājñāna.* For, it has to be admitted that in all things whether internal or external there exists this potency of nescience which is a "constant accompaniment of their inner nature". Without the admission of this fact, it would be otherwise impossible to explain the illusoriness of the objects perceived in erroneous cognitions[52]. Padmapāda says that nescience does not act as an obstruction in the manifestation of the insentient objects in their actual nature, since their non-apprehension results from the absence of the appropriate means of valid knowledge thereof. This is illustrated by the fact that *avidyā* exists both prior to and after the manifestation of silver in its real nature. *Avidyā* is therefore not to be seen as an obstructor, but rather as the cause of the manifestation of something as different from its real nature[53]. Elucidating Padmapāda's claim of non-contradiction between the beginninglessness of Nescience (*ajñāna*) and its being an effect, Prakāśātman says that the beginninglessness of Nescience (*ajñāna*) resides in its being the material cause of superimposition, born as it were, of the uninterrupted succession of Adhyāsa. And in the form of individual objects (of illusory) cognition it is the efficient cause[54].

Advocating the theory that Nescience (*Ajñāna*) has the (inner) self as its locus, Prakāśātman says that the words "*avaśyam*" and "*eṣā*" are here (to be taken as) proofs for this theory. Firstly, through direct perception, one is seen to undergo the immediate experience, "I am ignorant", "I do not know myself, "I do not know (that) other (thing)" etc. This cannot be said to be an example of absence of knowledge, since this is as good an example of immediate experience as the cognition, "I am happy", etc. (This is given as an example of immediate experience or intuition, illustrative of the meaning of '*eṣā*' referred to above[55]). Secondly, this theory is proved by means of "*Anupalabdhi* (the sixth means of knowledge), as for example, in the cognition, "I do not know the meaning of what you said", or "I do not know the number", or "I do not know the meaning of the text", etc. Having experienced such type of Nescience with regard to an object of cognition, one sets out to get to know it. (This is given as an example of reasoning to illustrate the meaning of the word *"avaśya"* referred to in the text mentioned above[56]). Thus, Prakāśātman believes that the locus of "*avidyā*" (Nescience) is the inner self, be it in the case of immediate experience or external perception[57]. Moreover, he declares that both knowledge (*jñāna*) and nescience (*ajñāna*) have the inner self as their common substrate and that there is no contradiction in this. He believes that all objects, whether known or unknown to the cognizer, are illumined by the inner self. Known objects require the mediacy of an instrument (of knowledge) for their illumination, but unknown objects rest always illumined either in the form of universals or as particulars. Prakāśātman concludes that Nescience (*ajñāna*) is perceived as existing in the inner self by means of the perception of nescience (*ajñānapratyakṣa*)[58]. Prakāśātman says further that the cause of superimposition or false cognition must itself have falsity as its nature, or else, if the cause be real, superimposition (*adhyāsa*) would also be real, the effect being of same nature as the cause. And should the cause though being false be taken to be originated, then would set in (the defect of) infinite regress, since the cause of that cause too would need to be looked for elsewhere, and *ad infinitum*. It is, therefore, proper to acknowledge beginningless nescience as the cause of wrong cognition, as discussed earlier[59]. Explaining the nature of illusory appearance, Prakāśātman says that appearance occurs as a result of superimposition of the object of cognition on consciousness under the influence of Nescience. It has already been seen that, according to Prakāśātman (and Padmapāda), Nescience (*Avidyā*) functions as a potency (*śakti*) which influences empirical activities in two ways, viz., by concealing the actual natue of the object, and by superimposing another attribute on it. Prakāśātman says that the substrate of an illusory cognition cannot be said to be concealed by Nescience, since Nescience according to him, does not reside in the object of cognition (*viṣaya*). (Should it be so, i.e., should Nescience reside in the object, the latter, says Nṛsiṁhāśrama, would never be cognized, there being no means of cognition of Nescience[60]). An insentient object, says Prakāśātman, cannot by itself have the potency to conceal an object[61].

Expatiating on the problem of Consciousness being the locus of Nescience, and not the external objects, Prakāśātman says that if, on the other hand, Nescience, with the Self as its locus, were to conceal the external object, then, on the termination of the concealment, with the object becoming known, the Nescience residing in the self should be eliminated. But since this is not so, it has to be admitted that while Nescience is directly given to consciousness, an object may remain unmanifest, not being directly given to consciousness as in the case of Nescience. Nescience, says Prakāśātman, may however take different forms of manifestation, and as such does not completely desert an individual even during the states of deep sleep and dream, much less during the wakeful state[62]. Prakāśātman suggests two alternatives on the question of the elimination of Nescience. He differentiates between the Nescience about the Self and the Nescience about an external object. According to him "*Ajñāna*" (Nescience) is always about (the) Self, i.e, Consciousness (in the first case). The illusion of silver and its content are effects of an *ajñāna* (nescience). When the person under illusion comes to perceive the mistaken thing in its rue nature, the illusory content and the "*vṛtti*" (mode) thereof merely get dissolved into its material cause, the *ajñāna* about the self[63].

The second alternative, says Prakāśātman, would be to admit that *Ajñāna* about the Self and "*Ajñāna*" (Nescience) about a particular object, say, the shell, are not the same". This has to be taken to be so "because the knowledge of the shell destroys or annuls ignorance about the shell while it is only knowledge of the self in its true nature which annuls the ignorance about the self[64].

It is noteworthy that according to the first alternative proposed by Prakāśātman, there is only one "*ajñāna*", and that is about the Self. This "*ajñāna*" gets annulled therefore only on the dawn of the Right Knowledge of the Sef. While as per the second alternative suggested above, the '*ajñāna*' is described as "*mūlājñāna*" when it concerns the Self, and as "*avasthājñāna*" when it concerns the external objects. The word "*avasthājñāna*" is interpreted also to stand for that '*ajñāna*' which is only an '*avasthā*' or a state of '*mūlājñāna*'. The part '*mūla*' of the compound '*mūlājñāna*' should here be understood as that which has states[65].

Śaṅkara in his commentary says that not only are external objects superimposed on the self and vice-versa, but that the attributes of the external world are also superimposed on the self. Thus, says he, in the cognition, "I am deaf", deafness is the attribute of the organ of hearing, imposed on the self. And this is because of non-discrimination between the one and the other. Padmapāda, elucidating the form that superimposition takes, says that the experience, "This am I", or "This is mine", is the first (form of) superimposition (*adhyāsa*) wherein the 'ego-notion' takes shape. Explaining this point, he says that when the notion of ego as agent is admitted to be a case of superimposition, then alone does it become evident that its auxiliary also is an erroneous notion, i.e., when the inner self which is manifested in the ego is erroneous, then the body also, its instrumentality, cannot but be erroneous,..... All empirical activities begin thus with the ego as the agency, after superimposing on the self (*ātman*) the notions of doership, etc. though the *ātman* is itself essentially eternal, pure, self-luminous and free[66].

Padmapāda says that the influence of Nescience (*avidyā*) is such that though all empirical activities are erroneous in essence, yet there is no consciousness of this fact unlike ordinary superimposition, as is illustrated in the illusory cognitions of shell-silver, two moons, etc. It is only on the sublation of the wrong apprehension that the erroneousness of empirical activities becomes known. But in the case of the erroneous cognition of I-ness, such (true) knowledge is not seen to dawn. Hence the continuity of the experience of "I"-ness, etc. at the empirical level[67]. Commenting on this, Prakāśātman says that nescience at the level of the self cannot be sublated by means of knowledge like Perception, Inference and actual experience; for that, Scriptural knowledge is required, for the superimposition of the not-Self on the Self is known only through the Scriptures. Reasoning etc., says he, are helpful in the ascertainment of superimposition at the empirical level, but at the spiritual level, there being no such means of ascertainment of superimposition, the very nature of the falsity of knowledge cannot be determined (and hence its sublation also is not possible)[68].

Citsukhācārya observes in this connection that '*Avidyā*' is that which can be removed only through the "Right knowledge"; "*Bhrānti*" is that which is in the form of appearance; '*Adhyāsa*' is the 'coupling of the 'real and the unreal'; and *Mithyā*' is that which is (inexpressible through and therefore) different from the 'Real and the unreal'[69].

Throwing more light on the functioning of Nescience at the spiritual level, Padmapāda says that "in the inner self which is of the nature of pure intelligence, and as such self-illuminating, since the non-manifestation of *Brahman* cannot be accounted for by any other means, it must be admitted that its non-manifestation is due to the obstruction caused by the potency of Nescience which is existent therein (i.e., in *Brahman*) and is beginningless. Hence it is that the Primal Nescience obstructs the manifestation of the real nature of "*Brahman*" in the inner-Self (i.e., the *Jīva*) and it becomes the cause of the appearance of something other than its nature, like 'I'-ness, etc.. In the state of deep sleep too, having remained in the residual state of mere impressions of "I"-ness, etc., which are the outcome of its projective power (*vikṣepa-śakti*), it revives again (during the waking state). Hence, though the superimposition as evidenced in empirical experiences, such as "I", "mine", etc., is beginningless, (since its cause, *Avidyā*, is beginningless), it is said to have false knowledge (*"mithyā-jñāna"*) as its cause. By saying so, the adventitiousness of superimposition is discarded[70].

Explaining this, Prakāśātman says that the fact that even though at the empirical level there is the experience that the "Self exists and is (self) luminous", there is yet seen the empirical usage of the like, "He is non-existent and is (therefore) non-luminous". And this, says Prakāśātman, cannot be attributed to something else except the concealing potency (of Nescience) residing positively in the self. Much so because it is seen in actual experience that on the satisfaction of all necessary conditions (in its manifestation) and in the absence of the concealing potency, there is manifestation of the 'pot'. It follows that in the case of the self as well, the cognition, "the self is non-existent and is non-luminous" can be justified only by admitting by implication or by inference, the positiveness of Nescience[71].

Elucidating the points raised above, Vidyāraṇya argues as follows : what is the nature of the concealing potency (*āvaraṇa*) residing in the self ? Is it in the form of destruction of luminosity (of the self) or is it in the form of an impediment or obstruction in the manifesting capacity of Consciousness or is it something else? It cannot be the first, since luminosity is the very essence of Consciousness. It cannot be the second or the third, since it is not admissible that the manifestation of an external object be the result of any means other than the modes of the internal organ. It is thus quite proper to say that the nature of this concealing potency is indescribable, for it is indeed of the nature of the indeterminable Nescience (*Avidyā*). This can be explained through inference as well. It is but the nature of unintelligent people to reason like this : there is no existence and luminosity of any entity bereft of the attribute of enjoyership, etc., and having as its essence the intelligent Self. Vidyāraṇya says that this kind of usage is possible only on the admission of positive concealing potency with the self as its substrate, since there is seen to be the usage of an opposite nature in the presence of appropriate factors, leading to the experience, 'He is in existence and is conscious'. It cannot be said also that there is no proof for the existence of such an entity, for the Eternal, Real Consciousness is self-manifest[72].

In what sense is superimposition a remembrance, clarifying this point, Padmapāda says that in the definition of '*Adhyāsa*' given by Śaṅkara, viz., "*smṛtirūpaḥ paratra pūrvadṛṣṭāvabhāsaḥ*", the word '*paratra*', i.e., "in some other object", implies that the manifestation is of something other than the presented object. As for the phrase "being of the nature of remembrance" (*smṛti-rūpaḥ*) it is attributive of the word '*paratra*', i.e., elsewhere. 'Recollection' or 'remembrance' here means 'what is remembered' or 'recollected'. "This construction is justified on the ground of usage, for the termination *"Ghañ"*, etc., is sometimes used in the sense of a *"Kāraka"* which is not denotative of 'agent' though its sense is derivative. The manifested object only resembles the object remembered, but is not the thing actually recollected. In other words, this means that the '*rūpa*' (form) of the superimposed object is only similar to the appearance of the recollected object, but is not that object '*per se*'. This is clear from the fact that what is represented to the sense organ (and not what is remembered) is what is manifested. That the '*adhyāsa*' *resembles* recollection is corroborated by the explanation that it is the manifestation of what was perceived in the past. There can be no manifestation of silver to one in direct sense-contact with the shell, who has not seen silver before"[73].

Elucidating this point further, Padmapāda adds that from this definition it is implied that the knowledge ('*avabhāsa*') of the illusory object is of the same nature. Says he, "The manifestation of the illusory knowledge is similar to the manifestation of recollection itself, since the knowledge of the particular object (say, silver) given in past cognition does not manifest itself as that experienced before, or else, the illusory cognition would have been of the form '*tad rajatam*', i.e., 'that silver', and not '*idaṁ rajatam*', i.e. 'this silver'. The similarity in nature of the knowledge (of the illusory object) is due to its arising through the experience in a past cognition. This is also due to the fact that there can be no knowledge of an object without the sense-contact unless such knowledge originates through the impression of a past-experience with regard to the same object[74].

Prakāśātman refuting the objection to the effect that there can be no manifestation of an object in its (i.e., the object's) absence, says that the existence of an object is ascertained only through the reflection of it in consciousness. It cannot be said that it is the reflection in consciousness which depends on the ascertainment of the existence of the object, for in that eventuality there would arise the dependence of the acertainment of the existence of the object otherwise, and '*ad infinitum*'. It cannot also be said that in the illusory cognition, 'This is silver', the sublating cognition 'This is not silver' arising afterward, proves the non-existence also of the object cognized earlier, for that would be in contradiction to the earlier manifestation in consciousness of the object (as being one in existence)[75].

Vidyāraṇya says in this context that 'superimposition, which constitutes error, may be defined in two ways. From the point of view of the thing which is superimposed, superimposition may be defined as "that which is similar to what is remembered and (which) appears as of the nature of a different thing". From the point of view of the cognition, superimposition is that "cognition similar to memory, which is the presentation of one thing as of the nature of another"[76].

Explaining the phenomenon of the manifestation of (silver) even on there being sense-contact only with 'shell', Padmapāda says that it is not that the memory which is caused by the mental impressions (*saṁskāra*) and which is divested of the knowledge that it is memory, arises (as) distinct from the cognition arising from sense-contact (viz., of the "this")[77]. On the contrary, it is a unitary cognition, arising from the sense in contact with the mental impressions. The vitiated cause having obstructed its potency to produce the proper effect (here, knowledge), revives at the same time the (type of) mental impression (conducive to or) giving rise to illusory cognition. It is from the effect that the potency of the vitiated cause is inferred. Hence the impression so generated, in association with the vitiated cause, acts as the single means in the production of the illusory cognition. Hence, the single cognition and the single result[78]. Padmapāda says further that 'of that cognition which has arisen through the instrumentality of the particular impression received by some defective cause, the illusory object 'silver' manifests itself as the object in front (viz., shell). Hence, that cognition which has something false as its object is erroneous cognition, for falsity cannot be attributed to cognition as such, since, its sublation does not take place[79].

Concluding this discussion on the nature of illusory cognition, Padmapāda says that there is nothing wrong in admitting that a single cognition is produced by different instrumets serving as the cause of different apprehensions. This is so because the 'apprehensions of the *probans* and the mental impressions of the concomitance between the *probans* and the *probandum* conjointly produce the inference. Recognition also arises both from sense-contact and mental impression (*saṁskāra*). In both the cases (of inference and recognition)there is only a single valid cognition having close relation with memory. For without the revival of the impressions it is impossible that the inference or the recognition could arise. Hence it must be said that it is only the perception of the *probans* that, having recalled the impression of *vyāpti-jñāna* (i. e., the *saṁskāra* left by the former experience of the concomitance between the *probans* and the *probandum*) generates the inferential cognition in association with it[80]. Padmapāda observes that the same reasoning holds good for recognition. This can be exemplified by the "unitary cognition" of a portrait drawn from a variety of colours such as blue, red, green, etc. which serve as causes of separate cognitions. There is however, this much difference: cognitions of the nature of inference, recognition and cognition of complex colours (i.e., a portrait) manifest themselves as being true to (empirical) reality because they originate from non-defective causes. Here, however, in the case of the cognitions of illusory silver, snake, etc., due to defects in the causes, the cognitions are not true to reality. There is thus no contradiction to actual experience, for this false cognition has false silver as its object. Therefore, silver thus cognized is but a product of Nescience[81].

Refuting an objection as to the positiveness of Nescience, Prakāśātman argues that it is not proper to say that there is nothing like positive Nescience (*ajñāna*) other than the non-apprehension of difference, or false-cognition, or the impression generated by such non-apprehension and false cognition, and that these are the very factors responsible for the obstruction of the manifesting capacity of the self, though Itself self-luminous. The objection is untenable because during the state of deep sleep there remains the potency of Nescience in residual form, and not the impressions, etc. referred to above. This is so because the non-manifestation of the self-luminous consciousness in its true nature even in deep sleep cannot be attributed to the incongruity of cognizer, as is the case with the cognitions apprehended by different persons, there being, in the former case, continuity (or consistency) of experience by the same person. False knowledge also cannot be said to be responsible for the obstruction mentioned above, it being not there in that state. Nor could the obstruction be said to be caused by the impressions left by the latter, for the impressions of doubts are not known to cause obstruction to the manifestation of consciousness, as is illustrated by the fact that despite the impressions left behind by the doubt regarding silver in the silver-in-shell cognition, there is (seen to be) the cognition of shell (and hence the manifestation of consciousness therein). Non-apprehension also cannot be held accountable for the obstruction in question, since there is uninterrupted apprehension of the true-nature of the self owing to the fact that accidental (or occasional) non-apprehension of the true nature of the self-luminous consciousness does not obstruct the manifestation of the self.... It follows, therefore, that in deep sleep the non-apprehension of the true nature of the self cannot be said to be caused by any of the factors mentioned above, but by something else, and that is Nescience[82].

Driving home the notion of the indefinability of illusory objects and their cognitions, Prakāśātman holds that there are three levels of reality - the Absolute Reality of the Supreme being (*Brahman*), the empirical reality impregnated by *Māyā* and qualified by the potency of meaningful activity, such as that of the sky, etc., and the illusory reality having '*Avidyā*' as its base, such as that of the illusory silver, etc. Of these, the indefinability of illusory objects and their cognitions due to their being illusorily real in comparison to the Absoluteness of the Reality of *Brahman*, is not contradictory to world experience[83].

Elucidating the 'nescienceness' (*māyāmayatva*) of the illusory object, Padmapāda says that the cognition of negation (or sublation) which takes the form (of) 'this is not silver', is indicative of the fact that it, (silver) is (only) a product of 'Māyā'- (Nescience). This is to be understood by the fact that it is verily through that sublating cognition that, "the fact that the origin of the shell-silver is *māyā* is brought to mind, preceded by the negation of its (the silver's) very existence". "Witness the nature of the cognition that arises after sublation, viz., 'this is not Silver; what manifested itself was false". Such cognition would be inappropriate if the shell-silver is admitted to exist in its real nature in some form or the other, such as the one in the market, just as it would be much less inappropriate to negate the shell in front with which there is sense-contact[84].

Clarifying the concept of negation (or sublation) referred to above, Prakāśātman says that sublation consists in the removal (or elimination) of "*ajñāna*" as it is presented (to the cognizer) in the form of an effect (the illusory object), by '*jñāna*' (true cognition). Sublation is thus known "as" sublation on the removal of the absence of true knowledge of the nature referred to above[85].

Commenting on this, Vidyāraṇya says that it would be equally right to regard the cognition of 'shell' itself as the sublating cognition, it being the remover of the illusory object (silver) together with its material cause. But there is a difference: while the shell-cognition is a subordinate cause therein (i.e., in the sublation of the illusory silver), the sublating cognition "this is not-silver", in the form of true-knowledge, is to be considered as the sublation-'*par-excellence*', it being the cause of the elimination of the desire to act (with regard to the acquisition of the illusory silver), by the fact that it arouses in the person intent upon procuring the silver with the belief that it is real, the knowledge of its absence (in that particular spot)[86].

Refuting an objection in connection with Superimposition, Padmapāda points out its double function, and also its sublatability by *Vidyā* (true knowledge). Says he, ...Superimposition in its causal form of Nescience (*Avidyā*) has the potency to distort reality, i.e., to make things appear different from what they are. It is this 'causal potency to produce the ills of life by projecting something other than the real object, i.e. the "*Vikṣepa-śakti*", which is highlighted by the term *Avidyā*, in contrast to the term *Adhyāsa*, which highlights its potency to conceal the real nature of things (viz., the "*Āvaraṇa-śakti*"). Again , by terming it *Avidyā*, says Padmapāda, its sublatability by "*Vidyā*" alone is rendered explicit. And since superimposition is dispelled by knowledge, it has to be made more explicit, (says Śaṅkara) that, where something is superimposed on something else, the substrate of the illusory cognition, (say, the shell) is not the least affected either by the bad effects or the good effects resulting from that "*Adhyāsa*". The unreality of the ills as well (of enjoyership, etc.) is implied here, or else, says Padmapāda, the claim by Śaṅkara that the sublation of *Adhyāsa*, and of its effects, by knowledge (*jñāna*) would be void[87].

Elaborating on this, Prakāśātman says that when it is said that the substrate of *Avidyā*, viz., the self, is not affected by the good or bad effects of "*Avidyā*", what is meant is that no change whatsoever takes place in the substratum, i.e., the self, it being changeless on the one hand, and the changes referred to above not being real as such, on the other; this is so, says Prakāśātman, because the beginningless '*Avidyā*' in the form of nescience is always manifested by Consciousness which is itself eternal (and therefore not subject to any change). This means that the changes that are seen to take place in the world have only an empirical reality and are therefore ephemeral in nature. At the absolute level such changes are non-existent, since they are inconceivable at that level owing to there being no ground for such changes at that level. Changes, good or bad, take place with regard to illusory objects only. These changes that occur *per accidens*, says Prakāśātman, have for their cause Nescience which is associated with the self. Owing to this association of Nescience with self, its effects (viz., these changes) have the self as their substratum[88]. It is due to this (i.e., due to the effects of Nescience having the self as their substratum) that they are sublatable by knowledge (of the true nature of the self). So says Akhaṇḍānanda Muni[89].

III. Summary

The Advaita theory of error is a logical consequence of the failure of the non-Advaitic theories in providing an adequate explanation of the phenomenon of error. These rival theories suggest, as has been seen, three possibilities with regard to the nature of the illusory object, namely, either it is real, or unreal, or real and unreal. We have seen how none of these is acceptable to the Advaitin-s, who reject them all as untenable. If nacre-silver were real, its cognition could not be illusory, say both the Bhāmatī and the Vivaraṇa; nor could it be sublated. And even if the nacre-silver were to be absolutely real when it appears, it would then be possible for even those who are free from any defect to apprehend it. And to crown it all, there is the sublating cognition, "This is not silver", which negates the very existence of the illusory silver there and then. Therefore, because of the fact that the nacre-silver is not apprehended by those who are free from defect, and owing also to its sublatability by the negating cognition, the illusory silver cannot be said to be real. Nor can it be said to be unreal. The very fact that the silver is cognizable proves that it cannot be unreal. Were it absolutely unreal, as in the case of the hare's horn, it would not be cognizable at all, and least still would it be sublatable. There is also the fact that an absolutely unreal object cannot lead to illusion followed by sublation, as is the case with the nacre- silver which is the cause of illusion in actual experience. It cannot therefore be said that the silver appearing in an illusory cognition is unreal. Due to its cognizability it is not unreal, and due to its sublatability it is not real. Also, it cannot be both real and unreal at the same time, this being contradictory, and therefore against experience. Hence the theory of indeterminability ("*anirvacanīyatā*") propounded by the Advaitin-s to explain the phenomenon of erroneous cognition and its object. Accordingly, the illusory silver is indeterminable as real or unreal. And since the object of an illusory cognition is indeterminable, the cognition cannot but be indeterminable as well. And to pursue the same logic, the material cause of error, viz., Nescience, is also indeterminable as real or unreal, because the cause cannot be of a different nature than the effect. For, were Nescience to be taken as real, then its effect the erroneous cognition, as well as the illusory object, would be real, and there would thus be no illusion at all, which would be contrary to experience. And were it to be unreal, then too there would be no illusion as in the preceding case, which would again be contrary to experience. It is, therefore, conclusively inferred by the Advaitin-s that neither Nescience nor the illusory object can be defined as real or unreal or still as real and unreal, but as indeterminable ("*anirvacanīya*").

In the Adhyāsabhāṣya, Śaṅkara defines "*Adhyāsa*" as *Avidyā* (Nescience), *Mithyā* (false), *Anādi* (beginningless), *Ananta* (endless), *Nairsargika* (natural), *Mithyā pratyaya* (false-cognition), *kartṛtva-bhoktṛtva-pravartaka* (instigator of the notion of doership, enjoyership, etc.), *Anartha-hetu* (cause of evil) and as being within the purview of experience of one and all (*sarvalokapratyakṣa*)[90]. It is indeed quite significant that Śaṅkara attributes the qualitative "endlessness" to Nescience, apart from that of "beginninglessness". Explaining this passage, Vācaspati specifies that 'endless' here means "not being destructible in the absence of true knowledge[91].

Bhāmatī further says that the cause of the beginninglessness and endlessness is stated as being "natural" (*"naisargika"*); and commenting on the meaning of *'naisargika'*, Vācaspati, as it has already been seen, says that "this process (of superimposition) is beginningless, like the succession of the seed and the sprout"[92]. The Vivaraṇa school is quite close to Bhāmatī in its interpretation of the term "*ananta*" referred to above. Padmapāda says in this context that "its (the Adhyāsā's) end is brought about either by itself or by some other cause. Hence what is intended to be conveyed by the statement that the study of "all the Vedānta texts is undertaken for the destruction of what is endless", is that this alone (i.e., Vadāntic study alone) is presumably the cause of its removal. If that Vedāntic study be absent it is evident that *Adhyāsa* will be endless[93]. So far as Prakāśātman is concerned, he is silent on the question of endlessness of *Adhyāsa*, implying by this that he acquiesces in the line taken by his mentor[94].

As regards the *mithyātva* (i.e., falsity) of *Adhyāsa*, Vācaspati says that what is meant is that "illusion" signifies 'concealment'. What the Bhāmatīkāra means by this is that illusion 'conceals' the real nature of the objects of cognition giving rise to non-apprehension of difference between the real and the unreal objects, which in turn results in erroneous activities[95].

The Vivaraṇa school on the other hand interprets "*mithyā*" as "*apahnavavacana*" having its meaning as "concealment", but adds to it the sense of 'inexpressibility'as well. Padmapāda says also that "it is reasonable to ascribe non-existence to superimposition alone"[96]. So, it can be seen that while the Bhāmatī school explains superimposition by the description of it as non-apprehension of difference due to concealment of the real nature of the object of cognition by (the *Āvaraṇa-śakti* of) Nescience, the Vivaraṇa school hints at the sublatability of illusion, and therefore at its non-existence '*per se*'.

Describing the functioning of *Adhyāsa*, Śaṅkara, as shown above, adds that it functions by "coupling the true with the untrue" ("*satyānṛte mithunīkṛtya*")[97], giving rise to "natural empirical usages ("*naisargika-lokavyavahāra*"), like, "I am this", "this is mine", etc ("*ahamidam*", "*mamedam*", etc). He says further that superimposition is of some thing existing in the form of remembrance ("*smṛtirūpa*")[98] it being the appearance elsewhere of what had been cognized earlier ("*paratra pūrva-dṛṣṭāvabhāsa*")[99]. Śaṅkara illustrates this by giving the examples of the illusory cognition of silver-in-shell and of the apprehension of two moons, etc[100].

To the Bhāmatī school, "*avabhāsa*" is that appearance which is subject to termination or sublation by a stronger (i.e., real) cognition[101]. Vācaspati is of the opinion that superimposition results from the coupling of the true ("*satya*"), i.e., the intelligent self, with the untrue ("*anṛta*"), i.e., the intellect, the organs, the body, etc. As a matter of fact, says the Bhāmatī, the coupling of the "Real" with the phenomenal being impossible, the coupling of that nature which takes place at the empirical level cannot but be illusory, and therefore false[102]. The Vivaraṇa School believes that superimposition resulting from the coupling of the "not this", i.e. consciousness (*anidaṁ caitanyam*) with the sense "thou", i.e. the insentient world (*"yuṣmadartha"*)[103], takes the form of the erroneous association of the evils of doership and enjoyership, etc., with the self[104]. And this error is beginningless, says Padmapāda, as it is indicated by the (use of the) suffix "*cvi*" (which is not used in this context to show precedence of one action over the other[105]. What is meant is that the superimposition of the true, the real upon the untrue, the unreal , i.e. superimposition of the Self upon the not-Self, of Consciousness on the insentient worlds, and vice-versa, is a beginningless process, and continues in a natural way until it is stopped by True Knowledge, which consists in the discrimination of the Self from the not-Self, resulting in the realization of the unitariness of the soul.

Describing the manner in which Nescience functions in actual experience, Śaṅkara says that, "that which is called superimposition is 'the cognition of something as what it is not". ("*Adhyāso nāma atasmiṁstadbuddhiḥ*")[106]. Illustrating this concept, he discusses how all empirical activities are the sequel of superimposition. This is interpreted by the Bhāmatī school as an elaboration showing Nescience as the cause of all evils. Vācaspati says that in the illustrations of superimposition given by Śaṅkara, such as "I am myself sound or unsound", "I am fat", "I am lean", "I am fair", "I stand", "I go", "I am dumb", one-eyed, impotent, deaf, blind", etc.[107], the "I", which is the superimposition of the nature of the substrate alone, cannot be the cause of evil without generating the sense of "*mine*", i.e., the superimposition of the attributes. Hence, according to the Bhāmatī school, the direct cause of the evils of the world is the superimposition of the substrate "I" alone[108]. The Vivaraṇa follows suit, declaring that what is meant by "*atasmiṁstadbuddhiḥ*", is the presentation of the not-self denoted by "thou" or "this", in the Self, denoted by "not-thou" or "not-this"[109].

It is from this very Nescience (*Avidyā*), says Śaṅkara conclusively, that in the form of reciprocal superimposition of the Self and the not-Self, proceed all empirical activities, inclusive of the means of valid knowledge, and also all the sacred teachings in respect of prescription, prohibition and release[110].

Prakāśātman observes in this context that as far as Nescience is concerned, Śaṅkara alludes to it by the terms "*Avidyā*", "*Māyā*" "*Avidyātmikā Māyā-Śakti*" (potency of *Māyā* in the form of *Avidyā*) etc., synonymously. The Vivaraṇa proclaims that there is no difference between "*Māyā*" and "*Avidyā*", claiming that the Scriptures, Padmapāda and the author of the *Brahmasiddhi* are also of the same opinion.

According to the Vivaraṇa school there is no disparity between "*Māyā*" and "*Avidyā*" as such, but for the sake of differentiating between the two potencies of Nescience, the term "*Māyā*" is utilised with reference to its "Projective" potency, and the term "*Avidyā*" is utilised with regard to its "concealing" potency. The discrimination is hence, more for the sake of convenience than as a matter of fact[111].

The Bhāmatī school also acknowledges the existence of one Nescience, calling it the beginningless and positive *Avidyā*[112]. But due to intervening adjuncts in the form of preceding impressions, that One *Avidyā* appears to have differing forms, assuming the forms of particularized Nescience having as its loci the individual souls[113]. Defending further the position taken above as to the locus of *Avidyā*, Vācaspati declares that, should *Brahman* be taken to be the locus of Nescience, then the latter, as the (creative) power of *Brahman*, would be the cause of (the origin of) the world; and in this eventuality, even the liberated souls would find themselves in bondage anew, their being, in the form of *Brahman*, the substrate (s) of the (beginningless) *Avidyā*. And on the other hand, there would arise also the eventuality of the dissolution of the whole world on the eradication of that one Nescience. The question of the liberated soul being bound anew cannot arise, says Vācaspati, owing to the seed of their origin, the potency of *Avidyā*, being destroyed by *Vidyā*, the True Knowledge. And hence, the bold proclamation of the Bhāmatī school, viz., "we do not propound the pervasiveness of a single *Avidyā* in all individual souls...., but rather separate *Avidyā* in each individual soul. Hence, the plausibility of the liberation of only that individual soul on whom True Knowledge (*Vidyā*) dawns leading to the sublation of his individual *Avidyā* and not of others. And this is so because of the difference in the substrates of *Vidyā* and *Avidyā*"[114]. Vācaspati therefore concludes this debate on the locus of *Avidyā*, saying that *Brahman* cannot be the locus of *Avidyā*, the latter being indefinable as real or unreal (and hence, it cannot have the Real (*Brahman*) as its locus). *Brahman* being therefore Eternal and Pure, the locus of *Avidyā* cannot be but *Jīva*, the individual soul[115].

The Vivaraṇa School on the other hand, believes that the locus of *Avidyā* is "*Brahman*", and not "*Jīva*", though like the Bhāmatī School, it too acknowledges two kinds of "*Avidyā*", viz., "*Mūlāvidyā*" and "*Tūlāvidyā*". While the former, beginningless in character, is one and rests in "*Brahman*", the latter, which Prakāśātman describes as "*Avasthājñāna*", is multiple and rests in the external objects[116]. The Vivaraṇa School argues that since *Avidyā* is sublatable by True Knowledge alone, i.e. by the realization of the true nature of *Brahman*, it cannot but have the latter as its locus[117].

The view of the Bhāmatī School, that the individual soul is the locus of "*Avidyā*", raises a difficulty in that *Avidyā* presupposes the appearance of the individual soul, and hence, by implication, the *Jīva* cannot be justifiably held to be its locus. The *Jīva-Brahman* distinction, as such, is itself the result of *Avidyā* and persists only till Brahman is not realized. It follows, therefore, that while the notion of the individuality of the soul emanates from *Avidyā*, *Avidyā* on the other hand, is not dependent on the notion of the individuality of the soul for its existence. The notion of the individuality of the soul being thus antecedent to "*Avidyā*", the *Jīva* cannot be said to be its locus. In the state of deep sleep also, the fact that there is direct experience of *Avidyā*, due to the absence of the notion of individuality in that state, proves that the locus of *Avidyā* is not the individual soul. Such direct experience of *Avidyā* has for evidence the recollective cognitions on waking up, of the nature, "I did not know anything when I was asleep",

"Being enveloped by *Avidyā*, I was incapable of understanding anything", etc. The reference to *Avidyā* in such cognitions proves its presence at that state, and the absence of the notion of individuality of soul at that state proves the incapability of the *Jīva* to be the locus of *Avidyā*. Hence, *Brahman* alone is the locus of *Avidyā*[118].

Referring to the sublation of *Avidyā* and all the 'evils' resulting therefrom, Śaṅkara says at the end of the Adhyāsabhāṣya that, "it is for the removal of this cause of evil, for the attainment of the knowledge of the oneness of the Self, that (all) the (discussions on the) Vedānta are commenced"[119]. To Śaṅkara, therefore, the removal of *Avidyā* cannot but be by "the attainment of the knowledge of the oneness of the Self" through the study of Vedānta. The Vivaraṇa school believes in this context, that it is indeed from the destruction of the cause that there results the total destruction of the effect.... For, what is sought after (here), is the unique knowledge which arises from the intuitive comprehension of the "*Mahāvākya*"-"*Tattvamasi*" (That Thou Art). And that knowledge, says Padmapāda, arises while revealing at the same time the real nature of *Brahman*, and dispelling Nescience, which, by concealing the true nature of Consciousness, brings about the notion of the indivduality of the soul.... From True knowledge arises the elimination of the cause of evil together with its effects, the notions of enjoyership. etc. Since the experience of "I" -ness is also beginningless, says Padmapāda, and is in close association with the entire bodily aggregate which is also beginningless, the superimposition cannot be eradicated by merely discriminating between the Self and the not-Self....[120]

Elucidating further the question of the removal of Nescience as a pre-requisite for the identification of *Jīva* with *Brahman*, Padmapāda notes that, "if the eradication of "*Avidyā*" which is the cause of evil must necessarily precede the knowledge of *Jiva-Brahman*-identity, then "*Śabda*" is not operative there.... For it is indeed impossible to determine the real nature of a thing cognized illusorily, without the eradication of the illusion. Hence, the "*Mahāvākya*", (i.e. "*Śabda*") establishes the reality only by first removing Nescience...."[121]

Illustrating the manner in which, on the eradication of Nescience, knowledge dawns of its own, Padmapāda says that,

"....without first negating its opposite, the cognition "*Tattvamasi*" would be incompetent to give rise to the '*Jīva-Brahman*'-identity, just as the act of raising one scale-pan of a balance necessarily lowers the other scale-pan, without any additional effort. For, the act of raising cannot bring about the contact of its object with the space above without at the same time effecting the other pan's contact with the space below". Padmapāda adds that it is not to be supposed that the effort of the hand, etc., which serves as the cause in the raising is also the cause of the lowering, for this is against practical experience[122].

Emphasizing the simultaneity of the elimination of Nescience and the dawning of True Knowledge, Prakāśātman says that though the difference in nature of the Self and the not-Self may be known through empirical means of knowledge, True Knowledge, however, cannot be realized through any empirical means nor even through the mere study of Scriptures, they being themselves the product of Nescience. Hence, the necessity of the removal of Nescience and the realization of he *Jīva-Brahman*-identity simultaneously[123].

As for the Bhāmatī school, the removal of Nescience, which is the cause of all evils in this world, has for purpose the attainment of the knowledge of the oneness of the self, (establishing thereby the *Jīva-Brahman*-identity), and not *merely* for incantation or engaging in rites, etc. The oneness of the Self, says Vācaspati, is in effect the entire dissociation from the universe, while existing in the form of bliss. The Vedāntas, which indubitably bring about the Knowledge of the *Jīva-Brahman*-identity, destroy superimposition from its very root. This is so since the experience of "I" -ness, which is the fruit of superimposition, and which serves as the base for all empirical (and hence, erroneous) activities, is removed by True Knowledge, The 'real', notes in this context Vācaspati, cannot be removed, reversely, by untrue knowledge, just as, for example, the rope-nature of the rope cannot be negated by even a thousand continuous apprehensions of snake (in that rope). The superimposed form in an illusory cognition can, however, be negated by True Knowledge. As for the impressions left by illusory cognitions, these are removable, however strong they may be, by counter impressions produced through the unintermittent and prolonged repetition of True

Knowledge"[124].

Both the Bhāmatī school and the Vivaraṇa school hence, it may be said, postulate that "*Avidyā*" is sublatable by the knowledge of *Brahman* alone. It is also the shared belief of both the schools that the substrate of illusory cognition is not the least affected by either the good or the bad effects of illusion, still less is *Brahman* affected by *Avidyā* or *Māyā*. The Vivaraṇa, moreover, avers that while the apprehension of the true nature of the object in front is the subordinate cause of the sublation of the illusory cognition, the main cause thereof is the sublating cognition, owing to its being the cause of the elimination of the very desire to act erroneously[125].

NOTES

1. The Vedānta-Sūtras, Part-I-Tr. George Thibaut, Motilal Banarsidass, 1962-p.4, Vide, "कोऽयमध्यासो नामेति। उच्यते स्मृतिरूप: परत्र पूर्वदृष्टावभास:।" —The Brahmasūtra Śāṅkara Bhāṣya, Op. Cit. pp.17-18.
2. The Bhāmatī of Vācaspati, Op. Cit p.16; Vide, "अवसन्न: अवमतो वा भास: अवभास:। प्रत्ययान्तरबाधश्चास्य अवसादोऽवमानो वा। एतावता मिथ्याज्ञानमित्युक्तं भवति।" —Bhāmatī on Adhyāsabhāṣya, Loc. Cit., p.16.
3. George Thibaut, Loc. Cit., pp.3-4, Vide,

   "युष्मदस्मत्प्रत्ययगोचरयोर्विषयविषयिणोस्तम:प्रकाशवद्विरुद्धस्वभावयोरितरेतरभावानुपपत्ति: इत्यतोऽस्मत्प्रत्यगोचरे विषयिणि चिदात्मके युष्मत्प्रत्ययगोचरस्य विषयस्य तद्धर्माणां चाध्यास:, तद्विपर्ययेण विषयिणस्तद्धर्माणां च विषयेऽध्यासो मिथ्येति भवितुं युक्तम्। तथाप्यन्योन्यस्मिन्नन्योन्यात्मकतामन्योन्यधर्मांश्चाध्यस्येतरेतरा विवेकेनात्यन्त विविक्तयोर्धर्मधर्मिणोर्मिथ्याज्ञाननिमित्त: सत्यानृते मिथुनीकृत्य अहमिदं ममेदमिति नैसर्गिकोऽयं लोकव्यवहार:।"

   —Adhyāsabhāṣya.
4. The Bhāmatī of Vācaspati, Op. Cit. p.5.
5. इदमस्मत्प्रत्ययगोचरयोरिति वक्तव्ये युष्मद्ग्रहणमत्यन्तभेदोपलक्षणार्थम्। यथा ह्यहंकारप्रतियोगी त्वंकारो नैवमिदंकार: 'एते वयम्, इमे वयम् आस्महे' इति बहुलं प्रयोगदर्शनादिति। चित्स्वभाव आत्मा विषयी, जडस्वभावा बुद्धीन्द्रियदेहविषया विषया:।" —Bhāmatī on Adhyāsabhāṣya, Loc. Cit., p.6.
6. "इतरेतरभाव: इतरेतरत्वम्, तादात्म्यमिति यावत्।.... मा भूद्धर्मिणो: परस्परभाव:; तद्धर्माणां तु जाड्यचैतन्यनित्यत्वादीनाम् इतरेतराध्यासो भविष्यति। दृश्यते हि धर्मिणोर्विवेकग्रहणेऽपि तद्धर्माणामध्यास:, यथा कुसुमाद्भेदेन गृह्यमाणेऽपि स्फटिकमणावतिस्वच्छतया जपाकुसुमप्रतिबिम्बोद्ग्राहिणि 'अरूण: स्फटिक: इत्यारुण्यविभ्रम इति।" -Ibid.
7. "अध्यासो भेदाग्रहेण व्याप्त:"। -Ibid.
8. The Bhāmatī of Vācaspati, Op. Cit., p.7, Vide,

''भवेदेतदेवं यदि 'अहम्' इत्यनुभवे आत्मतत्त्वं प्रकाशेत। न त्वेतदस्ति। तथा हि समस्तोपाध्यनवच्छिन्नानन्तानन्दचैतन्यैकरसमुदासीनमेकमद्वितीयमात्मतत्त्वं श्रुतिस्मृतीतिहासपुराणेषु गीयते''। —Bhāmatī on Adhyāsabhāṣya, Loc. Cit., p.7.

9. ''अहमनुभवस्तु प्रादेशिकमनेकविधशोकदुःखादिप्रपञ्चोपप्लुतमात्मानमादर्शयन् कथमात्मतत्त्वगोचरः कथं वानुपप्लवः। -Ibid, p.8.
10. Vide, "The Bhāmatī of Vācaspati, Op. Cit., p.10.
11. Ibid, p.11.
12. ''अहमिहैवास्मि सदने जानानः इति सर्वव्यापिनः प्रादेशिकत्वेन ग्रहणात् (न (अहंकारस्य) तात्त्विकत्वमभ्युपेतव्यम्)।.... न चेदं देहस्य प्रादेशिकत्वमनुभूयते न त्वात्मन इति सांप्रतम्। न हि तदैवं भवति 'अहम्' इति, गौणत्वे वा न ''जानानः'' इति।.... न त्वहंकारस्य मुख्योऽर्थो निर्लुठितगर्भतया गौणेऽपि न गौणत्वाभिमानः सार्षपादिषु तैलशब्दवदिति वेदितव्यम्। तत्रापि.... सर्षपादीनां तैलशब्दवाच्यत्वाभिमानः, न त्वर्थयोस्तैलसार्षपयोरभेदाध्यवसायः। तत्सिद्धं गौणत्वमुभयदर्शिनो गौणमुख्यविवेकविज्ञानेन व्याप्तम्, तदिह व्यापकं विवेकविज्ञानं निवर्तमानं गौणतामपि निवर्तयतीति।'' —Bhāmatī on Adhyāsabhāṣya, Loc. Cit., pp. 10-11.
13. ''न च बालस्थविरशरीरभेदेऽपि 'सोऽहम्' इत्येकस्यात्मन प्रतिसंधानाद्देहादिभ्यो भेदेनास्त्यात्मानुभव इति वाच्यम्। परीक्षकाणां खल्वियं कथा न लौकिकानाम्। परीक्षका अपि हि व्यवहारसमये न लौकिकसामान्यमतिवर्तन्ते। वक्ष्यति.... हि भगवान्भाष्कारः, ''पश्वादिभिश्चाविशेषात्'' इति।.... तत्पारिशेष्याच्चिदात्मगोचरमहंकारम् अहमिहास्मि सदने इति प्रयुञ्जानो लौकिकः शरीराद्यभेदग्रहादात्मनः प्रादेशिकत्वमभिमन्यन्त नभस इव घटमणिक मल्लिकाद्युपाध्यवच्छेदादिति युक्तमुत्पश्यामः। —Ibid.
14. ''विज्ञानालम्बनत्वेऽपि अहंप्रत्ययस्य भ्रान्तत्वं तदवस्थमेव, तस्य स्थिरवस्तुनिर्भासत्वादस्थिरत्वाच्च विज्ञानानाम्। एतेन स्थूलोऽहम् अन्धोऽहम् गच्छामि इत्यादयोऽपि अध्यासतया व्याख्याताः''। —Ibid, p.12
15. The Bhāmatī of Vācaspati, Op. Cit., p.12
16. ''तदेवं सर्वप्रवादश्रुतिस्मृतीतिहासपुराणप्रथितमिथ्याभावस्याभावस्याहंप्रत्ययस्य स्वरूपनिमित्तफलैरुप-व्याख्यानम्....। अन्योन्यस्मिन्धर्मिण्यात्मशरीरादौ अन्योन्यात्मकतामध्यस्य - अहमिदं शरीरादीति। 'इदम्' इति च वस्तुतः, न प्रतीतितः।...... ''इति'' शब्दसूचितश्च शरीराद्यनुकूलं च.... तदुपादानपरिवर्जनादिः।'' —Bhāmatī, Ibid.
17. ''अन्योन्यधर्मांश्चाध्यस्य अन्योन्यस्मिन्धर्मिणि देहादिधर्मान् जन्ममरणजराव्याध्यादीनात्मनि धर्मिणि अध्यस्तदेहादिभावे समारोप्य तथा चैतन्यादीनात्मधर्मान् देहादावध्यस्तात्मभावे समारोप्य ममेदं जरामरणपुत्रपशुस्वाम्यादि' इति व्यवहारो व्यपदेशः।'' —Ibid.
18. ''.... इति समानकर्तृकत्वेन अध्यस्य व्यवहारः इत्युपपन्नम्। पूर्वकालत्वसूचितमध्यासस्य व्यवहारकारणत्वं स्फुटयति - मिथ्याज्ञाननिमित्तः व्यवहारः इति। मिथ्याज्ञानमध्यासः तन्निमित्तः, तद्भावाभावानुविधानाद् व्यवहारभावाभावयोरित्यर्थः। —Ibid.
19. ''तदेवमध्यासस्य स्वरूपम्....उक्त्वा.... तदेवम.... तस्य निमित्तमाह - इतरेतराविवेकेन इति। विवेकाग्रहणेनेत्यर्थः।....परमार्थतो धर्मिणोरतादात्म्यं विवेकः धर्माणां चासंकीर्णता विवेकः।'' —Ibid.
20. ''विविक्तयोर्वस्तुसतोर्भेदाग्रहनिबन्धनस्तादात्म्यविभ्रमो युज्यते शुक्तेरिव रजताद्भेदाग्रहे रजततादात्म्यविभ्रमः। —Ibid. p.14.
21. "The Bhāmatī of Vācaspati, Op. Cit., p.14.,Vide,

"सत्यं चिदात्मा अनृतं बुद्धिन्द्रियदेहादि"। —Bhāmatī, Ibid.

22. "न च संवृतिपरमार्थसतोः पारमार्थिकं मिथुनमस्तीत्यभूततद्भावर्थस्य च्वेः प्रयोगः।" —Ibid.

23. "ततश्च मिथुनभावोऽप्यवास्तव इत्यर्थः।"
—Vedāntakalpataru, The Brahmasūtra Śāṅkara Bhāṣya, Op. Cit., p.17.

24. The Bhāmatī of Vācaspati, Op. Cit., p.15, Vide,
"नैसर्गिक इति स्वाभाविकः अनादिरयं व्यवहारः। व्यवहारानादितया तत्कारणस्याध्यासस्य अनादितोक्ता"। —Bhāmatī, Op. Cit., p.15.

25. "पूर्वदृष्टस्यावभासः पूर्वदृष्टावभासः। मिथ्याप्रत्ययश्च आरोपविषयारोपणीयमिथुनमन्तरेण न भवतीति पूर्वदृष्टग्रहणेनानृतमारोपणीयमुपस्थापयति। तस्य च दृष्टत्वमात्रमुपयुज्यते न वस्तुसत्तेति दृष्टग्रहणम्"। —Bhāmatī, Op. Cit., p.17.

26. ".... वर्तमानं दृष्टं दर्शनं नारोपोपयोगीति पूर्व इत्युक्तम्। तच्च पूर्वदृष्टं स्वरूपेण सदप्यारोपणीयतया अनिर्वाच्यमित्यनृतम्। आरोपविषयं सत्यमाह परत्र इति। परत्र शुक्तिकादो परमार्थसति"। —Ibid.

27. "असंनिहित विषयत्वं च स्मृतिरूपत्वम्। संनिहितविषयं च प्रत्यभिज्ञानं समीचीनमिति"। —Ibid, p.18.

28. The Bhāmatī of Vācaspati, Op. Cit., p. 18, Vide,
"एवम् 'पीतः शङ्खः, तिक्तो गुडः' इत्यत्राप्येतल्लक्षणं योजनीयम्। तथा हि - बहिर्विनिर्गच्छदत्यच्छनयनरश्मिसंपृक्तपित्तद्रव्यवर्तिनीं पीततां पित्तहितामनुभवन्, शङ्खं च दोषाच्छादितशुक्लिमानमनुभवन् पीततायाश्च शङ्खासंबन्धमननुभवन् असंबन्धाग्रहणसारूप्येण पीतं तपनीयपिण्डं पीतं बिल्वफलम् इत्यादौ पूर्वदृष्टं सामानाधिकरण्यं पीतत्वशङ्खत्वयोरारोप्याह पीतः शङ्ख इति। एतेन तिक्तो गुडः इति प्रत्ययो व्याख्यातः।" —Bhāmatī, Op. Cit., p.18.

29. The Bhāmatī of Vācaspati, Op. Cit., pp.18-19, Vide,
"एवं विज्ञातृपुरुषाभिमुखेष्वादर्शोदकादिषु स्वच्छेषु चाक्षुषं तेजो लग्नमपि बलीयसा सौरेण तेजसा प्रतिस्रोतः प्रवर्तितं मुखसंयुक्तं मुखं ग्राहयत् दोषवशात्तद्देशतामनभिमुखतां च मुखस्याग्राहयत् पूर्वदृष्टाभिमुखादर्शोदकदेशतामाभिमुख्यं च मुखस्यारोपयतीति प्रतिबिम्बविभ्रमोऽपि लक्षितो भवति। एतेन द्विचन्द्रदिङ्मोहालातचक्रगन्धर्वनगरवंशोरगादिविभ्रमेष्वपि यथासंभवं लक्षणं योजनीयम्।" —Bhāmatī, Op. Cit., pp.18-19.

30. "तत्किं मरीचिषु तोयनिर्भासप्रत्ययस्तत्त्वगोचरः। तथा च समीचीन इति न भ्रान्तो नापि बाध्येत।... न चारोपितं स्वरूपं वस्त्वन्तरम्। तद्धि मरीचयो वा भवेद् गङ्गादिगतं तोयं वा। पूर्वस्मिन्कल्पे मरीचयः इति प्रत्ययः स्यात् न तोयम् इति। उत्तरस्मिंस्तु गङ्गायां तोयम् इति स्यात् न पुनः इह इति। देशभेदास्मरणे तोयम् इति स्यात् न पुनः इह इति। न चेदमत्यन्तमसत् निरस्तसमस्तस्वरूपमलीकमेवास्तु इति सांप्रतम्, तस्यानुभवगोचरत्वानुपपत्तेः....। तस्मान्न सत् नासत् नापि सदसत् परस्परवरोधात् इत्यनिर्वाच्यमेवारोपणीयं मरीचिषु तोयमास्थेयम्। तदनेन क्रमेणाध्यस्तं तोयं परमार्थतोयमिव अत एव पूर्वदृष्टमिव तत्त्वतस्तु न तोयम्। न च पूर्वदृष्टम्। किंतु अनृतम् अनिर्वाच्यम्। " —Ibid, pp.21-23.

31. "एवं च देहेन्द्रियादिप्रपञ्चोऽपि अनिर्वाच्यः। अपूर्वोऽपि पूर्वमिथ्याप्रत्ययोपदर्शित इव परत्र चिदात्मन्यध्यस्त इति उपपन्नम् अध्यासलक्षणयोगात्। देहेन्द्रियादिप्रपञ्चबाधनं च उपपादयिष्यते। चिदात्मातु श्रुतिस्मृतीतिहासपुराणगोचरः तन्मूलतदविरुद्धन्यायनिर्णीतशुद्धबुद्धमुक्तस्वभावः सत्त्वेनैव निर्वाच्यः।" —Ibid, p.23.

32. "प्रत्यगात्मन्यनात्माध्यास एव सर्वानर्थहेतुः न पुना रजतादिविभ्रमा इति स एवाविद्या।.... यस्मात्प्रत्यगात्मन्यशनायादिरहिते अशनायाद्युपेतान्तःकरणाद्यहितारोपेण प्रत्यगात्मानमदुःखं दुःखाकरोति तस्मादनर्थहेतुः।" ..... अविद्या हि सर्वानर्थबीजमिति श्रतिस्मृतीतिहासपुराणादिषु सुप्रसिद्धम्। —Ibid, p.44.
33. "इयमनादिरतिनिरूढनिबिडवासनानुबद्धा अविद्या न शक्या निरोद्धुम्.... इति.... मन्यन्ते।.... प्रत्यगात्मनि खलु अत्यन्तविविक्ते बुद्ध्यादिभ्यः बुद्ध्यादिभेदाग्रहनिमित्तो बुद्ध्याद्यात्मत्वतद्धर्माध्यासः। तत्र.... विवेकज्ञानं.... विवेकाग्रहे निवर्तिते अध्यासबाधात्मकं वस्तुस्वरूपावधारणं विद्या चिदात्मरूपं स्वरूपे व्यवतिष्ठत इत्यर्थः।" —Ibid, p.45.
34. "तत्र अहमिति धर्मितादात्म्याध्यासमात्रं 'मम' इत्यनुत्पादितधर्माध्यासं नानर्थहेतुरिति धर्माध्यासमेव ममकारं साक्षादशेषानर्थ-संसार-कारणमुदाहरणप्रपञ्चेनाह तद्यथा पुत्रभार्यादिषु इति। देहतादाम्यमात्मन्यध्यस्य देहधर्म.... आरोप्याह- अहमेव विकलः सकलः इति।.... देहादप्यन्तरङ्गाणामिन्द्रियाणामध्यस्यतीति....।" —Ibid, p.57-58.
35. "मिथ्याप्रत्ययरूपः मिथ्याप्रत्ययानां रूपमनिर्वचनीयत्वम्। तद्यस्य स तथोक्तः अनिर्वचनीय इत्यर्थः।" —Ibid, p.59.
36. Vide, D. Venkataramiah, The Pañcapādikā of Padmapāda, Baroda, 1948-p.8.
37. Ibid. Vide,

"अध्यासो नाम अतद्रूपे तद्रूपावभासः। सः मिथ्येति भवितुं युक्तम् इति मिथ्याशब्दो द्व्यर्थः अपह्नवचनः अनिर्वचीयतावचनश्च। अत्र अयमपह्नववचनः। मिथ्येति भवितुं युक्तम् अभाव एवाध्यासस्य युक्त इत्यर्थः।"

—Pañcapādikā (and Pañcapādikāvivaraṇa), Madras Government Oriental Series, 1958, p.23.
38. Ibid. Vide,

"अन्यस्य अन्यात्मतावभासः अविद्या इति"। आत्मनि कर्तृत्वभोक्तृत्वदोषसंयोग एवं अध्यासः। तत्र भोक्तृत्वाध्यासः कर्तृत्वाध्यासमपेक्षते। अकर्तुर्भोगाभावात्। कर्तृत्वं च रागद्वेषसंयोगाध्यासमपेक्षते। तद्रहितस्य कर्तृत्वाभावात्। दोषसंयोगश्च भोक्तृत्वमपेक्षते। अनुपभुक्ते अतज्जातीये वा रागाद्यनुपपत्तेः एवं बीजाङ्कुरवत् हेतुपरम्परया अनादित्वात् अध्यासस्य नैसर्गिकत्वमिति।"

—Vivaraṇa, p.63; pp.61-62.
39. "अस्यानर्थहेतोः प्रहाणाय आत्मैकत्वविद्याप्रतिपत्तये सर्वे वेदान्ता आरभ्यन्ते।" —Adhyāsabhāṣya, Op. Cit., p.45.
40. The Pañcapādikā, of Padmapāda, Op. Cit., p. 2; Vide,

"ब्रह्मज्ञानं हि सूत्रितमनर्थहेतुनिबर्हणम्। अनर्थश्च प्रमातृताप्रमुखं कर्तृत्वभोक्तृत्वम्। तत् यदि वस्तुकृतं न ज्ञानेन निबर्हणीयम्। यतः ज्ञानमज्ञानस्यैव निवर्तकम्। तत् यदि कर्तृत्व-भोक्तृत्वमज्ञानहेतुकं स्यात् ततः ब्रह्मज्ञानमनर्थहेतुनिबर्हणमुच्यमानमुपपद्यते।" —Pañcapādikā, Loc. Cit., p.11.
41. विचारसाध्यज्ञानस्य प्रयोजनमाकाङ्क्षन् विचारविधिः अधिकारिविशेषणं मोक्षं प्रयोजनत्वेन प्रमिमीते इत्यर्थः।" —Vivaraṇa, Loc. Cit; p.40.
42. "तथा हि चित्रावयविनि नीलविशिष्टद्रव्यज्ञानं स्वविषयं वा स्वविषसमवेतं वा रसादिकं विरोधिनं वा पीतिमादिगुणं न निवर्तयति स्वविषयानवबोध एव केवलः तेन निवर्त्यते।.... न च आश्रयविषयोभयसम्बन्धि वस्तु ज्ञानेन निवर्तते। आत्मनः शरीरविषयज्ञानेन देहात्म-सम्बन्धाद्यनिवृत्तेः इति।" —Ibid, p.41.
43. The Pañcapādikā of Padmapāda, Op. Cit., p.3.

44. "तथा चास्य शास्त्रस्य ऐदम्पर्यं सुखैकतानसदात्मक-कूटस्थचैतन्यैकरसता संसारित्वाभिमतस्यात्मनः पारमार्थिकं स्वरूपमिति वेदान्ताः पर्यवस्यन्तीति प्रतिपादितम्। तच्च अहं कर्त्ता सुखी दुःखी इति प्रत्यक्षाभिमतेन अबाधितकल्पेन अवभासेन विरुध्यते।" - Pañcapādikā, Loc. Cit; pp. 12-13.
45. "ब्रह्मात्मैकत्वे वेदान्ताः पर्यवस्यन्तीति यदिहं वेदान्तशास्त्रस्य ऐदम्पर्यं तत् सूत्रभाष्याभ्यां प्रतिपादितमिति तन्त्रार्थं प्रदर्श्य तस्य अध्याससिध्द्यधीनतया अध्यासस्य प्रथमवर्णनीयतां दर्शयति-तच्चाहं कर्त्ता सुखी दुःखी इति।" —Vivaraṇa, Loc. Cit; p.47.
46. "अस्मत्प्रत्यये यः अनिदमंशः चिदेकरसः तस्मिन् तद्बलनिर्भासितया लक्षणतो युष्मदर्थस्य मनुष्याभिमानस्य सम्भेद इव अवभासः स एव अध्यास।" —Pañcapādikā, Loc. Cit; p.60.
47. "अस्मत्प्रत्ययगोचरस्य चैतन्यस्यबलेन निर्भास्यत्वात् अहङ्कारादेः प्रतिभासतो युष्मदर्थत्वाभावेऽपि अपरोक्षतया अवभास्यत्वेन लक्षणेन युष्मदर्थभावो युज्यते इत्यर्थः।.... अन्तःकरण-वृत्त्युपाधौ नानेव अवभासन्ते इत्यर्थः।" —Vivaraṇa, Loc. Cit; p.60.
48. The Pañcapādikā of Padmapāda, Op. Cit; p.10.Vide, "मिथ्याज्ञाननिमित्तः इति मिथ्या च तदज्ञानं च मिथ्याज्ञानम्। मिथ्येति अनिर्वचनीयता उच्यते। अज्ञानमिति च जडात्मिका अविद्याशक्तिः ज्ञानपर्युदासेन उच्यते। तन्निमितः तदुपादानः इत्यर्थः।" —Pañcapādikā, Loc. Cit; p.26.
49. "तत्र अज्ञानम् इत्युक्ते ज्ञानाभावमात्रम् उक्तं स्यात्, मिथ्या इत्युक्ते भ्रान्तिज्ञानम् इति स्यात्। तदुभयव्यावृत्त्यर्थं निरुच्य पदार्थौ दर्शयति मिथ्या च तत् अज्ञानं च इत्यादिना। ननु कथं मिथ्याज्ञानम् अध्यासस्य उपादानम् तस्मिन् सति अध्यासस्य उदयात् असति च अनुदयात् इति ब्रूमः ।" —Vivaraṇa, Loc. Cit; pp.64-65.
50. "ननु क्लृप्तं विषयेन्द्रियादिदोषः कारणम् इति। सत्यम् निमित्तं तु तत्। उपादानापेक्षायाम् अज्ञानमनुप्रविशति।" —Ibid., p.68.
51. सर्वं च कार्यं सोपादानम्, भावकार्यत्वात्, घटादिवत्, इत्यनुमानात्।" -Ibid. p.69.
52. "कथं पुनः नैमित्तिकव्यवहारस्य नैसर्गिकत्वम्? अत्रोच्यते। अवश्यमेषाविद्याशक्तिः बाह्याध्यात्मिकेषु वस्तुषु तत्स्वरूप-सत्तामात्रानुबन्धिनी अभ्युपगन्तव्या। अन्यथा मिथ्यार्थावभासानुपपत्तेः।"-Pañcapādikā, Loc. Cit; p.27.
53. "सा च न जडेषु वस्तुषु तत्वस्वरूपावभासं प्रतिबध्नाति। प्रमाणवैकल्यादेव तदग्रहणसिद्धेः। रजतप्रतिभासात् प्राक् ऊर्ध्वं च सत्यामपि तस्यां स्वरूपग्रहणदर्शनात्। अतः रूपान्तरावभासहेतुरेव केवलम्।" —Ibid
54. Vivaraṇa, Loc. Cit; p.74. "तत्र प्रथमं तावत् अध्यासप्रवाहजन्मना उपादान-कारणरूपेण नैसर्गिकत्वं कार्यव्यक्तिरूपेण नैमित्तिकत्वम् इति अविरोधम्....।"
55. Tātparyadīpikā on Vivaraṇa, Loc. Cit; p.74.
56. Ibid
57. ".....आत्मनि भावरूपमज्ञानं साधयति अवश्यमेषा अविद्याशक्तिः इति। अवश्यम् इति एषा इति च प्रमाणद्वयसत्तामाह। प्रत्यक्षं तावत् अहमज्ञः मामन्यं च न जानामि इत्यपरोक्षावभासदर्शनात्। ननु ज्ञानाभाव-विषयः अयमवभासः। न, अपरोक्षावभासत्वात् अहं सुखी इतिवत्। अभावस्य च षष्ठ प्रमाण-गोचरत्वात्।.... त्वदुक्तमर्थं संख्या वा शास्त्रार्थं वा न जानामि इति विषयव्याकृत्तमज्ञानपमनुभूय तच्छ्रवणादौ प्रवर्तते।" —Vivaraṇa, Loc. Cit; pp. 75-76.
58. सर्वं वस्तु ज्ञाततया वा अज्ञाततया वा साक्षिचैतन्यस्य विषयः एव। तत्र ज्ञाततया विषयः

प्रमाणव्यवधानमपेक्षते अन्यस्तु सामान्याकारेण विशेषाकारेण वा अज्ञानव्यावर्तकतया सदा भासते इति उपपत्तिसहितम् अज्ञानप्रत्यक्षं भावरूपमेव आत्मनि अज्ञानं गमयति इति सिद्धम् ....ततश्च ज्ञानेन समानाश्रयविषयं भावरूपमज्ञानं सिद्धम्।'' —Ibid, pp. 83-89.

59. ''विशुद्धब्रह्मात्मनि शुक्तिकायां च अहङ्काररजताध्यासस्य अर्थज्ञानात्मकस्य मिथ्याभूतस्य मिथ्याभूतमेव किंचित् उपादानमन्वेषणीयम्। सत्योपादानत्वे कार्यस्य कारणस्वभावतया अध्यासस्यापि सत्यत्वप्रसङ्गात्। तस्यापि मिथ्योपादानस्य सादित्वे तथाविधोपादानान्तरकल्पनाप्रसङ्गात् अनाद्येव तत् मिथ्योपादानम् इति कल्पनीयम्।'' —Ibid, pp.89-90.

60. Bhāvaprakāśikā on Vivaraṇa, Loc. Cit; p.96.

61. ''विषयैः सह साक्षिचैतन्ये अज्ञानाध्यासात् प्रतिभासः। न च अध्यस्तस्य आवरणमस्ति।...... नास्ति अनात्मनि आवरणे प्रमाणम्। न च स्वयमेव प्रकाशहीनस्य जडस्य आवरणार्थताऽपि सम्भवति। तस्मात् अतिशयाभावात् न अज्ञानविषयः अनात्मा इति।'' - Vivaraṇa, Loc. Cit; p.96.

62. Sukharanjan Saha, Loc. Cit; p.76; Vide,
''यदि आत्माश्रयम् अज्ञानम् अनात्मावरणं स्यात् तदा आवरणविनाशमन्तरेण विषयावभासायोगात् विषयज्ञानेन आत्माज्ञानं निवर्तेत। अतः सत्यामेव आत्मनि अविद्यायां त्रिष्वपि कालेषु विषयस्वरूपप्रतिभासदर्शनात् न अनात्मावरणम् अज्ञानमिति भावः।'' —Vivaraṇa, Loc. Cit; p.97.

63. Sukharanjan Saha, Loc. Cit; p.81; Vide,
''....शुक्तिकादिज्ञानेन रजताद्यध्यासानां स्वकारणे प्रविलयमात्रं क्रियते मुसलप्रहारेणेव घटस्य।'' —Vivaraṇa, Loc. Cit; pp 98-99.

64. Sukharanjan Saha, Loc. Cit; p.82; Vide,
''अथवा मूलाज्ञानस्यैव अवस्थाभेदाः रजताद्युपादानानि शुक्तिकादिज्ञानैः सहाध्यासेन निवर्तन्ते इति कल्प्यताम्।'' —Vivaraṇa, Loc. Cit; p.99.

65. Sukharanjan Saha, Loc. Cit; p.82.

66. The Pañcapādikā of Padmapāda, Loc. Cit; pp. 13-14, Vide,
'' अहमिति तावत् प्रथमोऽध्यासः।.... यदैव अहङ्कर्ता अध्यासात्मकः तदैव तदुपकरणस्यापि तदात्मकत्वसिद्धिः।.... एवम् अहङ्कर्तृत्वप्रमुखक्रियाकारकफलात्मको लोकव्यवहारः अध्यस्तः नित्यशुद्धबुद्धमुक्तस्वभावे आत्मनि।'' —Pañcapādikā, Loc. Cit; pp.31-32.

67. Ibid, pp. 33-34; Vide,
''न देहेन्द्रियादिषु अहंममाभिमानवत एव प्रमातृत्वप्रदर्शनमात्रेण तस्य अध्यासात्मकता सिध्यति। लोके शुक्तिरजतद्विचन्द्रादिवत् अध्यासानुभवाभावात्। बाधे हि सति स भवति। नेह स विद्यते।''—Vivaraṇa, Loc. Cit; p.115.

68. ''बाधानुपपत्तिर्मिथ्यात्वे प्रमाणं प्रत्यक्षानुमानव्यवहारानुपपत्त्यागमाः आत्मन्यनात्मावभासे प्रमाणम्....। यौक्तिकज्ञानादिना परोक्षविवेकमाश्रित्य परस्परात्मनाऽवभासनिश्चयः अपरोक्षबाधस्य भ्रान्तिप्रतिभासोच्छेदिनोऽभावात् न स्पष्टो मिथ्यात्वाध्यवसायः इति भावः।'' —Vivaraṇa. Loc. Cit, p.115.

69. ''अत्र च सम्यग्ज्ञानैकनिवर्त्यतवात् अविद्यात्वम्, प्रतिभासमात्रशरीरत्वात् भ्रान्तित्वम्, सत्यानृतमिथुनीकरणरूपत्वात् अध्यासत्वम्, सदसदादिप्रकारवैलक्षण्यात् मिथ्यात्वम् इति।'' —Tātparyadīpikā on Vivaraṇa, Loc. Cit, p.115.

70. The Pañcapādikā of Padmapāda, Op. Cit; pp.11-12, Vide,
''प्रत्यगात्मनि तु चितिस्वभावत्वात् स्वयं प्रकाशमाने ब्रह्मस्वरूपानवभासस्य अनन्यनिमित्तत्वात् तद्गतनिसर्गसिद्धाविद्याशक्तिप्रतिबन्धादेव तस्य अनवभासः। अतः सा प्रत्यक्चिति ब्रह्मस्वरूपावभास

प्रतिबध्नाति अहङ्काराद्यतद्रूपप्रतिभासनिमित्तं च भवति सुषुप्त्यादौ च अहङ्कारादि विक्षेपसंस्कारमात्रशेषं स्थित्वा पुनरुद्भवति, इत्यतः नैसर्गिकोऽपि अहङ्कारममकारात्मको मनुष्याद्यभिमानो लोकव्यवहारः मिथ्यात्मको ज्ञाननिमित्तः उच्यते न पुनः आगन्तुकत्वेन''। -Pañcapādikā, Loc. Cit; pp.29-30.

71. ''अस्ति प्रकाशते इत्याद्यभिज्ञादिव्यवहारपुष्कलकारणे सति नास्ति न प्रकाशते च इति योऽयम् आत्मतत्त्वालम्बनो व्यवहारः सः भावरूपेण केनचित् आत्मनि आवरणमन्तरेण नोपपद्यते सति पुष्कलकारणे असति च आवरणे सन्निहिते घटे प्रकाशते इत्यादिव्यवहारदर्शनात्। अतः नास्ति ब्रह्म न प्रकाशते च इति व्यवहारः अन्यथानुपपत्त्या भावरूपमज्ञानं गमयति इति अर्थापत्तिः अनुमानं वा समुदायार्थः।'' -Vivaraṇa, Loc. Cit; p.104.

72. ''नन्वात्मन्यप्यावरणं नाम किं प्रकाशनाशः किं वा प्रकाशस्य विषयप्राकट्यकार्योत्पादने प्रतिबन्ध उत तत्रैव सहकार्यन्तरप्रतीक्षा। नाद्यः। प्रकाशस्य नित्यात्मचैतन्यरूपत्वात्। नापि द्वितीयतृतीयौ। अन्तःकरणवृत्तिव्यक्तचित्प्रकाशमन्तरेण विषये पृथक् प्राकट्यानङ्गीकारात्। ततो दुर्निरूपमावरणस्वरूपमिति चेत्। सत्यमेतत् अत एवावरणस्यानिर्वाच्याविद्यारूपत्वमङ्गीकर्तव्यं न तु दुर्निरूपत्वमात्रेण तदपलापो युक्तः। अनुमानसिद्धत्वात्। तथा हि। अस्ति तावन्मूढानामेवं व्यवहारः। अशनायाद्यतीतं विवेकिप्रसिद्धमात्मतत्त्वं नास्ति न प्रकाशते चेति। सोऽयं व्यवहार आत्मनि भावरूपावरणनिमित्तो भवितुमर्हति अस्ति प्रकाशत इत्यादिव्यवहार पुष्कलकारणे सति तद्विपरीतव्यवहारत्वाद् यत्रैवं तन्नैवं यथास्ति प्रकाशते घट इति व्यवहारः। न च कारणपौष्कल्यमसिद्धं नित्यसिद्धस्वप्रकाशचैतन्यातिरेकेणात्रान्यापेक्षाभावात्।'' —Vivaraṇa Prameya Saṅgraha, Op. Cit; pp.20-21.

73. Pañcapādikā of Padmapāda, Op. Cit., pp. 17-18, Vide, ''परत्र इत्युक्ते अर्थात् परस्य अवभासमानता सिद्धा। तस्य विशेषणं स्मृतिरूपत्वम्। स्मर्यते इति स्मृतिः। असंज्ञायामपि अकर्तरि कारके घञादीनां प्रयोगदर्शनात्। स्मर्यमाणरूपमिव रूपमस्य न पुनः स्मर्यते एवं स्पष्टं पुरोऽवस्थिततत्वावभासनात्। पूर्वदृष्टावभासः इति उपपतिः स्मृतिरूपत्वे। न हि पूर्वम् अदृष्टरजतस्य शुक्तिसम्प्रयोगे रजतम् अवभासते।'' —Pañcapādikā, Loc. Cit; pp.39-40.

74. ''अर्थात् तद्विषयस्य अवभासस्यापि इदमेव लक्षणमुक्तं भवति। कथम्? तदुच्यते। स्मृतेः रूपमिव रूपमस्य न पुनः स्मृतिरेव। पूर्वप्रमाणविषय विशेषस्य तथाऽनवभासकत्वात्। कथं पुनः स्मृतिरूपत्वम्। पूर्वप्रमाणद्वारा समुत्थत्वात् न हि असम्प्रयुक्तावभासिनः पूर्वप्रवृत्ततद्विषयप्रमाणद्वारा समुत्थत्वमन्तरेण समुद्भवः सम्भवति''। —Ibid, pp. 41-22.

75. ''अर्थाभावे कथमपरोक्षा संविदिति चेत्। न। यथासंविदवभासाधीनत्वादर्थसत्ता निश्चयस्य। न हि अर्थसत्ता निश्चयाधीनः संवित्सत्तानिश्चयः। अर्थसत्तानिश्चयस्यापि निश्चयान्तराधीनत्वप्रसङ्गात्। ननु नेदं रजतम् इत्युत्तरसंवेदनादर्थाभावोऽपि निश्चितः। न। तत्रापि पूर्वसंवेदनेन सद्भावविषयेण विरोधात्।'' —Vivaraṇa, Loc. Cit; p.121.

76. T. M. P. Mahadevan, The Philosophy of Advaita, Arnold-Heinemann, N. Delhi; 1976, p.107.
''द्विविधो ह्यध्यासो ज्ञानविशिष्टोऽर्थोऽर्थविशिष्टं ज्ञानं चेति। तत्रार्थस्य तावत् स्मर्यमाणसदृशोऽन्यात्मनाऽवभास्यमानोऽन्योऽर्थोऽध्यास इति लक्षणम्। ज्ञानस्य तु स्मृतिसमानोऽन्यस्यान्यात्मतावभासोऽध्यास इति।'' —VPS, Loc. Cit., p.26.

77. PPD, Op. Cit., pp.27-28.

78. न इन्द्रियज्ञानम् संस्कारजं स्मरणं पृथगेव स्मरणाभिमानशून्यं समुत्पन्नम्। किन्तु एकमेव संस्कारसहितात् इन्द्रियात्।.... कारणदोषः कार्यविशेषे तस्य शक्तिं निरुन्धन्नेव संस्कारविशेषमपि

उद्बोधयति। कार्यगम्यत्वात् कारणादोषशक्तेः। अतः संस्कारदुष्टकारणसंवलिता एव सामग्री। सा च एकमेव ज्ञानम् एकमेव फलं जनयति।'' —Pañcapādikā, Loc Cit; pp. 51-52.

79. PPD, Op. Cit; pp.28-29; Vide,
''तस्य च दोषोत्थापित-संस्कार-विशेषसहित-सामग्रीसमुत्पन्नज्ञानस्य उचितमेव शुक्तिमिथ्यारजतमालम्बनमवभासते। तेन मिथ्यालम्बनं ज्ञानं मिथ्याज्ञानं, न स्वतो ज्ञानस्य मिथ्यात्वमस्ति बाधाभावात्।'' —Pañcapādikā, Loc. Cit; pp. 52.

80. ''भिन्नजातीयज्ञानहेतुसामग्र्योः कथमेकज्ञानोत्पादनमिति चेत् नैष दोषः। दृश्यते हि लिङ्गज्ञानसंस्कारयोः सम्भूय लिङ्गिज्ञानोत्पादनं प्रत्यभिज्ञानोत्पादनञ्च अक्षसंस्कारयोः। उभयत्रापि स्मृतिगर्भमेकमेव प्रमाणज्ञानम्। संस्कारानुद्बोधे तदभावात्। तस्मात् लिङ्गदर्शनमेव सम्बन्धज्ञानसंस्कारमुद्बोध्य तत्सहितं लिङ्गिज्ञानं जनयतीति वक्तव्यम्।'' —Pañcapādikā, Loc. Cit; p.53.

81. ''अयमेव च न्यायः प्रत्यभिज्ञानेऽपि। न पुनः ज्ञानद्वये प्रमाणमस्ति। तथा भिन्नजातीयज्ञानहेतुभ्यो नीलादिभ्य एकं चित्रज्ञानं निदर्शनीयम्। तत्र लैङ्गिज्ञानप्रत्यभिज्ञाचित्रज्ञानानामदुष्टकारणारब्धत्वाद् यथार्थमेवावभासः। इह तु कारणदोषादतथाभूतार्थवभासः इति विशेषः। एवञ्च सति नानुभवविरोधः। प्रतिभासमानस्य रजतस्यैवालम्बनत्वात्। अतो मायामयं रजतम्।'' -Ibid, p.54.

82. ''ननु अग्रहणमिथ्याज्ञानतत्संस्कारेभ्यः अन्यत् अज्ञानं नाम न पश्यामः। ते एव च जीवस्य स्वयंप्रकाशमानमपि ब्रह्मस्वरूपावभासं प्रतिबध्नन्ति इति। नेत्याह सुषुप्त्यादौ च इति। तत्रापि अविद्याशक्तिः संस्कारशेषं तिष्ठति न संस्कारादय एवम् अज्ञानम् इत्यर्थः। कथम्। न तावत् सुषुप्त्यादौ स्वयंप्रकाशब्रह्मस्वरूपानवभासः पुरुषान्तरसंवेदनवत् द्रष्टुर्भिन्नत्वात् इति शक्यं वक्तुम्। एकत्वश्रुतेः। नापि मिथ्याज्ञानप्रतिबन्धात्। तत्र तस्याभावात्। नापि तत्संस्कारप्रतिबन्धात्। भ्रान्तिसंस्काराणां तत्त्वावभासप्रतिबन्धकत्वाभावात् सत्स्वपि रजतभ्रमसंस्कारेषु शुक्तिकावबोधदर्शनात्। नापि अग्रहणप्रतिबन्धात्। स्वरूपग्रहणस्य नित्यत्वात् स्वयम् अप्रतिबन्धकदर्शनात्। नापि अग्रहणप्रतिबन्धात्। स्वरूपग्रहणस्य नित्यत्वात् स्वयंप्रकाशमाने संवेदने तद्विषयकादाचित्काग्रहणस्य अप्रतिबन्धकत्वात्।... तस्मात् सुषुप्त्यादौ स्वरूपानवभासव्यवहारः अग्रहणमिथ्याज्ञानतत्संस्कारकर्मभ्यः अन्यदेव किंचित् प्रतिबन्धकम् अज्ञानं कल्पयतीत्यर्थः।'' —Vivaraṇa, Loc. Cit, pp. 105-108.

83. ''त्रिविधं सत्त्वं परमार्थसत्त्वं ब्रह्मणः अर्थक्रियासामर्थ्यसत्त्वं मायोपाधिकमाकाशादेः अविद्योपाधिकसत्त्वं रजतादेः इति परमार्थसत्त्वापेक्षया अनिर्वचनीयमिति नानुभवविरोधः यथानुभवमर्थसत्त्वाभ्युपगमात्। —Ibid, p.165.

84. PPD, Op. Cit; p.32; Vide,
''किञ्च नेदं रजतम् इति बाधेऽपि मायामयत्वमेव सूचयति। कथम्। तेन हि तस्य निरुपाख्यतापादनपूर्वकं मिथ्यात्वं ज्ञायते। नेदं रजतं मिथ्यैवाभासिष्ट इति। न च तत् केनचिद् रूपेण रूपवत्त्वेऽवकल्प्यते। सम्प्रयुक्तशुक्तिवत् निरस्यमानविषयज्ञानवच्च।'' —Pañcapādikā, Loc. Cit; p.55.

85. ''अज्ञानस्य स्वकार्येण वर्तमानेन प्रविलीनेन वा सह ज्ञानेन निवृत्तिबोधः। तथाविधानवबोधनिवृत्तौ बाधप्रसिद्धेः। —Vivaraṇa, Loc. Cit., p.178.

86. ''नन्वेवं सति शुक्तिज्ञानमेव मिथ्यारजततदुपादानयोर्निवर्त्तकत्वाद्बाधकं स्यात्। सत्यमेवं रहस्यमेतत् तथापि परमार्थरजतबुद्धया प्रवर्तमानस्य तदभावबोधनेन प्रवृत्त्याकाङ्क्षोच्छेदित्वान्नेदं रजतमिति ज्ञानमपि बाधकत्वेन व्यपदिश्यते।'' - VPS, Loc. Cit., p.39.

87. PPD, Op. Cit; pp. 105-106; Vide,
''अविद्येत्येवोच्यमाने आच्छादकत्वं नाम यत् तस्यास्तत्त्वं तदेवाभिहितं स्यात् न अतद्रूपावभासितया अनर्थहेतुत्वम्। अतोऽतद्रूपावभासित्वमध्यासशब्देन प्रकृतोपयोगितया उपक्षिप्य पुनस्तस्याविद्याशब्दतया

विद्यामात्रापनोदनार्हत्वं दर्शनीयम्। तदेतदाह 'तत्र यदध्यासः तत्कृतेन दोषेण गुणेन वा अणुमात्रेणापि स न सम्बध्यते इत्यवास्तवमनर्थं दर्शयति। वास्तवत्वे हि न ज्ञानमात्रात् तद्विगमः इति प्रतिज्ञा हीयेत।'' —Pañcapādikā, Loc. Cit., p.138.

88. ''अविद्याध्यासविषयत्वप्रयुक्तस्तावद् गुणदोषाभावः सिद्धः। अत्राध्यासपरिणामितयाऽऽश्रयत्वप्रयुक्तगुणदोषाभावः कथ्यते। कथम्। अनाद्यविद्याध्यासस्य नित्यचैतन्यावभास्यत्वान्न तत्राध्यासपरिणामः कदाचित्काध्यासपरिणामस्यविद्योपादानत्वादविद्यासंभेदादात्माश्रयत्वादिसिद्धिरिति।'' —Tattvadīpana on Vivaraṇa, Loc. Cit., p.347.

89. ''आगन्तुकाध्यासस्याविद्याश्रयत्व आत्मनो नित्यमुक्तत्वाद् ज्ञानवैयर्थ्यमित्याशङ्कयाऽविद्यातत्कार्ययोरात्मन्यध्यस्तत्वाद् ज्ञानस्यार्थवत्त्वमित्याह।'' —Vivaraṇa, Loc. Cit., pp.346-347.

90. Adhyāsabhāṣya, Brahmasūtra Śāṅkara Bhāṣya-Parimal Sanskrit Series, Delhi, pp.16-45.

91. तत्त्वज्ञानमन्तरेणाशक्यसमुच्छेदः —Bhāmatī, Op. Cit., p.59.

92. Supra, (Bhāmatī).

93. The Pañcapādikā of Padmapāda, Op. Cit., p.124.

94. ''ननु....कथम् (अध्यासः) अनन्तः? अन्तवत्त्वेऽपि तर्हि कथम्? स्वतोऽन्यतो वा तत्सिद्धेः। तस्मात् अनन्तस्य प्रहाणाय वेदान्ता आरभ्यन्ते इत्युक्ते अर्थादेष एव प्रहाणहेतुः असत्यस्मिन् अनन्तः इति निश्चीयते।'' —Pañcapādikā, Loc. Cit., pp.160-161.

95. ''मिथ्याशब्दः अपह्नववचनः। एतदुक्तं भवति-अध्यासो भेदाग्रहेण व्याप्तः।.... स (भेदग्रहः) भेदाग्रहं निवर्तयंस्तद्व्याप्तमध्यासमपि निवर्तयतीति।'' —Bhāmatī, Op. Cit., p.7.

96. Supra, (Vivaraṇa).

97. Adhyāsabhāṣya

98. Supra, (Bhāmatī).

99. Ibid.

100. ''शुक्तिका हि रजतवदवभासते एकश्चद्रः सद्वितीयवदिति।'' —Ibid.

101. Supra, (Bhāmatī).

102. Ibid.

103. Vide, Pañcapādikā, Loc. Cit., p.25.

104. Supra, (Vivaraṇa).

105. Vide, Pañcapādikā, Loc. Cit., p.25.

106. Adhyāsabhāṣya, Op. Cit., p.56.

107. ''पुत्रभार्यादिषु विकलेषु सकलेषु वा अहमेव विकलः सकलो वा....। स्थूलोऽहम् कृशोऽहम्, गौरोऽहम्, तिष्ठामि, गच्छामि....। मूकः काणः क्लीबो बधिरोऽन्धोऽहम् इति''। —Ibid. p.56-57.

108. Supra (Bhāmatī).

109. ''अतस्मिन् अयुष्मदर्थे अनिदंचिति तद्बुद्धिः युष्मदर्थावभासः इत्यर्थः।'' —Pañcapādikā, Loc. Cit., p.152.

110. ''तमेतमविद्याख्यमात्मानात्मनोरितरेतराध्यासं पुरस्कृत्य सर्वे प्रमाणप्रमेयव्यवहारा लौकिकाः प्रवृत्ताः सर्वाणि च शास्त्राणि विधिप्रतिषेधमोक्षपराणि।'' —Adhyāsbhāṣya, Op. Cit., p.44.

111. न च शास्त्रव्यवहारात् मायाविद्याभेदः। .... भाष्यकारेण च ''अविद्या माया'' ''अविद्यात्मिका मायाशक्तिः इति तत्र तत्र निर्देशात्। टीकाकारेण च ''अविद्या मायाऽक्षरम्'' इत्युक्तत्वात्। ब्रह्मसिद्धिकारेण च ''एवमेवेयमविद्या माया मिथ्याप्रत्ययः'' इत्युक्तत्वात् तस्मात् लक्षणैक्यात् वृद्धव्यवहारे च एकत्वावगमादेकस्मिन्नपि वस्तुनि विक्षेपप्राधान्येन माया आच्छादनप्राधान्येन

अविद्येति व्यवहारभेदः इच्छाधीनत्वतद्वैपरीत्येन वा व्यवहारभेदः इति युक्तं मायामयमिति।'' —Vivaraṇa, Op. Cit., pp.172-173.

112. ''एका ह्यविद्या अनादिर्भावरूपा।'' —Supra, (Bhāmatī).

113. ''... अन्या पूर्वपूर्वविभ्रमसंस्कारः तदविद्याद्वितयं सत्वासत्त्वाभ्यामनिर्वाच्यम्।.... तत्सचिवता ब्रह्मणस्तद्विषयता तदाश्रयास्तु जीवा एवेति।'' —Ibid.

114. ''यदि ब्रह्मणोऽविद्याशक्त्या संसारः प्रजायते हन्त मुक्तानामपि पुनरुत्पादप्रसङ्गः तस्याः प्रधानवत्तादवस्थ्यात्। तद्विनाशेऽपि वा समस्तसंसारोच्छेदः तन्मूलाविद्याशक्तेः समुच्छेदादित्यत आह-मुक्तानां च पुनः बन्धस्य अनुत्पत्तिः। कुतः ? विद्यया तस्या बीजशक्तेर्दाहात्। अयमभिसन्धिः -न वयं प्रधानवदविद्यां सर्वजीवेष्वेकामाचक्ष्महे....। किंत्वियं प्रतिजीवं भिद्यते। तेन यस्यैव जीवस्य विद्योत्पन्ना तस्यैवाविद्याऽपनीयते व जीवान्तरस्य भिन्नाधिकरणयोर्विद्याऽविद्ययोरविरोधात्।'' —Bhāmatī on SB. I.4.3, Op. Cit., pp.377-378.

115. ''नाविद्या ब्रह्माश्रया किंतु जीवे सा त्वनिर्वचनीयेत्युक्तं तेन नित्यशुद्धमेव ब्रह्म।'' -Ibid, I.1.4, p.126.

116. Supra, (Vivaraṇa).

117. Ibid.

118. Vide, R. Subrahamanian, Loc. Cit., pp.88-89.

119. The Bhāmatī of Vācaspati, Op. Ciṭ, pp.59-60. Vide, ''अस्यानर्थहेतोः प्रहाणाय आत्मैकत्वविद्याप्रतिपत्तये सर्वे वेदान्ता आरभ्यन्ते।'' -Adhyāsa-bhāṣya.

120. The Pañcapādikā of Padmapāda, Op. Cit., pp.125-126, Vide, Pañcapādikā, Loc. Cit., pp.162-163.
''हेतोः प्रहाण्या हि हेतुमतः प्रहाणिरात्यन्तिकी यतः ।... तत्त्वमसीत्यादिवाक्याद् ब्रह्मस्वरूपावगाहि-ज्ञानान्तरोत्पत्तेरिष्टत्वात्। तद्धि ब्रह्मणोऽवच्छिद्यैव चैतन्यस्य ब्रह्मरूपत्वप्रच्छादनेन जीवरूपत्वापादिकामनादिसिद्धामविद्यामहङ्कारादिविक्षेपहेतुं निराकुर्वदेवोत्पद्यते। ततः कारणनिवृत्तौ तत्कार्यमहमिति जीवे भोक्तृरूपता सपरिकरा निवर्तते इति युज्यते। अहंप्रत्ययः पुनरनादिसिद्धोऽनादि-सिद्धेनैव कार्यकरणमात्रेण सहभावादविरोधात् न स्वरूपविवेकमात्रेण निवर्तते।''

121. Pañcapādikā of Padmapāda, Op. Cit., pp. 128-129, Vide,
''(यद्येवं) ब्रह्मात्मावगतिनान्तरीयकम्! अनर्थहेतोरविद्यायाः प्रहाणं न शब्दस्य तत्र व्यापारः। न हि विपर्यासगृहीतं वस्तु तन्निरासादृते तत्त्वतो निर्णेतुं शक्यम्। तस्मात् पूर्वावसितमतद्धर्मं निरस्यदेव तत्त्वावद्योति वाक्यं तत्त्वमवसाययति।''।
-Pañcapadikā, Loc. Cit., pp. 165-166.

122. The Pañcapādikā of Padmapāda, Op. Cit., pp.129-130, Vide,
''इह पुनः विज्ञानमेव तादृशमुत्पन्नं यत् विरोधिनिराकरणमन्तरेण न स्वार्थं साधयितुमलम् तुलोन्नमनव्यापार इव आनमननान्तरीयकः। तथा हि उन्नमनव्यापारः स्वविषयस्य तुलाद्रव्यस्योर्ध्वदेशसम्बन्धं न साधयितुमलं तत्कालमेव तस्याधोदेशसम्बन्धमनापाद्य। न चोन्नमनकारकस्य हस्तप्रयत्नादेरानमनेऽपि कारकत्वम्। प्रसिद्ध्यभावादनुभवविरोधाच्च।'' -Pañcapādikā, Loc. Cit., pp. 166-167.

123. ''....अज्ञानादिसत्यमिथ्यावस्तु साधारणेन साक्षिमात्रेण वेद्यत्वात् प्रपञ्चस्य प्रमित्या न बाध्यते। तस्मात् अविद्यातत्कार्यप्रपञ्चप्रतिभासाभावस्यतद्विरोधादेव ब्रह्मात्मविशेषणत्वेन प्रमातुमशक्यत्वात्! ब्रह्मात्मावगति नान्तरीयकतया प्रातिभासिकबन्धनिवृत्तिरिति सूक्तम्।'' - Vivaraṇa, Loc. Cit., p.389.

124. The Bhāmatī of Vācaspati, Op. Cit., pp.60-61, Vide, Bhāmatī, Loc. Cit., pp.60-61.

"आत्मैकत्वविद्याप्रतिपत्तये....। प्रतिपत्तिः प्राप्तिः तस्यै न तु जपमात्राय नापि कर्मसु प्रवृत्तये। आत्मैकत्वं विगलितनिखिलप्रपञ्चत्वम् आनन्दरूपस्य सतः। तत्प्रतिपत्तिं निर्विचिकित्सां भावयन्तो वेदान्ताः समूलघातमध्यासमुपघ्नन्ति।.... आरोपितं हि रूपं तत्त्वज्ञानेनापोद्यते न तु वास्तवमतत्त्वज्ञानेन। न हि रज्ज्वा रज्जुत्वं सहस्रमपि सर्पधाराप्रत्यया अपवदितुमुत्सहन्ते। मिथ्याज्ञानप्रसञ्जितं तु रूपं शक्यं तत्त्वज्ञानेनापवदितुं मिथ्याज्ञानसंस्कारश्च सुदृढोऽपि तत्त्वज्ञानसंस्कारेणादरनैरन्तर्यदीर्घकालासेवित-तत्त्वज्ञानाभ्यासजन्मनेति।"

125. Supra, (Vivaraṇa).

CHAPTER V

THE ADVAITIC CONCEPTS OF JĪVA, ĪŚVARA AND JAGAT

The Advaitic concepts of *Jīva* (individual self), *Īśvara* (the Lord) and *Jagat* (the world) are intimately linked to the phenomenon of superimposition discussed in the preceding chapters. Advaita Vedānta does not deny outright the plurality of souls, i. e., of individual selves, at the empirical level. Each individual self is a complex entity consisting of the self (Ātman) and the mind-sense-body-complex. To Advaita Vedānta, the self by its very nature is consciousness and is impartite, eternal, and self-luminous, while the mind-sense-body-complex, which is *not-self*, is composite, ephemeral and therefore perishable. And that which is perishable cannot be real, says the Advaita Vedānta. The not-self serves as a limiting factor, an adjunct (*upādhi*) to the self, resulting in a multitude of apparently limited, deluded individual selves called *Jīva*-s. The self constitutes the essential nature of the *Jīva-s* in much the same way as one and the same thread permeates individual beads having characteristics of their own that differentiate the one from the other. 'It is because of this difference in the adjuncts that each *Jīva* exists and functions as a separate unit of action and centre of experience'[1]. The Advaita Vedānta proves on the basis of Scriptural evidence that there is no plurality[2] of souls as such, but rather unity in diversity[3], as the self (*Jīva*) is no other than *Brahman* itself[4]. Hence, "the *Jīva qua* self should be reckoned not as a separate real entity different from *Brahman*, but as *Brahman* itself"[5].

What is true of the individual Self (*Jīva*) is true of the Universal Self (*Īśvara*) at a higher level. "*Īśvara* or God is the personal aspect of impersonal *Brahman*. As *Saguṇa Brahman*, He is the abode of all good qualities (*aśeṣakalyāṇaguṇa-saṁpanna*). He is the perfect-personality. He is the material cause (Upādāna

Kāraṇa) as well as the efficient cause (*Nimitta Kāraṇa*) of this Universe, consisting of individual selves (*Jīva*-s) and the objective world"[6]. As he is the Lord of *Māyā*, the covering or concealing power (*āvaraṇa-śakti*) of *Māyā* cannot operate on him and does not therefore conceal his nature. He controls the projecting power (*vikṣepa-śakti*) of *Māyā* through which He appears as the individual selves and the objective world[7].

The Jīva is said to possess three bodies – causal, subtle, gross. "The causal body of the *Jīva* is Nescience, and as qualified by that body, it is known as *prājña*. The causal body (*kāraṇa-śarīra*) is so called because, as a particular aspect of *Prakṛti* which is the parent of the subtle and gross bodies, etc., it is the cause (*kāraṇa*), and because it is destroyed (*śīryate*) by true knowledge"[8]. "The subtle body (*sūkṣma-śarīra*) consists of the five organs of sense, the five of action, the five vital airs, mind and intellect. From the *tamas*-predominant *prakṛti* the five great elements, viz., ether, air, fire, water and earth spring forth. From the *sattva*-parts of these five elements are born respectively the five organs of sense; and those parts together produce the internal organ, which owing to a difference in function is divided into mind (*manas*) that deliberates, and intellect (*buddhi*) that decides"[9]. "From the *rajas*-parts of the five elements are created respectively the five organs of action; and from them as a collective whole the five vital airs are derived. These seventeen factors go to make up the subtle body of the *Jīva* which, as having conceit therein, comes to be called *taijasa*"[10]. "The gross body (*sthūla-śarīra*) of the *Jīva* is its particular physical frame which is a composite of the quintuplicated elements. When the *Jīva* has conceit in its physical body, it is called *viśva*"[11]. "Thus the three forms of the *Jīva* are conditioned by the three vestures it wears. There is also another way of characterizing the three forms of the *Jīva*. The *pāramārthika* (absolute) Self is the substrate of the subtle and gross bodies. The *prātibhāsika* (apparent) Self is the subject of the dream world. And the *vyāvahārika* (empirical) self is the agent and enjoyer of the waking experience"[12]. 'The subject element in *Jīva* is *Sākṣin* (witness) which is Pure Consciousness and is identical with *Brahman*. Hence *Īśvara*, *Sākṣin* and *Jīva* are in fact non-different from *Brahman*, their apparent difference is due to their association with *Māyā* or

Avidyā in different degrees, and this association too is finally unreal as the fact of illusion is also illusory. The phenomenal character of God is realized when *Brahman* is directly experienced, and then there is neither *Īśvara*, nor *Jīva*, nor the world[13]. The law of causation applies wholly to the empirical creation, whereby there are numerous appearances simultaneously or successively from one and the same reality through *Avidyā*'. As per this law, destruction or dissolution would be the merging back of the effects into their respective causes. The same applies to all empirical materials also, "which seem to come into and pass out of existence sooner or later"[14]. 'Thus all things, when destroyed, revert to their own basic substances, that is, their respective causes, after having existed for some time as diverse appearances thereof and concealing or enshrouding them for a shorter or longer period of time but not for ever. In the last analysis, however, the ultimate basis, common cause or underlying essence of all evolutes or appearances cannot but be admitted to be one only, which has no further cause of its own and is not, therefore, an appearance of anything else, and as such it must be only one and unrelated. This ultimate cause is the reality proper, which, unrealized on account of *Avidyā* and, as appearing in and through the latter and its modifications, gives rise to appearances of an unending diversity, i.e., empirical entities of the universe and thereby of further illusions also. So the one way of explaining the appearance of the universe and its undeniable producibility and perishability sooner or later in consonance with its nature, analogous to that of illusions, is to hold all empirical entities to be so many diverse appearances of only one Reality, which is technically known in Advaita terminology as *Brahman*. From the stand-point of *Avidyā*, this one Reality may be envisaged to be the ultimate cause of the universe only so long as appearing in and through it, but from the stand-point of Itself, It is One, Undifferentiated and Unrelated unity, Pure Being or bare Essence (all others being its various appearances in the empirical order and unexceptionally unreal as such in the true sense of Reality)[15].

Since the Ultimate Reality or Principle, i.e. *Brahman*, and the world stand in the relation of the Real and the '*apparent*', whereby the latter is the effect of the former, it becomes imperative that the nature of this relationship be examined in the light of Advaita Vedānta. The followers of Śaṅkara have given different explanations for the relationship subsisting between the Self and the not-Self and its nature, which may be conveniently classified under three schools, viz. (i) *Ābhāsa- vāda* (the Theory of Appearance), (ii) *Pratibimba-vāda* (the Theroy of Reflection) and (iii) *Avaccheda-vāda* (the Theory of Limitation).

Ābhāsa-vāda

According to Sureśvara, the main exponent of *Ābhāsa-vāda*, 'the universe with all its phenomenal truths or pseudo-realities is as much appearances as illusions, but with this difference that the former are *primary appearances* and as such "recognized" to be "real"; while the latter are *secondary appearances* and as such are considered to be 'unreal ordinarily' even in the realm of relativity of the plane of phenomenalism. Just as to a man in a state of trance certain appearances are known as real, while these same apearances are known to him as illusory in the normal state of mind, in like manner the phenomenal appearances or pseudo-reals of the universe seem to be real for all intents and purposes to the *Avidyā*-ridden person (i.e., *Jīva*), but cease to appear as real to the same (*Jīva*) on the realization of the Absolute Reality (i.e. *Brahman*), which instantaneously sublates *Avidyā* and all that it projects and entails. 'The *Primordial Appearance*, immured in *Avidyā*, is the perennial source or inexhaustible medium of all other *manifold Appearances*, answering to the multiple modifications or possible projections of *Avidyā*. *Avidyā* is both the *modifying medium* and the *effectuating principle*. It is the energising power and the diversifying force responsible for eliciting diverse *Appearances* from the Absolute Reality, corresponding and suitable to itself and its multifarious modifications. *Avidyā* and its innumerable modifications serve as the various backgrounds, receptacles and media of the said *Reality-Appearances* and thus account for diversities or innumerable varieties of the universe. In other words, Reality as appearing primarily and directly or indirectly in *Avidyā* and its numerous modifications constitutes the backbone of all further outer appearances. These *original Appearances* of Reality ensconced in their *receptacles* (i.e. *Avidyā* and its manifold modifications), emerge into further outer and fresh appearances, diversely known as phenomenal or empirical entities and into still further ones, recognized as illusions. These *animating Appearances* are, so to say, the 'Elixir of Life' and the sustaining power, so far as *Avidyā* and its modifications are concerned in as much as they enliven and sustain their said receptacles or backgrounds. It is they, which ceaselessly bubble out into pseudo-realities in multifarious forms over the calm and constant bottom of the Absolute Reality. They together with their media and receptacles, (i.e. *Avidyā* and its manifold modifications), bolster up *de novo* appearances that collectively constitute what is denoted by the term 'universe', ordinarily differentiated into animate and inanimate, real and illusory, etc. Thus every object of the universe is a *de novo* appearance of the Ultimate Reality, the *Brahman*, through the said process and all causal factors and conditions involved in various forms in the evolution of manifold appearances are summed up in one term, i.e., *Avidyā*[16].

The *Ābhāsa-vāda* described above, is distinguishable from the other two schools in a number of ways. '*Pratibimba* or reflectional appearance is taken to be identical with the *prototype*, i.e. the *Bimba*, and hence as much real as the Original. And in the case of an *Avaccheda*, i.e. 'limitary appearance', only limitation is conceptual and unreal, but what comes to appear as limited is essentially unlimited and real. *Ābhāsa*, i.e., a seeming appearance on the other hand, is *neither identical with the underlying reality nor is itself real* in any sense. What appears through the reflection of Reality in *Avidyā* and its modifications is essentially nothing but Reality Itself, but what emerges from the Appearance of Reality in and through *Avidyā* is not Reality Itself but something *de novo* inexplicably elicited therefrom and appearing to be an established fact or a veritable entity only until the realization of Reality. It is an apparent and fresh eventuation or externalisation lasting upto realization of Reality. Reflection is real substantially all the time, but appears to be unreal on account of (it) being misjudged as distinct from its original, while appearance proper is at no time real (considered from the standpoint of Reality), but, being a further and fresh elicitation from Reality (it) *appears* to be as good as real. Thus production or manifestation is only an apparent emanation of something indescribable from Reality through *Avidyā* and destruction or termination is either submergence and absorption thereof into its said source of appearances or sublation of all appearances once for ever instantaneously on the realization of Reality respectively as it is either the case of Dissolution or that of Emancipation (i.e., *Pralaya or Mukti*)"[17].

Pratibimba-vāda

The theory of *Pratibimba-vāda* (theory of Reflection as referred to above), advocated by Padmapāda, Prakāśātman and others of the Vivaraṇa School, 'seeks to establish the undivided oneness of the Absolute by showing that the relation between the Absolute and the selves is like that of the original (i.e. the Prototype or *Bimba*) and its reflection. "To put it in other words, just as the original appears as separate and distinct from itself by way of reflection, in the same way the Absolute when reflected in the numerous adjuncts (*upādhi*-s) in the form of intellects, said to be the modifications of *Ajñāna* (*Avidyā*, Nescience), appears as many individual selves". "Madhusūdana Sarasvatī drives this point home more effectively when he urges upon us to clearly understand, by the example of face and its reflection in the mirror, that self and *Brahman* are identical. Those who admit that there is difference between the face and its reflection in the mirror explain their point of view with the example of *Caitra* and his shadow. They further clarify that it is evident to the person who is sitting near, that his (Caitra's) face and the reflection in the mirror are distinct. Moreover, even in the absence of any other person sitting near, the distinction between the original and its reflection becomes evident to the person himself when he takes into consideration his own hand and its reflection in the mirror. Madhusūdana Sarasvatī does not accept it and points out that the difference between the original and its reflection is apparent, and not real. He further points out that, if it were scrutinized closely, it would become absolutely clear that it is due to the mirror that the face is superimposed on it or that the face occasions its own reflection in the mirror. It is the experience of one and all that everybody understands and says that it (reflection) is the same as the original (face, in the present case). In this way when the point at issue is investigated properly, it becomes crystal clear that the original and its reflection are not essentially different and it is on this basis that the analogy of the original and its reflection is offered to establish the indentify of the self with Absolute"[18].

Avaccheda-vāda

"The limitation-theory (*Avacchedavāda*) as propounded by Vācaspati Miśra is also an attempt to establish that self is none but the Absolute. As per this view, the One Undivided and Unlimited Ultimate Reality comes to be viewed as limited on account of different limiting adjuncts (*upādhi-s*). It is based on the pot-space analogy. The space in a pot and (the) space (outside) are interlocked in a relation of identity with each other. In a similar way the relation between the individual self and the Absolute is that of identity. The individual self is not a part or modification of the Ultimate (Self) just as the pot space cannot be termed as a part or modification of space"[19].

"The individual self gets its name because of the body in the same manner as the pot-space gets its name on account of the pot. Śaṅkara uses this analogy as if to clarify the point at issue. He says that it is due to adjuncts that the Absolute is said to give rise to the emergence of many individual selves just as different parts of space are apparently perceived to arise when space is limited by pots, etc. and dissolved back into space when pots, etc. disappear. What is worth noticing in the illustration is that space is held to be the cause in both the situations. In this way *Avacchedavāda*, too, seeks to demonstrate that the Absolute is One Undivided Whole and the apparent emergence of many selves is due to numerous limitors in the form of *Upādhi-s* (adjuncts) which are said to be the modifications of *Avidyā*"[20].

I. The Bhāmatī's concept of Jīva, Īśvara and Jagat

The notion of individual self (*Jīva*) emanates from the mutual superimposition of the Self on the not-Self and of the not-Self (the mind-sense-body-complex) on the Self (*Brahman*) as has already been discussed. This superimposition which has *Avidyā* (Nescience) as its essence, results in the empirical experience of "I"-ness (*ahaṁpratyaya*), which in turn is the cause of agency, enjoyership, etc.[21] Expatiating on the concept "I", Vācaspati Miśra says that, "that in which the psychosis, the concept "I" occurs, i.e., the internal organ, that is the denotation of the concept "I" (*ahaṁpratyayin*); that is superimposed on the inner Self, which on account of its intelligence and indifference, is the witness of the processes of the internal organ"[22].

Vācaspati says further that "the inner self defined by the internal organ, etc., the intelligent being compounded of the "this" and the "not-this", is the *Jīva,* the agent, the enjoyer, the support of the two kinds of Nescience—the result and the cause, —the substrate "I"-ness, the transmigrator, the vessel of the entire host of woes, the material cause of reciprocal superimposition; the material cause of that again is superimposition"[23].

It is quite significant that the *Bhāmatī* considers *Jīva* to be the support of the two kinds of Nescience–*Māyā* and *Avidyā,* for it is only the *Jīva*-s that are at the mercy of the concealing and projecting powers of Nescience which render them finite (though only apparently). *Īśvara,* as will be seen, is not swayed by Nescience, being itself the 'Lord" of Nescience. *Māyā* indeed operates at the empirical level through its dual potencies at the behest of *Īśvara,* resulting in the apparent plurality of souls. The *Jīva-s* therefore, owe their individuality to Nescience operating under the "Lordship" of *Īśvara*[24]. As to the (wrong) notion that self (*Jīva*) is finite, etc., Vācaspati says that this is due to the apprehension of non-difference between the self and not-self, i.e., the mind-sense-body-complex, just as space is cognized as finite when it is apprehended as (apparently) limited by pot, ewer, basin, etc[25]. Throwing further light on the nature of the individuality of the soul, i.e. of *Jīva,* the *Bhāmatī* declares that though the inner-self (*Brahman*) is self-manifest, and hence, cannot be an object of cognition, yet as *Jīva,* it appears as though limited by the qualities superimposed by indeterminable and beginningless Nescience, such as intellect, mind, body, senses, etc. In like manner though undifferentiated, it appears as differentiated; though not an agent, it appears as an agent; though not enjoyer, it appears as enjoyer; though not an object, it apears as an object of the "I" -cognition. And this happens in the same manner as space appears differentiated by the adjuncts such as pot, ewer, basin, etc. though in reality it is devoid of any such differences[26].

Vācaspati says furthermore, that even when at the empirical

level intelligence is apprehended, nothing at the Absolute level remains unapprehended as such, the self being the very essence of Intelligence. It cannot also be said (of the *Jīva*) that on the apprehension of its intelligence, its other (essential) qualities such as Bliss, eternality, pervasiveness, etc. remain unapprehended, for, in reality, these qualities are not different from (i.e. are non-differentiable) from Its essence of Intelligence. Though apprehended, yet, because of superimposed differences or adjuncts, they appear to be non-discriminated, and therefore, non-apprehended.[27]

It is moreover claimed by the *Bhāmatī* that the difference existing between the self and the intellect, etc. cannot be said to be real, so that on the apprehension of the Intelligent self that difference too is apprehended. For in effect, the intellect, etc. (i.e. not-Self) being indeterminable, the difference subsisting between the self and the not-Self also is indeterminable (it being an effect of indeterminable Nescience). (The apprehension of difference between the self and the not-Self would imply the reality of both the Self and the not-Self, which would be in violation of the Advaitic doctrine of one Reality)[28]. Unravelling the link (of identity) existing between the inner-Self, the individual self (*Jīva*) and the "I"-cognition, Vācaspati claims that it is the Intelligent Self itself that, owing to the non-apprehension of the difference between Its real nature (of "Self-manifest", "Undefined", etc.) and the mind-sense-body-complex, appears as the finite *Jīva* as a result of superimposition on It of the attributes of the intellect, etc. The consequence of this is the appearance of the Self as the "object" of the "I"-cognition, though It is itself of the nature of "not-this", i.e. non-object. The outcome of this (superimposition of the "not-this", on the "this", and the non-apprehension of difference therein) is the appearance of the intelligent Self as agent and enjoyer in the "I"-cognition[29]. The *Jīva*, says the *Bhāmatī*, cannot as such possess the potency to act or to enjoy, being in essence the Inner Self which is indifferent to activity and enjoyment. The capacities of agency and enjoyership *per se* belong to the not-Self, to the intellects, to the mind-sense-body-complex, which do not have intelligence as their essence. And since activity, enjoyership, etc. requires intelligence, it can therefore be inferred that the potencies to act, to enjoy, etc. are superimposed on the individual self due to it being associated with the complex of mind-sense body. It is thus that the self, though self-manifest, yet due to its being confused with objects such as the intellect, etc., becomes cognizable as the object of the "I"-cognition, which is the substrate of "I" -ness. It is hence that the self becomes known as *Jīva* or *Jantu* (creature, or still as *Kṣetrajña* (the "knower of the field"). It is therefore evident that the *Jīva* is not different from the Intelligent Self, but is the Intelligent Self in *reality*. This fact has for support the Scriptures which declare" ... in its own nature as that Jīva", etc. Thus, has it been shown that though self-manifest it being non-different from the Self, the *Jīva* is rendered "fit for empirical usage as agent and enjoyer by the "I"-cognition. And consequent upon this, the *Jīva* is erroneously said to be the substrate of the "I"-cognition.[30]

Discarding an objection with regard to the fallacy of reciprocal dependence between *Jīva*-hood and superimposition, Vācaspati clarifies that the process of objectification of the self being the effect of superimposition, and the objectification of the self being the cause of superimposition, as is the case with the seed and the sprout, it cannot be said that the theory suffers from the fallacy of reciprocal dependence, this being a beginningless process. Furthermore, says Vācaspati there is no inconsistency in holding that every subsequent superimposition has for its object that which was the content of each earlier superimposition and its impressions (*vāsanā-s*), for this has been indicated by the Commentator (Śaṅkara) himself in the text - "this natural empirical usage (*naisargiko' yam lokavyavahāraḥ*)". It is therefore settled that the self (*Jīva*) is apprehensible as an object (of cognition) while in its conditioned form, though it is essentially intelligent and self-manifest, being non-different from the Intelligent-self[31].

Justifying the Advaitic doctrine that *Brahman*, though One and Immutable, appears as many (in the form of individual souls), Śaṅkara says that, "Just as, at the empirical level it is found that though stones possess the common attribute of having been formed from earth, yet there is a great diversity among them (in colour and shape and value), ..., or just as .... though all seeds grow on the same soil, yet there is a great variety in their leaves, flowers, fruits, colour, taste, etc., ..., or just as from the same chyle originate different products like blood, etc., so it is justifiable even for the Non-dual *Brahman* to have such distinctions as becoming the embodied soul (s) and God, and the different products (of the material world, like earth, etc.)"[32]. And this is backed by Scriptural authority, such as, "The modifications have speech alone as their origin"– ("…. *vācāraṁbhaṇaṁ vikāro nāmadheyaṁ….* ")–(Ch. UP. VI. 1.4)[33].

As Vācaspati is in agreement with Śaṅkara on this point, he simply observes that should the world be taken to be an actual transformation of *Brahman* (*Vivarta*), then like the *Jīva*-s, everything else (i.e. even the insentient objects) would be intelligent (i.e., conscious)[34].

The individual souls, says Śaṅkara owe their birth and death, etc. to God (*Parameśvara*) who is invested with *Brahman's* power of *Māyā*. The state of *Jīva* is compared by him to a kind of "deep slumber in which the transmigrating souls sleep without being conscious of their real nature. The individuality of the *Jīva*-s is due to the influence of *Māyā* which is also known as *Avyakta* and which acts as a limiting adjunct. Śaṅkara observes further that *Māyā* or *Avyakta* is of the nature of Ignorance, and it is because of the possession of this ignorance by the individual souls that all kinds of empirical behaviour continue for ever. Liberation, therefore, is possible only when the potential power of *Māyā* is burnt away by knowledge[35].

Vācaspati notes on this that the *Advaitin-s* do not hold that there is only One Nescience (*Avidyā*) at the base of all the *Jīva*-s, but rather one *Avidyā* at the base of each *Jīva*. Hence, the liberation of one *Jīva* on his attaining knowledge, does not entail the liberation of the rest. He says further that this doctrine does not suffer from the fallacy of reciprocal dependence by arguing that the distinctness of the *Jiva*-s is due to the adjuncts of *Avidyā* and the adjuncts of *Avidyā* are dependent on the distinctness of the *Jiva*-s; for both are beginningless like seed and sprout[36]. According to Vācaspati, *Avidyā*, the substrate of the individuality of the soul, is dependent on *Īśvara* either as the efficient cause thereof or as object; in the same manner, *Īśvara* is the material cause of the world-illusion, just as rope is the material cause of the snake-illusion. This is so, says Vācaspati, because the insentient cannot, on its own, be active without being dependent (for its activity) on the sentient; hence, its dependence on *Īśvara*, either because of *Īśvara* being its efficient cause or its material cause, for *Īśvara* is verily the substrate of the world-illusion, just as rope is the substrate of the snake-illusion[37].

Citing the views of Kāśakṛtsna, Śaṅkara says that the Supreme Self Himself appears as the individual soul-s without undergoing any transformation. And this, says Śaṅkara, "is in accord with the Upaniṣads, for it agrees with the instruction sought to be imparted, as stated in such texts as, "That Thou Art", and from this standpoint, (of non-difference), the attainment of immortality as a result of the Knowledge of the Self is quite in order"[38]. Śaṅkara observes further that should the individual soul be taken to be created, then the Scriptural assertion of the attainment of immortality through Knowledge of the Supreme Self would become meaningless, because 'the modification of a substance loses itself on merging into its material cause. Moreover, says Śaṅkara, name and form cannot be the "natural appendages of the individual soul, for, in reality, name and form belong to the limiting adjuncts". This is why, continues Śaṅkara, the allusion made in the Upaniṣads to the origin of the individual soul, while referring to the simile of sparks darting out of fire, should be understood as referring to the adjuncts alone, and not to the *Jiva*-s as such[39].

Throwing more light on the *Jīva-Brahman* identity described above by Śaṅkara, Vācaspati says that there is no indication whatsoever in the Scriptures with regard to the creation of the *Jīva-s* in the same way as fire is described as being an evolute (of Prakṛti). He maintains that there is no relation of cause and effect between *Jīva* and *Brahman*. The *Jīva-Brahman*-absolute-identity being real, the apparent difference resulting from beginningless Nescience is eradicable through True knowledge that dawns on the realization consequent upon "Listening to, Meditating upon and intense contemplation of" the Upaniṣadic teaching, "That Thou Art", just as the appearance of snake-in-rope is removed upon the dawning of the knowledge of the real nature of rope[40]. Vācaspati says further that if *Jīva* were a real transformation of *Brahman*, then as a consequence of knowledge, meditation, etc., on the *Jīva* merging back into its cause, there would subsist no hope whatsoever of its attaining immortality, defeating thus the very aim of life, and this would be in opposition also to the teaching of the Scriptures[41]. Moreover, argues the Bhāmatī, the notion of agency, etc., imposed upon *Jīva* is also amenable to cancellation owing, on the one hand, to the establishment in the Scriptures of Absolute identity, and on the other, to the negation of agency, etc., in the Scriptures, in the form of texts such as, "who is to be seen , and by whom", "The Omniscient is to be known by whom", etc[42].

In addition to this, the Bhāmatī declares that the defects such as birth, death, fear, etc., associated apparently with the individual souls, are all negated by the Scriptures in the texts, such as, "(It is) Great, Unborn, etc." And in the case of the doctrine of *Pariṇāma-vāda* also, whereby the *Jīva*-s are considered to be real transformations or transfigurations of *Brahman*, there too, the doctrine stands contradicted by Scriptural texts establishing Absolute identity of *Jīva*-s and *Brahman*, as in, "(It is) One without a Second", etc., and by other Scriptural texts condemning dualism, as in, "Anyo' anyo' sāvanyo' hamasmi", etc[43].

Emphasizing further still the oneness of the Self, Śaṅkara says that "when the full illumination about the oneness of the Supreme Self and the self witnessing the body becomes established, such terms as "the witness of the body", "the Supreme Self" betray a mere difference in terminology, and hence the insistence in the theory that this witness of the body is different from the Supreme Self and the Supreme Self is different from the "witness of the body", that centres round the idea of difference of the two selves, is meaningless.. For the Self is but One, though spoken of differently on the basis of difference in mere nomenclature. Not that the text, "*Brahman* is Truth, Knowledge, Infinite"; "He who knows that *Brahman* as existing in the cavity of the intellect" (Tai. Up. II.1), is spoken of in relation to any particular cavity; nor does anything else but *Brahman* exist in the cavity (of the intellect) since we hear of the entry of the Creator Himself, in text such as, "Having created that, He entered into that" (Tai. Up. II.6). Those who insist on difference shut the door to the understanding of the purport of the Upaniṣads and thereby shut out full illumination itself that leads to Liberation"[44].

Commenting on the nature of *Jīva-Brahman*-identity referred to above, Vācaspati says, using the example of reflection, that just as the reflections of one clear object appear variegated due to intervening adjuncts despite the identity of the object and the reflections, in the same may the *Jīva-s* too, though non-different from *Brahman*, appear differentiated due to intervening adjuncts such as the intellect, etc. In the same manner (may be explained), says Vācaspati, in spite of the absolute non-difference between the Essentially Pure Supreme Being and the *Jīva-s*, the *Jīva-s* appear to be different from *Brahman* due to the intervening influence of indeterminable and beginningless Nescience, and consequently there are empirical usages of the like, "The Supreme Being is Pure, Intelligence, Bliss and these *Jīva*-s are subjected to ignorance, grief, suffering"[45].

Elucidating the nature of the individuality of *Jīva*, Vācaspati says that just as, with regard to the (one) object jewels, swords, etc., are "caves" (*guhā-s*), in like manner, with regard to the one *Brahman*, the *Avidyā* subsisting in each individual *Jīva* is the cave. Just as the one object though non-different from the reflections, appears hidden in them (and is therefore apparently unknown), in the same manner, though One and Non-different from the *Jīva-s*, the one *Brahman* appears 'hidden" in them all (and remains therefore apparently unknown (to them)[46].

The Bhāmatī, following Śaṅkara, propounds the doctrine of non-ephemerality of the *Jīva-s* and declares that the *Jīva-s* are not affected at all by birth, death, etc., which in reality, affect only the body, not the soul. Vācaspati says in this context that the nomenclature "Devadatta", etc., cannot be said to apply to the soul, for were it so, then in the case of 'Devadatta' being born or being dead, the association with him of the fruits of (his) actions, such as heaven, etc, as promised by the Scriptures, would be impossible, thus rendering ineffective the Scriptural claim to that effect. Moreover, says Vācaspati, the Purificatory acts, such as *Jātakarma*, etc., are not meant for the removal of impurities associated with the *Jīva*, but rather for the removal of impurities associated with the body, as is declared by the 'Smṛti-s', "Thus is destroved the sin arising from birth, ...etc." It is thus established, says the Bhāmatī, that the *Jīva-s* are neither born nor do they die with the birth or death of the body[47].

Strengthening further its position on the question of non-origination of the *Jīva-s*, the Bhāmatī declares that the *Jīva-s* could have been said to originate like space, etc., if only they were any different from *Brahman*. But the fact is that they are non-different from *Brahman*, as is established by the Scriptures. Due also to the fact that differences are dependent on adjuncts, as is to be seen in the case of the origination of pot, cup, etc., the *Jīva*-s cannot be said to be associated with birth, death, etc. On account also of the repeated declarations in the Scriptures of the eternality of the soul-s, and due to Scriptural declarations, such as, "The one God is present... in all created beings", it is therefore settled that the *Jīva*-s are not evolutes, and neither does the Advaitic doctrine suffer from any contradiction in this regard[48].

Refuting the views that *Jīva* is of atomic size etc., Śaṅkara says that it has already been stated that *Jīva* is but the Highest *Brahman*, because there is no mention in the Scriptures about its creation and because the Scriptures declare that *Brahman* Itself entered (the created entities such as the *Jīva*), and also because of the instruction that there is complete identity (of *Jīva* and *Brahman*). If *Jīva* is the Highest *Brahman*, then it should be of the same size as that of the Highest-*Brahman*, and as the Highest *Brahman* has been declared by the Scriptures to be All-pervading, *Jīva*, therefore, cannot but be all-pervading as well[49].

The Bhāmatī says on its part that were the *Jīva-s* of atomic size, the experience of cold, pain etc., by it throughout the body would not be possible. Only the all-pervading *Jīva* can experience cold, pain, etc., throughout the body through the sense of touch when the skin comes into contact with cold-water, etc. But the *Jīva* of limited-size would be able to experience cold, etc., at only that spot in the body where it is located, not throughout the body, due to such *Jīva* not pervading the whole body[50].

Vācaspati says further, that the association of the feelings of desire, hatred, etc., with the *Jīva*-s, also cannot be said to be natural, for the *Jīva*-s, being of the nature of *Brahman*, are unattached and eternal. This association (of the feelings of desire, hatred, etc.) is in effect the result of the superimposition on the *Jīva*-s of the attributes of the intellect, etc., due to non-apprehension of difference, just as through the reflection of the moon in the water contained in a jar, the moon is identified with the water-in-jar, so that when the water gets agitated there is the erroneous cognition that the moon is shivering. In the same way, the alleged atomic size of the *Jīva*-s is but the result of superimposition on the *Jīva*-s of the attribute of atomicity of the intellect, etc., just as a multitude of size and form is superimposed on space due to intervening adjuncts in the form of pots, etc[51].

Śaṅkara says at this point that it is necessary to consider, with regard to agentship etc., of the *Jīva*-s which depends on the limiting adjuncts under the influence of Nescience, whether the *Jīva*-s are independent or whether they are dependent on *Īśvara.* Śaṅkara says that during the condition of Nescience, when the *Jīva*-s are blinded by the darkness of ignorance, and are unable to distinguish themselves from the mind-sense-body-complex, this transmigratory existence, characterized by the *Jīva*-s being agents and experiencers, deserves to be the result as sanctioned by *Īśvara* who resides in all beings, presides over all their actions, is the immediate witness of everything, and quickens intelligence in everybody, resulting in Final Release by means of True knowledge'[52]. Śaṅkara says further that 'though the *Jīva*-s are contaminated with faults and are equipped with all the necessary paraphernalia of means, and though in the ordinary world it is not seen that *Īśvara* is the means or cause of such activities as agricultural pursuits, etc., yet it is conclusively understood from the Scriptures that *Īśvara* is the motivating cause of all tendencies of the *Jīva*-s'[53].

The Bhāmatī observes in this context that it is not proper to hold *Īśvara* responsible for engaging the *Jīva*-s in agentship etc. when this can be conveniently attributed to passion, etc., which is of the nature of action-instigating. *Īśvara* also cannot be said to be responsible for engaging the *Jīva*-s in good and bad actions, for He being Just, Compassionate and Impartial, would rather cause all the *Jīva*-s to engage in righteous acts alone, not in unrighteous acts, and consequently the *Jīva*-s so engaged would all be righteous and therefore happy, and none would be miserable. On the other hand, left to their own care, the *Jīva*-s would engage themselves in righteous and unrighteous actions impelled by their own passion, etc., leading thus to the experience by them of manifoldness in the world. This would also take care of the meaningfulness of Vedic Injunctions and Prohibitions which, if otherwise the *Jiva*-s were to be dependent on *Īśvara* for their actions, would fall into disutility[54].

Further to the discussion on the relation obtaining between *Jīva* and *Īśvara*, the Bhāmatī proceeds with a discussion on the relation subsisting between *Jīva* and *Brahman*. Refuting the view that *Jīva*-s are "*limbs*" or *parts* (*aṁśa*) of *Brahman*, the Bhāmatī says that it is not proper to assign to *Jīva-Brahman* a relationship of Master and servant or of controller and controlled or still of substrate and object, etc., there being a relationship of identity and non-difference of *Jīva* and *Brahman*[55].

Vācaspati notes moreover that if the *Jīva*-s were to be regarded as 'limbs' or 'parts' of *Brahman*, then all their sufferings would be those of *Brahman*, just as the pain occurring in Devadatta's foot, etc. is said to occur to him. In this eventuality, when on attaining release, the *Jīva*-s would attain *Brahman*, they would inherit sufferings etc., and in that conjuncture it would be better for them, says Vācaspati, to stay in the world itself after Liberation. For, while in the world, they would experience their own sufferings only, not the accumulation of sufferings of other *Jīva*-s as well, as would be the case in *Brahman*. Would result also from such a situation the futility of attaining Liberation itself[56].

The Bhāmatī gives another reason for the rejection of the theory of 'parts and whole' relationship between the *Jīva*-s and *Brahman* and for the claim of a relationship of identity-cum-difference between the *Jīva*-s and *Brahman*. Vācaspati says that the means of knowledge, specially Verbal Authority, are meant for the cognition of the hitherto unknown thing. And difference (between *Jīva* and *Brahman*) being known already to everyone cannot be the object of cognition of Verbal Authority. As for non-difference, that being unknown, it is fit to be made known on the basis of what is known already in the form of difference. The Upaniṣads are therefore seen in this context to preach non-duality from the beginning till the end, establishing that the *Jīva*-s though non-different from *Brahman*, appear different from it due to the adjunct of the indeterminable and beginningless Nescience, in the same way as reflections appear different from the "prototype" due to the intervening adjuncts in the form of mirror, etc[57].

Vācaspati observes in conclusion that Liberation also cannot be said to be meaningless for, just as reflections are apparently endowed with qualities such as blackness, brightness, etc., in like manner, the *Jīva*-s are associated with sufferings of all kinds, while *Brahman* is absolutely free from any such defects, very much like the "spotless prototype". Furthermore, just as on the removal of the mirror the reflections merge back into the original object, and not in the sword, etc., in the same manner, on the removal of the adjunct of Nescience the *Jīva*-s are one with *Brahman*. Thus is established the fact that the *Jīva-s* are like the parts of *Brahman*, not parts *per se*[58].

II. The Vivaraṇa's concept of Jīva, Īśvara and Jagat

Like the Bhāmatī school the Vivaraṇa school also subscribes to the view that *Jīva* is identical with *Brahman*, and that the manifestation of difference being the effect of Nescience, is unreal and contrary to the nature of Consciousness. Just as the moon though one is apprehended as double due to the influence of visual defects, etc., *Brahman* also, though one, appears as many in the form of *Jīva-s* due to the influence of the adjuncts of Nescience. The illustration of the double-moon, says Padmapāda, is used to point out that the (appearance of) difference between *Jīva* and *Brahman*, between *Jīva* and *Īśvara*, and between *Jīva* and *Jīva* is false[59].

[It is worthy of note here that the double-moon-illusion is known as "*sopādhikādhyāsa*", while that of the shell-silver is known as "*nirūpādhikādhyāsa*". While "*nirupādhikādhyāsa*" disappears the moment True Knowledge is achieved, "*sopādhikādhyāsa*" persists even after the dawning of True Knowledge, until the removal of the adjuncts (*upādhi*)][60].

Padmapāda says that if the *Jīva-Brahman*-identity is not admitted, then *Jīva* being distinct from *Brahman*, and being of finite intelligence, the concealing effect of *Avidyā* described in the Scriptures would become meaningless, and so would be the Scriptural teaching of identity (*tādātmyopadeśa*). It has, therefore, to be admitted that *Brahman*, of the nature of "'homogeneous consciousness", is the substratum of the appearance of innumerable *Jīva*-s which are under the influence of beginningless Nescience[61].

Thus conditioned by *Avidyā*, says Padmapāda, the *Jīva*, though non-different from *Brahman*, fails to discover its real nature. It is, therefore, said in the Scriptures that, "when the *Jīva* is awakened from the sleep of the beginningless *Māyā*, it understands itself to be the unborn, the ever-awake, the dreamless, the 'one without a second'–(Gauḍapāda-Kārikā, VII.16)[62].

Prakāśātman observes in this connection that it is the concealing potency of Nescience that is verily the material cause of the appearance of *Jīva-Brahman*-difference while it is the (individual)*Ajñāna* which is the efficient cause of the particularization of the *Jīva*-s. He says that since the bifurcation of the "partless" *Brahman* is not permissible, the association of agentship, etc, with *Jīva*-s having been shown to be the beginningless succession of superimposition, its material cause i.e., Nescience, also is ought to be beginningless, as the seed and the sprout-relationship. And the cause of the beginningless appearance of difference is also the beginningless Nescience (*Avidyā*), not the intellect, etc[63(i)]. The Vivaraṇa is of the view that *Avidyā* itself has to be postulated as the cause of the superimposition of plurality on the Supreme Soul through its 'concealing' potency. Otherwise on admitting the contrary characteristics, only the absence of apprehension would result, there being no instance of the one Omniscient, self-luminous *Brahman*[63(ii)].

The Vivaraṇa says that due to *Brahman* being impartible, the difference appearing between *Jīva* and *Brahman* cannot be ascribed to the relationship of 'parts and whole'. Consequently, *Avidyā* has to be admitted as constituting the efficient cause of appearance of difference[64].

As to the question concerning the basis on which *Avidyā* functions as the efficient cause, the Vivaraṇa holds the view that just as in the case of the reflection in the mirror the face serves as the basis, in the same manner, *Brahman* Itself is the basis for the functioning of *Avidyā* as the efficient cause of empirical difference between *Jīva* and *Brahman*[65].

Elaborating on the nature of *Jīva-Brahman*-relationship in further detail, Padmapāda says that, as regards the illustration of the reflection of the face in the mirror as well as of the moon in water, what is intended to be brought home is the fact that the 'not-this' (*Jīva*), as expressed in the cognition 'I am doer' etc., is an entity not distinct from *Brahman* but on the contrary it is That (*Brahman*) Itself, just as the reflected image is not distinct from the prototype. It is to point out that in the case of the mirror, the only elements to be regarded as illusory are their appearance as two distinct entities (i.e. the reflection as distinct from the prototype), and appearance as being contrariwise (i.e., the prototype and the reflection appearing (as) opposite to each other)[66]. Padmapāda, answering an objection as to the proof of identity therein, says that the reflection is known to be the same as the object (reflected) because of the cognition of the essentially identical object. For example, just as Devadatta is found inside his house with the same individual traits with which he is found outside (the house), in like manner, it is a matter of common experience that the Devadatta reflected in the mirror is the same as the one outside the mirror. If it were a different object, then the recognition of the reflection as identical to the object outside would be unintelligible. It cannot also be said that the mirror itself underwent a transformation caused by the vicinity of the object, for in such an instance, the thus transformed mirror would remain the same (i.e. the reflection would persist) even on the removal of the object[67].

Padmapāda gives another reason to prove the identity of the object and its reflection, and that is the non-sublation of the image. Reacting to an objection to the effect that sublation of the reflection (*Jīva*) is evident in the *Mahā-vākya*, "Tat Tvamasi" (That Thou Art), he says that what is intimated in the *Mahā-vākya* is that the reflection (*pratibimba*) in the form of *Jīva* is of the same nature as the object in the (*bimba*) form of *Brahman*. Otherwise, says he, the teaching of the Upaniṣad would have been 'thou art not", like 'silver is not", instead of "That Thou Art", were there any sublation[68].

Reacting to the assertion that just as even when the identity of the reflection with the prototype is cognized the erroneous manifestation of separateness, etc., persists, in the same manner, even on the cognition of the *Jīva-Brahman*-identity, the erroneous manifestation of separateness persists, Padmapāda says that the reason for this is that in the example given above, what is reflected is only Devatta's insentient part.... Just as the duskiness of the mirror affects the reflected.image, in the same way influenced by the inertness of the mirror, the reflection of Devadatta's face does not cognize its identity with the prototype.... this is so because the reflection cannot move without the movement of the original object[69].

The Vivaraṇa, addressing itself to the issue under discussion, says that in the cognition, "This is not silver", the very existence of silver is sublated, while in the cognition, "There is no silver here, etc.", the location only is sublated, resulting in the non-recognition of the real silver. And due to the non-recognition of silver there arises its illusory apprehension. But in the case of the reflection, there is no sublating cognition in the form, "This is not (my) face". There is rather the cognition, "This face here is not verily mine", and this is not sublated[70]. Prakāśātman says in addition that there cannot be in the mirror etc., the cognition, "This is (the face of) another person", due to the absence there of its cause, just as the hare's horn (cannot be cognized due to the absence of its cause)[71].

Padmapāda observes, furthermore, that when indeed illusion arises in a person whether concerning himself or something else, that illusion is sublatable by the right knowledge dawning on himself. Moreover, Devadatta, while understanding his identity with the reflection in the mirror etc., is unaffected however, by any defects therein. More so, the mere knowledge of identity does not for that matter sublate the reflection, its cause (i.e. the mirror) being empirically real[72].

Throwing light on this, the Vivaraṇa says that the appearance of difference is not sublated by the mere dawning of knowledge because that appearance is not a product of the reflection, but is caused rather by the adjuncts, which not being of the nature of wrong-cognition, are not sublatable by knowledge[73].

Padmapāda notes also that the *Jīva*, which may be likened to the reflection, is of the nature of '*Cit*' (Consciousness), as is known to one and all. The *Jīva*, which is not affected by the inertness of the inner sense (*antaḥkaraṇa*), considers itself to be the enjoyer, etc., but is not conscious of its oneness with *Brahman*, which is like the prototype vis-a-vis the reflection. Hence it is quite in order that the illusion should disappear on the dawning of the knowledge of its real nature, when the inertness of *antaḥkaraṇa* ceases to influence the consciousness[74].

The Vivaraṇa observes in this connection that the *Jīva* is the reflection of (and therefore identical with) Consciousness, as this is not only proclaimed by the Scriptures, but is also within the experience of one and all through direct perception. Due also to the fact that just as the formless sky together with the stars and the clouds is reflected in water and it is possible to apprehend in knee-deep water that far off and far stretched sky, in the same way the formless *Brahman* also can be reflected. It cannot be said also that it is the sky itself which is apprehended in water, with the reflections of stars and clouds etc., (this being contrary to experience)[75].

Padmapāda says that "because the *Jīva* assumes the nature of object of the "I-"cognition ("*aham-pratyaya*"), it is called by different names in the Scriptures, though it is "not-this", i.e. it is of the nature of consciousness. Conditioned as the 'ego' in the waking and dream states, and conditioned in deep sleep by Nescience, which carries the traces of its past impressions, the *Jīva* keeps "going forward and backward", and as such it is termed as *Saṁsārī, Jīva, Vijñānaghana, Vijñānātman, Kartā, Bhoktā, Kṣetrajña,* etc"[76].

Refuting the theory of Limitation, according to which Consciousness is limited or modified by *Avidyā* giving rise to the individuality of souls, Prakāśātman says that this cannot be accepted, for it implies a contravention of the principle of Omniscience and Omnipotence of *Brahman.* He asserts that if the existence of individual *Jīva*-s were to be explained by the illustration of pot-space, whereby the one undivided space is particularized due to external adjuncts such as pots, etc., then *Brahman* would have to be conceived as characterised by universal and particular adjuncts (such as *samaṣṭi* form and *vyaṣṭi* form, etc.[77]). In such an eventuality, it being the totality of all the limited *Jīva*-s, there would arise the conjuncture of the unmodified aspect of *Brahman* existing aloof of the Universe of individualized souls, whereby would set in the contradiction referred to above[78].

Prakāśātman says further that it is not plausible to conceive of the Unlimited and Unmodified *Brahman* as co-existing with the limited and modified *Jīva*-s, for that again would violate the principle of *Brahman* being the Controller of all creatures[79]. The Theory of Reflection on the other hand, says the Vivaraṇa, does not suffer from these defects. For, indeed in this case, the reflection of the sky being apprehended in its natural (i.e.

unmodified) form in water, it is feasible to conceive of both the *Jīva*-form and the *Brahman*-form of the Supreme being as existing in a single location, without violating the principle of indivisibility and All-Controllership of *Brahman*[80]. The Vivaraṇa says also that the *Jīva*-forms of *Brahman* as conditioned by adjuncts are but the result of illusion. Hence, the dissolution of individuality on the removal of the adjuncts following the dawning of True knowledge[81]. Clarifying the theory that the *Jīva-Brahman*-difference has *Avidyā* as its substrate, the Vivaraṇa says that there being Absolute non-difference between the *Jīva*-s and *Brahman* the very notion of *Avidyā* serving as the substrate of beginningless difference is but imaginary or illusory. Hence also, the plausibility of the indefinability and beginninglessness of all that have *Avidyā* as their substrate, such as the *Jīva-Brahman*-difference[82]. The Vivaraṇa says also that the fact that difference is caused by adjuncts (and is therefore not absolutely real), is illustrated by the fact that the appearance of difference between face, sky, etc. and their reflections, has mirror, water in the pot, etc., as substrates and is therefore false[83].

Some argue that the *Jīva-Brahman* relationship is one of identity-cum-difference, reports the Vivaraṇa. This being so, there is eternal non-attachment in the case of *Brahman* while in the case of *Jīva*, there is eternal attachment. This needs to be so because if *Brahman-Jīva* were to be assumed to be absolutely non-different, then it would not be possible to explain how *Brahman* would create the world with a plurality of souls. And in case of absolute difference the Pure *Brahman* would incur the defect of impurity. In reply to this argument, Prakāśātman queries as to what is the nature of this relationship of identity-cum-difference. It cannot be one of universal and particular, neither one of cause and effect, not even one of whole and part, there being none of such relationships between *Brahman* and *Jīva*[84]. It cannot also be claimed that the Scriptures themselves proclaim the theory of identity-cum-difference in such passages as, "(There is) my own part (essence) in the world of the selves", for this is contradicted by other Scriptural passages, such as, "(This *Brahman*) (is) without parts (and) without activity", etc; And also, because of the intention of indicating the limited character (of the *Jīva*-s) expressed in such passages as, "All creatures are but

His foot", etc. There is also the fact that other passages declare the eternality of *Brahman*. Were *Brahman* to be assumed as consisting of parts (in the form of the *Jīva*-s), there would arise in it the defect of origination in the same manner as cloth, etc[85].

The Vivaraṇa argues further that though *Brahman* is as per its nature partless, it cannot be said to be partitioned by adjuncts such as the intellect, etc. for then it would follow that the *Jīva*-s are created by the partition of *Brahman* by adjuncts, which is not conceivable, just as partless space is not seen to be partitioned despite its being pierced by sword, etc. Even if *Brahman* were to be conceived as creating the world (of *Jīva*-s) by the partitioning of Itself by adjuncts, it would then give rise to perplexity (*vyāmoha*) within Itself (which again would be contradictory to the fact that *Brahman* is free of all defects). It cannot also be said that the adjuncts are created through some other means, for such other means are non-existent. Due also to the 'non-otherness' of the *Jīva*-s, who, prior to getting bound in *Jīva*-hood are but one with *Brahman*[86].

Concluding the debate on the nature of *Jīva* and its relationship with *Brahman*, the Vivaraṇa raises a question as to who is this *Jīva* who is referred to figuratively by means of the term "Thou" (in "*Tat Tvam Asi*" – i.e., "That Thou Art") and which is resolved ultimately as being *Brahman* itself. The reply that Prakāśātman gives is no less emphatic : *Jīva*, says he, is but *Brahman* itself reflected in (or through) *Avidyā*[87]. Then, on the elimination of all traces of adjuncts from it, the notion "Thou", which figuratively refers to the real nature of the self, gets absorbed into *Brahman* Itself, Which is referred to by the term "That", due to the identity of meaning of both the terms[88].

Coming again to the charge, the opponent queries the *Advaitin* as to why should the (Upaniṣadic) sentence (*"Tat Tvam Asi"* - "That Thou Art"), not have as meaning identity -cum-difference, In reply, the Vivaraṇa says that this is not acceptable, because, were it so, then on the term "Thou", which has attributes such as the body, the senses, etc., being realized as having as purport the Supreme Being with which *Jīva* entertains a relationship of identity-cum-difference, there would arise the eventuality of non-sublation of superimposition even on the attainment of Right Knowledge, since the aforesaid sentence being interpreted likewise, would also culminate into identity-cum-difference[89]. Moreover, says the Vivaraṇa, in a state of identity-cum-difference, there would arise the problem of non-elimination of the element of difference even after the realization of Truth, due to the failure of True Knowledge in destroying ignorance in the form of apprehension of difference[90].

The Vivaraṇa castigates those who believe that as per the theory of identity-cum-difference, Knowledge, Liberation, etc. could be attained through identity or non-difference, while through difference, the performance of action, etc. could be entertained (for the subsequent attainment of True knowledge). In such a situation, says Prakāśātman, if the *Jīva* itself be (taken to be) the whole and to be constituted of parts, then *Brahman* would be a part of *Jīva*, which is contradictory to reality. And in the case of the non-*Brahman* (i.e., *Jīva*) itself being of the nature of non-difference, then would arise a situation of absolute difference (which would again be contradictory to reality)[91]. It cannot also be said that *Jīva* itself is the substrate of both identity and difference, says the Vivaraṇa, for this would lead to a state of unreality. And in the conjecture of *Jīva* itself being the non-different element, *Brahman* would then be reduced to the state of being a mere *Jīva*, which again would be contradictory[92].

Prakāśātman says that the propounder of the doctrine of identity-cum-difference cannot also claim that difference pertains to one *Jīva*, and non-difference to another, for this would result into the being of two kinds of *Jīva*-s, which again cannot be accepted. The *Jīva*, on the other hand, cannot be conceived of as being different from *Brahman*, for this would give rise to a situation of absolute difference resulting in the ineffectiveness of Right Knowledge, Liberation, etc.[93].

The Vivaraṇa closes this debate on the doctrine of identity-cum-difference, saying that this doctrine only appeals to the ordinary man bereft of wisdom. He says that the sentences, "This is that Devadatta" ("*So'yaṁ Devadattaḥ*"), "That Thou Art", ("*Tat Tvam Asi*") etc. establish the fact that there is only one Reality, but due to adjuncts such as name and forms, etc., as "Devadatta" etc., there is an appearance of differene, giving rise to the individuation of selves. On the realization of the falsehood of difference and on its removal through contemplation on the above-mentioned "*Mahāvākya-s*", the oneness of *Jīva-Brahman* is established, leading simultaneously to the dissolution of the adjuncts of the *Jīva*-s[94].

III. Summary

According to Advaita Vedānta, Reality is "One without a second"[95], though there is apparent plurality at the empirical level due to the concealing and projective influences of *Māyā*. Śaṅkara says that *Brahman* or *Sat* is "that entity which is mere *esse* (*astitāmātram*)—Subtle, devoid of specification, All-pervading, One, Taintless, Impartite, Consciousness, as understood from the Vedānta texts[96].

The physical world being a mere appearance of *Brahman* and having *Māyā* as its substrate, is not real, says the Advaitin. '*Brahman* and the world are related as cause and effect in the same way as rope and the illusory snake are related as cause and effect'. Advaita believes in two kinds of material cause–transformative material cause (*pariṇāmyupādāna-kāraṇa*) and transfigurative material cause (*vivartopādāna-kāraṇa*). 'While clay is the material cause of pot, etc. the latter being a real modification of the former, rope, on the other hand, is the material cause of the illusory snake, the latter being but a transfiguration of the former without its (the former) undergoing any modification whatsoever. Clay is thus the transformative cause (*pariṇāmyupādāna-kāraṇa*) of pot, etc., whereas rope is the transfigurative cause (*vivartopādāna-kāraṇa*) of the illusory snake. 'Rope, which does not undergo any change whatsoever, is said to be the substratum (*adhiṣṭhāna*) for the superimposition of the illusory snake thereon. From the Advaitic point of view, it is the rope-snake relation which best illustrates the *Brahman*-world-relation, and not the clay-pot-relation. The implication is that according to Advaita Metaphysics *Brahman* is the transfigurative material cause (*vivartopādāna-kāraṇa*) of the world, and not the transformative material cause (*pariṇāmyupādāna-kāraṇa*), because It does not undergo the least change, It being Changeless, Impartite, Eternal. But even while attributing material causality to *Brahman* it needs to be emphasized that *Brahman* is not the cause *per se* of the world, but it is rather *Brahman-in-association-with-Māyā* that is the actual material cause thereof[97].

That the plurality experienced at the empirical level is not real is proved by Advaita in two ways. Referring to the illustration of clay and pot given above, the Scriptures declare that 'clay' alone is real therein ("*mṛttiketyeva satyam*") which implies that pot, etc., being a mere product of clay, does not have a separate identity, and is therefore not real. 'It may be noted in this context that even the reality accorded to clay is but relative, for it is real only with reference to its product (s); but with reference to its cause, it has no separate identity, and is therefore not real. And what is true of clay is true of all material objects—they all have a relative reality in their character as cause, but as effects, they are unreal, their actual identity being with their respective cause. And just as all material causes are ultimately identifiable with *Māyā*, in like manner the individual selves are also identical with *Brahman*, their having no separate identity (or reality) of their own–such is the claim of Advaita Vedānta[98].

'The analysis of the cause-effect-relation suggests another reason to show that the world is not real.The effect, both in the case of the theories of Transformation (*Pariṇāmavāda*) and Transfiguration (*Vivartavāda*), has no reality or existence of its own apart from the reality or existence of its cause. It is true that there is a basic difference between the cause-effect-relation through transformation (*pariṇāma*) and that through transfiguration (*vivarta*). Cause and effect have the same ontological status in the case of *pariṇāma*, whereas they have different ontological status in the case of *vivarta*. Clay is empirically real, and the pot which is a modification of clay is also empirically real in the sense that both of them possess empirical reality (*vyāvahārika-sattā*). The position is different in the case of *vivarta*. While rope has empirical reality (*vyāvahārika-sattā*), the rope-snake has only phenomenal or apparent reality (*prātibhāsika-sattā*). It means that the cause and effect in this case do not have the same ontological status because of the difference between *vyāvahārika-sattā* and *prātibhāsika-sattā*. Notwithstanding this basic difference between these two kinds of cause-effect-relation, the effect in both the cases is immaginary (*kalpita*) or unreal (*asatya*) or illusory (*mithyā*), and so it has no reality or existence of its own apart from the reality or existence of its cause.' Since the pluralistic universe is an effect of *Brahman* (through *Māyā*), it is not real. It is said to be *mithyā* (illusory), or *asatya* (unreal) or *kalpita* (imaginary). It cannot therefore be reckoned as real in addition to *Brahman*'[99].

At the level of Consciousness, however, *Jīva* and *Īśvara* are considered to be mere reflections or appearances of the One, Impartite *Brahman*; they have no identity separate from *Brahman*, they being essentially identical with *Brahman*. Of the three schools that evolved within the fold of Advaita Vedānta with regard to the status of *Jīva* and *Īśvara* vis-a-vis *Brahman*, the *Ābhāsavāda* of Sureśvara *et al* propounds the theory that the *Jīva*-s are as real as *Brahman*, the Ultimate Reality, they being 'primary appearances' *in and through Avidyā*, while the objects of the world are unreal, they being *secondary appearances*, i.e. mere reflections of the primary appearances. 'Reality as appearing primarily and directly or indirectly in *Avidyā* and its numerous modifications constitutes the backbone of all further outer appearances. These original Appearances of Reality emerge into further outer and fresh appearances, directly known as the Phenomenal or empirical entities and into still further ones, recognized as illusions[100]. Thus is established the reality of the Primary appearances (*Jīva-s, Īśvara*) and the unreality of the secondary appearances (the material objects, etc.).

The Vivaraṇa School on the other hand, upholding the theory of reflection (*bimba-pratibimba-vāda*), regards *Jīva*-s and *Īśvara* to be *Brahman* Itself reflected in the numerous adjuncts (*upādhi-s*), such as the intellect-sense-body-complex. According to this theory, the One Absolute Reality appears as numerous selves due to the intervening adjuncts and their cause Avidyā. Just as the reflections appearing in mirror, etc. are identical with the prototype, in the same way *Jīva*-s also are identical and one with *Brahman*. The same holds good for *Īśvara* also, but with this difference that while the *Jīva*-s are affected by the dual potencies of *Māyā*, the latter (i.e. *Īśvara*) is above such influences, He being Himself the Lord of *Māyā* (and also, Lord of the *Jīva*-s). Prakāśātman argues that though the reflections are false within themselves, yet what appears in them (viz. Consciousness) is True in its essence[101].

The Bhāmatī School on its part, propounding the theory of Limitation (*Avacchedavāda*), considers the *Jīva*-s to be *Brahman* Itself, but appearing as though limited by the adjuncts, such as the mind-sense-body-complex. Vācaspati says that just as space, though one and undivided, appears as though multiplied and differentiated, by a variety of objects, such as jars, pots, etc., in the same manner, *Brahman*, One and Impartible, appears as though many and differentiated by the intervening adjuncts such as intellect, sense, body, etc. But, just as on the removal of the jars, etc., the appearance of variegated space disappears, resulting into the apprehension of space in its natural form, in like manner, on the removal of the *Upādhi*-s (adjuncts) such as the intellect, etc., the *Jīva*-s which are essentially and ceaselessly identical with *Brahman*, regain as though their real nature—that of identity with the Absolute[102].

Closely connected with the theories of the illusory appearance of *Brahman* as many, is the question as to whether *Jīva* or *Brahman* is the locus of *Avidyā*. The Bhāmatī, as discussed already[103], holds the view that the *Jīva*-s are the locus of their respective *Avidyā*, implying that there are as many *Avidyā*-s as there are *Jīva*-s. This particular stand taken by the Bhāmatī school with regard to *Jīva*-s vis-a-vis *Avidyā*, renders easy the Bhāmatī's task of accounting for the liberation of one *Jīva* on the dawning of Right Knowledge, while other *Jīva*-s still reeling under the spell of Nescience remain in bondage[104].

The Vivaraṇa School on the other hand, advocates the doctrine of singularity of *Avidyā*, which is located in *Brahman*[105], and not in *Jīva*. This doctrine inevitably results in a contradiction at the empirical level, where the advocates of the Vivaraṇa-view are faced with the problem of plurality of *Jīva*-s, while there is but one *Avidyā*. This problem is solved by the Vivaraṇa by postulating two types of *Avidyā*-s or *Ajñāna*-s, namely, *Mūlājñāna* and *Avasthājñāna*-s. This School holds the view that while *Mūlājñāna* operates at the level of *Brahman*, *Avasthājñāna*-s operate at the level of the individual selves, and external objects, accasioning thus a plurality of *Jīva*-s.

As a matter of fact, it is seen from the analysis of the Bhāmatī views and those of the Vivaraṇa as concerns the individual selves, as well as their nature and their relation with *Brahman*, that both of the schools postulate more or less the same doctrines. Both share the docrine of *Jīva-Brahman*-identity and both hold *Avidyā* and its products—the *upādhi*-s (adjuncts) such as intellect, sense, body, etc., to be responsible for the apparent sense of finitude and perishability of the *Jīva*-s. Both of the Schools also believe in the purity and eternality of the selves and in their being essentially free from agentship, enjoyership, etc. Both also postulate True Knowledge as the means to Liberation of the *Jīva*-s. Where they do not seem to agree, is the question as to the locus and number of *Avidyā*, and also as regards the *Jīva-Brahman*-relation. These differences however, it may be observed, are more apparent than real, there being *per se* no plurality whatsoever as far as *Brahman* is concerned. The apparent plurality of selves, whether interpreted as reflections of *Brahman* or as *Brahman* in the form of limited entities, is but illusory, and therefore unreal.

NOTE

1. R. Bālasubramanian (Ed.), The Tradition of Vedānta (TOV), p.46.
2. "नेह नानास्ति किञ्चन।" -Bṛh. UP. - IV.4.19.
3. "सर्वं खल्विदं ब्रह्म।" - Ch. UP. - III.14.1.
4. "अयमात्मा ब्रह्म।" - Bṛh. UP. - II.5.19.
5. R. Bālasubramanian, Loc. Cit., p.47.
6. C.D. Sharma, The Advaita Tradition in Indian Philosophy (ATIP), p. 189.
7. Ibid. p.190.
8. T.M.P. Mahadevan, The Philosophy of Advaita (P.A.), p.208, quoting from PD I.17.
9. Ibid. pp. 208-209.
10. Ibid. p.209, quoting from PD, I.18-24.
11. Ibid. quoting from PD, I.29.
12. Ibid. p.209.
13. C.D. Sharma, Loc. Cit. p.190
14. Veermani Prasad Upadhyaya, Lights on Vedānta (LV), pp.17-18.
15. Ibid. pp.18-19.
16. Ibid. pp.41-42.
17. Ibid. pp. 42-43.
18. Kanshi Ram, Integral Non-Dualism, pp.51-52; See also, "तथा जीवब्रह्मणोः मुखप्रतिमुखवत् बिम्बप्रतिबिम्बरूपत्वादप्यभेदोऽवगन्तव्यः। ननु दृष्टान्ते नाभेदः संप्रतिपन्नः चैत्रतच्छाये भिन्ने इतिवत् चैत्रतत्प्रतिबिम्बे भिन्ने इत्येव पार्श्वस्थितेन ग्रहणात् स्वेनापि स्वकरतत्प्रतिबिम्बे भिन्ने इति ग्रहणाच्चेति चेन्न। आपाततो भेदप्रतीतावपि सयुक्तिकप्रत्यक्षेण बिम्बप्रतिबिम्बयोरैक्यसिद्ध्या दृष्टान्तत्वोपपत्तेः.....ग्रीवास्थं मुखं यत्स्वलक्षणकं प्रतिपन्नं दर्पणस्थमपि तथेत्यवधार्य तथैवेदं मुखमिति स एवायं कर इति च स्वपर-साधारणप्रतीतिरप्यनुभवसिद्धा।" —Advaita Siddhi, Parimal Publications, Delhi, 1982, p.847.
19. Kanshi Ram, Loc. Cit. pp.52-53; See also, "न जीव आत्मनोऽन्यः। नापि तद्विकारः किन्त्वात्मैवाविद्योपधानकल्पितावच्छेदः। आकाश

इव घटमणिकादिकल्पितावच्छेदो घटाकाशो मणिकाकाशो न तु परमाकाशादन्यस्तद्विकारो वा... ।" —Bhāmatī on SB-I.4.22, Op. Cit. p.416.

20. Kanshi Ram, Loc. Cit., p.53; See also, यथा आकाशस्य सुषिरभेदोत्पत्ति-प्रलय-निमित्तत्वं घटाद्युपाधिकृतमेव तद्वदक्षरस्यापि नाम रूपकृतदेहोपाधिनिमित्तमेव जीवोत्पत्तिप्रलयनिमित्तत्वम् ।" —SB on Muṇḍaka UP. II.14.

21. एवमयमनादिरनन्तो नैसर्गिकोऽध्यासो मिथ्याप्रत्ययरूप: कर्तृत्वभोक्तृत्वप्रवर्तक: सर्वलोकप्रत्यक्ष: ।" Adhyāsabhāṣya, Loc. Cit., pp.44-45.

22. Bhāmatī of Vācaspati, Op. Cit., p.58; See also; अहंप्रत्ययो वृत्तिर्यस्मिन्नन्त:करणादौ सोऽयमहंप्रत्ययी, तं स्वप्रचारसाक्षिणि अन्त:करणप्रचारसाक्षिणि, चैतन्योदासीनताभ्यां प्रत्यगात्मन्यध्यस्य" —Bhāmatī, Ibid, p.58.

23. Ibid, p.59; See also, "तदनेन अन्त:करणाद्यवच्छिन्न: प्रत्यगात्मा इदमनिदंरूपश्चेतन: कर्त्ता भोक्ता कार्यकारणा-विद्याद्वयाधारोऽहंकारास्पदं संसारी सर्वानर्थसंभारभाजनं जीवात्मा इतरेतराध्यासोपादान: तदुपादानाश्चाध्यास इति"। —Ibid, p.59.

24. Ibid. (Parimal Edition), p.620; See also,
(i) "...सर्वथा जीवा अस्वतन्त्रा ईश्वरेणैव प्रवर्त्यन्ते इति..."। "...यद्यप्ययमीश्वरो वीतरागस्तथापि पूर्वपूर्वजन्तुकर्मापेक्षया जन्तून् धर्माधर्मयो: प्रवर्तयन् न द्वेषपक्षपाताभ्यां विषम: नापि निर्घृण:"। —Bhāmatī on SB. II. 3.42.
(ii) "जीवब्रह्मभेदाभेदश्रुतिविरोधसंदेहे पूर्वत्र जीवनियन्तेश्वर इत्युक्तम् ।" —Kalpataru, Ibid, p.621.

25. ...आत्मगोचरमहंकारम्, 'अहमिहास्मि सदने' इति प्रयुञ्जानो लौकिक: शरीराद्यभेदग्रहादात्मन: प्रादेशिकत्वमभिमन्यते नभस इव घटमणिकमल्लिकाद्युपाध्यवच्छेदादिति... ।" —Bhāmatī, Ibid. p.14.

26. Ibid. p.38. Vide, "सत्यं प्रत्यगात्मा स्वयंप्रकाशत्वादविषयोऽनंशश्च। तथापि अनिर्वचनीयानाद्यविद्यापरिकल्पितबुद्धिमन:-सूक्ष्मस्थूलशरीरेन्द्रियावच्छेदकभेदेन अनवच्छिन्नोऽपि वस्तुतोऽवच्छिन्न इव अभिन्नोऽपि भिन्न इव अकर्तापि कर्तेव अभोक्तापि भोक्तेव अविषयोऽप्यस्मत्प्रत्ययविषय इव जीवभावमापन्न: अवभासते नभ इव घटमणिकमल्लिकाद्युपाध्यवच्छेदभेदेन भिन्नमिवानेकविधंधर्मकमिवेति।" —Bhāmatī on Adhyāsabhāṣya.

27. "न हि चिदेकरसस्यात्मन: चिदंशे गृहीते अगृहीतं किंचिदस्ति। न खलु आनन्दनित्यविभुत्वादय: अस्य चिद्रूपाद्वस्तुतो भिद्यन्ते येन तदग्रहे न गृह्येरन्! गृहीता एव तु कल्पितेन भेदेन न विवेचिता इत्यगृहीता इवाभान्ति। —Ibid.

28. "न च आत्मनो बुद्ध्यादिभ्यो भेदस्तात्त्विक: येन चिदात्मनि गृह्यमाणे सोऽपि गृहीत एव भवेत् बुद्ध्यादीनामनिर्वाच्यत्वेन तद्भेदस्याप्यनिर्वचनीयत्वात्। —Ibid.

29. "तस्माच्चिदात्मन: स्वयंप्रकाशस्यैव अनवच्छिन्नस्य अवच्छिन्नेभ्यो बद्ध्यादिभ्यो भेदाग्रहात् तदध्यासेन जीवभाव इति। तस्य च अनिदमिदमात्मन: अस्मत्प्रत्ययविषयत्वमुपपद्यते। तथा हि कर्ता भोक्ता चिदात्मा अहंप्रत्यये प्रत्यवभासते"। —Ibid. pp.38-39.

30. "न च उदासीनस्य तस्य क्रियाशक्तिर्भोगशक्तिर्वा संभवति। यस्य च बुद्ध्यादे: कार्यकारणसंघातस्य क्रियाभोगशक्ती न तस्य चैतन्यम्। तस्माच्चिदात्मैव कार्यकारणसंघातेन ग्रथितो लब्धक्रियाभोगशक्ति: स्वयंप्रकाशोऽपि बुद्ध्यादिविषयविच्छुरणात् कथंचिदस्मत्प्रत्ययविषय: अहंकारास्पदं जीव इति च जन्तुरिति च क्षेत्रज्ञ इति च आख्यायते। न खलु जीवश्चिदात्मनो भिद्यते। तथा हि

श्रुतिः- "अनेन जीवेनात्मना इति।" तस्माच्चिदात्मनोऽव्यतिरेकात् जीवः स्वयंप्रकाशोऽपि अहंप्रत्ययेन कर्तृभोक्तृतया व्यवहारयोग्यः क्रियते इत्यहंप्रत्ययालम्बनमुच्यते।" —Ibid. p.39.

31. Bhāmatī of Vācaspati, Loc. Cit. p.41; See also, "न च अध्यासे सति विषयत्वं विषयत्वे च अध्यासः इत्यन्योन्याश्रयत्वमिति सांप्रतम् बीजाङ्कुरवदनादित्वात्, पूर्वपूर्वाध्यासतद्वासनाविषयीकृतस्योत्तरोत्तराध्यासविषयत्वाविरोधादित्युक्तम्-नैसर्गिकोऽयं लोकव्यवहारः इति भाष्यग्रन्थेन।.... जीवो हि चिदात्मतया स्वयंप्रकाशतया अविषयोऽपि औपाधिकेन रूपेण विषय इति भावः।" —Bhāmatī on Adhyāsabhāṣya, Loc. Cit, p.39.

32. Vide, Swami Gambhirananda, Brahma-Sūtra Bhāṣya, Advaita Ashrama, pp.349-350.

33. यथा च लोके पृथिवीत्वसामान्यान्वितानामप्यश्मनां केचिन्महार्हा मणयो वज्रवैदूर्यादयोऽन्ये.... पाषाण इत्यनेकविधं वैचित्र्यं दृश्यते, यथा चैकपृथिवीव्यपाश्रयाणामपि बीजानां बहुविधं पत्रपुष्पगन्धरसादिवैचित्र्यं.... उपलक्ष्यते यथा चैकस्याप्यन्नरसस्य.... विचित्राणि कार्याणि भवन्ति एवमेकस्यापि ब्रह्मणो जीवप्राज्ञपृथक्त्वं कार्यवैचित्र्यं चोपपद्यते... ।...श्रुतेश्च प्रामाण्याद्विकारस्य च वाचारम्भणमात्रत्वात्.... इत्यभ्युच्चयः।" —S.B. on BS-II.1.23, Loc. Cit. p.473.

34. "यदि ब्रह्मविवर्तो जगत्, हन्त सर्वस्यैव जीववच्चैतन्यप्रसङ्ग इति।" —Bhāmatī, (Parimal, Ed.), Loc. Cit. p.473.

35. Vide, Sw. Gambhirananda, Loc. Cit. pp.249-250; See also, "परमेश्वराधीना त्वियमस्माभिः प्रागवस्था जगतोऽभ्युपगम्यते, न स्वतन्त्रा। ....नहि तया विना परमेश्वरस्य स्रष्टृत्वं सिध्यति शक्तिरहितस्य तस्य प्रवृत्त्यनुपपत्तेः।.... अविद्यात्मिका हि बीजशक्तिरव्यक्तशब्दनिर्देश्या परमेश्वराश्रया मायामयी महासुप्तिः यस्यां स्वरूपप्रतिबोधरहिताः शेरते संसारिणे जीवाः। अव्यक्ता हि सा माया। ....तदियं 'महतः परमव्यक्तम्' तु जीवो महान् तदाप्यव्यक्ताधीनत्वाज्जीवभावस्य-महतः परमव्यक्तमित्युक्तम्। अविद्यावत्त्वेनैव जीवस्य सर्वः सर्वव्यवहारः संततो वर्तते।... विद्यया तस्या बीजशक्तेर्दाहात्... मुक्तानां च पुनरनुत्पत्तिः।" —SB on BS - I 4.3, Loc. Cit. (Parimal), pp.377-380.

36. "न वयं प्रधानवदविद्यां सर्वजीवेष्वेकामाचक्ष्महे, किंत्वियं प्रतिजीवं भिद्यते। तेन यस्यैव विद्योत्पन्ना तस्यैवाविद्याऽपनीयते न जीवान्तरस्य।... न च अविद्योपाधिभेदाधीनो जीवभेदो जीवभेदाधीनचाविद्योपाधिभेद इति परस्पराश्रयादुभयासिद्धिरिति सांप्रतम्, अनादित्वाद्-बीजाङ्कुरवदुभयसिद्धेः।" —Bhāmatī on SB - I.4.3, Loc. Cit. pp. 377-378.

37. "न ह्यचेतनं चेतनानधिष्ठितं कार्याय पर्याप्तमिति स्वकार्यं कर्तुं परमेश्वरं निमित्ततया वोपादानतया वाऽश्रयते, प्रपञ्चविभ्रमस्य हीश्वराधिष्ठानत्वमहिंविभ्रमस्येव रज्ज्वधिष्ठानत्वम् तेन यथाऽहिविभ्रमो रज्जूपादानः एवं प्रपञ्चविभ्रम ईश्वरोपादानः। तस्माज्जीवाधिकरणाप्यविद्या निमित्ततया विषयतया वेश्वरमाश्रयतः।" —Ibid.

38. SW. Gambhirananda, Loc. Cit., p.287; See also, "काशकृत्स्नस्याचार्यस्याविकृतः परमेश्वरो जीवो नान्य इति मतम्। ...तत्र काशकृत्स्नीयं मतं श्रुत्यनुसारीति प्रतिपिपादयिषितार्थानुसारात् 'तत्त्वमसि' इत्यादि श्रुतिभ्यः एवं च सति तज्ज्ञानादमृतत्वमवकल्पते।" —SB On BS - I.4.22, (Parimal ed.) Loc. Cit. p.417.

39. SW. Gambhirananda, Loc. Cit., p.287; See also, "विकारात्मकत्वे हि जीवस्याभ्युपगम्यमाने विकारस्य प्रकृतिसंबन्धे प्रलयप्रसंङ्गान्न तज्ज्ञानादमृतत्वमवकल्पेत। अतश्च स्वाश्रयस्य नामरूपस्यासंभवादुपाध्याश्रयं नामरूपं जीव

उपचर्यते। अत एवोत्पत्तिरपि जीवस्य क्वचिदग्निस्फुलिङ्गोदाहरणेन श्रावयमाणोपाध्याश्रयैव वेदितव्या। —SB on BS - I.4.22, Loc. Cit. p.417.

40. ''आत्यन्तिके हि जीवपरमात्मनोरभेदे तात्त्विकेऽनाद्यविद्योपाधिकल्पितो भेदस्तत्त्वमसीति जीवात्मनो ब्रह्मभावतत्त्वोपदेशश्रवणमननिदिध्यासनप्रकर्षपर्यन्तजन्मना साक्षात्कारेण विद्यया शक्यः समूलकाषं कषितुम् रज्ज्वामहिविभ्रम इव रज्जुतत्त्वसाक्षात्कारेण।'' —Bhāmatī, Loc. Cit. p.417.

41. ''अपि च जीवस्यात्मविकारत्वे तस्य ज्ञानध्यानादिसाधनानुष्ठानात् स्वप्रकृतावप्यये सति नामृतत्वस्याशास्तीत्यपुरुषार्थत्वममृतत्वप्राप्तिश्रुतिविरोधश्च।'' —Ibid.

42. ''ऐकान्तिके हि खल्वद्वैते आत्मनोऽन्यकर्मकरणे ''केन कं पश्येत्'' इति आत्मनश्च कर्मत्वं 'विज्ञातारमरे केन विजानीयात्' इति शक्यं निषेद्धुम्।'' —Ibid.

43. ''जननजरामरणभीतयो विक्रियास्तासां सर्वासां ''महानजः'' इत्यादिना प्रतिषेधः। परिणामपक्षेऽन्यस्य चान्यभावपक्षे, ऐकान्तिकाद्वैतप्रतिपादनपराः 'एकमेवाद्वितीयम्' इत्यादयो द्वैतदर्शननिन्दापराश्च 'अन्योऽसावन्योऽहमस्मिइत्यादयः श्रुतय उपरुध्येरन्।'' —Ibid. p.419.

44. Sw. Gambhīrānanda, Loc. Cit. pp.290-291; See also,
''स्थिते च क्षेत्रज्ञपरमात्मैकत्वविषये सम्यग्दर्शने क्षेत्रज्ञः परमात्मेति नाममात्रभेदात्, क्षेत्रज्ञोऽयं परमात्मनो भिन्नः परमात्मायं क्षेत्रज्ञाद्भिन्न इत्येवंजातीयक आत्मभेदविषयो निर्बन्धो निरर्थकः। एको ह्ययमात्मा नाममात्रभेदेन बहुधाभिधीयते इति। न हि 'सत्यं ज्ञानमनन्तं ब्रह्म। यो वेद निहितं गुहायाम्' इति काचिदेवैकां गुहामधिकृत्यैतदुक्तम्। न च ब्रह्मणोऽन्यो गुहायां निहितोऽस्ति, 'तत्सृष्ट्वा तदेवानुप्राविशत्' इति स्रष्टुरेव प्रवेशश्रवणात्। ये तु निर्बन्धं कुर्वन्ति ते वेदान्तार्थं बाधमानाः श्रेयोद्वारं सम्यग्दर्शनमेव बाधन्ते।'' —SB on BS - I.4.22, Loc. Cit. pp.420-421.

45. ''यथा बिम्बादवदातात्तात्त्विके प्रतिबिम्बानामभेदेऽपि नीलमणिकृपाणकाचाद्युपधानभेदात्काल्पनिको जीवानां भेदो बुद्धिव्यपदेशभेदौ वर्तयति, इदं बिम्बमवदातमिमानि प्रतिबिम्बानि नीलोत्पलपलाशश्यामलानि वृत्तदीर्घादिभेदभाञ्जि बहूनीति, एवं परमात्मनः शुद्धस्वभवाज्जीवानामभेद ऐकान्तिकेऽप्यनिर्वचनीयानाद्यविद्योपधानभेदात्काल्पनिको जीवानां भेदो बुद्धिव्यपदेशभेदावयं च परमात्मा शुद्धविज्ञानानन्दस्वभाव इमे च जीवा अविद्याशोकदुःखाद्युपद्रवभाज इति वर्तयति''।।
—Bhāmatī on SB - I.4.22, Loc. Cit. pp.422-421.

46. ''यथा हि बिम्बस्य मणिकृपाणादयो गुहा एवं ब्रह्मणोऽपि प्रतिजीवं भिन्ना अविद्या गुहा इति। यथा प्रतिबिम्बेषु भासमानेषु बिम्बं तदभिन्नमपि गुह्यमेवं जीवेषु नासमानेषु तदभिन्नमपि ब्रह्म गुह्यम्।'' —Ibid. p.421.

47. ''...मृतो देवदत्तो जातो देवदत्त इति व्यपदेशस्य मुख्यत्वं मन्वानस्य पूर्वः पक्षः, मुख्यत्व-शास्त्रविरोधाल्लौकिकव्यपदेशो भाक्तो व्याख्येयः।...जातकर्मादि च गर्भबीजसमुद्भवजीवपापप्रक्षयार्थं, न तु जीवजन्मजपापक्षयार्थम्। अत एव स्मरन्ति 'एवमेनः शमं याति बीजगर्भसमुद्भवम्' इति। तस्मान्न शरीरोत्पत्तिविनाशाभ्यां जीवजन्मविनाशाविति सिद्धम्।'' - Ibid. p.600.

48. ''भवेदेवं यदि जीवा ब्रहाणो भिद्येरन्। न त्वेतदरित। 'तत् सृष्ट्वा तदेवानुप्राविशत्', 'अनेन जीवेन' इत्याद्यविभागश्रुतेः, औपाधिकत्वाच्च भेदस्य घटकरकाद्याकाशवद्विरुद्धधर्मसंसर्गस्योपपत्तेः।
.... श्रुत्याऽविभागस्य च 'एको देवः सर्वभूतेषु गूढः' इति श्रुत्यैवोक्तत्वान्नित्या जीवात्मनो न विकारा न चाद्वैतप्रतिज्ञाविरोध इति सिद्धम्। —Ibid. P.602.

49. V.M.Apte, Brahma-Sūtra, Śāṅkara-Bhāṣya, pp.464-65; See also,
''नैतदस्त्यणुरात्मेति। उत्पत्त्यश्रवणाद्धि परस्यैव तु ब्रह्मणः प्रवेशश्रवणात्तादात्म्योपदेशाच्च परमेव ब्रह्म जीव इत्युक्तम्। परमेव चेद्ब्रह्म जीवस्तस्माद्यावत्परं ब्रह्म तावानेव जीवो

भवितुमर्हति। परस्य च ब्रह्मणे विभुत्वमाम्नातम्। तस्माद्विभुर्जीवः।" —SB on BS-II 3.29, Loc.Cit. p.609.

50. "न चाणोर्जीवस्य सकलशरीरगता वेदनोपपद्यते। यद्यप्यन्तःकरणमणु तथापि तस्य त्वचा संबद्धत्वात्त्वचश्च समस्तशरीरव्यापित्वादेकदेशऽप्यधिष्ठिता त्वगधिष्ठितैवेति शरीरव्यापी जीवः शक्नोति सर्वाङ्गीणं शैत्यमनुभवितुं त्वगिन्द्रियेण गंगायाम्। अणुस्तु जीवो यत्रास्ति तस्मिन्नेव शरीरप्रदेश तदनुभवेन्न सर्वाङ्गीणम्, तस्यासर्वाङ्गीणत्वात्।" —Bhāmatī on SB - II.3.29, Loc. Cit., p.609.

51. "न च ब्रह्मस्वभावस्य जीवात्मनः कूटस्थनित्यस्य स्वत इच्छाद्वेषानुषङ्गसंभव इति बुद्धिगुणानां तेषां तदभेदाध्यासेन तद्धर्मत्वाध्यासः, उदशरावाध्यस्तस्येव चन्द्रमसो बिम्बस्य तोयकम्पे कम्पवत्त्वाध्यास इति...। तथा च बुद्ध्याद्युपाधिकृतमस्य जीवत्वमिति बुद्धेरन्तःकरणस्याणुतया सोऽप्यणुव्यपदेशभाग्भवति, नभ इव करकोपहितं करक परिमाणम्।" —Ibid. pp.610-611.

52. V.M. Apte, Loc. Cit., p.483; See also,
"यदिदमविद्यावस्थायामुपाधिनिबन्धनं कर्तृत्वं जीवस्याभिहितं तत्किमनपेक्ष्येश्वरं भवत्याहोस्विदीश्वरापेक्षमिति भवति विचारणा।... अविद्यावस्थायां कार्यकारणसंघाताविवेकदर्शिनो जीवस्याविद्यातिमिरान्धस्य सतः परस्मादात्मनः कर्माध्यक्षात्सर्वभूताधिवासात्साक्षिणश्चेतयितुरीश्वरात्तदनुज्ञया कर्तृत्वभोक्तृत्वलक्षणस्य संसारस्य सिद्धिः, तदनुग्रहहेतुकेनैव च विज्ञानेन मोक्षसिद्धिर्भवितुमर्हति।" —S.B. on BS - II 3.41, Loc. Cit., p.620.

53. V.M. Apte, Loc. Cit., p.483; See also,
"यद्यपि दोषप्रयुक्तः सामग्रीसंपन्नश्च जीवः, यद्यपि च लोके कृष्यादिषु कर्मसु नेश्वरकारणत्वं प्रसिद्धम् तथापि सर्वास्वेव प्रवृत्तिष्वीश्वरो हेतुकर्तेति श्रुतेरवसीयते।" —SB on BS-II 3.41, Loc. Cit., p.620.

54. "यदेतज्जीवानामौपाधिकं कर्तृत्वं तत्प्रवर्तनालक्षणेषु रागादिषु सत्सु नेश्वरमपरं प्रवर्तकं कल्पयितुमर्हति अतिप्रसंगात्। न चेश्वरो द्वेषपक्षपातरहितो जीवान् साध्वसाधुनि कर्मणि प्रवर्तयितुमर्हति.... स हि स्वतन्त्रः कारूणिको धर्म एव जन्तून् प्रवर्तयेन्नाधर्मे। ततश्च तत्प्रेरिता जन्तवः सर्वे धार्मिका एवेति सुखिन एव स्युर्न दुःखिनः। स्वतन्त्रास्तु रागादिप्रयुक्ताः प्रवर्तमाना धर्माधर्मप्रचयवन्तो वैचित्र्यमनुभवन्तीति युक्तम्। एवं च विधिनिषेधयोरर्थवत्त्वमितरथा तु सर्वथा जीवा अस्वतन्त्रा ईश्वरेणैव प्रवर्त्यन्त इति कृतं विधिनिषेधाभ्याम्।" —Bhāmatī on SB - II.3.41, Loc. Cit. Pp.619-620.

55. "ईशितव्येशितृभावश्चान्वेष्यान्वेष्टृभावश्च ज्ञेयज्ञातृभावश्च नियम्यनियन्तृभावश्चाधाराधेयभावश्च न जीवपरमात्मनोरभेदेऽवकल्प्यते।" —Ibid. SB - II. 3.43, Loc. Cit. pp.621-622.

56. "जीवानां ब्रह्मांशत्वे तद्गता वेदना ब्रह्मणो भवेत्। पादादिगता इव वेदना देवदत्तस्य। ततश्च ब्रह्मभूयंगतस्य समस्तजीवगतवेदनानुभवप्रसङ्ग इति वरं संसार एव मुक्तेः। तत्र हि स्वगतवेदनामात्रानुभवान्न भूरि दुःखमनुभवति। मुक्तस्तु सर्वजीवगतवेदनाभागिति प्रयत्नेन मुक्तिरनर्थबहुलतया परिहर्तव्या स्यादिति।" —Ibid. p.622.

57. "अनधिगतार्थावबोधनानि प्रमाणानि, विशेषतः शब्दः। तत्र भेदो लोकसिद्धत्वान्न प्रतिपाद्यः। अभेदस्त्वनधिगतत्वादधिगतभेदानुवादेन प्रतिपादनमर्हति।... उपनिषदश्चाद्वैतोपक्रमतत्परामर्शतदुपसंहारा अद्वैतपरा एव युज्यन्ते। ....तस्मादद्वैते भाविके स्थिते जीवभावस्तस्य ब्रह्मणोऽनाद्यनिर्वचनीयाविद्योपधानभेदादेकस्येव बिम्बस्य दर्पणाद्युपाधिभेदात् प्रतिबिम्बभेदाः। —Ibid. pp.622-623.

58. "न च मोक्षस्यानर्थबहुलता, यतः प्रतिबिम्बानामिव श्यामतावदाततादिजीवानामेव नानावेदनाभिसंबन्धो ब्रह्मणस्तु बिम्बस्येव न तदभिसंबन्धः। यथा च दर्पणापनये तत्प्रतिबिम्बं बिम्बभावेऽवतिष्ठते

न कृपाणे प्रतिबिम्बितमपि। एवमविद्योपधानविगमे जीवे ब्रह्मभाव इति सिद्धं जीवो ब्रह्मांश इव तत्तत्रतया न त्वंश इति तात्पर्यार्थः" —Ibid. p.623.

59. "द्विचन्द्रोदाहरणेन जीवेश्वरयोः जीवानां चानात्मरूपो भेदावभासः इति दर्शितम्।" —Pañcapādikā, Loc. Cit. p.71.

60. Vide, D. Venkataramiah, The Pañcapādikā of Padmapāda, Loc. Cit. p.46.

61. "ननु न जीवो ब्रह्मणोऽन्यः इत्युक्तम्। बाढम्। अत एवऽर्थाज्जीवे ब्रह्मस्वरूपप्रकाशाच्छादिका अविद्या कल्प्यते। अन्यथा परमार्थतस्तत्स्वरूपत्वे तदवबोधोऽपि यदि नित्यसिद्धः स्यात् तदा तादात्म्योपदेशो व्यर्थः स्यात्। अतः अनादिसिद्धाविद्यावच्छिन्नानन्तजीवनिर्भासास्पदमेकरसं ब्रह्मेति अभ्युपगन्तव्यम्।" —Pañcapādikā, Loc. Cit. pp.73-74.

62. D. Venkataramiah, Loc. Cit. pp.73-74; See also, "अतो मायावच्छिन्नरूपत्वादनन्यदपि ब्रह्मरूपमात्मनो न वेत्ति। तथा चोक्तम् - "अनादिमायया सुप्तो यदा जीवः प्रबुद्ध्यते। अजमनिद्रमस्वप्नमद्वैतं बुध्यते तदा॥" इति।" —Pañcapādikā, Loc. Cit, p.75.

63. Ibid. p.215.
   (i) "आत्मावरणमात्माज्ञानमेव जीवब्रह्मविभागाद्यध्यासोपादानं यतः अतो जीवावच्छेद-निमित्तमज्ञानमिति अवच्छेदस्यापि प्रातिभासिकाध्यासस्य तदुपादानत्वात्। सत्यतो निरवयवस्य द्वैधीभावायोगात् कर्तृत्वभोक्तृत्वदोषसंयोगानां बीजाङ्कुरवदनादिप्रवाहस्य दर्शितत्वात् तदुपादानमप्यज्ञानमनादि। अनादिजीवविभागाध्यासप्रवाहस्यानाद्यविद्यैव कारणं नान्तःकरणादि....।"
   (ii) "ऐक्ये स्वयंप्रकाशत्वे सर्वज्ञत्वे च सत्येवानवभासदर्शनादाच्छादिका अविद्या कल्प्यते। अन्यथा भेदजाड्यकिंचिज्ज्ञत्वे ग्रहणाभावमात्रमेव स्यात्।"

64. "निरंशत्वात् न अंशाशिभावेन भेदः संभवति। तस्मादविद्यैव भेदाध्यासनिमित्तमिति।" —Ibid. p.218-219.

65. "ननु विद्या किंसंबन्धिनी भेदनिमित्तम् ? ननु दर्पणादिद्रव्यं वा किंसंबन्धि बिम्बभेदनिमित्तम्? मुखमात्रसंबन्धिनी चेत्? इहापि चित्स्वरूपमात्रसंबन्ध्यज्ञानं तत्र जीव-ब्रह्मव्यवहारभेदं प्रवर्तयति"। —Ibid. p.219.

66. Vide, D. Venkataramiah, Loc. Cit. p.72; See also, "यत् पुनः दर्पणजलादिषु मुखचन्द्रादिप्रतिबिम्बोदाहरणं तत् अहङ्कर्तुरनिदमंशो बिम्बादिव प्रतिबिम्बं न ब्रह्मणो वस्त्वन्तरं किंतु तदेव तत्, पृथगवभासविपर्ययस्वरूपतामात्रं मिथ्या इति दर्शयितुम्।" —Pañcapādikā, Loc. Cit. p.104.

67. Vide, D. Venkataramiah, Loc. Cit. pp.72-7; See also, "कथं पुनस्तदेव तत्? एकस्वलक्षणतावगमात् । तथा च यथा बहिः स्थितो देवदत्तो यत्स्वलक्षणः प्रतिपन्नः तत्स्वलक्षण एव वेश्मान्तः प्रविष्टोऽपि प्रतीयते तथा दर्पणतलस्थितोऽपि। न तत् वस्त्वन्तरत्वे युज्यते। अपि च अर्थात् वस्त्वन्तरत्वे सति आदर्श एव बिम्बसन्निधावेव तदाकारगर्भितः परिणतः इति वाच्यम्।.... तथा सति बिम्बसन्निधिलब्धपरिणतिरादर्शः तदपायेऽपि तथैनावतिष्ठेत।" —Pañcapādikā, Loc. Cit, pp.104-105.

68. "ननु तत्त्वमसिवाक्यात् बाधो दृश्यते। मैवम्, तत्र तत्त्वमिति बिम्बस्थानीयब्रह्मस्वरूपता प्रतिबिम्बस्थानीयस्य जीवस्योपदिश्यते। अन्यथा न तत्त्वमसीति स्यात्, किन्तु न त्वमसीति भवेत् न रजतमस्तीतिवत्।" —Ibid. p.108.

69. Vide, D. Venkataramiah, Loc. Cit. p.76; See also, "ननु सत्येव बिम्बैकतावगमे प्रतिबिम्बस्य तद्गतो विच्छेदादिमिथ्यावभासः तथा ब्रह्मैकतावगमेऽपि जीवस्य विच्छेदादिमिथ्यावभासो न निवर्तितुमर्हति। उच्यते—देवदत्तस्याचेतनांशस्यैव प्रतिबिम्बत्वात्

सचेतनांशस्यैव प्रतिबिम्बत्वे प्रतिबिम्बहेतोः श्यामादिधर्मेणेव जाड्येनाप्यास्कन्दितत्वात् न तत् प्रतिबिम्बं बिम्बैकरूपतामात्मनो जानाति अचेतनत्वात्। तथा च.... न बिम्बचेष्टया विना प्रतिबिम्बं चेष्टते इति'' —Pañcapādikā, Loc. Cit, p.110.

70. ''तत्र नेदं रजतमिति रजतस्वरूपमेव बाध्यते, नात्र रजतं किंतु तदिदं रजतमिति देशमात्रबाध्या सत्यरजतेनैकतया न प्रत्यभिज्ञायते। अतो रजतेऽभिज्ञाबाधात् प्रत्यभिज्ञा विभ्रम इत्यर्थः। इह तु नेदं मुखमिति न स्वरूपेण बाध्यते। किंतु नात्र मुखं मदीयमेवेति प्रत्यभिज्ञायते। न च सा बाध्यते। —Vivaraṇa on PPD Adhyāsabhāṣya, Loc. Cit. p.283.

71. ''न दर्पणादौ मुखव्यक्त्यन्तरमस्ति, तज्जन्मकारणशून्यत्वात्, शशमस्तके विषाणवदिति।'' —Ibid. p.283.

72. ''यस्य हि भ्रान्तिरात्मनि परत्र वा समुत्पन्ना तद्गतेनैव सम्यग्ज्ञानेन सा निवर्तते। यस्तु जानीते देवदत्तः प्रतिबिम्बस्यात्मनोऽभिन्नत्वं न स तद्गतेन दोषेण संस्पृश्यते। नापि ज्ञानमात्रात् प्रतिबिम्बस्य निवृत्तिः तद्धेतोः दर्पणादेः पारमार्थिकत्वात्।'' —Pañcapādikā, Loc. Cit. pp.110-111.

73. "ननु एकतावगमेऽपि न तत्र विच्छेदविभ्रमो निवर्तते। सत्यम्, न प्रतिबिम्बकृतं तत् किंतु उपाधेरज्ञानाजन्यत्वाज्ज्ञानानिवर्त्यत्वकृतमिति"। —Vivaraṇa, Loc. Cit. p.289.

74. ''जीवः पुनः प्रतिबिम्बकल्पः सर्वेषां नः प्रत्यक्षश्चिद्रूपः, नान्तःकरणजाड्येनास्कन्दितः। स चाहंकर्तृत्वमात्मनो रूपं मन्यते न बिम्बकल्पब्रह्मैकरूपताम्। अतो युक्तस्तद्रूपावगमे मिथ्यापगमः'' —Pañcapādikā, Loc. Cit. p.111.

75. ''....श्रुतिस्मृतिसूत्रैः जीवस्य प्रतिबिम्बभावस्य दर्शितत्वात्, अमूर्तस्य चाकाशस्य साभ्रनक्षत्रस्य जले प्रतिबिम्बवदमूर्तस्य ब्रह्मणोऽपि प्रतिबिम्बसम्भवात्, जानुमात्रप्रमाणेऽपि जले दूरविशालाकाशदर्शनात्, जलान्तराकाश एवाभ्रादिप्रतिबिम्बयुक्तो दृश्यते इति वक्तुमशक्यत्वात्। तत्प्रतिबिम्बत्वं चिद्रूपत्वं च शास्त्रप्रतिपन्नं प्रत्यक्षप्रतिपन्नं च न निराकर्तुं शक्यते इति भावः।'' —Vivaraṇa, Loc. Cit.p.289.

76. ''तदेवमहङ्कारग्रन्थिरस्मच्छब्दसंशब्दितः प्रत्ययश्चासौ आदर्श इव प्रतिबिम्बस्य अनिदञ्चित्सम्बलितत्वेन तस्याभिव्यक्तिहेतुत्वात्। अतः तस्य विषयवत् भवतीत्युपचारेण अनिदञ्चिदात्मधातुरस्मत्प्रत्ययविषय उच्यते। स पुनरेवम्भूतो जाग्रत्स्वप्नयोरहमुल्लेखरूपेण सुषुप्ते तत्संस्काररञ्जिताग्रहणाविद्याप्रतिबद्धप्रकाशत्वेन च गतागतमाचरन् संसारी जीवः विज्ञानघनः विज्ञानात्मा प्राज्ञः शरीरी शारीरः आत्मा सम्प्रसादः पुरुषः प्रत्यगात्मा कर्ता भोक्ता क्षेत्रज्ञः इति च श्रुतिस्मृतिप्रवादेषु गीयते।'' —Pañcapādikā, Loc. Cit. pp.133-135.

77. Vide, Tātparayadīpikā, Loc. Cit. p.290.

78. ''ननु घटाकाशवदुपाध्यवच्छिन्नो जीवः किं न स्यात्? न, सामान्यविशेषाभ्याम् उपाधिभिरण्डान्तर्वर्तिब्रह्मणः सर्वात्मना जीवभावेनावच्छिन्नत्वादनवच्छिन्नस्य ब्रह्मणोऽण्डाद् बहिरेव सद्भावप्रसङ्गात् तत्र सर्वगतसर्वनियन्तृत्वादि ब्रह्मणो न स्यात्''। - Vivaraṇa, Loc. Cit., pp.289-290.

79. ''अवच्छिन्नप्रदेशेष्वनवच्छिन्नस्य द्विगुणीकृत्य वृत्त्ययोगात्।'' —Ibid.

80. ''प्रतिबिम्बपक्षे तु जलगतस्वाभाविकाकाशे सत्येव प्रतिबिम्बाकाशदर्शनादेकत्रैव द्विगुणीकृत्य वृत्त्युपपत्तेः जीवावच्छेदेषु ब्रह्मणोऽपि नियन्तृत्वादिरूपेणावस्थानमुपपद्यते इति प्रतिबिम्बपक्ष एव श्रेयानिति।'' —Ibid. pp.291-292.

81. ''उपाधिस्वरूपमपि भ्रान्त्यैवावभासते....। अतः तत्त्वज्ञानेनोपाधिनिवृत्तेः विच्छेदापायः....।'' —Ibid. p.292.

82. ''ननु जीवब्रह्माश्रयो विभागः कथमविद्यातन्त्रः, स्यात्? उच्यते - अनाद्यविद्याविशिष्टं

चैतन्यमनादिजीवभावेन काल्पनिकानादिभेदस्य आश्रयः, न स्वरूपेण, तस्यैकत्वात्।... अविद्यातन्त्राणां चानिर्वचनीयत्वमनादित्वं चाविद्या सम्बन्धवन्न विरुध्यते।'' —Ibid. P.294.

83. ''लोके च दर्पणघटादिविशिष्टयोरेव मुखाकाशयोः मिथ्याभेदावभासो न स्वरूपेण इत्युपाधितन्त्रता भेदस्योच्यते।'' —Ibid.

84. ''अत्र कश्चिदाह-ब्रह्मणो भिन्नाभिन्नोऽयं जीवः, ततश्च ब्रह्मणो नित्यमुक्तवता जीवस्य च नित्यबद्धता व्यवस्थामश्नुते। अत्यन्ताभेदे तु ब्रह्मैव स्वसंसाराय कथं जगदुत्पादयेत् विरुद्धा च विशुद्धस्य अशुद्धताप्रतिपत्तिरिति। अत्रोच्यते-किमात्मिकेयं भिन्नाभिन्नता ? न तावत् जातिव्यक्तिगुणगुणिकार्यकारणविशिष्टस्वरूपांशाशिभावनिबन्धना। जीवब्रह्मणोः तेषामभावात्।'' —Vivaraṇa, Loc. Cit. p.754.

85. ''ममैवांशो जीवलोके इति स्मृतेः अंशांशितेति चेत् न- 'निष्कलं निष्क्रियं इति श्रुतिविरोधात्। 'पादोऽस्य सर्वा भूतानि' इति च अल्पतामात्रविवक्षयोक्तम्। वाक्यस्य ब्रह्मानन्त्यप्रतिपादनपरत्वात्। सांशत्वे च पटादिवत् अवयवारभ्यत्वप्रसङ्गात्।'' —Ibid.

86. ''ननु स्वाभाविकी निरवयवता बुद्ध्याद्युपाधिनिमित्तं सांशत्वमिति चेत्, न तावदुपाधिना विदार्य पृथक् क्रियते जीवः। खड्गधारासमाविद्धेऽप्याकाशे निरवयवे भेदनादर्शनात्। उपाधिभिश्च स्वात्मानं विदार्य संसारमनुभावयता ब्रह्मणा स्वात्मनि व्यामोह एव प्रकटितः स्यात्। न च उपाधीनामन्यार्थतया सृष्टिः। अन्याभावात्। प्रागभिन्नानां जीवानामन्यत्वाभावात्।'' —Ibid.

87. ''ननु कोऽयं जीवो नाम यस्य स्वरूपं त्वंपदेन लक्ष्यमाणं ब्रह्मैव वाक्यार्थः सम्पद्यते। - ब्रह्मैवाविद्याप्रतिबिम्बितमिति वदामः।'' —Ibid. Loc. Cit. p.760.

88. ''ततश्च त्वंपदेन अशेषोपाधिनिराकरणेन आत्मस्वरूपमेव लक्ष्यमाणं तत्पदोपलक्ष्यं ब्रह्मैव पदद्वयसामर्थ्यात् सम्पद्यते।'' —Ibid.

89. ''ननु भिन्नाभिन्नता वाक्यार्थः किं न स्यात् न- तथा सति शरीरेन्द्रियविशिष्टस्यैव त्वंपदार्थस्य ब्रह्मणो भिन्नाभिन्नत्वात् तथैव वाक्यार्थसिद्धे : लक्षणया ब्रह्मात्मज्ञानेन अध्यासबाधो न स्यात्।'' —Ibid, Loc. Cit. p.761.

90. ''भिन्नाभिन्ने च वाक्यार्थे न तत्त्वज्ञानात् भेदांशनिवृत्तिः। तस्य स्वविषयानाशकत्वात्।'' —Ibid.

91. ''यदि भेदाभेदाभ्यामंशी जीवोऽभेदांशश्च ब्रह्मैव स्यात् तदा सावयवो जीवो जीवांशश्च ब्रह्मेति पण्डितम्मन्यस्य विपरीतोऽर्थः सम्पद्यते। अभेदांशस्य अब्रह्मत्वे अत्यन्तभेद एव स्यात्।'' —Ibid.

92. '' न च अंशद्वयसमुदायो जीवः, अवस्तुत्वप्रसङ्गात्। न चाभेदांश एव जीवः, ब्रह्मण एव जीवत्वप्रसङ्गात्।'' —Ibid.

93. ''न च उभावंशौ, जीवद्वयप्रसङ्गात् न च भेदांश एव जीवः; अत्यन्तभेदप्रसङ्गात्, यत्र तत्त्वज्ञानमोक्षादिव्यवहारासिद्धिः''। —Ibid.

94. ''तस्मात् मन्दमतिसन्तोषमात्रप्रयोजनतया बहुवेणुभारपीडितचेतसा अयं भेदाभेदपक्षः समादीयत इति। तस्मादेकमेव ब्रह्म देवदत्तवदुपाधिभेदनिमित्तविभागपरामर्शेन प्रत्यस्तमितविभागं वाक्येन प्रतिपाद्यत इति शोभनम्।'' —Ibid, Loc. Cit. p.763.

95. ''एकमेवाद्वितीयं तद्धैक आहुः''। —Ch. UP. VII. 2.1

96. Vide, R. Balasubramanian, Loc. Cit., p.44, See also. सदैव सदिति अस्तितामात्रं वस्तु सूक्ष्मं निर्विक्षेपं सर्वगमेकं निरञ्जनं निरवयवं विज्ञानं यदवगम्यते सर्ववेदान्तेभ्यः।'' —SB on Ch. UP. VI. 2.1

97. Vide, R. Balasubramanian, Loc. Cit., p.47.

98. "जीवेश्वरौ मायिकौ विज्ञाय सर्वविशेषं नेति नेतीति विहाय यदवशिष्यते तदद्वयं ब्रह्म।" —Advaytāraka-Upaniṣad-2- Vide, Upaniṣad Vidyabhawan, Varanasi, 1990, p.196.
99. Vide, R. Balasubramanian, Loc. cit., p.49.
100. Supra, p.173.
101. Supra, p.176.
102. Supra, p.196.
103. Supra, p.185.
104. Supra, Ibid.
105. Supra, p.199.

CHAPTER VI

THE ADVAITIC CONCEPT OF BRAHMAN

It has been suggested in the last chapter that there is a relation of cause and effect between *Brahman* and the world in so far as *Brahman* is the substrate of Nescience. The question that arises next is what then is the nature of *Brahman,* the Ultimate Reality.

"The Scriptures define *Brahman,* the Ultimate Reality in two ways - in terms of Its essential nature as well as in terms of its accidental attributes. *Brahman,* the Absolute Reality, is described as "the Real Knowledge, Infinite," by the Scriptures[1]. When the Upaniṣad says that *'Brahman* is that from which all beings come into existence, that by which they live after coming into existence, and that towards which they move and into which they merge'[2], it defines *Brahman* in terms of Its accidental attribute, because causality of the world is an external qualification or attribute of *Brahman,* which is meaningful only in the context of its relation to the world. It is not a definition of what *Brahman* is in Itself; on the contrary, it is a definition of *Brahman* in relation to something else"[3].

Brahman is therefore viewed from two stand-points. From the point of view of *Brahman* Itself and from the point of view of the world. "Viewed in Itself, It is called the Absolute, (i.e. *Brahman*) and viewed in relation to the world, It is called God (i.e. *Īśvara*). It means that God is the Absolute from the cosmic point of view, and the absolute is God from the acosmic point of view. So long as we are at the vyāvahārika (empirical) level, which is relative and relational, we cannot but speak of the Ultimate as god. We try to relate the world with the Ultimate as the cause of it. But the dualism of God and world, which is inherent in the category of causality, does not satisfy the demands of reason, and has, therefore, to be transcended. It is for this reason that the dualist position of theism, even though methodologically significant and valuable, is not final.

Unless the Ultimate is known in Itself, there is no overcoming of the *vyāvahārika* realm of dualities. It follows that the metaphysics of Advaita, which is transtheistic and not anti-theistic, is oriented towards the discovery of the Ultimate"[4].

Advaita Vedānta believes in the manifestation of *Brahman* in two forms : as *Apara-Brahman* (Lower Brahman) and *Para-Brahman* (Supreme Reality). In Its Pure untainted form, *Brahman* is *Nirviśeṣa* (Unqualified), *Niṣprapañca* (Transcendent), *Nirguṇa* (Indeterminate), *Anirvacanīya* (Indescribable). But in association with *Māyā,* It appears as though possessing qualities, and as such is referred to as being *Saguṇa* (Determinate), *Śaviśeṣa* (Qualified), *Saprapañca* (Immanent).

"Śaṅkara makes (in this connection) a distinction between the description (i.e., *taṭastha-lakṣaṇa*) of a thing and its definition (*Svarūpa-lakṣaṇa*). The former gives only the accidental qualities or modes of a thing, while the latter reveals its essential nature"[5]. The *Brahma-Sūtra* (I.1.2) says that *Brahman* is the cause of the creation, preservation and dissolution of this universe. Commenting upon this, Śaṅkara says that this is merely a description of *Brahman;* it is not Its definition as such[6]. "Being the cause of this universe consisting of individual selves and external objects is an accidental quality of *Brahman* and not Its essential nature. Causality is a category of thought which has empirical validity but not final reality. It connot be really attributed to *Brahman*"[7].

When the Upaniṣads declare that *Brahman* is *Sat* (Reality), *Cit* (Consciousness), *Ānanda* (Bliss), these (terms) should not be taken to represent Its qualities, but rather Its very essence, or else the contingency of dualism would creep in due to the emergence of two realities—the qualificand and the qualifier, which would be contradictory to the doctrine of non-dualism of the Śāṅkara school of thought.

In Advaita terminology the term *Brahman* is suggestive of vastness, all-pervasiveness, unlimitedness, absolute indivisibility. Whatever division is attributed to It in philosophical disquisition is only a concession to the limitations of normal experience of thought and senses; hence so long as the world of thought and senses persists, the Absolute Reality, Which is One and Undifferentiated, cannot but be regarded in dual and interrelated aspects of immanence and distinctions.... So, as the Ultimate

Cause of all appearances, *Brahman* has to be described as both immanent in, and also as distinct from, all appearances so long as these appearances linger on in the empirical state of existence. "*Brahman* is thus the only Reality in its true sense, all others being only Its appearances. This aspectless *Brahman* is a synonym of what has been referred to repeatedly as the one Ultimate and underlying Reality, the non-realization of which has resulted in all kinds of empirical and illusory appearances, beginningless and interminable, making up the whole universe"[8].

Of the two theories of Reflection and Limitation invoked by the Advaitin-s to prove the illusory nature of the plurality of selves and the consequent undivided oneness of the Absolute, "Śaṅkara makes use of the latter theory on the analogy of pot and space to explain that the Absolute seems to assume differentiations on account of Its being limited by the intellects, sense-organs, bodies, etc. The limitation which causes differentiation is due to *Ajñāna*, 'Primal Ignorance'. The Absolute in reality remains one undivided whole like space. The principle of *Ajñāna* which generates the illusion of distinctions is also sought to resolve the contradictions among Scriptural statements which declare the individual self to be both identical with, and different from, the Absolute"[9].

As a matter of fact, *Brahman* is not the least connected with the act of creation. It is only in Its apparent association with *Avidyā* or *Māyā* that It is said to evolve the world out of Itself. 'But since this association is but illusory, there is no actual evolution (*pariṇāma*) of *Brahman* into the world, as of milk into curd. There is only an illusory appearance (*vivarta*) of *Brahman* as the world, like the appearance of the rope as the snake. Hence *Brahman* is not in the least affected by the so-called evolution and reabsorption of the world'[10]. Śaṅkara says in this context that 'the cause is not affected by the effect and its qualities, because the latter are the mere fallacious superimpositions of Nescience'. And what is true of creation holds good with regard to dissolution as well[11]. But even when *Brahman* is conceived as the creative and preservative cause of the world process, Its role consists in merely 'casting a glance' which is sufficient to set *Māyā* into motion[12]. The entire process goes on spontaneously, without any active participation of *Brahman* as such. It is thus that *Brahman* is described by the Bhāmatī as having "the Vedas as Its breath, the five elements as Its looks, the entire world of sentient and insentient creatures as Its smile, and ultimate dissolution (of the world) as Its dreamless-sleep"[13].

'*Brahman* is also described as the teleological Principle. The world reveals to us a wonderful plan and order of existence, and this plan is consistent only with the existence of a Conscious Power behind it'[14]. Śaṅkara says in this regard that this world cannot be conceived as coming out of a blind force, implying that there exists a rational power or consciousness behind the world order, and that is *Brahman*[15].

According to Advaita Vedānta, *Brahman* is Omniscient and this consists in Its capacity of manifesting everything in the world. 'Just as the lamp is capable of illuminating everything in its vicinity, in the same way *Brahman* is to be conceived as ceaselessly illumining everything in the world, It being the material cause of everything and everything being permeated by It'[16].

Brahman is also defined as '*Anugata*' (i.e. Immanent in all worldly entities), *Vyāvṛtta* (i.e., Distinct from the worldly entities), *Ananugata-vyāvṛtta* (i.e., transcending even those two aspects). "The use of such terms is merely a formal attempt at distinguishing and analysing logically, what is in reality 'Indistinguishable', 'Indivisible' and Absolutely One and above all logical analysis"[17]. "*Brahman* as *Immanent* is involved in the world as its source and sustenance through Its Incidences or Appearances, and as Transcendent, It is concerned with, and absolutely unrelated to, anything; It is utterly conspicuous by its absence from the stand-point of Reality. This statement is neither paradoxical nor involves any logical inconsistency, as the two positions are clearly based on two different stand-points of "*Vastu-vṛtta*" and "*Tamo-vṛtta*" (i.e., stand-points of Reality and *Avidyā* respectively). In other words, the representation of one and the same Reality-Consciousness-Bliss *Brahman* as *Immanent*, that is pervading, permeating and pulsating through all worldly entities and as Transcendent, i.e., beyond the reach of all of them, is not any assertive proposition but only explanatory or reconciliatory of two apparent contradictions : the world appearing to be real to normal human experience on the one hand, and *Brahman*, the only Reality recognized by the Upaniṣadic texts, on the other. Thus the Transcendent, Absolute and Aspectless *Brahman,* as recognized by the system, is not only essentially One, Unrelated, Unlimited, Immutable, Inexhaustible but also free from the logical and metaphysical incongruities, involved in its dynamic conception as held by some...... school of Indian Philosophy"[18].

"Immanence is truth or reality in relation to all appearances of the world and so is 'Distinction' too till the dualism of *Ātman* and *Anātman* or *Pratyak* and *Parāk* is not dissipated by supreme *Brahman*-realization. Both "Immanence" and "Distinction" appears to be true so long as Truth or Reality Itself has not been realized.... When Reality Proper is fully realized, not only *Avidyā* but also the universe with all its apparent truths and empirical realities are sublated and *Brahman—Transcendent, Absolute* and *Aspectless*—remains the One Truth-in-Itself or the only Reality in its absolute sense"[19]. It is thus that *Brahman,* which is described by Advaita Vedānta as "One without a Second", is bereft of any form of differentiation, be it *sajātīya-bheda* (i.e., difference subsisting between two (different) objects of the same class—*Brahman* being only one); *vijātiya-bheda* (i.e., difference subsisting between two objects of different classes—there being no object existing apart from *Brahman*); and *svagatabheda* i.e., internal distinction—*Brahman* being One whole, Impartite, Indivisible and Unchangeable). "According to Advaita, there is nothing like or unlike the Ultimate. It means that there is no plurality of reals. Also, the ultimate is free from internal differentiation. It is neither a whole consisting of parts nor a substance possessing attributes. The three words in the Upaniṣadic text, "*Ekam*" (one), "*eva*" (only), and "*advitīyam*" (without a second), are intended in respect of the Ultimate Reality. So the Ultimate is One and Non-dual, Homogenous, Infinite and without beginning and end"[20]. *Brahman* thus defies all descriptions and definitions, all comparisons, and contrasts, and being so, all that can be said about It is that It is not like anything in this world. This is why the Upaniṣads describe It as simply "*neti*" "*neti*", "not this", "not this"[21].

II. The Bhāmatī's concept of Brahman

The Bhāmatī declares from the very outset that the Supreme Being (*Brahman*) is Immortal, and is of the nature of immeasurable Bliss and Knowledge. It is both the efficient cause and the material cause of this univese of sentient and insentient creatures of all kinds, since this all issued forth verily from It, and since, with the assistance of indeterminable Nescience, the five elements—ether, air, fire, water and earth—are illusorily manifested from It[22]. Vācaspati further says that the Self alone is called *Brahman,* because It is great or because It is the cause of growth[23]. It has 'light' as Its essence and is Self-luminous, One, Immutable, Eternal, Impartite. *Brahman* Itself is indeed the inner self[24]. Justifying the necessity of undertaking a discussion on *Brahman,* Śaṅkara says that such a discussion is necessitated by the fact that though *Brahman* is always manifest, being Self-luminous, yet It is as though unmanifest and unknown to the individual self due to the influence of beginningless Nescience, resulting in the individuation of the self accompanied by the paraphernalia of pains and sufferings. It is indeed to ward off such ignoble influences of Nescience and to re-establish, so to say, the individual self in its true nature, thus releasing it from all forms of bondage and suffering, that the deliberation on the true nature of the self as identical with *Brahman* is ought to be undertaken[25]. The Bhāmatī says in this regard that just as a person becomes aware of the presence around his neck of an apparently lost (or absent) necklace only on its being pointed out to him by somebody else, despite its having been there even before, in the same manner, due to Nescience, the self though always illumined and manifest, is as though unknown and unrealized, and becomes as though known to the seeker on his being expressly made to discover It by a (Self-realized) Preceptor[26].

Raising a question regarding the very existence of such an entity as *Brahman,* Śaṅkara says that *Brahman* should be either known or unknown to justify Its being or not being the subject of investigation. The unambiguous reply given by Śaṅkara himself puts to rest all doubts whatsoever as regards the existence of *Brahman.* Says he, 'there does exist *Brahman* who is in essence eternally Pure, Intelligent and Omniscient, and endowed with all powers that be'. He declares further, that the concept of *Brahman's* having eternality, purity etc. as Its essence is in conformity with the sense conveyed by the verbal root "*Bṛh*". This is evident also from the fact of Its being the self of all beings, since existence, and not non-existence, of oneself is cognized by everyone. Were the Self not known to be in existence, the whole world would have the cognition, "I do not exist". And that self, says Śaṅkara, is *Brahman* verily[27].

Pre-empting a further query as to the proof of the existence of *Brahman,* the Bhāmatī says that the Scriptures or Verbal Testimony, i.e., the Vedas, which are not of human origin, should be understood to be the means of knowing *Brahman,* for no other means of valid knowledge is applicable to the knowledge about It. And also because the authoritativeness of the Scriptures resides in that only (i.e., in the revelation of the knowledge of *Brahman*)[28]. Clarifying this position taken by him as to the veracity of verbal Testimony, Vācaspati Miśra says that the concept of *Brahman* endowed with Eternality, Purity, etc., becomes clear even prior to undertaking the enquiry into *Brahman,* by the mere study of the Vedas together with Etymology, Grammar, etc. which renders explicit the meaning of Scriptural texts, such as those starting with "Truth alone was there in the beginning" and ending with "That thou art[29]." Vācaspati remarks in this context that the term "*Brahman*" used here is indicative of that knowledge only whose content is *Brahman,* and not (*Brahman* as such) since That *Brahman* is known only through the proper inquiry. As to the terms such as "Eternal" and "Pure" used in connection with *Brahman,* the Bhāmatī clarifies that these are meant to exclude from the concept of *Brahman* such defects as non-eternality and misery resulting from association with adjuncts like the body, etc., respectively, while the term "intelligent" "exhibits It as Blissful and not (as) illumined by an external object"[30]. According to the Bhāmatī School therefore, the study of the Scriptures leads to the rise only of the knowledge about *Brahman,* and not to Its realization, as such.

Distinguishing between the "adjunctless" form of *Brahman* and Its form qualified by the adjunct of Nescience, the Bhāmatī says that *Brahman* without adjuncts is always free and pure, but appears as though non-different from the body, etc. Vācaspati observes that the attributes such as Omniscience, Omnipotence etc., project *Brahman* as the Cause of the world through Nescience, since causality presupposes the presence of power, and vice-versa[31]. It is clear from this that the Bhāmatī views *Brahman* from two angles—one, as Pure *Brahman*, free from Nescience, and the other, causal *Brahman*, having Nescience as Its adjunct (for the purpose of creation, preservation and dissolution of the world.

The Pure *Brahman*, described as Eternal, Intelligent, always Free, etc., says Bhāmatī, is denoted by the word "That", while the self is denoted by the word "thou" (in the Vedānta text-"That thou art"). This is indicated by Śaṅkara when be says that, "And because of being the self of all, the existence of *Brahman* is known even to the ploughman, because of his own cognition, "I exist". Vācaspati says (furthermore) that 'because of the appositional relation of "That" to "thou", the self is proved to be *Brahman* Itself. Hence, the purity, intelligence, etc. of the denotation of the "That" being known from the Scriptures, and the *Jīva* denoted by the "thou" being known from perception, it is intelligible that the realization of the denotation of the term 'thou' as being of the nature of *Brahman* results from the text "That thou art"[32].

Śaṅkara defines "*Brahman*" as the Omniscient and Omnipotent Cause Whence there is the creation, preservation and dissolution of this universe characterized by name and form, containing many agents and enjoyers, the abode of what is definitely regulated in respect of place, time, cause, action and fruit, the nature of whose design cannot even be conceived by the mind[33]. Śaṅkara says in addition that the true nature of a thing cannot be cognized through human intellect, but rather through the thing itself. Clarifying this point, Śaṅkara says that just as the cognition of one and the same post does not take the form, "this is a post or something else or a man," this being an illusory cognition, but takes rather the definite form, "This is certainly a post". This latter cognition is indeed the true cognition of the post, for it depends on the post itself. Thus, says Śaṅkara, the validity of a cognition having an existent entity as content depends solely on that entity and not on the intellect. Therefore, the knowledge of *Brahman* is dependent on *Brahman* Itself because that knowledge too has an existing entity as its content"[34].

Vācaspati says on his part that one cannot object to the nature of *Brahman* being defined by the knowledge of things coming within the range of human experience on the ground that such things are as per their nature opposed to the nature of *Brahman,* It being eternally Pure and Intelligent, while the former are limited, impure, non-intelligent and destructible. It is true that the Eternal cannot be defined as having the world of created objects as Its attributes or as being identical to It, say Vāscaspati, but It can be defined as being at Its origin, just as the movement of the sun is defined in terms of the attainment (by it) of different spheres (in the sky)[35]. Vācaspati observes further, that the objection to the effect, that when causality could be attributed to so many other entities such as Pradhāna (Primal nature), Time, planetary deities (Graha Lokapāla), Chance, Non-existence, etc., why postulate *Brahman* Itself as the cause, is also untenable because what needs to be postulated as the cause is an Intelligent entity, and not non-intelligent entities such as Pradhāna, etc. This, says the Bhāmatī, is indicated by Śaṅkara by the use of the term differentiation, meaning thereby that what is characterized by name and form is verily caused by an intelligent entity as is seen in the case of pot, etc[36].

Strengthening the notion of Omniscience of *Brahman* as referred to above, Śaṅkara says that *Brahman* is not only the cause of this material world of names and forms, but also of the vast body of Sacred Knowledge which comprises the Ṛg Veda, etc., together with its multitude of disciplines, and which, like a torch illuminates all things in this world, resembling as though the Omniscient Itself. The origin of such Sacred teaching as constituting the Ṛg Veda, etc., itself of the nature of Omniscience, cannot be an entity other than an Omniscient Being, says Śaṅkara." When a Sacred teaching with an extensive theme originates from a particular person, for example, the sacred teaching of Grammar etc., from Pāṇini, etc., although its content be only a part of what is to be known, he possesses more extensive knowledge than that — this is well known in experience"[37]. In the same way, that from which originates without the slightest effort, the ocean of all knowledge the Ṛg Veda, etc., constituting various branches of knowledge, and which is the cause of distinctions such as gods, man, animals etc., has as its cause the Omniscient and Omnipotent *Brahman*. And this has for support Scriptural texts such as, "Of that Great Being this is the breath, which is the Ṛg Veda", etc[38].

Elucidating the magnificence of the Sacred Knowledge constituting the Ṛg Veda, etc. with a view to substantiating the natures of Omniscience and Omnipotence of *Brahman*, Vācaspati says that texts such as the Ṛg Veda, etc. are Scriptures (*Śāstra-s*) as they give instructions with regard to the performance of all categories of acts, namely, obligatory, occasional and optional, with reference to the *Varṇa-s* and *Āśrama-s*, (beginning with the *Garbhādhāna-saṁskāra* and ending with funeral rites), as well as acts to be performed at different periods of the day; and due also to the fact that they teach the truth about *Brahman* which teaching is not obtainable from any other source. Hence, as they are concerned with great themes they are indeed of great importance. This is so also owing to their having many auxiliary sciences (*Aṅga-s* and *Upāṅga-s*), supplemented by innumerable disciplines, such as the Purāṇa-s, Nyāya, etc. Their authoritativeness is also established by the fact of their being recognized as such by great sages, authors of works such as the Purāṇa-s, etc[39].

The Bhāmatī says in conclusion that the unsurpassed omniscience and omnipotence of *Brahman* from which the Vedas originated, need not be pointed out, it being too evident to be emphasized,. Moreover, what requires great effort on the part of divine beings to accomplish, does not require the slightest effort on the part of *Brahman*. From this only Its supremacy is to be inferred. That even the creation of the Veda requires no effort whatsoever on the part of *Brahman* is corroborated by the Scriptures also in texts such as, "Of This Great Being", etc[40]. The Ṛg Veda, etc., says Śaṅkara in addition, is thus the source of the nature of *Brahman*. What is sought to be emphasized here is that the Veda being a creation of *Brahman* and being the repository of all Sacred Knowledge, is the sole authority as far as the nature of *Brahman* is concerned[41].

Averring that the nature of *Brahman* is known through the Scriptures, Śaṅkara says that the whole of the Vedānta literature also has for its content the nature of *Brahman*. All Vedāntic texts teach that *Brahman*, the Omniscient, the Omnipotent, is the cause of the creation, preservation and dissolution of the universe. And in this teaching, says he, there is absolute harmony among all the Vedānta texts. Illustrating this fact, Śaṅkara cites a few such texts as have for purport the nature of *Brahman,* viz., "All this was existence alone in the beginning" (Ch. UP. VI.2.1); "(That *Brahman*) is One, without a second" (Ibid); "The Self alone as One was there in the beginning" (Ait. Up. II. 1.1.1) etc[42]. Śaṅkara observes in this context that it would not be proper to assume something else as the main theme of the Vedānta, for that would amount to abandoning that which is expressly mentioned to be the main content while assuming something arrived at indirectly to be the main content of the Vedāntic texts[43].

Vācaspati says on his part, that the subject with which a statement starts and with which it ends, that itself is to be considered as the content of the statement, and not something subsidiary. In Vedānta also, says he, because *Brahman* is the subject of discussion in the beginning and the same is the subject of discussion in the end, *Brahman* itself is the content of Vedānta. This is made more explicit by Vācaspati by referring to the Vedāntic texts, "All this was existence alone in the beginning" and 'That thou art', which mark respectively the introductory and the concluding parts of Vedānta, showing there by that the Vedāntic texts have for purport the nature of *Brahman*[44]. According to Śaṅkara, though *Brahman* is of the nature of an already existent Entity, It cannot be said to be known through the empirical means of knowledge, such as Perception, etc. This is so because *Brahman,* Which is identical with the self, cannot be known through any other means except the Scriptures. It cannot also be said of *Brahman* that It can be known only through contemplation for It is the object of the injunction of contemplation. *Brahman* is One, says Śaṅkara, and as such, It is not amenable to any injunction, involving duality such as action, doership, etc. And also because once duality with respect to *Brahman* is dispelled (through Self-realization), there is no revival of the notion of duality, which otherwise, Brahman being the object of the injunction of contemplation, would have been possible[45]. Clarifying the fact of *Brahman* not being an object of injunction, Vācaspati says that as regards human goals, their attainment is an indirect result of the understanding of the Vedic injunctions. But as regards *Brahman*, Its realization is the direct outcome of the understanding of Vedānta texts such as, "That thou art", without any external aid, just as the realization of the reality of rope, which is a direct consequence of the knowledge, "This is not a snake; this is a rope." The superiority of *Brahman* to the knowledge resulting from injunctions is thus established[46]. Vācaspati says moreover, that contemplation presupposes the threefold difference of the contemplated, the contemplator and contemplation. *Brahman* being devoid of all kinds of differences, cannot be the object of the injunction of contemplation for that would be contradictory to Its nature[47].

Śaṅkara, concluding the discussion on the authoritativeness of the Scriptures as regards the nature of *Brahman*, observes that it is a fact that in other cases the authoritativeness of the Vedic text is plausible with respect only to injunctions. But with regard to *Brahman*, this is not the case, for the realization of the true nature of *Brahman* results directly from the knowledge of the Self which has for authority only the sacred teachings. Śaṅkara also remarks that the authoritative nature of the Sacred Text cannot be established through inference, etc. due to the absence of any example seen elsewhere that may be quoted to support the inferential argument. Thus is established the authoritativeness of the Scriptures with respect to the nature of *Brahman*[48]. Clarifying this point further, Vācaspati says that the non-dependence of *Brahman*-knowledge on injunction is also due to the difference in nature between the empirical means of knowledge and Verbal Authority. Says he, "the authoritativeness of the means of valid knowledge consists in their generating knowledge which is unsublated, not already understood, and indubitable; and that is intrinsic. Though the generation of this kind of knowledge is known by presumptive implication from the nature of the effect, yet, in the generation of that knowledge, they (i.e. the means of knowledge) do not depend on any other means of valid knowledge, not even this presumptive implication, as otherwise reciprocal dependence would result; hence it is said to be intrinsic"[49]. The same applies to the Vedānta-s (i.e. the Sacred Scriptures) too as regards *Brahman*, and hence their authoritativeness and the intrinsic nature of Verbal Authority, which if not accepted, would amount to saying that since any other sense organ is not seen to manifest colour, the sense of sight too does not manifest colour[50].

Making explicit the difference between *Brahman* and the world, the *Bhāmatī* says that the Self is absolutely Real, It being declared to be so by the Scriptures, the traditional Codes, the Epics, the Purāṇa-s, and by reasoning not in conflict with them. As for the world, it is not absolutely real, being itself an emanation from beginningless Nescience. That which is Real, says the *Bhāmatī,* is the material cause of this world, just like the real *rope* is the material cause of the illusory *snake,* which is but a modification. Being but a modification, this world is perishable and therefore unstable. Even a thousand causes cannot together make unreal the self which is Absolutely Real, just as even a thousand craftsman cannot convert a pot into cloth. In this world therefore all modifications are of a perishable nature while the self alone is imperishable, as is the case with the silver-in-shell and the snake-in-rope which are perishable upto the level short of the real shell and the real rope respectively. In this manner, says the *Bhāmatī,* amidst the multitude of modifications in the world, the self is the sole Truth, the Infinite, the Imperishable[51].

Explaining further why *Brahman* cannot be associated with injunction of any kind, Vācaspati says that since the pure form of *Brahman,* viz., that of the *witness* in contrast to the *Jīva* form, is not apprehensible through other means of knowledge, It has for authority the Sacred Texts, viz., the Upaniṣads alone. And the self, says Vācaspati, is not meant for any injunction, for everything is indeed meant for it, and not it for everything else, as is evoked by the Scripture itself: "everything here is liked not for its own sake; but for the sake of the self it is that everything is liked". And for that very reason, i.e. for being the self of all, it transcends the very notions of acceptance and rejection. Thus, *Brahman* being the true Self of the entire universe, none can talk of the rejection of one's nature since that nature cannot be rejected, nor can one talk of its acceptance, since that is present already. Therefore, the true nature of the self is not amenable to prescription and prohibition which are of the nature of acceptance and rejection respectively. Hence, *Brahman* alone is the Truth of the universe[52].

Refuting the Sāṅkhya view that insentient *Pradhāna* is the cause of the universe, and not *Brahman* as is claimed by the

Advaitin-s, Śaṅkara says that this is not acceptable as it is in opposition to what is taught by the Upaniṣad-s. The Vedānta texts are quite emphatic about *Brahman's* being the cause of the Universe. Starting with statements such as "before its creation this universe was but Existence (i.e. *Brahman*) which is One without a second", they establish irrevocably that *Brahman* itself visualized thus, "I shall be many, I shall appear as many". And following this, it created fire. Śaṅkara observes here that in that text, the universe, manifested as names and forms and referable by the word 'it', is first ascertained to be identified with Existence (i.e. *Brahman*) 'before its creation', then the text shows that the creatorship of fire, etc., that follows the visualization of future creation, belongs to that very entity, called existence, which is under consideration'[53]. The Upaniṣadṣ say also that in the beginning this universe was but the Self itself, and that there was nothing else whatsoever that was in existence then[54]. Śaṅkara notes in this context that creation took place only after its being 'visualized' by *Brahman*, Whom some texts declare as possessing '*sixteen limbs*'. The texts such as, "From Him who is Omniscient....Whose austerity (i.e. creative effort) is constituted by knowledge, emerged this *Brahmā* (i.e. *Hiraṇyagarbha*) as well as name, form and food"[55] have for purport the Omniscient *Brahman* as the cause of the universe.

Refuting another objection as to the omniscience of *Brahman*, Śaṅkara says that it is illogical to argue that *Brahman* cannot have omniscience in the primary sense on the ground that It is an Eternal Knower and as such cannot have any 'independence as regards the act of knowing'. He asks, how can It lose its Omniscience just by possessing the act of knowing eternally. It is contradictory to assert that *Brahman* possesses eternally the knowledge having the potency of illuminating each and everything and yet It is not Omniscient. Should such knowledge be non-eternal, says Śaṅkara, the possessor would sometimes know and would not know at other times, in which eventuality there would arise non-omniscience. But as far as *Brahman* is concerned, this is not the case, for knowledge as such is eternal[57].

Vācaspati says on his part that *Pradhāna, atoms,* etc. cannot be considered to be the cause of the universe since they differ from the effects. The effects being non-different from their cause, it is possible to know the entire effects through the knowledge of the cause, just as all earthen objects become known through knowledge of clay, their cause, which would not be possible, were there difference between the cause and the effects. This is substantiated by the Scriptures themselves, says Vācaspati, which, through texts such as, "One without a second", "There is no plurality here whatsoever", "From death he attains death", etc. negates the existence of the universe, as existent apart from *Brahman,* thereby establishing a conscious cause of the Universe, even as the rope is the material cause of the superimposed snake[58].

As to the concept of *Brahman* having 'sixteen limbs', the *Bhāmatī* clarifying this says that *Brahman* is conceived as an animal having four legs, eight hoofs and sixteen *limbs'* as follows: the first four limbs are the four cardinal points; *Brahman* is self-luminous;' luminosity itself is therefore Its first leg. The four gross elements represented by the earth, space, heavens (sky) and the ocean (s) are Its other limbs. *Brahman* is Eternal : Eternality is therefore Its second leg. In the same way fire, sun, moon and lightning are Its other four limbs. Its brilliance is defined as Its other leg. Similarly It also has breath, eyes, ears and tongue, i.e. breathing, seeing, hearing and speech are Its other four limbs.. *Brahman* is the substratum or abode of all : this is what is meant when it is said that It has a fourth leg. Thus, says Vācaspati, *Brahman* is described as possessing sixteen limbs and sixteen parts and as such is made an object of worship by some Scriptures[59].

Refuting another objection to the effect that it is *Pradhāna,* and not *Brahman* that is referred to as Existence, "having as attributes the acts of 'seeing', etc. in texts such as "That fire saw", "These waters saw", etc., Śaṅkara says that it is wrong to say so, owing to the use of the word "Self" with reference to the said texts. After the statements referred to above, the same text, refers to that very Existence as well as the word "deity", as is testified by texts such as, "That Deity, which is such, saw....., Now then let me manifest name and form by Myself entering into these three deities as the *Jīva* (individual soul) that is but (My) Self"[60]. Śaṅkara observes that had *Pradhāna* been the entity referred to here, it would have been alluded to in the texts, and in that case, the Deity would not refer to the *Jīva* as Its own self. Moreover, how can the *Jīva* be the self of the insentient *Pradhāna*. It follows therefore that it is *Brahman,* not *Pradhāna,* which is the subject of the texts under discussion[61].

According to Śaṅkara, "*Brahman* is known in two aspects—one, as possessed of the limiting adjunct constituted by the diversities of the universe which is a modification of name and form, and the other, free from all conditioning factors and opposed to the earlier"[62]. It is only due to Nescience that *Brahman* becomes as though within the scope of empirical activities involving the three-fold divisions of the meditator, meditation and the meditated. Śaṅkara says in the context of worship or meditation, that the results of such activities differ in accordance with the qualities attributed to the One God, the Supreme Self, as is claimed by the Scriptures themselves: "One becomes as what one worships It"[63]. Vācaspati remarks on this that although *Brahman* is devoid of all adjunct - related forms, yet it cannot be deliberated upon merely on the basis of that Supreme form. Hence the necessity of referring to It as having adjuncts in order to render easier the deliberation on Its nature. But the purpose of attributing to *Brahman* different kinds of adjuncts vary from person to person. Some, for example, do so for the sake of attaining spiritual emancipation; some for gradual liberation, (*Krama-mukti*), and some others for "*Karma-Samṛddhi*"[64]. The Bhāmatī says moreover that although the Self is one, Supreme and of the form of Knowledge and Bliss, yet due to the influence of beginningless Nescience It appears to be as though unreal at one time and real at the other. For what reason is this so, asks Vācaspati. In reply to this he says that this is due to the varying influence of the blinding effect of Nescience. Illustrating this variation in the influence of Nescience resulting in apprehension of *Brahman* in a variety of forms, the Bhāmatī says that just as the sun in the form of superior light fills all the directions and the sky with one single (undivided and unvariegated) light, but still in the rainy season the same light is said to be 'dim', while during summer it is said to be 'very bright', in the same way One *Brahman* is apprehended variously due to a variety of adjuncts under the influence of Nescience[65].

Śaṅkara, quoting from the Śvetāśvatara-Upaniṣad, says that *Brahman* is the all-knowing God, the Cause of the Universe. 'In this universe It has no master, no ruler; It has neither any distinguishing sign. It itself is the cause and the Ordainer of the masters of the senses. It has no originator nor any ordainer. *Brahman,* the Ominiscient, is therefore the cause of the Universe, and none else[66]. The Bhāmatī says in this connection that all the Scriptures advocate the Ominiscient and Omnipotent *Brahman* as the cause of the origin, sustennence and dissolution of the universe, and that there is no portion of the Vedānta-texts which says anything contradictory to this claim[67].

Highlighting another aspect of *Brahman,* Śaṅkara says that the Self is of the nature of Bliss as has been repeatedly asserted by the Scriptural texts such as, "The enlightened man is not afraid of anything after realizing the Bliss of *Brahman*", "*Brahman* Itself is Bliss, thus did he realize"; and there are also other texts which identify Bliss with *Brahman,* such as, "Knowledge, Bliss, *Brahman*[68]". Following Śaṅkara, Vācaspati says that the fact of *Brahman's* being of the nature of Bliss is also evident from the corroborating texts of the *Mantra* and *Brāhmaṇa* portions of the Veda-s[69]. He says further that Bliss cannot be the essence of any other entity, such as *Jīva,* etc. due to the inappropriateness of such an assertion. Moreover, says the Bhāmatī, the *Jīva* as far as Bliss is concerned entails the sense of 'attainer' as per scriptural texts, such as "*Jīva becomes* happy on coming in contact with Bliss", while the One having Bliss as its essence inheres the sense of "attainablity", and as such differs from the former. Hence, since *Jīva* is different from the One having Bliss as Its essence, it is settled that *Brahman* alone is Bliss[70]. Replying to an objection as to how *Brahman* can here be said to be 'attainable' by *Jīva* which is essentially non-different from It, the Bhāmatī says that it is true that in the absolute sense there is no difference between *Jīva* and *Brahman,* yet due to the influence of Nescience, there is the compatibility of the sense of 'attainer' and 'attainable', between *Jīva* and *Brahman*[71].

Hinting at the Omnipresence of *Brahman,* Śaṅkara says that *Brahman* Itself is the potency present in all the sense organs such as the eyes, etc., as is reported in texts such as, "That One Puruṣa who is the Self, and who is Immortal and Fearless, is Himself to be seen in the eye...". That the Self referred to here cannot be but *Brahman* is inferable from the number of attributes mentioned here, which attributes, says Śaṅkara, can belong to *Brahman* alone. This is also evident from the fact that *Brahman* is taught as being the self in the Scriptures, in texts like "He himself is the self" (and) "That thou art". Śaṅkara says that the Scriptures abound in examples where *Brahman* is described as "Immortal" and "Fearless". Moreover, in the texts such as, "That One (indeed) is the Ordainer of all effulgence, for it is the One that shines in all the worlds"[72], etc., *Brahman* Itself is described as being the 'resort of all blessings'. It therefore follows that *Brahman* Itself and not a 'shadow being', or the intellect, or any divine being, is the force described here as "the one inside", says Śaṅkara[73]. Commenting on this, the Bhāmatī says that the "eyes" have here been alluded to as God's "abode" because of the fact that the eyes, just as *Brahman,* are unattached. The idea intended to be driven home here is that just as the eyes move freely in the eye-lids and do not remain attached to one state therein, so is *Brahman* totally detached from this universe, thought It is present everywhere. This is why, though *Brahman* is Omnipresent, it has been alluded to as seated in the eyes[74]. Vācaspati says in addition that *Brahman* is Itself the cause of the good results of the actions performed in this world; this is why the Scriptures refer to It as *Vāmanī* ("carrier of good results"). In the same manner, It being the source of light and effulgence, is called *Bhāmanī,* in consonance with the Upaniṣadic declaration that "when That One shines, shineth the whole universe; all this here is illumined by Its very Light"[75].

Pursuing the discussion on the omnipresence of *Brahman,* Śaṅkara says that the Supreme Self is also the Internal Ruler of all beings. This is made obvious by frequent references to this characteristic of *Brahman* in the Scriptures. This is also evident from the fact of Its being the source of all creation whereby It inheres also the potency of internal rulership. This is specially due also to Its having created all things by 'entering into them'. In the text, "This is the Internal Ruler, your own Immortal Self" (Bṛ. UP. III. 7.3)[76], the terms "immortal" and "self" are meaningful only with reference to *Brahman,* says Śaṅkara. He says that the objection to the fact that *Brahman* cannot be the internal ruler due to Its having no body, etc., is untenable owing to Its having the potency of omnipresence, especially of being present in all things that are within Its control[77]. In support of this, the Bhāmatī says that all the Scriptures unanimously declare That 'Omniscient' and 'Omnipotent' *Brahman* to be the origin of the universe, and this fact cannot be falsified by mere inference or reasoning contradictory to the Scriptures. *Brahman* being thus the creator of all beings, the totality of the things created through Its potency (i.e. through beginningless Nescience) is Its body, organs, etc. It is indeed through the deities of earth, etc., which are themselves the cause of the gross elements from which are produced the material things, that *Brahman* can be said to be the internal Ruler of all things[78]. There is no incidence of infinite regress here, says Vācaspati, since the question of a separate ruler having control over *Brahman* does not arise. This is so because the *Jīva,* which is known as the controller or ruler at the empirical level, is verily that Supreme Self, differentiated illusorily by adjuncts, as has been pointed out so many times in the Scriptures. This separate rulership is denied also by the Scriptures in texts like, "There is no Seer other than This (self)"[79]. Furthermore, says Vācaspati, the Scriptures characterized by differentiations such as the *knower,* the *knowable,* etc., together with the empirical means of knowledge and all empirical experiences, as well as Scriptures characterized by injunctions and prohibitions, are all grounded in the apparent differentiation of *Jīva* and *Brahman* caused by *Avidyā*[80]. In this manner it has to be understood, says the Bhāmatī, that all the natural and supernatural forces also have for Internal Ruler that One *Brahman* alone, as is claimed by the Scriptures themselves, in statements such as "He who rules over the worlds", "He who rules over all the Vadās", "He who rules over all the sacrifices"; "He who rules over all beings" etc. Hence it is settled that it is *Brahman,* and not *Jīva,* etc., that is the Internal Ruler of the whole universe[81].

III. The Vivaraṇa's Concept of Brahman

In the invocatory verse of the Pañcapādikā, Padmapāda describes *Brahman* as Beginningless, Bliss, Changeless, and of the nature of Knowledge, Eternity and Existence; It is also the Witness of this world of duality[82]. As for the meaning of the word '*Brahman*' itself, Padmapāda says that with reference to the root *Bṛh*' (to be great) from which it is derived, the word *Brahman* is denotative of an entity possessed of unexcelled magnitute'[83], which meaning alone fits in with other appellations namely, Absolute Existence (*Satyam*), Consciousness (*Jñānam*), Infinite (*Anantam*), as per the Vedānta text—"*Satyam Jñānam Anantam Brahma* "[84]. Hence, says Padmapāda, because of the absence of the sense of limitedness occasioned by the delimitation of time, some entity that is constant and therefore eternal is intimated by the term *Brahman*[85]. The word *Brahman* conveys the sense of homogeneity and non-dualism, says the Pañcapādikā[86]. The verbal root '*Bṛh*' inheres also the sense of consciousness, says Padmapāda. This is inferable from the fact that all things save consciousness belong to the sphere of experience, and hence, are inferior and subordinate to the experiencer, i.e. Consciousness itself. And Consciousness (being 'One without a second') is subordinate to none; it is therefore obvious that '*Brahman*', with reference to the meaning of the root '*Bṛh*' stands for the entity which is most excellent and which is Consciousness in essence[87]. '*Brahman*', embraces also the sense of 'freedom', says Padmapāda. This is also inferable from the fact that ordinary beings are seen to be at the mercy of Nescience, lust and the urge to act and become rendered wretchedly helpless by the same and as such are comparable to animals, caught up as they are, in the bondage of birth and death. On the other hand the word *Brahman* reveals the sense of greatness, and also that of eternal freedom (from the grip of Nescience, etc.)[88]. Padmapāda observes also that '*Brahman*' is endowed with the essence of omniscience and omnipotence since every thing is known to It and since there is no single instance where any other entity is seen to surpass or even to equal It in Its potency. In case of the contrary, it would mean that Its excellence is but relative, which would go against the very sense of the term "*Brahman*" established by no other means of knowledge except the Scriptures or Verbal Authority. Were '*Brahman*'s greatness to be established by empirical means of knowledge, then Its "Greatness" too would be relative. But this is not the case since *Brahman* is self-revelatory. Its relation with the other components of the said sentence (*Vākya*) also is cognizable only through the direct cognition of the meaning of '*Brahman*'[89]. The author of the Pañcapādikā says concludingly that 'the meaning of the root '*Bṛh*' will be complete only if the whole of the universe lies within the scope of (*Brahman's*) Consciousness or omniscience, and is under Its control'[90], as Śaṅkara himself says : 'There verily exists an entity referred to as *Brahman* having Eternity, Purity, Consciousness, Freedom, Omniscience and Omnipotence as its characteristics, as is revealed by the root '*Bṛh*' itself'[91].

Prakāśātman says that the term '*eternal*' used in the above-mentioned sentence applies equally to the other three words, viz., Purity, Consciousness and Freedom, meaning thereby that these are not the qualities of *Brahman,* but rather Its very essence and are therefore non-exhaustible features of *Brahman.* The words 'Consciousness', etc. says he, are meant to emphasize the Absolute greatness of *Brahman* Which does not suffer from defects such as ignorance, limitedness, impotence, etc. as ordinary beings[92]. In the same manner, the words 'Omniscience and 'Omnipotence' are used here to eliminate any possibility of the limitation of knowledge and potency with respect to *Brahman,* justifying thereby Its absolute control over the whole universe[93]. As regards the fact that the meaning of the word *Brahman* is self-revelatory and not dependent on any other means of knowledge, Prakāśātman observes that whether a word carries the sense of smallness or of greatness depends on which one of the two meanings is assignable to it as per the means of knowledge through which it is cognized. But as for the words whose meaning is not dependent on any empirical means of knowledge, the sense of greatness, etc. embodied by them is known directly by their primary sense. Hence the sense of greatness of the word '*Brahman*' is known directly, It being self-revealed, and as such is free from the possibility of ambiguity[94].

Śaṅkara, by asserting the existence of the Self (*Ātman*) and by identifying it with *Brahman,* proves the existence of the Supreme Being. This, he says, is very much within the experience of one and all or else, instead of the cognition "I am", everyone would have the cognition "I am not", which is absurd[95]. Reacting to this, Padmapāda says that *Ātman* is identifiable with *Brahman* on account of the assertion by the Vedānta texts in this sense. And this *Ātman* is indeed the entity designated by the ego (*aham*) in this empirical world. Hence, the ego itself is *Brahman*[96]. Clarifying this point further, the author of the Pañcapādikā says that 'the word *aham* means Consciousness divested of all limiting adjuncts'. It is this purified form of the self that is revealed in deep sleep that takes the form of the recollection of happiness, such as 'I slept happily' 'nothing was cognized by me', etc.[97] Such an experience, says Padmapāda, is not a product of mental impressions, but rather arises directly as a result of the absence of pain in that state[98]. As for Prakāśātman, he says in this regard that the 'I'-cognition in the state of deep-sleep is not influenced by adjuncts such as enjoyership, etc. What is, if at all, recalled is merely 'I'-ness-which is but the *Ātman* itself[99]. During deep-sleep the Self is revealed in Its pure form, being rid of all adjuncts in that state, says Prakāśātman[100]. That Supreme Self is beyond the reach of verbal description and empirical perception, being devoid of form. Having known that changeless *Brahman*, one is freed from the grip of death for ever, adds the Vivaraṇa[101].

With a view to throwing further light on the nature of *Brahman*, Padmapāda, following Śaṅkara, says that *Brahman* is Omniscient and Omnipotent and It alone is the origin of this world 'the nature of whose design cannot even be thought of'. The complexity of the nature of the world is itself an indication of the supremacy of its source which cannot be ascribed to any other entity such as *Pradhāna* or *Hiraṇyagarbha*, etc., whose potency is but of limited scope[102]. The Vivaraṇa observes in this context that it cannot be argued that the cause of the universe is *Īśvara* and not *Brahman*, there being no such indication in the texts. Or else the texts would have raised the doubt about *Īśvara* being Himself *Pradhāna* or '*atom*'. There being no such doubt in the texts, it is but logical that the doubt as regards the origin of the universe should arise as it does, in respect of the body and the senses etc., due to the wrong identification of the self with the latter[103]. Prakāśātman says that in fact on the removal of superimposition of the Self on the body, mind etc. there follows the cessation of the sense of being perceiver etc., which leads to the self's detachment from the world and to the experience of the absence of duality[104]. Hence, concludes the Vivaraṇa, the eradication of all sense of doership, etc., resulting in the cessation of the apprehension of duality justifies the investigation into the nature of *Brahman* which is Infinite Bliss and Light in essence[105].

The Vivaraṇa is of the view that *Brahman* is both the efficient cause and the material cause of the universe. That *Brahman* is the material cause is inferable from the fact that the five gross elements have one common cause—viz., *Prakṛti* and that all evolutes are of the same nature as their material cause, just as pots, etc. are essentially identical with clay, etc. Moreover, all material objects, though diverse in nature, have *Prakṛti* as their essence. Hence, for brevity's sake, says Prakāśātman, it is but logical to postulate one common material cause of all objects[106]. In the same manner, *Brahman* Itself is the efficient cause of the universe. This is inferable from the fact that all effects have an intelligent entity as their cause and all feelings such as pleasure, pain, like, dislike, etc. have the self as their substratum. It cannot be said of pots, etc. that they have different material and efficient causes, for there too, the postulation of the singularity of cause is plausible[107]. Padmapāda says in this context that the origin of the earth is known by experience to be some intelligent Entity. But since there is no means of ascertaining singularity or plurality of causation, the matter is settled through Scriptural evidence, such as "from whence proceed these beings"[108], which points towards the singularity of causation. This is so because the word denoting the cause (*yataḥ*) is in the singular number and because the purpose of the text—"*Yato vā imāni*" is to denote only that (singularity of causation)[109], It is also to be understood by presumption that the entity from which the world originated is Omniscient and Omnipotent, in pursuance of the text, "That has the desire to understand", followed by the statement "That is *Brahman*"[110]. This statement, says Padmapāda, is indicative of the fact that the cause of the world is characterized by freedom from all limitations[111]. The Pañcapādikā further adds that the text, "for indeed from Bliss only (beings are born; when born they live by Bliss and on death they enter into Bliss) points to the fact that *Brahman* is of the essence of Bliss, while the text relating to *Brahman*, viz., "Whence these beings are born, etc.", defines *Brahman* only by indirect indication and as such does not establish any contact of the aggregate of attributes such as origination etc. with It. It follows from this that *Brahman* is Omniscient, Omnipotent and Supreme Bliss[112].

The Vivaraṇa holds that though it is not possible to establish through reasoning the existence of *Brahman* of the nature of Knowledge, Bliss, Omniscience etc., yet it is possible to do so on the basis of Scriptural texts having *Brahman* as their content. In support Prakāśātman adds that it is possible to infer the singleness of the cause of the world from texts making such claims and from the fact that effects cannot be determined in isolation from their cause as is illustrated by the example of clay, etc.[113] Moreover, the examples such as the reflection of redness in crystal, the snake in rope, the pot-space, etc. apart from illustrating the illusoriness of agentship, etc. superimposed on the self, illustrate as well the *Jīva-Brahman*-identity, and also the fact that the world cannot exist independently of *Brahman*. Through the aforesaid illustrations the non-attached nature of *Brahman* is also made explicit, which points equally to the purity and non-dual nature of the self[114].

As to the means of ascertaining the existence of *Brahman* of the nature discussed above, the Vivaraṇa school, as indeed its counterpart the Bhāmatī, believes in the sole authority of the Vedas in that regard. The Vedas are like *Brahman* without beginning and remain unaltered throughout. That *Brahman,* says the Pañcapādikā, is to be ascertained from the Vedānta *Śāstra* since the Vedānta texts are congruent in having It (i.e. *Brahman*) as their purport... The proposition that *Brahman* having the attributes of omniscience, etc, is known from the *Vedānta Śāstra,* is stated in the words 'because they are congruent'[115]. The term "*samanvaya*", says Padmapāda, conveys the sense that all Vedānta texts are in agreement as far as their purport, i.e. *Brahman,* is concerned[116].

The Vivaraṇa concludes the discussion on *Brahman* by saying that it is thus established that *Brahman* is Omniscient and is the efficient as well as the material cause of the universe. But divergent views still persist as to the relation of *Brahman* with *Jīva* and its impact on the conceptualization of the world. He says that some are of the view that *Brahman* as the prototype, with *Māyā* as its implement, is the Cause of the world, while the *Jīva*-s are connected with their own individual *avidyā*-s[117]. Some others, says he, believe that *Brahman* as reflected through *Māyā* and *Avidyā* is the Cause of the world, while the Pure Self is the substratum of eternity, and the *Jīva*-s are bound by *avidyā*[118]. There are still others who advance the theory that the *Jīva*-s themselves are *Brahman* in the form of the diversified world creatures; there is the appearance of duality despite actual unity among all things of the world, just as the moon, though one is illusorily perceived as double by many[119]. There are still others who hold the view that *Brahman* Itself takes the form of the world without undergoing any fundamental change, just as dreams, etc. Hence, impelled by Its own *Māyā* or *Avidyā*, *Brahman* Itself gets modified (into the world of form and name)[120].

IV. Summary

It has thus been seen in the foregoing discussion, that the Advaita Vedānta propounds the theory of one Reality, which is 'without a second'. This Reality i.e. the Absolute Being, is called *Brahman* due to Its All-pervasiveness, All-comprehensiveness, Omnipotence, Omniscience and Omnipresence. That Itself is the All-Bliss Entity, the Consciousness of all beings, the unique source of Eternal Happiness[121]. That Supreme Self, though One and Undivided and Impartible, appears as though differentiated in the forms of *Īśvara* and *Jīva*-s. And this, aver both the Bhāmatī and the Vivaraṇa, is but the conception of *Brahman* in a relative sense: *Brahman* itself is *Īśvara* in relation to the Universe, and *Jīva* in relation to the individual body. What is true of the *Jīva*-s vis-a-vis the body is true of *Īśvara* vis-a-vis the universe. Such a postulation does not constitute any contradiction as to the All-rulership and Omnipotence of *Brahman*, for *Jīva* and *Īśvara* are but *Brahman* Itself : the one reeling under the influence of Nescience, the other having Nescience under His control[122]. Thus, what is known as *Brahman* at the *pāramārthika* or *Absolute* level, is known as *Īśvara* or *Jīva* at the *vyāvahārika* or empirical level, viewed respectively from the universal and individual angles. It is thus that the eternally free *Brahman*, the One Reality, is projected as illusorily the *Jīva* due to the influence of beginningless Avidyā. Hence the description of *Brahman* first as free from all adjuncts and then as apparently limited by the adjuncts of *Avidyā*, in which instance It is said to be "*Omniscient*" and "*Omnipotent*". The point that Vācaspati Miśra wants to drive home here is that even the conception of *Brahman* as *Omniscient* and *Omnipotent* is but the result of Nescience[123].

Both the schools under review are emphatic about the fact that the nature of *Brahman* can be known only through the Scriptures. Verbal Testimony is therefore postulated as the sole means of knowledge with regard to *Brahman,* since It cannot be known through any of the empirical means of knowledge[124]. Even the Scriptures cannot but describe It negatively, i.e., as what It is not, and not positively as what it is. This is evident from the fact that all attempts at the description of *Brahman* are confined to the phrase *neti neti,* which conveys the idea that *Brahman* cannot be described in actual terms, It being beyond the scope of thought and imagination[125]. This is what Vācaspati tries to intimate when he says that *Brahman* is *anirvācya*[126]. Advaita Vedānta indeed postulates that *Brahman* is devoid of attributes of any kind, of distinguishing features, contrary to empirical entities, It being the sole Reality, "One without a Second[127]", the Origin and Substratum of the whole Universe. Hence, *Brahman* is also without name and form, without parts, and is not subject to any change whatsoever. *Brahman* is not susceptible to any kind of limitations and divisions, It being beyond space and time[128].

Both the Bhāmatī and the Vivaraṇa schools postulate that *Brahman* is the Efficient cause as well as the Material cause of the world. They both agree to Its being a sheer "witness" to the origination, preservation and dissolution of the world, all this being but consequential to the reflection of *Brahman* in *Māyā.* That is to say that the actual acts of creation, preservation and dissolution pertain to *Māyā*—acting at the behest of and in the proximity of *Brahman.* It is noteworthy that *Māyā* being fundamentally inert, becomes active only by being in the proximity of *Brahman*[129].

According to both schools, *Brahman* is Self-luminous requiring no external instrumentality for Its illumination or for It to become known. "All knowledge is self-affirmation". But the *Brahman* of Advaita Vedānta is beyond this self-affirmation. It is something that transcends determination. It is Indeterminate; It is the Unknown and the Unknowable. It is that entity which "being (itself) presupposed in all knowledge is incapable of being caught in any determinate mode of knowledge. This determinate self-affirmation, too, is (eternally) *completed* or *accomplished;* (it) is beyond the self-affirming activity. The consciousness of such limited agent or subject as (illusorily) identified with the self (which is really *absolute,* not only in the sense of being above duality but above all determination also) is (what may be called)......"empirical self-consciousness".[130] "The self is manifested in self-affirmation or Knowledge; Knowledge is manifested by the self-affirming activity of the self-conscious individualized self; the activity is that of the interpretation of the sense-manifold, given as one apprehension".[131]

That *Brahman* is Omniscient and Omnipotent is illustrated by both the Bhāmatī and the Vivaraṇa by the fact that the *Veda-s,* the book of knowledge *par excellence,* the repository of all knowledge, has its origin in *Brahman.* Śaṅkara says that for the Supreme Being the origination of the *Vedas* is as natural as the act of inhaling and exhaling. What this means is that knowledge being the very essence of *Brahman* its 'origination' is but figuratively alluded to for the sake of convenience, since knowledge in the form of *Vedas* has no origination and is not subject to destruction as such, it being eternal, without beginning and without end[132]. Prakāśātman observes on this that the fact that the *Veda*-s have *Brahman* as their origin sets at rest the contention that the eternality of the *Veda*-s is but relative. The *Veda*-s, says he, are beginningless as *Brahman* Itself, and as such are immutable and eternal[133]. He also says that the *Veda-s* are in fact the mere *vivarta* of *Brahman.* This much only is meant to be conveyed by the allusion to the origination of the Veda-s, asserts the Vivaraṇa[134].

Brahman, according to the Vivaraṇa, is subordinate to none, It being indeed second to none. It is Constant, Changeless and is not subject to any kind of alteration. The term "*Brahman*" itself, says Prakāśātman, conveys the sense of homogeneity and non-duality. Hence it is that Consciousness or *Brahman* is eternally free from (the influence) (of) Nescience[135]. *Brahman* is Itself the Internal Ruler and Lord of all beings[136], every thing having originated from It, and there being nothing in existence outside That One Reality, says the Bhāmatī on its part. Hence also the denial of plurality whatsoever here by both the schools[137]. Both, the Bhāmatī and the Vivaraṇa agree with Śaṅkara that it is only by realizing the real nature of *Brahman* that eternal freedom from the influence of Nescience can be achieved, and for that purpose no external action is enjoined by the Scriptures, *Brahman* being as such already and eternally "*attained*" . There is, however, this much of difference between the Bhāmatī and the Vivaraṇa on this issue : while the latter holds that *Brahman*-knowledge is attainable directly from Verbal Testimony, the former believes that Verbal Testimony can only lead to an indirect knowledge of *Brahman*[138].

NOTES

1. "सत्यं ज्ञानमनन्तं ब्रह्म"। - Tai. UP.II. 1.1.
2. "यतो वा इमानि भूतानि जायन्ते। येन जातानि जीवन्ति॥ यत्प्रयन्त्यभिसंविशन्ति। तद्विजिज्ञासस्व। तद् ब्रह्मेति॥" —Tai. UP. III. 3.1.
3. Vide, R. Bālasubramanian, Loc. Cit., p.31.
4. Ibid, p.32.
5. C.D. Sharma, Loc. Cit., p.186.
6. "जन्माद्यस्य यतः।" -B.S. I.1.2.
7. C.D. Sharma, Loc. Cit., p.186.
8. Veeramani Upadhyāya, Loc. Cit., p.54.
9. Kanshi Ram, Loc. Cit., p.22.
10. T.P. Ramachandran,. The concept of the Vyāvahārika in Advaita Vedānta, Univ. of Madras, 1980 - p. 237.
11. "एवमवस्थात्रयसाक्ष्येकोऽव्यभिचार्यवस्थात्रयेण व्यभिचारिणा न संस्पृश्यते।....तत्र यदुक्तमपीतौ कारणस्यापि कार्यस्येव स्थौल्यादिदोषप्रसङ्गः इत्येतदयुक्तम्।" —SB on BS-II.1.9.
12. Vide, M. Sircar, Vedāntic Thought and Culture, p.101.
13. "निःश्वसितमस्य वेदा वीक्षितमेतस्य पञ्चभूतानि। स्मितमेतस्य चराचरस्य च सुप्तं महाप्रलयः॥" —Bhāmatī - Introductory Verse (no. 2).
14. M. Sircar, Loc. Cit., p.103.
15. "अतो रचनानुपपत्तेश्च हेतोर्नाचेतनं कारणमनुमातव्यं भवति।" —SB on BS-II. 2.1.
16. "यथा प्रकाशद्रव्यस्य प्रदीपस्य स्वसन्निहिताशेषवस्तुप्रकाशिता एवं प्रकाशस्वरूपस्य ब्रह्मणः सर्वोपादानतया सर्वसंसर्गिणः स्वसन्निहिताशेषवस्तुप्रकाशिता नित्यवत् भवतीति युक्तं सामर्थ्यानुसारेण सर्वज्ञत्वम्।" —Vivaraṇa, Loc. Cit., pp.690-691.
17. Vide, Lights on Vedānta, Op. Cit., p.55.
18. Ibid. pp.55-56.
19. Ibid. pp-56-57.
20. Vide, B. Bālasubramanian, Loc. Cit., p.34.
21. "नेति नेति नह्येतस्मादिति नेत्यन्यत्परम्।" —Bṛh. UP. II. 3.6.
22. "अनिर्वाच्याविद्याद्वितयसचिवस्य प्रभवतो। विवर्ता यस्यैते वियदनिलतेजोऽबवनयः॥ यतश्चाभूद्विश्वं चरमचरमुच्चावचमिदम्। नमामस्तद्ब्रह्मापरिमितसुखज्ञानममृतम्॥ —Bhāmatī- Introductory Verse (no. 1).
23. "बृहत्त्वाद्बृंहणत्वाद्वात्मैव ब्रह्मेति गीयते।" —Bhāmatī on *Adhyāsabhāṣya*, Parimal

Ed., p.5.

24. "तदयं प्रकाश एव स्वयंप्रकाश एकः कूटस्थो नित्यो निरंशः प्रत्यगात्मा।" —Ibid. p.37.

25. "एवमयमनादिरनन्तो नैसर्गिकोऽध्यासो मिथ्याप्रत्ययरूपः कर्तृत्वभोक्तृत्वप्रवर्तकः सर्वलोकप्रत्यक्षः। अस्यानर्थहेतोः प्रहाणाय आत्मैकत्वविद्याप्रतिपपत्तये सर्वे वेदान्ता आरभ्यन्ते।" —Adhyāsabhāṣya, Loc. Cit., p.45.

26. "तच्च प्राप्तमप्यनाद्यविद्यावशादप्राप्तमिवेति प्रेप्सितं भवति। यथा स्वग्रीवागतमपि ग्रैवेयकं कुतश्चिद्भ्रमान्नास्तीति मन्यमानः परेण प्रतिपादितमप्राप्तमिव प्राप्नोति।" —Bhāmatī on SB-I.1.1, Loc. Cit. p.46.

27. "तत्पुनर्ब्रह्म प्रसिद्धमप्रसिद्धं वा स्यात्। यदि प्रसिद्धं न जिज्ञासितव्यम्। अथाप्रसिद्धं नैव शक्यं जिज्ञासितुमिति। उच्यते—अस्ति तावद्ब्रह्म नित्यशुद्धबुद्धमुक्तस्वभावं सर्वज्ञं सर्वशक्तिसमन्वितम्। ब्रह्मशब्दस्य हि व्युत्पाद्यमानस्य नित्यशुद्धत्वादयोऽर्थाः प्रतीयन्ते; बृहतेर्धातोरर्थानुगमात्। सर्वस्यात्मत्वाच्च ब्रह्मास्तित्वप्रसिद्धिः। सर्वो ह्यात्मास्तित्वं प्रत्येति न नाहमस्मि इति। यदि हि नात्मास्तित्वप्रसिद्धिः स्यात् सर्वो लोकः 'नाहमस्मि' इति प्रतीयात्। आत्मा च ब्रह्म।" —SB on BS. I.1.1, Loc. Cit., pp.79-81.

28. "वेदान्तेभ्योऽपौरुषेयतया स्वतःसिद्धप्रामाण्येभ्यः (ब्रह्म) प्रसिद्धमप्रसिद्धं वा स्यात्।.... शब्दो हि तस्य प्रमाणं वक्तव्यम्। .... स चेत.... न्नावबोधयति कुतस्तस्य तत्र प्रामाण्यम्? न च प्रमाणान्तरं ब्रह्मणि प्रक्रमते।" —Bhāmatī on SB-I.1.1., p.79.

29. "प्रागपि ब्रह्ममीमांसाया अधीतवेदस्य निगमनिरुक्तव्याकरणादिपरिशीलनविदितपदतदर्थसंबन्धस्य 'सदेव सोम्येदमग्र आसीत्' इत्युपक्रमात् 'तत्त्वमसि' इत्यन्तात्संदर्भात् नित्यत्वाद्युपेतब्रह्मस्वरूपावगमस्तावदापाततो विचाराद्विनाप्यस्ति।" —Ibid.

30. The Bhāmatī of Vācaspati, Op. Cit., pp.110-111. See also, "अत्र च ब्रह्मेत्यादिनावगम्येन तद्विषयमवगमं लक्षयति, तदस्तित्वस्य सति विमर्शे विचारात्प्रागनिर्णयात्। नित्येति क्षयितालक्षणं दुःखमुपक्षिपति। शुद्धेति देहाद्युपाधिकमपि दुःखमपाकरोति। बुद्धेत्यपराधीनप्रकाशमानन्दात्मानं दर्शयति आनन्दप्रकाशयोरभेदात्"। —Ibid, pp.79-80.

31. "सदैव मुक्तः सदैव केवलोऽनाद्यविद्यावशात्तु भ्रान्त्या तथावभासत इत्यर्थः। तदेवमनौपाधिकं ब्रह्मणो रूपं दर्शयित्वा अविद्योपाधिकं रूपमाह—सर्वज्ञं सर्वशक्तिसमन्वितम्। तदनेन जगत्कारणत्वमस्य दर्शितम्, शक्तिज्ञानभावाभावानुविधानात्कारणत्वभावाभावयोः।" —Bhāmatī on SB-I.1.1, Loc. Cit., P.80.

32. The Bhāmatī of Vācaspati, Op. Cit., p.113, Vide, "तदेवं तत्पदार्थस्य शुद्धत्वादेः प्रसिद्धिमभिधाय त्वंपदर्थस्याप्याह - सर्वस्यात्मत्वाच्च ब्रह्मास्तित्वप्रसिद्धिः। .... आत्मत्वात्... सर्वस्य... हालिकस्यापि ब्रह्मस्तित्वप्रसिद्धिः।... न न प्रत्येति 'अहमस्मि' इति, किंतु प्रत्येत्येवेति। . . . आत्मा च ब्रह्म, तदः त्वमा सामानाधिकरण्यात्। तस्मात्तत्पदार्थस्य शुद्धबुद्धत्वादेः शब्दतः त्वंपदार्थस्य च जीवात्मनः प्रत्यक्षतः प्रसिद्धेः पदार्थज्ञानपूर्वकत्वाच्च वाक्यार्थज्ञानस्य, त्वंपदार्थस्य ब्रह्मभावावगमः तत्त्वमसि इति वाक्यादुपपद्यत इति भावः।" —Bhāmatī on SB-I.1.1.

33. The Bhāmatī of Vācaspati, Op. Cit., pp. 121-122, Vide, "अस्य जगतो नामरूपाभ्यां व्याकृतस्य अनेककर्तृभोक्तृसंयुक्तस्य प्रतिनियतदेशकालनिमित्तक्रियाफलाश्रयस्य मनसाप्यचिन्त्यरचनारूपस्य जन्मस्थितिभङ्गं यतः सर्वज्ञात्सर्वशक्तेः

कारणाद्भवति तद्ब्रह्मेति।'' —SB on BS-I.1.2.

34. ''न वस्तुयाथात्म्यज्ञानं पुरुषबुद्ध्यपेक्षम्। किं तर्हि ? वस्तुतन्त्रमेव तत्। न हि स्थाणावेकस्मिन् 'स्थाणुर्वा पुरुषोऽन्यो वा इति तत्त्वज्ञानं भवति। तत्र 'पुरुषोऽन्यो वा' इति मिथ्याज्ञानम्। 'स्थाणुरेव' इति तत्त्वज्ञानम्, वस्तुतन्त्रत्वात्। एवं भूतवस्तुविषयाणां प्रामाण्यं वस्तुतन्त्रम्। तत्रैवं सति ब्रह्मज्ञानमपि वस्तुतन्त्रमेव भूतवस्तुविषयत्वात्।'' —SB on BS. I.1.2, Loc. Cit., p.91.

35. ''तत्र यद्यावदनुभूयते तत्सर्वं परिमितमविशुद्धमबुद्धं विध्वंसि च; न तेनोपलब्धेन तद्विरुद्धस्य नित्यशुद्धस्वभावस्य ब्रह्मणः स्वरूपं शक्यं लक्षयितुम्। न हि जातु कश्चित्कृतकत्वेन नित्यं लक्षयति। . . . (तं) परिहरति . . . मा भूदनुभूयमानं जगत्तद्धर्मतया तादात्म्येन वा ब्रह्मणो लक्षणम्; तदुत्पत्त्या तु भविष्यति देशान्तरप्राप्तिरिव सवितुर्व्रज्याया इति तात्पर्यार्थः।'' —Bhāmatī on SB-I.1.2, Loc. Cit., pp.84-85.

36. ''प्रधानकालग्रहलोकपालक्रियायादृच्छास्वभावाभावेषूपप्लवमानेषु सत्सु सर्वज्ञं सर्वशक्तिस्वभावं ब्रह्म जगज्जन्मादिकारणमिति कुतः संभावनेत्यत आह - अस्य जगत इति। अत्र नामरूपाभ्यां व्याकृतस्य इति चेतनभावकर्तृकत्वसंभावनया प्रधानाद्यचेतनकर्तृकत्वं ... व्यासेधति। यत्खलु नाम्ना रूपेण च व्याक्रियते तच्चेतनकर्तृकं दृष्टं, यथा घटादि। विवादाध्यासितं च जगन्नाम्ना रूपेण च व्याकृतम्, तस्माच्चेतनकर्तृकं संभाव्यते।'' —Bhāmatī on SB-I.1.2, Loc. Cit., p.85.

37. The Bhāmatī of Vācaspati, Op. Cit., pp.137-138.

38. ''महत ऋग्वेदादेः शास्त्रस्य अनेकविद्यास्थानोपबृंहितस्य प्रदीपवत्सर्वार्थावद्योतिनः सर्वज्ञकल्पस्य योनिः कारणं ब्रह्म। न हीदृशस्य शास्त्रस्य ऋग्वेदादिलक्षणस्य सर्वज्ञगुणान्वितस्य सवर्ज्ञादन्यतः संभवोऽस्ति। यद्यद्विस्तारार्थं शास्त्रं यस्मात् पुरुषविशेषात्संभवति, यथा व्याकरणादि पाणिन्यादेः, ज्ञेयैकदेशार्थमपि, स ततोऽप्यधिकतरविज्ञान इति प्रसिद्धं लोके। किमु वक्तव्यम् - अनेक-शाखाभेदभिन्नस्य देवतिर्यङ्मनुष्य.... विभागहेतोः ऋग्वेदाद्याख्यस्य सर्वज्ञानाकरस्य अप्रयत्नेनैव लीलान्यायेन पुरुषनिःश्वासवत् यस्मात्महतो भूताद् योनेः संभवः - 'अस्य महतो भूतस्य निःश्वसितमेतत् यदृग्वेदः इत्यादिश्रुतेः—तस्य महतो भूतस्य निरतिशयं सर्वज्ञत्वं सर्वशक्तिमत्त्वं चेति।'' —SB on BS-I.1.3, Loc. Cit., pp.96-99.

39. ''चातुवर्ण्यस्य चातुराश्रम्यस्य च यथायथम्। निषेकादिश्मशानान्तासु ब्राह्ममुहूर्तोपक्रम-प्रदोषपरिसमापनीयासु नित्यनैमित्तिककाम्यकर्मपद्धतिषु च ब्रह्मतत्त्वे च शिष्याणां शासनात् शास्त्रमृग्वेदादिः। अत एव महाविषयत्वात् महत्। न केवलं महाविषयत्वेनास्य महत्त्वम् अपि त्वनेकाङ्गोपाङ्गोपकरणतयापि...। पुराणन्यायमीमांसादयो दशविद्यास्थानानि। तदनेन समस्तशिष्टजनपरिग्रहेणाप्रामाण्यशङ्काप्यपाकृता। पुराणादिप्रणेतारो हि महर्षयः शिष्टाः। तैः तया तया द्वारा वेदान् व्याचक्षाणैस्तदर्थं चादरेणानुतिष्ठद्भिः परिगृहीतो वेद इति। —Bhāmatī on SB-I.1.3, Loc. Cit., p.96.

40. ''वेदस्य यस्मात् महतो भूतात् योनेः संभवः तस्य महतो भूतस्य ब्रह्मणे निरतिशयं सर्वज्ञत्वं सर्वशक्तित्वं च किमु वक्तव्यम्। . . . देवर्षयो हि महापरिश्रमेणापि यत्राशक्ताः तदयमीषत्प्रयत्नेन लीलयैव करोतीति निरतिशयमस्य सर्वज्ञत्वं सर्वशक्तित्वं चोक्तं भवति। अप्रयत्नेनास्य वेदकर्तृत्वे श्रुतिरुक्ता 'अस्य महतो भूतस्य' इति।'' —Bhāmatī on SB-I.1.III. Loc. Cit., pp.97-98.

41. "अथवा यथोक्तमृग्वेदादिशास्त्रं योनिः कारणं प्रमाणमस्य ब्रह्मणे यथावत्स्वरूपाधिगमे। शास्त्रादेव प्रमाणात् जगतो जन्मादिकारणं ब्रह्माधिगम्यत इत्यभिप्रायः। —SB on BS-I.1.III, Loc. Cit, pp.99-100.

42. "तद्ब्रह्म सर्वज्ञं सर्वशक्तिजगदुत्पत्तिस्थितिलयकारणं वेदान्तशास्त्रादवगम्यते। कथम्? समन्वयात्। सर्वेषु हि वेदान्तेषु वाक्यानि तात्पर्येणैतस्यार्थस्य प्रतिपादकत्वेन समनुगतानि— 'सदेव सोम्येदमग्र आसीत्'। 'एकमेवाद्वितीयम्'। 'आत्मा वा इदमेक एवाग्र आसीत्'।...।" — SB on BS-I.1.IV-Loc. Cit., pp.102-103.

43. "न च तद्गतानां पदानां ब्रह्मस्वरूपविषये निश्चिते समन्वयेऽवगम्यमाने अर्थान्तरकल्पना युक्ता, श्रुतहान्यश्रुतकल्पनाप्रसङ्गात्।" —Ibid.

44. "येन हि वाक्यमुपक्रम्यते येन चोपसंह्रियते स एव वाक्यार्थ इति शाब्दाः। . . . एवमत्रापि सदेव सोम्येदम् इति ब्रह्मोपक्रमात् 'तत्त्वमसि' इति च जीवस्य ब्रह्मात्मनोपसंहारात् तत्परतैव वाक्यस्य। एवं वाक्यान्तराणामपि पौर्वापर्यालोचनया ब्रह्मपरत्वमवगन्तव्यम्।" —Bhāmatī on SB - I.1.IV, Loc. Cit., pp.103-104.

45. "न च परिनिष्ठितवस्तुस्वरूपत्वेऽपि प्रत्यक्षादिविषयत्वं ब्रह्मणः, तत्त्वमसि इति ब्रह्मात्मभावस्य शास्त्रमन्तरेणानवगम्यमानत्वात्। ...न तु तथा ब्रह्मण उपासनाविधिशेषत्वं संभवति एकत्वे हेयोपादेयशून्यतया क्रियाकारकादिद्वैतविज्ञानोपमर्दोपपत्तेः। न हि ब्रह्मैकत्वविज्ञानेनोन्मथितस्य द्वैतविज्ञानस्य पुनः संभवोऽस्ति येनोपासनाविधिशेषत्वं ब्रह्मणः प्रतिपाद्येत।" —SB on BS-I.1.IV, Loc. Cit., pp.105-108.

46. "विध्यर्थावगमात् खलु पारम्पर्येण पुरुषार्थप्रतिलम्भः। इह तु 'तत्त्वमसि' इत्यवगति-पर्यन्ताद्वावाक्यार्थज्ञानात् बाह्यानुष्ठानायासानपेक्षात्साक्षादेव पुरुषार्थप्रतिलम्भः, 'नायं सर्पो रज्जुरियम्' इति ज्ञानादिवेति सोऽयमस्य विध्यर्थज्ञानात् प्रकर्षः।" —Bhāmatī on SB-I.1.IV, Loc. Cit., p.107.

47. "उपास्योपासकोपासनादिभेदसिद्ध्यधीनोपासना न निरस्तसमस्तभेदप्रपञ्चे वेदान्तवेद्ये ब्रह्मणि संभवतीति नोपासनाविधिशेषत्वं वेदान्तानां तद्विरोधत्वात् इत्यर्थः"। —Ibid.

48. "यद्यप्यन्यत्र वेदवाक्यानां विधिसंस्पर्शमन्तरेण प्रमाणत्वं न दृष्टं तथाप्यात्मविज्ञानस्य फलपर्यन्तत्वान्न तद्विषयस्य शास्त्रस्य प्रमाण्यं शक्यं प्रत्याख्यातुम्। न चानुमानगम्यं शास्त्रप्रामाण्यं येनान्यत्र दृष्टं निदर्शनमपेक्ष्येत। तस्मात्सिद्धं ब्रह्मणः शास्त्रप्रमाणकत्वम्।" —SB on BS-I.1.4, Loc. Cit., p.108.

49. Vide, The Bhāmatī of Vācaspati, Op. Ciţ, p.159.

50. "ननु विध्यसंस्पर्शिनो वेदस्यान्यस्य न प्रामाण्यं दृष्टमिति कथं वेदान्तानां तदस्पृशां तद्भविष्यतीत्यत आह—न चानुमानगम्यमिति। अबाधितानधिगतासंदिग्धबोधजनकत्वं हि प्रमाणत्वं प्रमाणानाम् तच्च स्वत इत्युपपादितम्। यद्यपि चैषामीदृग्बोधजनकत्वं कार्यार्थापत्तिसमधिगम्यम्, तथापि तद्बोधोपजनने मानान्तरं नापेक्षन्ते नापीमामेवार्थापत्तिम्, परस्पराश्रयप्रसङ्गादिति स्वत इत्युक्तम्। ईदृग्बोधजनकत्वं दृष्टान्तानपेक्षं तेषां ब्रह्मणि प्रामाण्यं सिद्धं भवति । अन्यथा नेन्द्रियान्तराणां रूपप्रकाशनं दृष्टमिति चक्षुरपि न रूपं प्रकाशयेदिति।" —Bhāmatī on SB-I.1.IV, Loc. Cit., p.108.

51. "पुरुषो हि श्रुतिस्मृतीतिहासपुराणतदविरुद्धन्यायव्यवस्थापितत्वात्परमार्थसन्। प्रपञ्च-स्त्वनाद्यविद्योपदर्शितोऽपरमार्थसन्; यस्य परमार्थसन् असौ प्रकृतिः रज्जुतत्त्वमिव

सर्वविभ्रमस्य विकारस्य; अत एवास्यानिर्वाच्यत्वेनादृढस्वभावस्य विनाशः। पुरुषस्तु परमार्थसन्। नासौ कारणसहस्रेणाप्यसन् शक्तः कर्तुम्। न हि सहस्रमपि शिल्पिनो घटं पटयितुमीशत इत्युक्तम्। तस्मादविनाशिपुरुषान्तो विकारविनाशः शुक्तिरज्जुतत्त्वान्त इव रजतभुजङ्गविनाशः। पुरुष एव हि सर्वस्य प्रपञ्चविकारजातस्य तत्त्वम्। न च पुरुषस्यास्ति विनाशो यतोऽनन्तः।''
—Bhāmatī on SB-I.1.IV, Loc. Cit., p.135.

52. ''यद्यपि 'अनेन जीवेनात्मना' इति जीवपरमात्मनोः पारमार्थिकमैक्यम्, तथापि तस्योपहितं रूपं जीवः शुद्धं तु रूपं तस्य साक्षि। तच्च मानान्तरानधिगतमुपनिषद्गोचर इति।... विधिशेषत्वं वा नेतुं न शक्यः। कुतः ? आत्मत्वादेव। न ह्यात्मा अन्यार्थः, अन्यत्तु सर्वमात्मार्थम्। तथा च श्रुतिः, 'न वा अरे सर्वस्य कामाय सर्वं प्रियं भवति, आत्मनस्तु कामाय सर्वं प्रियं भवति इति।' अपि चातः सर्वेषामात्मत्वादेव न हेयो नाप्युपादेयः। सर्वस्य हि प्रपञ्चजातस्य ब्रह्मैव तत्त्वात्मा। न च स्वभावो हेयः, अशक्यहानत्वात् न चोपादेयः, उपात्तत्वात्। तस्माद्धेयोपादेयविषयौ विधिनिषेधौ न तद्विपरीतमात्मतत्त्वं विषयीकुरुत इति सर्वस्य प्रपञ्चजातस्यात्मैव तत्त्वमिति।''
—Bhāmatī on SB-I.1.IV, Loc. Cit., p.134-135.

53. Vide, Swami Gambhirananda, Loc. Cit., p.47.

54. ''न सांख्यपरिकल्पितमचेतनं प्रधानं जगतः कारणं शक्यं वेदान्तेष्वाश्रयितुम् अशब्दं हि तत्।... कथम् ? एवंहि श्रूयते— 'सदेव सोम्येदमग्र आसीदेकमेवाद्वितीयम्' इत्युपक्रम्य 'तदैक्षत बहु स्यां प्रजायेयेति तत्तेजोऽसृजत' इति। तत्रेदंशब्द वाच्यं नामरूपव्याकृतं जगत् प्रागुत्पत्तेः सदात्मनावधार्य तस्यैव प्रकृतस्य सच्छब्दवाच्यस्येक्षणपूर्वकं तेजः प्रभृतेः स्रष्टृत्वं दर्शयति। तथान्यत्र 'आत्मा वा इदमेक एवाग्र आसीत्। नान्यत्किंचन मिषत्।'' —SB on BS-I.1.V-Loc. Cit., pp.168-169.

55. Swami Gambhirananda, Loc. Cit., p.48.

56. ''स ईक्षत लोकान्नु सृजा इति। स इमाँल्लोकानसृजत इतीक्षापूर्विकामेव सृष्टिमाचष्टे। क्वचिच्च षोडशकलं पुरुषं प्रस्तुत्याह—'स ईक्षांचक्रे। स प्राणमसृजत'इति। . . . तेन 'यः सर्वज्ञः सर्वविद्यस्य ज्ञानमयं तपः। तस्मादेतद्ब्रह्म नाम रूपमन्नं च जायते' इत्येवमादीन्यपि सर्वज्ञेश्वरकारणपराणि वाक्यान्युदाहर्तव्यानि।'' —Ibid, p.169.

57. ''यत्पुनरुक्तं-ब्रह्मणोऽपि न मुख्यं सर्वज्ञत्वमुपपद्यते नित्यज्ञानक्रियत्वे ज्ञानक्रियां प्रति स्वातन्त्र्यासंभवादिति। अत्रोच्यते—इदं तावद्भवान्प्रष्टव्यः, कथं नित्यज्ञानक्रियत्वे सर्वज्ञत्वहानिरिति ? यस्य हि सर्वविषयावभासनक्षमं ज्ञानं नित्यमस्ति सोऽसर्वज्ञ इति विप्रतिषिद्धम्। अनित्यत्वे हि ज्ञानस्य कदाचिज्जानाति कदाचिन्न जानातीत्यसर्वज्ञत्वमपि स्यात्। नासौ ज्ञाननित्यत्वे दोषोऽस्ति।'' —Ibid. p.170.

58. ''न च प्रधानं परमाणवो वा तदतिरिक्तसर्वज्ञेश्वराधिष्ठिता जगदुपादानमिति सांप्रतम्, तेषां भेदेन कार्यत्वात्। कारणात्कार्याणां भेदाभावात् कारणज्ञानेन समस्तकार्यपरिज्ञानस्य मृदादिनिदर्शनेनागमेन प्रसाधितत्वात्, भेदे च तदनुपपत्तेः। साक्षाच्च 'एकमेवाद्वितीयम्', 'नेह नानास्ति किंचन', 'मृत्योः स मृत्युमाप्नोति' इत्यादिभिर्बहुभिर्वचोभिर्ब्रह्मातिरिक्तस्य प्रपञ्चस्य प्रतिषेधाच्चेतनोपादानमेव जगत्, भुजङ्ग इवारोपितो रज्जूपादान इति सिद्धान्तः।'' —Bhāmatī on SB-I.1.5, Loc. Cit., p.168.

59. ''ब्रह्म चतुष्पादष्टाशफं षोडशकलम्। तद्यथाप्राची प्रतीची दक्षिणोदीचीति चतस्रः कलाः, ब्रह्मणः प्रकाशवान्नाम प्रथमः पादः। तदर्धशफः। तथा पृथिव्यन्तरिक्षं द्यौः समुद्र इत्यपराश्चतस्रः

कलाः, द्वितीयः पादोऽनन्तवान्नाम। तथाग्निः सूर्यचन्द्रमा विद्युदिति चतस्रः कलाः, स ज्योतिष्मान्नाम तृतीयः पादः। प्राणश्चक्षुः श्रोत्रं वागिति चतस्रः कलाः, स चतुर्थ आयतनवान्नाम ब्रह्मणः पादः। तदेवं षोडशकलं षोडशावयवं ब्रह्मोपास्यमिति श्रुत्यन्तरे षोडशकलं ब्रह्मेति प्रसिद्धम्।'' —Bhāmatī, Ibid, p.169.

60. Swami Gambhirananda, Loc. Cit., p.53.

61. ''यदुक्तं प्रधानमचेतनं सच्छब्दवाच्यं तस्मिन्नौपचारिक ईक्षतिः, अप्तेजसोरिवेति तदसत्! कस्मात्-आत्मशब्दात्। 'सदैव सोम्येदमग्र आसीत्' इत्युपक्रम्य 'तदैक्षत तत्तेजोऽसृजत' इति च तेजोऽबन्नानां सृष्टिमुक्त्वा तदेव प्रकृतं सदीक्षितृ तानि च तेजोऽबन्नानि देवताशब्देन परामृश्याह 'सेयं देवतैक्षत हन्ताहमिमास्तिस्रो देवता अनेन जीवेनात्मनानुप्रविश्य नामरूपे व्याकरवाणि इति। तत्र यदि प्रधानमचेतनं गुणवृत्त्येक्षितृ कल्प्येत तदेव प्रकृतत्वात्सेयं देवतेति परामृश्येत। न तदा देवता जीवमात्मशब्देनाभिदध्यात्। जीवो हि नाम चेतनः शरीराध्यक्षः प्राणानां धारयिता। ....स कथमचेतनस्य प्रधानस्यात्मा भवेत्। आत्मा हि नाम स्वरूपम्। नाचेतनस्य प्रधानस्य चेतनो जीवः स्वरूपं भवितुमर्हति।'' —SB on BS. I.1.6 Loc. Cit., p.173.

62. Swami Gambhirananda, Loc. Cit., p.62.

63. ''द्विरूपं हि ब्रह्मावगम्यते, नामरूपविकारभेदोपाधिविशिष्टं, तद्विपरीतं च सर्वोपाधिविवर्जितम्।.... तत्राविद्यावस्थायां ब्रह्मण उपास्योपासकादिलक्षणः सर्वो व्यवहारः। ....एक एव तु परमात्मेश्वरस्तैस्तैर्गुणविशेषैर्विशिष्ट उपास्यो यद्यपि भवति तथापि यथागुणोपासनमेव फलानि भिद्यन्ते। 'तं यथा यथोपासते तदेव भवति' इति श्रुतेः।'' —SB on BS. I.1.11, Loc. Cit, pp.176-177.

64. ''यद्यपि तत्त्वतो निरस्तसमस्तोपाधिरूपं ब्रह्म, तथापि न तेन रूपेण शक्यमुपदेष्टमित्युपहितेन रूपेणोपदेष्टव्यमिति। तत्र च क्वचिदुपाधिर्विवक्षितः ....क्वचित्पुनरुक्तोऽप्युपाधिरविवक्षितः। ....तदुपासनानि च कानिचित् अभ्युदयार्थानि मनोमात्रसाधनतयात्र पाठितानि। कानिचित्क्रममुक्त्यर्थानि, कानिचित्कर्मसमृद्ध्यर्थानि।'' —Bhāmatī on SB-I.1.11, Loc. Cit, pp. 176-177.

65. ''यद्यपि निरतिशयमेकमेव रूपमात्मन ऐश्वर्यं च ज्ञानं चानान्दश्च तथाप्यनाद्यविद्यातमः समावृतं तेषु तेषु प्राणभृद्भेदेषु क्वचिदसदिव, क्वचिदत्यन्ताप्रकृष्टमिव, क्वचिदपकृष्टमिव, क्वचित्सत्, क्वचित्प्रकर्षवत्, क्वचिदत्यन्तकर्षवदिव भासते। तत्कस्य हेतोः? अविद्यातमसः प्रकर्षनिकर्षतारतम्यादिति। यथोत्तमप्रकाशः सविता दिङ्मण्डलमेकरूपेणैव प्रकाशेनापूरयन्नपि वर्षासु निकृष्टप्रकाश इव शरदि तु प्रकृष्टप्रकाश इव प्रथते, तथेदमिति।'' —Bhāmatī, Ibid.

66. ''स्वशब्देनैव च सर्वज्ञ ईश्वरो जगतः कारणमिति श्रूयते श्वेताश्वतराणां-मन्त्रोपनिषदि सर्वमीश्वरं प्रकृत्य—'स कारणं करणाधिपाधिपो न चास्य कश्चिज्जनिता न चाधिपः' इति। तस्मात्सर्वज्ञं ब्रह्म जगतः कारणं न....अन्यत् इति सिद्धम्।'' —SB on BS-I.1.11, Loc.Cit.,p.176.

67. ''...शास्त्रं च सर्वज्ञे सर्वशक्तौ जगदुत्पत्तिस्थितिप्रलयकारणे ब्रह्मण्येव प्रमाणं....। न चास्ति कश्चिद्वेदान्तभागो यस्तद्विपरीतमपि बोधयेदिति।'' —Bhāmatī on SB - I.1.12, Loc.Cit., P.179-180.

68. ''पर एवात्मानन्दमयो भवितुमर्हति। कुतः? अभ्यासात्। परस्मिन्नेव ह्यात्मन्यानन्दशब्दो

बहुकृत्वोऽभ्यस्यते। आनन्दमयं प्रस्तुत्य.....उच्यते—....आनन्दं ब्रह्मणो विद्वान् न बिभेति कुतश्चन इति। 'आनन्दो ब्रह्मेति व्यजानात्' इति। श्रुत्यन्तरे च-'विज्ञानमानन्दं ब्रह्म' इति ब्रह्मण्येवानन्दशब्दो दृष्टः।'' —SB on BS-I.1.12, Loc.Cit., p.179-180.

69. ''अपि च मन्त्रब्राह्मणयोरुपेयोपायभूतयोः संप्रतिपत्तेर्ब्रह्मैवानन्दमयपदार्थः। मन्त्रे हि पुनः पुनः 'अन्योऽन्तर आत्मा' इति परब्रह्मण्यान्तरत्वश्रवणात् तस्यैव च 'अन्योऽन्तर आत्मानन्दमयः' इति ब्राह्मणे प्रत्यभिज्ञानात् परब्रह्मानन्दमयमिति।'' —Bhāmatī on SB-I.1.12, Loc.Cit., p.180-181.

70. ''नेतरो जीव आनन्दमयः तस्यानुपपत्तेः। सोऽयं जीवात्मनो लब्धृभावः आनन्दमयस्य च लभ्यता नाभेद उपपद्यते। तस्मादानन्दमयस्य जीवात्मनो भेदे परब्रह्मत्वं सिद्धं भवति।'' —Bhāmatī on SB-I.1.12, Loc. Cit., p.183.

71. ''यदि न लब्धो लब्धव्यः, कथं तर्हि परमात्मनो वस्तुतोऽभिन्नेव जीवात्मना परमात्मा लभ्यत इत्यर्थः।.... सत्यम्, परमार्थतोऽभेदेऽप्यविद्यारोपितं भेदमुपाश्रितय लब्धृलब्धव्यभाव उपपद्यते।'' —Bhāmatī, Ibid.

72. Vide, Swami Gambhirananda, Loc.Cit, pp.126-127.

73. ''य एषोऽक्षिणि पुरुषो दृश्यत एष आत्मेति होवाचैतदमृतमभयमेतद्ब्रह्मेति। ....परमेश्वर एवाक्षिण्यभ्यन्तरः पुरुष इहोपदिष्ट इति। कस्मात्? उपपद्यते। उपपद्यते हि परमेश्वरे गुणजातमिहोपदिश्यमानम्। आत्मत्वं तावन्मुख्यया वृत्त्या परमेश्वर, ''स आत्मा तत्त्वमसि इति श्रुतेः। अमृतत्वाभयत्वे च तस्मिन्नसकृच्छ्रुतौ श्रूयते। ....एष उ एव भामनीरेष हि सर्वेषु लोकेषु भाति'' इति, अत उपपत्तेरन्तरः परमेश्वरः।'' —SB on BS - I.2.13, Loc.Cit., p.245-247.

74. ''ननु सर्वगतस्येश्वरस्य कस्माद्विशेषेण चक्षुरेव स्थानमुपदिश्यत इति।....। एतदुक्तं भवति-निर्लेपस्येश्वरस्य निर्लेपं चक्षुरेव स्थानमनुरूपमिति।'' —Bhāmatī on SB - I.1.13, Loc.Cit., p.247.

75. ''वामनीयानि संभजनीयानि शोभनीयानि पुण्यफलानि वामानि। संयन्ति संगच्छमानानि वामान्यनेनेति संयद्वामः परमात्मा। तत्कारणत्वात्पुण्यफलोत्पत्तेस्तेन पुण्यफलानि संगच्छन्ते। स एव च पुण्यफलानि वामानि नयति लोकमिति वामनीः। स एव भामनीः। भामानि भानानि नयति लोकमिति भामनीः। तदुक्तं श्रुत्या-'तमेव भान्तमनुभाति सर्वं तस्य भासा सर्वमिदं विभाति' इति।'' —Bhāmatī, Ibid.

76. Vide, Swami Gambhirananda, Loc.Cit, pp.134.

77. ''य इमं च लोकं परं च लोकं सर्वाणि च भूतानि योन्तरो यमयति इत्युपक्रम्य श्रूयते '....यः पृथिवीमन्तरो यमयत्येष त आत्मान्तर्याम्यमृतः' इति ...योऽन्तर्याम्यधिदैवादिषु श्रूयते स परमात्मैव स्यान्नान्य इति। कुतः? तद्धर्मव्यपदेशात्। तस्य हि परमात्मनो धर्मा इह निर्दिश्यमाना दृश्यन्ते।....'एष त आत्माऽन्तर्याम्यमृतः' इति चात्मत्वामृतत्वे मुख्ये परमात्मन उपपद्येते।.... यत्त्वकार्यकरणस्य परमात्मनो यमयितृत्वं नोपपद्यत इति। नैष दोषः; यान्नियच्छति तत्कार्यकरणैरेव तस्य कार्यकरणत्वोपपत्तेः। ....तस्मात्परमात्मैवान्तर्यामी।'' —SB on BS. I.2.18, Loc. Cit., p.252-253.

78. ''श्रुतिस्मृतीतिहासपुराणेषु तावदत्रभवतः सर्वज्ञस्य सर्वशक्तेः परमेश्वरस्य जगद्योनित्वमवगम्यते। न तत्पृथग्जनसाधारण्यानुमानाभासेनागमविरोधिना शक्यमपह्नोतुम्। तथाच सर्वं विकारजातं

तदविद्याशक्तिपरिणामस्तस्य शरीरेन्द्रियस्थाने वर्तते इति यथायथं पृथिव्यादिदेवतादिकार्यकरणैस्तानेव पृथिव्यादिदेवतादीन्छक्नोति नियन्तुम्।"—Bhāmatī on SB - on I.1.18, Loc. Cit., pp.253-254.

79. "न चानवस्था। नहि नियंत्रन्तरं तेन नियम्यते किंतु यो जीवो नियन्ता लोकसिद्धः स परमात्मैवोपाध्यवच्छेदकल्पितभेदस्तथा व्याख्यायत इत्यसकृदावेदितं, तत्कुतो नियन्त्रन्तरं कुतश्चानवस्था। तथाच 'नान्योऽतोऽस्ति द्रष्टा' इत्याद्या अपि श्रुतय उपपन्नार्थाः। परमार्थतोऽन्तर्यामिणोऽन्यस्य जीवात्मनो द्रष्टुरभावात्।" —Bhāmatī, Ibid.

80. "अविद्याकल्पितजीवपरमात्मभेदाश्रयास्तु ज्ञातृज्ञेयभेदश्रुतयः, प्रत्यक्षादीनि प्रमाणानि, संसारानुभवः, विधिनिषेधशास्त्राणि च। एवं चाविद्याधिदैवादिष्वेकस्यैवान्तर्यामिणः प्रत्यभिज्ञानं समञ्जसं भवति....।" —Bhāmatī, Ibid.

81. "तस्मात्परमात्मान्तर्यामी न जीवादिरिति सिद्धम्। पृथिव्यादिस्तनयित्न्वन्तमधिदैवम्। "यः सर्वेषु लोकेषु इत्यधिलोकम्।'यः सर्वेषु वेदेषु इत्यधिवेदम्।'यः सर्वेषु यज्ञेषु' इत्यधियज्ञम्।" 'यः सर्वेषु भूतेषु' इत्यधिभूतम्।" —Bhāmatī, Ibid.

82. "अनाद्यानन्दकूटस्थज्ञानानन्तसदात्मने। अभूतद्वैतजालाय साक्षिणे ब्रह्मणे नमः॥" —Pañcapādikā - Verse 1, Loc.Cit., p.1.

83. The Pañcapādikā of Padmapāda, Op. Cit., p.242.

84. "तदत्र ब्रह्मशब्दे व्युत्पाद्यमाने बृंहतेर्धातोर्वृद्धिकर्मणोऽर्थानुगमात् प्रयोगानुगमे वा असति विशिष्टार्थविषयस्यापेक्षिकमहत्त्वस्यापरिग्रहात् सर्वतो निरवग्रहमहत्त्वसम्पन्नं वस्तु वाक्यार्थान्वयि ब्रह्मपदादनुगम्यते।" —Pañcapādikā on Adhyāsabhāṣya, Loc. Cit., p.275.

85. "ततश्च कालकृतावच्छेदनिमित्तस्याल्पत्वस्याभावात्। सदा सत्त्वान्नित्यं किंचिद्वस्तु ब्रह्मपदात् प्रतीयते।" —Ibid.

86. "तस्मादेकरसमद्वैतं वस्तु ब्रह्मपदात् प्रतीयते।" —Ibid.

87. "बुद्धत्वं च बृहत्यर्थान्वयादेव। कथम्? अबोधात्मकं हि वस्तु भोग्यम्। अतो भोक्तारं प्रति शेषत्वान्निकृष्टम्। चेतनः पुनर्न कस्यचिद्गुणभावमेति। तेनोत्कृष्टं सर्वस्मात् बुद्धस्वरूपं किंचिदिति बृहत्यर्थान्वयमेवानुसृत्य गम्यते।" —Ibid, p.276.

88. "मुक्तमिति च। अविद्याकामकर्मपरतन्त्रः तैरितश्चामुतश्च पशुवन्नीयमानो निकृष्टो भवति। ब्रह्मशब्दस्तु स्वार्थप्रक्षेपेण वाच्यं किंचिद्गमयन् सदैवाविद्यादिसंसारबीजानाकलियता तस्योत्कृष्टमहत्त्वमावेदयति।" —Ibid.

89. "सर्वज्ञं सर्वशक्तिसमन्वितं च तदिति ब्रह्मशब्दादेवावगम्यते। कथम्? यदि किंचिदविदितं तेन कुतश्चिद्वा कार्यात् व्यावर्तते शक्तिः आपेक्षिकस्तदोत्कर्षः स्यात्। न तद्युक्तं अन्यतोऽसिद्धस्य वस्तुनः पदप्रयोगादेव प्रतिपत्तौ। सिद्धे हि वस्तुनि प्रयोगे तस्य यथासिद्धमेव महत्त्वं निरुच्यते। शब्दादेव तदर्थान्वयप्रतीतौ निरङ्कुश एवार्थोऽभ्युपेतव्यः।" —Pañcapādikā-Loc.Cit., pp.276-277.

90. The Pañcapādikā of Padmapāda, Op. Cit., p.244; Vide, "एवं च बृंहतेरर्थः परिपूर्णो भवति यदि सर्वमस्य साक्षादेव संविद्गोचरे वशे च वर्तेत।" —Pañcapādikā, Ibid, p.276.

91. "अस्ति तावत् ब्रह्म नित्यशुद्धबुद्धमुक्तस्वभावं सर्वज्ञं सर्वशक्तिसमन्वितम्। ब्रह्मशब्दस्य हि व्युत्पाद्यमानस्य नित्यशुद्धत्वादयोऽर्थाः प्रतीयन्ते। बृहतेर्धातोरर्थानुगमादिति।" —Ibid, p.277.

92. गुणहीनं दोषभूयिष्ठं च वस्त्वल्पमविद्यमानसमं मन्यन्ते। गुणभूयिष्ठं दोषहीनं च महान्तं कथयन्ति। अतो गुणतोऽल्पत्वनिराकरणेन महत्त्वं दर्शयितुं बोधगुणहीनस्य गुणतोऽपकृष्टतया अल्पत्वात् बुद्धत्वमनुगम्यत....।'' —Vivaraṇa, Loc. Cit., p.589.

93. ''चेतस्यापि मुक्तस्य सर्वविषयज्ञानाभावे सर्वकार्यनियमनादिशक्त्यभावे च परिशिष्टज्ञेयकार्य-विषयज्ञाननियमनशक्त्यभावात् ततोऽपकर्षात् अल्पता स्यात् तद्व्यावृत्त्यर्थमाह—सर्वज्ञं सर्वशक्तिसमन्वितं च तदित्यादिना।'' —Vivaraṇa, Ibid.

94. ''प्रमाणान्तरगृहीतेऽर्थे प्रयोगसामर्थ्यादेवार्थप्रतिपत्तावल्पं वा महद्वा यथा प्रमाणान्तरेण प्रतिपद्यते तथैव शब्दार्थः प्रतिपत्तव्यः, यदा पुनः प्रयोगसामर्थ्यमनपेक्ष्य शब्दावयवसामर्थ्यादेवार्थोऽनुगम्यते तदा प्रमाणान्तरोपपदप्रकरणानां संकोचहेतूनामभावात् यथासामर्थ्यं मुख्य एवार्थः प्रतिपत्तव्यः इति भावः।'' —Vivaraṇa, Loc.Cit., pp.590.

95. ''सर्वो ह्यात्मास्तित्वं प्रत्येति न नाहमस्मीति। यदि न आत्मास्तित्वप्रसिद्धिः स्यात् सर्वो लोको नाहमस्मीति प्रतीयात्। आत्मा च ब्रह्मेति।'' —(SB) Pañcapādikā, Loc. Cit., pp.277-278.

96. ''कथं पुनरात्मा ब्रह्म ? वेदान्तेष्वात्मनि ब्रह्मशब्दप्रयोगात्। आत्मानमेव च लोकः अहमिति व्यपदिशति। तदेवमहंप्रत्यये एव ब्रह्मणः प्रसिद्धत्वान्नाप्रसिद्धिशंका।'' —Pañcapādikā-Loc.Cit., p.278.

97. ''सुखमहमस्वाप्समिति', ''सुखं सुप्तो न किंचिन्मया चेतितम्।'' —Ibid, pp.95,97.

98. ''न तत् स्वापे सुखानुभवसंस्कारजं स्मरणम्। सुखावमर्शो दुःखाभावनिमित्तः।....स्वप्ने तावदस्त्येव दुःखानुभवः। सुषुप्ते तु तदभावात् सुखव्यपदेशः।'' —Ibid, p.96.

99. ''न सुषुप्तौ भोक्तृतयाऽप्यहमुल्लेखोऽनुस्मर्यते इति।....आत्मन्यनुस्मर्यमाणे तावन्मात्रस्याहंकारस्य अहमित्येव स्मृतिनियमः स्यादित्युक्तम्। —Vivaraṇa, Loc. Cit., p.261.

100. ''दृष्टश्च सुषुप्ते चेतस्य निष्प्रपञ्चता पुरुषार्थ इति।'' —Ibid, pp.385.

101. ''श्रुतं च अशब्दमस्पर्शमरूपमव्ययं....निचाय्य तन्मृत्युमुखात् प्रमुच्यते।'' —Ibid.

102. ''मनसाऽप्यचिन्त्यरचनारूपस्येति। ...जन्मस्थितिभंङ्गं यतः सर्वज्ञात् सर्वशक्तेः कारणात् भवति तद् ब्रह्मेति...।'''' अस्य जगतो नामरूपाभ्यां व्याकृतस्येत्याद्यभिहितविशेषणचतुष्टयस्य, यथोक्तविशेषणमीश्वरं मुक्त्वेति-सर्वज्ञं सर्वशक्तिं विहाय न अन्यतः परपरिकल्पितात् प्रधानादेरचेतनात् चेतनादपि परिच्छिन्नज्ञानक्रियाशक्तेः संसारिणो हिरण्यगर्भात् उत्पत्त्यादि सम्भावयितुमपि शक्यम्।'' —Pañcapādikā- Loc. Cit., pp.298 & 302.

103. ''जगत्कारणादीश्वरस्याभिन्नत्वात्तद्विप्रतिपत्तिरीश्वरविप्रतिपत्तिरिति चेत्, तर्हीश्वरः प्रधानं परमाणुर्वेतिविप्रतिपत्तिर्दर्शिता स्यात्। न तथा संशेरते जनाः। युज्यते तु प्रत्यगात्मनो ब्रह्मशब्दाभिधेयविशेषस्वरूपस्य शरीरेन्द्रियादिषु संशयः। तेषामात्मनि तादात्म्यावभासात्।'' —Vivaraṇa, Loc. Cit., pp.614-615.

104. ''सत्स्वपि पृथिव्यादिष्वन्तःकरणाध्यासनिवृत्तौ प्रमातृत्वाभावादात्मचैतन्यस्य स्वतो विषयोपरागाभावात् द्वैतदर्शनं न प्राप्नोति अनिन्द्रियस्येव रूपादिदर्शनमित्येकः पक्षः।'' —Ibid, p.621.

105. ''तस्मान्निरस्तसकलकर्तृत्वाद्यध्यासम् अपाकृतद्वैतदर्शनं अनतिशयानन्दप्रकाशमानब्रह्मस्वरूपावस्थानं निःश्रेयसं वेदान्तविचारस्य प्रयोजनमिति रमणीयम्।'' —Ibid.

106. ''निमित्तत्वस्याप्युपलक्षणमेतत्।....भूतपञ्चकस्य तावदेका प्रकृतिरनुमीयते। सद्वस्त्वेकस्वभावानुगमात्। तथा हि—महाभूतानि सद्वस्तुप्रकृतिकानि तत्स्वभावानुरक्तत्वे सति विविधविकारत्वात्

मृदनुस्यूतघटादिवत्। द्रव्यत्वाद्यभेदा अपि प्रकृतिस्वभावा एव सामान्यवदवभासन्ते। सद्वस्तु पुनः सर्वानुगमात् सर्वविकारप्रकृतिः।...अतः सर्वकार्योपादानमेकमेव लाघवादिति न्यायानुगृहीतानुमानेन सिद्धम्।" —Ibid, pp.630-634.

107. "तस्यैव च निमित्तकारणत्वमनुमानेन कल्प्यते। तथा च—इदं जगदभिन्ननिमित्तोपादानं भवितुमर्हति प्रेक्षापूर्वजनितकार्यत्वात् आत्मगतसुखदुःख-रागद्वेषादिवत्। न च घटादिष्वनैकान्तिकता; तत्राप्यभिन्ननिमित्तोपादानत्वकल्पनात्।" —Ibid, p.634.

108. Vide, Pañcapādikā of Padṃapāda, Op.Cit., p.275.

109. Ibid.

110. "....पृथिव्यादीनां जन्मादिदर्शनात् तत्कारणे एकत्वनानात्वयोरन्यतरावगमे प्रमाणाभावात् बुद्धिमत्कारणपूर्वतामात्रे प्रतिपन्ने यतो वा इमानीति कारणस्यैकवचननिर्देशात् तदर्थमात्रस्यैव विधित्सितत्वादर्थात् सर्वज्ञं सर्वशक्ति जगत्कारणमिति कारणविशेषो वाक्यादवगम्यते।" —Pañcapādikā-Loc.Cit., p.311.

111. Vide, Pañcapādikā of Padmapāda, Op. Cit.

112. "तस्मात् ब्रह्मपरे वाक्ये जन्मादिधर्मजातस्योपलक्षणत्वात् ब्रह्मसंस्पर्शाभावात् सर्वज्ञं सर्वशक्तिसमन्वितं परमानन्दं ब्रह्मेति जन्मादिसूत्रेण ब्रह्मस्वरूपं लक्षितमिति सिद्धम्।" —Pañcapādikā-Loc. Cit., pp.312-313.

113. "ज्ञानानन्दसर्वज्ञप्रत्यगात्मभूतं ब्रह्म निश्चाययितुमसमर्था अपि युक्तयः शब्दावगते ब्रह्मणि सामान्यद्वारेण सम्भावनाबुद्धिहेतवो भवन्ति। कथम्?। जगदुपादाने अद्वितीये शब्दावगते मृदादिदृष्टान्तैरुपादानव्यतिरेकेण कार्यस्यानिरूपणात् अद्वितीयता संभाव्यते।" - Vivaraṇa, Loc.Cit., p.668.

114. "स्फटिकलौहित्यप्रतिबिम्बरज्जुसर्पघटाकाशदृष्टान्तैरात्मनि कर्तृत्वादेरारोपितत्वं जीवब्रह्मैक्यं ब्रह्मव्यतिरिक्तप्रपञ्चस्वातन्त्र्याभावः असंगत्वद्वारेण विशुद्धाद्वितीयप्रत्यगात्मता सम्भाव्यते इति।" —Vivaraṇa, Loc.Cit., pp.668-669.

115. Vide, Pañcapādikā of Padmapāda, Loc. Cit.,p.284.

116. "तत्तु समन्वयात्। तत् ब्रह्म सर्वज्ञत्वादिगुणकं वेदान्तशास्त्रात् प्रतीयत इति प्रतिजानीते।.... तत्र तात्पर्येण वेदान्तवाक्यानां समन्वयादित्यर्थः।" —Pañcapādikā-Loc. Cit.,p.322.

117. "तस्माज्जन्मादिनिमित्तोपादानकारणं सर्वज्ञं ब्रह्मेति सिद्धम्। तत्र बिम्बस्थानीयं ब्रह्म मायाशक्तिमत्कारणं जीवाश्च प्रत्येकमविद्यानुबद्धाः इति केचित्।" —Vivaraṇa, Loc.Cit.,p.693.

118. "मायाविद्याप्रतिबिम्बितं ब्रह्म जगत्कारणम्, विशुद्धं ब्रह्म अमृतत्वालम्बनम् जीवाश्च अविद्याबद्धाः इत्यन्ये।" —Vivaraṇa, Ibid.

119. "जीवा एव स्वाविद्यया प्रत्येकं प्रपञ्चाकारेण ब्रह्माविर्भावयन्ति सादृश्याच्च प्रपञ्चैकतावभासः अनेकैरवगतद्वितीयचन्द्रवत् स्वरूपापेक्षया च ब्रह्म सर्वजगत्कारणम् इत्यपरे।" —Vivaraṇa, Ibid.

120. "ब्रह्मैकमेव स्वाविद्यया जगदाकारेण विवर्तते स्वप्नादिवदिति मतान्तरम्। तस्मात् ब्रह्मैव स्वमायया अविद्यया विवर्तत इति।" —Vivaraṇa, Ibid.

121. "अस्ति तावत् ब्रह्म नित्यशुद्धबुद्धमुक्तस्वभावं सर्वज्ञं सर्वशक्तिसमन्वितम्। —SB on BS-I.1.1, Loc. Cit., p.79.

122. "....यो जीवो नियन्ता लोकसिद्धः स परमात्मैवोपाध्यवच्छेदकल्पितभेदस्तथा व्याख्यायते....। तथा च 'नान्योऽतोऽस्ति द्रष्टा इत्याद्या अपि श्रुतय उपपन्नार्थाः। परमार्थतोऽन्तर्यामिणोऽन्यस्य

जीवात्मनो द्रष्टुरभावात्।" —Bhāmatī, Supra, fn. 79.

123. "सदैव मुक्तः सदैव केवलोऽनाद्यविद्यावशात्तु भ्रान्त्या तथावभासत इत्यर्थः। तदेवमनौपाधिकं ब्रह्मणो रूपं दर्शयित्वा अविद्योपाधिकं रूपमाह—सर्वज्ञं सर्वशक्तिसमन्वितम्।" —Bhāmatī, Supra, fn. 31.

124. "शब्दो हि तस्य प्रमाणं वक्तव्यम्।....स चेत्तन्नावबोधयति कुतस्तस्य तत्र प्रामाण्यम्। न च प्रमाणान्तरं ब्रह्मणि प्रक्रमते।" - Bhāmatī, Supra, fn.28.

125. "नेति नेति नह्येतस्मादिति नेत्यन्यत्परम्।" —Supra, fn.21.

126. Vide, Supra, fn.22.

127. "...एकरसमद्वैतं वस्तु ब्रह्मपदात् प्रतीयते।" —Pañcapādikā, Supra, fn.86.

128. "...कालकृतावच्छेदनिमित्तस्याल्पत्वस्याभावात् सदा सत्त्वान्नित्यं किंचिद्वस्तु ब्रह्मपदात् प्रतीयते।" —Ibid, Supra, fn.85.

129. "मायाविद्याप्रतिबिम्बितं ब्रह्म जगत्कारणम्....।" —Vivaraṇa, Supra fn. 118.

130. Vide, Studies in Philosophy, Op. Cit., p.45.

131. Ibid.

132. "महत ऋग्वेदादेः शास्त्रस्य अनेकविद्यास्थानोपबृंहितस्य प्रदीपवत्सर्वार्थावद्योतिनः सर्वज्ञकल्पस्य योनिः कारणं ब्रह्म। न हीदृशस्य शास्त्रस्य ऋग्वेदादिलक्षणस्य सर्वज्ञगुणान्वितस्य सर्वज्ञादन्यतः संभवोऽस्ति।" —SB on BS-I.1.3, Loc.Cit., p.96.

133. "नन्वेवं सति बुद्धिपूर्वत्वात् सापेक्षं स्यात्? न स्यात्। ब्रह्मवदनादित्वात् कूटस्थनित्यत्वात्।" —Vivaraṇa, Loc. Cit., p.315.

134. "नन्वेवं सति कथं सर्वज्ञता? तस्यैव ज्ञानशक्तिविवर्तात्मकत्वात्....।" —Ibid.

135. "चेतनः पुनर्न कस्यचिद्गुणभांवमेति। तेनोत्कृष्टं सर्वस्मात् बुद्धस्वरूपं किञ्चिदिति बृहत्यर्थान्वयमेवानुसृत्य गम्यते।" "मुक्तमिति च।" —Pañcapādikā, Supra, fn.87,88.

136. "...योऽन्तर्याम्यधिदैवादिषु श्रूयते स परमात्मेव स्यान्नान्य इति।" —Bhāmatī, Supra, fn.77.

137. "साक्षाच्च 'एकमेवाद्वितीयम्', 'नेह नानास्ति किञ्चन" ....।" —Bhāmatī, Supra, fn.58.

138. "निःश्रेयसफलं तु ब्रह्मज्ञानम्, न चानुष्ठानान्तरापेक्षम्।" —SB on BS-I.1.1, Loc.Cit., p.69.

CHAPTER VII

THE ADVAITA CONCEPT OF MOKṢA

Freedom from the grip of *Avidyā* or Nescience is what according to Advaita Vedānta constitues the very essence of *Mokṣa*[1], which may also be called *Brahmāvagati*. Śaṅkara says that the attainment of *Brahman-hood* is itself *mokṣa,* which he also calls *bodyless-ness* (*aśarīratvam*)[2]. He says that if the evil of non-discrimination of the Self from the non-Self and vice-versa, and its terrific paraphernalia of consequential pains and sufferings are to be transcended, it then becomes imperative to first undertake a serious contemplation of the nature of *Brahman,* followed by a judicious application of the knowledge so obtained until the attainment of final release[3]. All Vedānta texts, says Śaṅkara, are necessarily a contemplation on *Brahman* of the nature referred to above and all aim at the destruction of ignorance by attaining the Right Knowledge, which culminates in the realization of the *Jīva-Brahman-identity*. This itself, says Śaṅkara, is *mokṣa* or *Emancipation*[4].

"The quest for absolute freedom from pain is as universal as the longing to live for infinity. Almost every Indian philosophical system, therefore, legitimately attempts to define the nature of the *summum bonum* along with its metaphysical principles, which when thoroughly comprehended and imbibed, facilitate the *seeker* to pursue the *highest good*. The inculcation of conviction and faith which are consequent upon insight into the nature of the Ultimate Reality, is essential for him to overcome hindrances that are likely to be encountered in his pursuits to attain Liberation. For this insight to take effect, it is necessary that the status of an individual self during the state of liberation, (alongside) the nature of Liberation and the means to it are discussed and understood at some length"[5].

The Knowledge of *Brahman* is the only means through which *avidyā* or ignorance is removable, for, as discussed already, *avidyā* is *jñānanivartya,* and cannot be removed by any other means. But this knowledge *about* the true nature of *Brahman,* which is indeed the 'opposite' of *ajñāna,* "is not Pure Consciousness as such", but rather "Pure Consciousness reflected in the mental mode (i.e., *vṛtti*) arising from the (study of) Upaniṣadic texts. The mental mode inspired by the reflection of Pure Consciousness which is opposed to *avidyā* is not the locus of *avidyā,* and Pure Consciousness which is the locus of *avidyā* is not the opposite of *avidyā;* It is (but) its witness"[6]. The removal of *avidyā* is viewed variously by different schools within Advaita Vedānta. There are mainly three prominent views in this regard, viz., (a) the removal of *avidyā* is identical with *Brahman* (or) *Ātman;* (b) it is different from *Brahman* (*Ātman*), but is not indescribable (*anirvacanīya*), but is rather of a fifth kind (i.e. *pañcama-prakāra*); and (c) it is identical with the direct experience of *Brahman*[7].

According to Vimuktātman, the upholder of the second view, the removal of *avidyā* (*avidyā-nivṛtti*) is not real, for were it to be so, that would imply the existence of another real entity, which would be against Advaita-metaphysics. It cannot be said to be unreal either, for were it so it would never be achievable. It cannot also be said to be both real and unreal, for this is self-contradictory[8]. But this view is criticised by Madhusūdana Sarasvatī who holds that if *avidyānivṛtti* be said to be different from *Brahman* it would never be manifested unless it be associated somehow with *Brahman,* It being the only Self-luminous entity. But *Brahman* being "supra-relational", It cannot be conceived as having any real relation with *avidyā-nivṛtti.* Hence, says Madhusūdana Sarasvatī, it has to be admitted that there is only a superimposed relation between *Brahman* and *avidyā-nivṛtti,* which obviously reposes on *Avidyā.* Hence *avidyā-nivṛtti,* if it be held to be different from *Brahman,* would be indeterminable (*anirvacanīya*), and to say anything contrary to this would be contradictory[9].

As for the view that *avidyānivṛtti* is identical with *Brahman,* this is upheld even by Śaṅkara and is generally accepted by the Advaita School. Śaṅkara says that *Brahman* is indeed of the nature of '*annihilation of avidyā*', which is the cause of the universe[10]. Reacting to the objection that if *avidyā-nivṛtti* be taken to be identical with *Brahman,* it would be co-existent with *Brahman* and then the need for its attainment would not arise,

Nṛsiṁhāśrama says that *avidyā* is verily experienced so long as *Brahman* is not realized. It is only in that state, i.e., the state of the direct experience of *Brahman* that *avidyā-nivṛtti* is as though '*achieved*'[11]. Sarvajñātman says that 'the ground for the use of the expression "*avidyā-nivṛtti*" is the mental state', which arises from *Śravaṇa* of the Upaniṣadic texts with reference to *Brahman*. "As this mental state is not present at the time of empirical existence", i.e., so long as *avidyā* exists, "the expression "*avidyā-nivṛtti*" does not signify *Brahman* then". "The word "*nivṛtti*" no doubt conveys the sense of absence. But when compounded with the word *avidyā* it signifies *Brahman* through the medium (i.e.), the mental state in the form of *Brahman*"[12].

According to the view that *avidyā-nivṛtti* is identical with the direct experience of *Brahman*, nothing *as such* gets annihilated, for *avidyā-nivṛtti* means simply the *rise* of the true knowledge of *Brahman*. Just as the elimination of darkness does not mean the actual removal of something, but rather the dawning of light, in the same manner *avidyā-nivṛtti* is identical with *Brahmānubhūti* since both the phenomena take place simultaneously[13].

Śaṅkara lays down four conditions as a pre-requisite for *Brahmāvagati* or Self-realization. According to him the seeker of Truth, i.e. of the True Knowledge about the Self, should be able to firstly, discriminate between the Self and not-Self, i.e., between the eternal and the ephemeral. Secondly, he should renounce all desire for the fruits of his actions—whether with regard to this life or thereafter. Thirdly, he should have already acquired what is known as the six-fold ethical and spiritual 'wealth', namely, (a) self-restraint; (b) control over the senses; (c) detachment from worldly-pursuits; (d) the sense of forbearance and tolerance; (e) (ability for) concentration; and (f) undaunted faith. And fourthly, he should have already developed an intense desire for the realization of *Brahman*, i.e., for final release[14]. In pursuance of the above-mentioned essential requirements for the realization of *Brahman*, Sureśvara establishes a succession of stages leading to Liberation, as per the following table[15]:

1. Performance of compulsory or obligatory actions[16].
2. Purification of the mind[17].
3. Knowledge of the evanescence, utter unreality and valuelessness of the world and empirical life[18].

4. Desire for renunciation of the utterly unreal and worthless world[19].
5. Abandonment of all the three possible kinds of human seekings or aspirations in human life[20].
6. An ardent desire for Self-realization[21].
7. Actual renunciation of the world as far as practicable as a consequence of the said desire[22].
8. Resort to positive means, leading to the desired *Brahma*-realization, namely Listening, Meditating and attainment of equipoise with the mind fully purified[23].
9. Actual realization of *Brahman*[24] and complete renunciation of empirical life as a result of the seeker's awakening[25].
11. Attainment of the *summum bonum,* i.e. Liberation, or restoration of the *Jīva* to its real essence, that is, *Brahman*[26].

It is noteworthy that while Sureśvara, as seen above, postulates the performance of *karma-s* as a means for the purification of the mind, after which they outlive their utility, Vācaspati on his part also shares the same view, i.e., that the performance of *karma-s* is subservient to the desire for Self-realization. "It gives rise to an unseen possibility which originates in the *'seeker'* a will to acquire Knowledge (of the Self). It has no connection with Knowledge directly : it serves its purpose in creating.....a desire to *know* and that is all"[27]. The Vivaraṇa, on the other hand, holds that the purpose of peforming *karma-s* is "to beget a desire to know and through it, a desire to *hear* and *reflect* upon the Vedāntic discourse without obstruction, until the final stage of knowledge is reached. They not only create a desire for Knowledge, but help the seeker by removing obstacles from the path of Knowledge. While giving rise to an unseen possibility which dies away on the awakening of the desire to *know,* they also produce something else which is persistent in its effect so long as Knowledge is not obtained"[28].

As pointed out above, *Śravaṇa, Manana* and *Nididhyāsana* are recognized as the direct means to the realization of the Self, but to what extent they are instrumental in this process is a matter of dispute among different schools of Advaita Vedānta. The Bhāmatī, while rejecting any possibility of injunction with regard to them, holds the view that all of them are of a cognitive nature. But the Vivaraṇa on its part defines them in the light of *Niyama-Vidhi.* Accordingly, "*Śravaṇa* is the eliminative thought-process....which repudiates impediments such as *asambhāvanā-s* and *viparīta-bhāvanā-s* with regard to the verbal epistemological process through which the purport of the Vedānta-passages is ascertained to be the identity between *Brahman* and *Jīva*"[29]. "*Manana* sweeps off from the mind the defect of "*asambhāvanā*" as regards...the identity between *Brahman* and *Jīva* by setting aside all contrary proofs and reasonings about the same...". "*Nididhyāsana* purges the mind of all "*Viparīta-bhāvanā-s*" still standing in the way of the realization of Reality, i.e., *Brahman.* Despite the conviction of Absolute Oneness, firmly established by *Manana,* there may be now and then a reassertion of old habits of thoughts, deep-rooted instincts and false notions of empirical glories and pragmatic values—compatible with the confirmed Truth"[30].

But for Madhusūdana Sarasvatī *Śravaṇa* is but "reflection of the determining principles of purport such as *Upakrama, Upasaṁhāra,* etc., so as to yield and establish conclusively the purport of the *Vedānta-Vākya-s* to the said '*Brahmātmaikya',* i.e., identity between *Jīva* and *Brahman*". "*Manana*", according to him, is...... the assimilation of *yukti-s* (arguments) calculated to dissipate all doubts about the said purport or theme[31].

Sureśvara on the other hand believes that *Śravaṇa* is "that mental activity which leads to the conviction that Reality, i.e., *Brahman,* is One, as declared by the Vedānta-texts. *Manana* to him, is the mental operation that produces ratiocinative knowledge that refutes every possible contradiction from other sources of knowledge as regards the truth established by the Scriptural testimony through the process of *Śravaṇa. Nididhyāsana,* however, is for Sureśvara, the starting of non-rational and intuitive knowledge of *Brahman.* It is the consummation of the preceding stages of *Śravaṇa* and *Manana* and the commencement of *Brahma*-realization...It is explained by Sureśvara as the first intuitive experience, which sets a limit to the continued process of *Śravaṇa* and *Manana. Śravaṇa* leads to definite verbal conviction and *Manana* occasions advanced intellectual conviction but *Nididhyāsana* is the culmination of these decisive but indirect convictions into a conclusive and direct intuition about *Brahman.* Being of the nature of the first unshakable intuition about *Brahman,* arising from the most intense and exclusive mental concentration thereon, after which emerges the supreme revelation of the Ever-revealed and Self-shining Pure Consciousness, known as *Brahma*-realization proper, it is a goal or a high achievement in itself. But even *Nididhyāsana,* being only the first or preliminary stage of direct intuition, is only a means to the supreme and final or consumate *Brahma*-realization"[32].

As far as *Manana* is concerned, as discussed already, the method of *Padārthaśodhana* is postulated with reference to the realization of *Brahman* as arising out of the hearing of the *Mahāvākya-s.* "*Padārtha-śodhana* is the method of convincing oneself of the true significance of the words "*Tat*" and "*Tvam*" by means of eliminating adventitious and irrelevant elements, features or attributes, acquired or gathered around and associated with the bare meanings of these terms through superimposition. It seeks to discriminate between the *Ātman* and its empirical adjuncts and establish the sole reality of *Ātman* or *Brahman,* and consequent falsity of the entire phenomenal world." "It must, however, be clearly understood that this method of bringing out the true implication of the terms "*Tat*" and "*Tvam*" as one Reality, i.e., the Pure Consciousness, by eliminating the superficial significatory elements, is confined to *Padārtha*-s only and serves the purpose of convincing the "*seeker*" that such a Substratum or Reality must be there to explain the otherwise inexplicable appearances. But it does not and cannot convey an immediate and intuitive knowledge of the Ultimate Reality, i.e., *Brahman,* for realizing which the full import of the *Mahāvākya* is indispensable and that is possible only at the stage of *Nididhyāsana*"[33].

The import of a *Mahāvākya* such as "*Tat Tvam Asi*" is believed to be "*akhaṇḍārtha*", i.e., it is free from all differences and relations—superior indeed to ordinary sentences, which necessitate differences and relations for the proper comprehension of their import. The import of the *Mahāvākya*-s such as the one just referred to, imply Ultimate Purity and Oneness—devoid of all distinctions of subject, object, etc. The process of realizing the import of such *Mahāvākya-s,* i.e., the realization of the *Vākyārtha-s,* must of necessity be different from that of verbal testimony. "Sureśvara recognizes three kinds of relations for the realization of the import of the said *Mahāvākya,* i.e., of the *akhaṇḍārtha,* viz., (i) *Sāmānādhikaraṇya;* (ii) *Viśeṣaṇa*-

viśeṣya-bhāva and (iii) *Lakṣya-lakṣaṇa-bhāva.* He says that in sentences such *as "So'yam Devadattaḥ"* and *"Tat Tvam Asi"*, etc., although the words signify the qualified entities, yet they ultimately imply one bare object only as their final import. First of all there is an apposition or coherence of what are ordinarily or expressly conveyed by the two terms "*Saḥ*" and "*ayam*", and "*Tat*" and "*Tvam*" (i.e., *Sāmānādhikaraṇyānvaya*). Then comes the stage of unitary judgement, in which the two express meanings of the words are presented in a combined form, constituting together the relation of the substantive and the subjective (i.e., *Viśeṣaṇa-viśeṣyatā*). But the two senses related as such, when closely examined, are found to be partially or wholly unsatisfactory, being conflicting or incongruous and hence the express meanings have to be partially or wholly relinquished, as the case may be, and are succeeded by senses, which turn out to be abolutely one and the same, presented through implication whether wholly or partly exclusive of the primary significance, as explained above (i.e., *Lakṣya-lakṣaṇa-sambandha*). At this stage emerges the intuitional realization or immediate realization of Pure Consciousness (i.e., *Svarūpa-pratipatti*), sublating *Avidyā* and all that it produces"[34].

As regards the nature of the Self-realized, Śaṅkara is quite emphatic about the fact that though *Sañcita-karma* and *Sañcīyamāna-karma* are automatically eradicated on the attainment of True Knowledge, yet this is not the case with *prārabdha-karma.* This position of Śaṅkara thus paves the way for the attainment of *Brahman* knowledge even though all *prārabdha-karma-s* have not been totally consumed. Hence, the phenomenon of the intermediate stage of *Jīvan-mukti* prior to final Liberation, or *Brahmāvagati*[35].

II. The Bhāmatī's concept of Mokṣa

Śaṅkara says that the determination of the true nature of *Brahman* through discrimination of the Self from the non-Self is called knowledge[36]. Commenting on this, Vācaspati says that *Vidyā* is knowledge about the nature of *Brahman,* which does not contain any trace of doubt or contradiction[37]. He says further that the non-apprehension of difference between the Self and the non-Self, which is the effect of Nescience, can be done away with only by the cognition of difference. And this Right Knowledge, i.e., cognition of difference, is possible through (the) hearing (of) the Vedānta texts and through reflection thereon, etc. The knowledge obtained through this instrumentality, claims the Bhāmatī, leads to the sublation of Nescience, and also to the ascertainment of the nature of *Brahman* which in reality 'Stands forth in Its own nature'[38]. According to the Bhāmatī, therefore, *Mokṣa* is identical with ascertainment of the true nature of *Brahman,* which (ascertainment) again is of the nature of knowledge, obtained through *śravaṇa, manana,* etc. This is, therefore, in conformity with the view expressed earlier to the effect that the *Bhāmatī* postulates *śravaṇa* and *manana* as purported to create the desire to know and nothing more.

As to Śaṅkars's assertion that the deliberation on the meaning of Vedānta texts is meant for the attainment of the knowledge of *Jīva-Brahman* identity, Vācaspati remarks (on this) that the study of the Vedānta-texts is not meant for incantation or ritualism of any kind[39]. The purpose served by the study of Vedānta is solely and simply the realization of the *Jīva-Brahman*-unity. He interprets the "unity of self" as being synonymous with "That One Reality of the nature of Supreme Bliss" characterized by total dissociation from the world constituted of the five elements representative of Māyā. The study of Vedānta verily brings about such a knowledge which, simultaneously with its rise, occasions the aforesaid 'dissociation from the world'[40]. The Bhāmatī says moreover, that the knowledge of the true nature of *Brahman,* i.e., Self-realization, is of the nature of complete cessation of all pains and sufferings, and is of the essence of Bliss[41]. Vācaspati, therefore, defines 'Mokṣa' as 'liberation' from world-misery on the one hand, and as eternal Bliss, on the other.

As already described, Śaṅkara prescribes certain qualifications as a necessary condition for the study of Vedānta—the gateway to Self-realization. Among these pre-requisites, he acknowledges "*Svādhyāya*", i.e. study of one's portion of the Veda-s, as a pre-condition for a deliberation on *Brahman*[42]. Clarifying this point, Vācaspati says that what is meant here is that 'immediate succession to the study of the Vedas' is common to the desire to know *Dharma* and to the desire to know *Brahman.* This is evident also from the (Mīmāṁsā) text, "Then, therefore, the desire to know *Dharma*". Vācaspati says that here the word "*Dharma*" means by implication the entire Vedic Scriptures, and since *Brahman* is equally the import of the Vedas, the teaching about immediate succession to the study of the Vedas applies to the contemplation on *Brahman* as well, or to the desire thereof[43]. In support of his view, Vācaspati says that in the texts," They desire to know by sacrifice", etc., "sacrifice, etc., are applied to the knowledge of *Brahman* as its subsidiaries; for knowledge alone is primary as the object of desire, and other things which are not primary have to be related to what is primary. Even here, sacrifice, etc. are not subsidiary to the production of the knowledge of the meaning of the sentence, since the latter is produced by the sentence itself"[44]. He observes moreover, that sentences as the one given above do not require ritual as an auxiliary, for it is seen that knowledge of the meaning of a sentence is obtained (even though no rites whatsoever have been perfomed), especially by such persons as having a knowledge of the connection of words and their senses with a comprehension of the true nature of the "principles regulating the use of sounds", and as being aware also of the "relationships of the subsidiary and the principal, etc., with a knowledge of the requirements of expectancy, proximity and compatibility[45].

Deliberating further on the nature of Self-realization, Vācaspati says that those whose intellects are impure...cannot...understand the validity of the identity asserted by the text, "That thou art", between the *Jīva* denoted by '*thou*', whose nature is that of agent and enjoyer, and the Supreme Self, denoted by '*That*', whose nature is eternal Purity, Intelligence and Indifference, because of the certainty (on their part) that there is lack of compatibility between the denotations of the two terms. But those of pure intellect, whose internal impurities have undergone attrition by means of sacrifices, gifts, austerities, fasting, etc; and who are endowed with faith, having understood the compatibility of the terms "*that*" and "*thou*", will understand their identity without failure. Vācaspati says here that if this be the claim of those who favour the performance of rituals as a means to the attainment of *Brahman*, they need to say, whether such ascertainment of identity is a product of ritual, which in itself is not a means of valid knowledge, or whether they hold rituals too to be a means of knowledge, in addition to Perception, etc. If, says the Bhāmatī, the ascertainment of identity is brought about by reasoning not in conflict with the Scriptures, but rather based on them, then there is no need for rituals as a means thereof[46]. It is thus that having known the *Jīva* to be of the same nature as *Brahman* through the knowledge obtained by hearing texts such as, "That thou art", etc., and through confirmation of same by means of reasoning there is the intuitive knowledge of *Brahman* through the contemplation of that Truth, i.e, through "*Bhāvanā*", practiced for a long time uninterruptedly, supported by sacrifice, etc. And this has for evidence texts such as, "knowing That alone, the wise should perform contemplation (*Prajñā*)". Having thus obtained knowledge through Verbal Testimony supported by reasoning, one should (then alone) contemplate on the Self, argues the Bhāmatī[47].

Raising his voice against any kind of assistance obtained from the performance of rites in the realization of the true nature of the Self, Vācaspati says that it has to be admitted that the contemplation of *Brahman* brings about intuitive knowledge of the nature of *Brahman*. He says in this context that the intuition of *Brahman* brought about by contemplation is not the result of perception etc, as is the case with empirical objects such as pot, etc. *Brahman,* while not being dependent on anything else for Its illumination, is known through direct intuition which is of Its own nature. Such an intuition cannot be said to be a product. For indeed, any intuition brought about by contemplation, and yet different in nature from *Brahman* Itself, should be considered as being doubtful in nature, similar to a product of imagination, and as such it cannot be taken to be valid. Hence, since ritual does not bring about valid intuition of the said nature, it cannot be said to be of any assistance in the generation of any such intuition through contemplation. Furthermore, the Immutable, Eternal, and All-pervasive *Brahman* cannot be said to be subject to any form of modification, purification or even attainment as a result of contemplation[48]. Vācaspati asks in this context the question, "What is it that is referred to as contemplation of the Self?" Is it anything emanating successively from Verbal Testimony or is it a series of valid cognitions obtained from

Verbal Testimony? If it is the first, then even if it is put to repeated practice it would not negate Nescience for it is the ascertainment of truth and its repeated and uninterrupted cognition that can uproot Nescience with its paraphernalia of evil impressions, and not the repetition of doubts present in invalid cognitions. For indeed, the mere repetition of the doubtful cognition, "Is this a post or a man, or is it a tall big object", even a hundred times cannot verily lead to the uprooting of the doubt. That can be achieved only through valid cognition[49].

Vācaspati says in addition that rituals involving prohibitions are also not mandatory for any seeker of truth as far as contemplation over the nature of the Self is concerned. This is so, says he, because even those who have already known the truth about the nature of the Self do incur sin by indulging in prohibitory acts, no less than those, who being still bound in Nescience, are yet to realize the truth[50]. Rituals are not of any assistance even in the origination of the desire to contemplate on the Self once all doubts about the nature of the Self have been cleared through Verbal Testimony or hearing of the Scriptures. And this is what is meant to be driven home by texts such as, "Not by rituals nor by offspring nor by wealth, but by renunciation alone do they enjoy immortality"[51]. As to the query whether rituals have thus no significance whatsoever in Self-realization the Bhāmatī says that they do have their significance in being remote auxiliaries therein. "The obligatory rites purify the person by destroying sins already incurred", as is claimed by the Scriptures in texts like, "He verily is the *ātmayājin* who pleases the Self and who has understood the purport of instructions", such as, "By this is purified this part (i.e. the body) of mine, by this is my body made to grow". The words "*by this*" used herein refer to sacrificial and purificatory acts[52]. This is also supported by the *Smṛti-s* wherein it is said that, "He for whom there have been these forty-eight purificatory acts, etc"[53]. The Scriptures also refer to the attainment of Knowledge only by that person, who, though ignorant, has a purified intellect and in whom the desire to know the Self has taken root by the mere purging of the impurities of the mind through the observance of the four kinds of act—*nitya, naimittika, kāmya* and *niṣiddha,* as is claimed by the text "Being of purified intellect, he then sees the partless *Brahman* through contemplation".

This is backed by the *Smṛti-s* where it is said that, "Knowledge arises in those persons whose sins have been consumed through the performance of rites"[54]. Hence, says Vācaspati, it is settled that the observance of rites and rituals is auxiliary to the generation of Knowledge by being instrumental in the removal of impurities of the mind[55].

Touching on another aspect of the pre-requisites for Self-realization, Vācaspati says, in pursuance of Śaṅkara's claims in this connection as referred to earlier[56] that "to be eternal is to be true: that in which this is, that is eternal, true, and thus, it is in the sphere of desire. To be non-eternal is to be untrue; that in which this is, that is non-eternal, untrue; and thus, it is not in the sphere of desire. Of these, which are experienced and constitute the spheres of the concepts "*Thou*" and "*I*", the object and the subject, that which is established to be true, eternal, pleasant, that comes in the sphere of desire; that, however, which becomes non-eternal, untrue, encompassed by the three-fold misery, that is affected by impurities such as passion, etc., resulting in the sense-organs being involved in their respective objects[57]. And this in turn results in activities of all sorts that bind the self to their fruits of the nature of merit and demerit and hence, the cycle of birth and death in which the self finds itself caught. But once the mind has been brought under control through contemplation resulting in non-attachment, calmness is achieved which is the *sine qua non* for the investigation into the true nature of the self. This again leads to equanimity and to the other pre-requisites, such as, the desire to abandon objects of enjoyment, withdrawal from the same and faith in Truth[58]. Hence it is, that with the mind purged of all impurities, the desire for release from the world arises in him (the seeker). And having known through the study of the Scriptures, etc. that the Knowledge of *Brahman* which is eternally Pure, Intelligent and Free, constitutes within itself release from the world, there arises in him the intense desire to know *Brahman*[59]. This has for evidence, says Śaṅkara, texts like, "One who knows *Brahman* attains the Supreme"[60].

The realization of *Brahman* is verily the sole goal in life, says Śaṅkara; and this is so because that itself brings to an end all evils, miseries, etc. of the world that are caused by Nescience.

Brahman Itself is therefore that for which one needs to have the desire to know[61]. Vācaspati notes on this that mere knowledge is not that which needs to be desired for the elimination of miseries, but rather such knowledge as will culminate in the realization of *Brahman* through intuition. This is what is meant by the "*San*" suffix in the word "*jijñāsā*", for, says Vācaspati, a desire is meaningful only when the fruit is attained[62]. He says with reference to the realization of the Self, that though in the realization of the Self nothing new is generated, contrary to the practice at empirical level, yet, due to the influence of beginningless Nescience, *Brahman,* though Self-luminous, appears as though non-luminous and as such, illumined by an external agent. Hence, though It is different from the body, etc., It appears as though identified with it. This indeed being the cause of all evils and transmigration, so long as this is not eliminated, It is as though unattained, and on its extermination, It becomes as though attained. This much is what is sought for. This itself is Self-realization or Release[63].

The eradication of Nescience as referred to above is brought about by contemplation of the nature as discussed above, resulting in intuition, which, says the Bhāmatī, is a mode of the internal organ. Without such an intuitional knowledge Nescience, the cause of miseries, cannot be destroyed. And without the eradication of Nescience there cannot be the realization of *Jīva* as being identical with *Brahman,* devoid of all taints, and of the nature of Infinite Beatitude. Hence, those desirous of the eradication of Nescience and of the realization of the true nature of the Self should aspire after the above-mentioned knowledge[64].

Continuing the discussion on this issue, Vācaspati says that it is due to superimposed adjuncts that the *Jīva* fails to identify itself with *Brahman.* These superimposed adjuncts are removable indeed by intuitional knowledge of Truth alone, which uproots and destroys the superimposed. "Thus, in the bliss of *Brahman,* which through the superimposition due to Nescience has attained the state of *Jīva,* which is in reality devoid of grief, misery, etc., this state conditioned by superimposition is sublated by the true knowledge of the sense of the text "That thou art", culminating in the realization of the true nature of the Self. On the sublation of superimposition, the blissful nature, though eternally attained, becomes attained, as if not attained already; grief, misery, etc., though eternally abandoned, become abondoned, as if unabandoned already."[65]

As regards *Mokṣa* as such, Śaṅkara says that it ensues simultaneously with the knowledge of *Brahman* independent of any preceding act. This has for evidence Scriptural texts such as, "He who knows *Brahman* becomes *Brahman* itself"; "And his actions perish when He, the Higher and the Lower, is seen"; "He who knows the Bliss of *Brahman* has no fear from anything or from anywhere", "Verily, thou hast, Oh Janaka, reached fearlessness", "Therefore, one knew only the Self in the form, I am *Brahman*", "from That all this sprang", "Then, what delusion is there, what sorrow is there for one who has uniformly seen this Oneness?", etc.[66] With a view to emphasizing the denial of any action to be undertaken prior to the realization of *Brahman*, Śaṅkara quotes other texts to support his view, such as, "Verily the sage Vāmadeva seeing him, realized, "I became Manu and the Sun", "Thou indeed art our father, Thou who carried us to the other shore of ignorance", "To him whose sins are worn out, the revered Sanatkumāra shows the other side of darkness", etc.[67] These passages and yet many others too, says Śaṅkara, show that the knowledge of *Brahman* means in reality the removal of all obstacles to *Mokṣa*, as discussed above.[68] Śaṅkara quotes also another aphorism which lays down the succession of causes and effects till the attainment of final Release. Says he, "In the series of misery, birth, activity, defect, wrong or illusory knowledge, the elimination of each subsequent member therein precipitates the elimination of each preceding one, so that by the elimination of misery final Release is attained.[69] Vācaspati observes in this connection that each subsequent member of the series is the cause and each preceding one is the effect. Thus it is that on the cessation of birth there takes place the eradication of misery; on the cessation of activity there is the cessation of birth; on the destruction of defect there is the cessation of activity and on the elimination of illusory Knowledge there takes place the destruction of defect. Illusory knowledge which is the primal cause of rebirth through the generation of desire, etc. is itself sublatable by true knowledge only which consists of the realization of the identity of the self with *Brahman*. Hence, says Vācaspati,

Release consists in the manifestation of the true nature of *Brahman* which takes place by nothing but the removal of Nescience. The Bhāmatī notes here that the manifestation of the true nature of *Brahman* is by no means the effect of *Vidyā* or contemplation nor is it the effect of any act, etc. performed with regard to that. This is, says Vācaspati, what is meant by the aphorism mentioned above.[70]

Deliberating still deeper on the nature of Release, Śaṅkara says that the cognition of the oneness of the self and *Brahman* cannot be said to be of the form of an "imagined identification", because were it so, then there would be violation of the syntactical relation of the words in texts such as, "That thou art", "I am *Brahman*" and "This Self is *Brahman*", the purport of which is to propound the identity of the self and *Brahman.* Furthermore, this will contradict the Scriptural claim that knowledge of *Brahman* signifies the eradication of Nescience, as in texts like, "The knot of the heart is severed and all doubts are removed." And also in texts such as, "He who knows *Brahman* becomes *Brahman* Itself", the purport would be rendered unintelligible.[71] The Bhāmatī observes on this that there cannot be agentship for the "*that*" which, not being an object, is in apposition to, and therefore non-different from, the inner Self. Hence, on the cessation of Nescience, cease also the threefold distinctions of knowledge, knower and known.[72]

Śaṅkara says of the final Release, that it is not the result of purification of any kind since that would imply activity with respect to *Mokṣa,* which is not acceptable. This is so because purification may be attained either through merits or through the removal of defects. Neither of these is applicable with respect to *Brahman,* since *Brahman* being most Excellent, and eternally Pure is not amenable to further excellence or purity by additional excellence or by the removal of impurities.[73] Vācaspati says on this that, if the merit supposedly to be added to *Brahman* is of the nature of *Brahman* itself, the question of its being added does not arise; and if it is different from *Brahman,* then being of necessity something produced, its causality with regard to final Release is untenable, or else that would imply non-eternality of *Mokṣa.* He further says that there being no impurity in *Brahman* whatsoever, the question of its removal does not arise, contrary to the case with a mirror, which can be purified by the removal of impurities.[74]

Reacting to the charge that through purificatory acts involving such things as bathing, sipping of water, wearing of the sacred thread, etc., the *Jīva* becomes purified and hence fit for final Release, Śaṅkara says that all the purificatory acts have the body as their locus, but due to the influence of Nescience these are associated with the Self. It is only he who, under the sway of Nescience, associates himself with the body, has the cognition, "I am clean," "I am purified", etc. Thus, such a self cognizes himself as enjoying the fruits of the purificatory acts, as is symbolically suggested in the texts, "One of the two eats the delicious fruit, while the other just looks on without tasting of the fruit," "The wise men call that self the enjoyer who is associated with the body, the sense organs and the mind", "He who is all effulgent, Un-embodied, free from defects, Indubitable, eternally Pure and unafflicted by sins of any sort, pervaded all". These texts bear testimony to the fact that *Brahman*, being eternally Pure, cannot be purified any further. Becoming *Brahman* is itself *Mokṣa,* says Śaṅkara. Hence *Mokṣa* is not the result of purification.[75]

Vācaspati says in addition, that it is due to the apprehension of non-difference that the attributes of purification as described above are applied to the self. In truth, says he, the acts of purification do not apply to the self. And there is no other means by which it may be said that the final *Release* is the result of purification of any activity whatsoever. Hence, says the Bhāmatī, knowledge is the only means to *Mokṣa.*[76]

And to the claim that (True) Knowledge as well is an act, albeit mental, Śaṅkara says that this is not acceptable because of fundamental difference between mental acts, such as contemplation, etc. and Knowledge, as such contemplation, says he, being dependent on the person undertaking it, is open to three possibilities—it may be either undertaken as enjoined, or not undertaken at all, or undertaken but differently. Knowledge, on the other hand, being dependent on a valid means of knowledge which has for content that the thing itself, is not open to any such possibilities. Hence, not being dependent on a person nor on any injunction, knowledge of the Self is not an act.[77] The Bhāmatī says, with a view to throwing more light on the above, that it is true that Knowledge is a mental act, but like other forms of act, it does not produce any fruit, in *Brahman.* This is so because It being self-luminous cannot be (made) an object of cognition. Moreover, for one who has studied the Scriptures and has understood the words, their senses and the relation between them, there is verily the Knowledge of *Brahman* resulting from the testimony of texts beginning with "Existence alone was this all, etc.", and ending with, "That thou art." This is so because of the possibility of obtaining valid Knowledge through Verbal Testimony. Such a knowledge cannot indeed be dependent on man's will, nor on any injunction.[78] *Brahman* knowledge is dependent on *Brahman* Itself.

III. The Vivaraṇa's Concept of Mokṣa

Mokṣa, according to the Vivaraṇa School is of the nature of a unique Knowledge which, while unveiling the true nature of *Brahman,* arises from the realization of truth contained in the *Mahāvākya,* "That Thou Art". That Knowledge, says Padmapāda, dispels simultaneously as it arises, the very root of all evils, i.e., Nescience, which, by its concealing potency, is responsible for the non–manifestation of *Brahman* in its own nature, i.e., that of Consciousness.[79] For the Pañcapādikā, the mere discrimination between the Self and the non-self does not constitute Release, for that on its own does not bring about the eradication of superimposition. Actual knowledge is Knowledge of the Self as revealed by the Scriptures and so long as that is not achieved there is no Release. Hence, for the Vivaraṇa School, that itself constitutes *Mokṣa.*[80] That *Mokṣa* is of the nature of the eradication of Nescience, on the one hand, and of the nature of the true Knowledge of the Self on the other, has for evidence the declarations in the Scriptures equating knowledge of *Brahman* with eradication of evils. For example, where it is said that the means of attaining *Brahman* is the "knowledge of *Brahman* itself", there itself (i.e., in Vedānta) it is said that—"He who has known the Self is released from sorrow". The Scriptures also declare that, "He who knows *Brahman* becomes *Brahman* Itself", "When he sees...the Lord, the Great One, he is freed from all evils"[81].

The Pañcapādikā interprets Śaṅkara's statement, "for the cognition of the *Jīva–Brahman*–identity", as meaning that this unity of the Self is itself the subject–matter of Vedānta, and as such, *Mokṣa* itself, of the nature of the *Jīva's* identifying himself with *Brahman*, is the subject-matter of Vedānta. Hence, concludes Padmapāda, the attainment of Bliss does not consist in arriving at something external to the subject-matter.[82] By saying so the Pañcapādikā hints at the fact that *Mokṣa* is attainable by the study of Vedānta itself, and by no other means.

Prakāśātman says on his part that the realization of the *Jīva-Brahman*-identity itself is the attainment of Bliss. And this, he says, is achieved through the study of Vedānta which is enjoined by the Scriptures by means of an "*Adhyayana-vidhi.*" Says the Vivaraṇa, 'Having studied one's portion of the *Veda-s* regularly as ordained, the *seeker* comes to know from the very first exposition of the Vedānta-texts that, "Everything here is dear but for the sake of the self." With this as the starting point, he develops a sense of detachment from worldliness and after coming to the conclusion that, "The Self having been known, all else becomes known", "This itself is Immortality", he takes to the means of achieving Knowledge of the Self, that which is instrumental in the attainment of Immortality or Final Release. Prakāśātman says that for this purpose, i.e. for the purpose of attaining *Mokṣa, Śravaṇa* is enjoined upon the *seeker*, with *Manana* and *Nididhyāsana* as its auxiliaries.[83]

Padmapāda says that though the eradication of Nescience is instrumental in the attainment of *Mokṣa*, yet due to the fact that it cannot be effected through Verbal Testimony, i.e. by *Śravaṇa*, etc. of the *Mahāvākya-s*, it is not as such the subject-matter of Vedānta, and hence the separate mention of the eradication of 'the cause of all evils' by Śaṅkara. Pañcapādikā lays emphasis here on the point that eradication of Nescience is not the purpose of Vedānta and hence it cannot result from the study of the Scriptures. Though, says he, the eradication is brought about by the 'potency' of knowledge of *Jīva-Brahman*-identity, yet man's desire for *Mokṣa* should itself be regarded as its actual cause[84]. This is what Prakāśātman also means when he says that, "the objection to the fact that since Knowledge of *Brahman* is the *Summum Bonum* of *Vedānta*, there is no logic in holding the eradication of evil as the end to be achieved through the study, etc. of the Scriptures", is untenable. This is because though not resulting directly from the study of Vedānta, yet it does occur as an indirect result of the same through the desire for *Mokṣa* awakened by the study of Vedānta[85]. He says in this connection that it cannot be said of *Brahman*-Knowledge that it is acquired as though from outside (i.e. as an object foreign to and therefore, separate from) the *seeker*, just as is the case with the acquisition of material objects. This is so, he says, because *Brahman*-Knowledge rests essentially '*attained*' verily by the *seeker*, it being in the form of cognition, arising in him with himself as the locus. It manifests at the same time the object of cognition to him, which is in fact no other than his own Self[86]. As regards the incompatibility of the perception of a material object with the Knowledge of the Self, the Vivaraṇa says that in the former case cognition arises as a result of the illumination of the external object by consciousness through the sense-organs, while in the latter case the Self is itself the "illuminator" as well as the "illumined", (i.e. both the subject and the object). Hence, in the latter case, one cannot talk of knowledge being "attained" as in the former case[87].

Describing the nature of true Knowledge, Padmapāda says that "though knowledge arises in regard to the *Viṣaya* (*viz.*, *Brahmātman*-identity) it does not attain indubitable certainty because it (i.e., the *viṣaya*) is beset with improbability (and contrariety). Such is the experience of men, says he. When there is a rooted conviction that a particular object by its very nature cannot exist (say) in this region and at the present time, if it should somehow by sheer accident come to view, the person though perceiving it himself will not be convinced of its existence as long as he does not take the trouble to ascertain its probability. Hence the right Knowledge also (though it has arisen) not being indubitable as regards its *viṣaya* (i.e. its content, *viz.*, *Brahmātman*-identity) will be as if it did not encompass the *viṣaya*. As such the knowledge that arises from the (*mahā*) *vākya* calls in the aid of *tarka* (reasoning) for self-certainty (i.e., for securing indubitability of its context). Therefore, since logic clarifies and stabilises the knowledge derived from *Pramāṇa-s* those proficient in *tarka* aver that *tarka* is an indispensable aid to *Pramāṇa-s* (here Verbal Testimony)[88]. Commenting on this, the *Vivaraṇa* says that just as there is uncertainty in the cognition of things situated in places far away from the cognizer, such as in the case of the illusory cognition of mirage, etc., in the same way in the Knowledge of the Self, indubitable knowledge does not arise immediately due to the absence of any similar past-impression and due to the presence of impressions of an opposite nature[89]. As to the objection that a cognition not ascertainable by Verbal Testimony cannot be ascertained through reasoning, Prakāśātman says that there is no contradiction in this for it is but a matter of practice to achieve an end with the aid of additional implements[90]. Reacting to another objection to the effect that even if reasoning be considered to be a valid means of knowledge, how can two means of Knowledge ascertain one particular cognition, and if it be considered to be an invalid means of knowledge (as far as Self-realization is concerned) it cannot be held to be of any help therein, the Vivaraṇa says that here, too, there is no contradiction, for even as an invalid means of knowledge reasoning may be instrumental in the ascertainment of a cognition (here, the realization of the true nature of the self)[91]. This is what Padmapāda means when he says that "reasoning is of the nature of discriminating cognition by which the probability (or improbability) of *pramāṇa, śakti* and *viṣaya* (*viz.*, the identity of *Brahman* and the individual soul) is ascertained"[92].

Explaining the manner in which reasoning is helpful in the realization of the true Knowledge, and hence, of *Mokṣa*, Padmapāda says, "When the improbability regarding the *viṣaya* (i.e., the unity of the individual soul with *Brahman*) and the fruition of that kind of experience which brings about the destruction of *anartha* or the evils of life, has not arisen, *tarka* (i.e., reasoning) is useful in removing the obstacles to the *phala* (fruition) by pointing to its probability (*sambhava*). As such in the *mahāvākya* (*Tat tvam asi*) the meaning of '*tvam*' is the *Jīva* (or individual soul) and this *Jīva* presuming the improbability of his being identical with *Brahman* which the word '*tat*' denotes,.....thinking that he is of an opposite nature, fails to arrive at the truth, though the Knowledge (identity) has arisen, so long as he does not recognize the probability of his own self being identical with *Brahman*, having first through the aid of *tarka* removed the impediment. Hence, says Padmapāda, before rational enquiry, though the Knowledge of identity has arisen from the sentence (*Tat tvam asi*), it is as good as not having been acquired. The means to acquire it is pointed out in the Vedānta itself with a view to helping one (to) attain the *phala* of immediate experience"[93].

Explaining on his part the nature and cause of immediate cognition of the Self, Prakāśātman, putting forward the views of *Bhāṭṭa-vedāntins*[94], says that in actual practice there are three means of perceiving or cognizing an object, *viz.*, either through non-difference from consciousness or knowledge itself, or through the production of knowledge by the object itself by its unobstructed proximity with consciousness, or still through the normal empirical means of knowledge, i.e., through the contact of the sense-organ(s) with the object. Any other means of knowledge, such as Inference, etc., is effective in the production of indirect cognition. It is therefore fit to hold *Brahman* Itself as being primarily directly cognized due either to Its being non-different from that cognition or due to Its being the cause thereof. This is so, says Prakāśātman, because *Brahman* being Itself the material cause of all cognitions, Verbal Testimony is itself of the nature of *Brahman*[95]. Even then, due to the mind being of an atomic size and due also to its being affected by impressions of invalid or wrong knowledge, *Brahman*, as though bound, is cognized erroneously as an external object. It is with regard to such an erroneous cognition of *Brahman* that acts such as sacrifices etc. are undertaken, and purificatory acts, such as *śama, dama,* etc. are practiced, and also prescriptions such as *nididhyāsana,* etc. are enjoined. It is thus, that when the mind is rid of all impurities through the observance of sacrifices etc., when it is freed from the defects of opposite tendencies, etc., through the observance of *śama, dama,* etc.; when through *manana,* it becomes quite clear to it that the cognition of *Brahman* is the *prameya par excellence;* when, through *nididhyāsana* of the very subtle cognition of *Brahman,* there is developed in it the capacity of concentration, then, with the consequential eradication of the cause of the erroneous knowledge of the externality of *Brahman*-knowledge, from Verbal Testimony itself will arise the ascertainment of the immediacy of the Knowledge of the Self[96].

Discussing another view on this issue (probably his own), Prakāśātman says that it is not the case that, as reported above, on the removal of the said obstacles, there is direct cognition (of *Brahman*) in the very first instance, through Verbal Testimony;

but it is such that after the production of the cognition of *Brahman* as an external object, Verbal Testimony itself gives rise to the direct cognition of *Brahman in the second instance,* through the instrumentality of the mind purged in the manner described above. This, he says, happens in the same way as the contact (of the internal organ) with the external object first gives rise to apprehension; thereafter, through the impressions of previous experience, it gives rise to recognition. As far as the Self-luminous *Brahman* is concerned, indirect cognition cannot be said to be erroneous, claims the Vivaraṇa[97].

But even the desire to acquire the knowledge of *Brahman* cannot "*arise*" in the real sense of the word. This is so, says Padmapāda, because the Scriptures declare that with the knowledge of *Brahman* even the mind gets isolated and consequently all contact of the internal organ with the world is lost. This severance of contact brings in turn an end to all types of worldly happiness, whether it be lordship over the world or attainment of *Brahmaloka.* It also cannot be said that the state of Bliss is something attainable, and therefore one has to strive for it, as one does for obtaining any other object[98]. In reply to the contention that since even after *Brahman*-realization, the cognition of "I"-ness persists, there is no difference between the cognition of *Jīva-Brahman*-identity and the cognition of difference between the self and the body, etc., Padmapāda says that when *Brahman*-knowledge dawns, dispelling all illusions, it puts an end to all notions of agentship, enjoyership, etc. It is therefore untenable that the cognition of "I"-ness should continue even after Self-realization. But it is true that, due to mental impressions left back, *avidyā* continues for sometime to influence the individual soul even after Self-realization, as is the case with the fear generated by the illusion of snake, etc., which persists for sometime even when true knowledge (of the rope) has dawned. Hence the persistence of the I-cognition for sometime even after the realization of the true nature of the Self[99].

Prakāśātman says that there is seen the persistence of the aforesaid mental impressions even on its eradication through the realization of Truth due to the trace of Nescience left behind, similar to traces of darkness persisting even on the coming of light. This is, says the Vivaraṇa, what explains also the possibility of total release only on casting off the body, (*videha-mukti*), implying that empiricity persists for sometime, impelled by *prārabdha-karma,* until the total consummation of past actions. Hence, the incidence of *Jīvan-mukti* (self realization in this life-time itself)[100].

The Vivaraṇa School is of the view that the injunction to study one's section of the Veda ("*Svādhyāyo' dhyetavyaḥ*") is not mandatory in the realization of *Brahman.* This is so because even on the apprehension of the meaning of the Vedic texts as a result of the said injunction, there is no inducement to undertake an enquiry into the nature of *Brahman* with a view to Self-realization[101]. Clarifying this point, Prakāśātman says that even if it be granted that through the "*adhyayanavidhi*" the meaning of the *Veda* is to be acquired, yet it is through "*vicāravidhi*" that the actual meaning of the Vedānta text is to be apprehended, and this (i.e. "*vicāra*") is not enjoined by the "*Adhyayana-vidhi*"[102]. The reason for this, says the Vivaraṇa, is that before undertaking the study of the *Veda* (which is governed by the *Adhyayana-vidhi*) there cannot be ascertainment of the meaning of its purport; and without the ascertainment of the meaning, there can be no desire for its achievement. Hence it is settled that the *adhyayana-vidhi* does not apply to the ascertainment of the meaning of Vedānta, much less to the attainment of Knowledge of the Self[103]. Padmapāda says also that if it be argued that the ascertainment of the meaning of Vedic texts is a prerequisite to any enquiry into the nature of *Brahman,* then this too is not in contradiction to what has just been said, but rather gives weight to it since it becomes evident from this very fact that the determination of meaning of Vedic-texts (*Vākyārtha-nirṇaya*) is in no way instrumental in the inducement to an enquiry into the true nature of Brahman. The Knowledge of something cannot be the cause of an act of a different nature, says he[104]. Prakāśātman says conclusively following this that Sclf-rcalization or *Brahman*-Knowledge is not governed by any injunction whatsoever[105].

As regards the role of *Karma-s* (enjoined actions) in the realization of *Brahman,* Padmapāda says that these may be helpful in the attainment of worldly happiness or its means, but as far as the Knowledge of *Brahman* is concerned, they are of no use at all. Says he, "For him who wishes to climb to the top of a mansion the flight of steps gradually ascended becomes the means of gaining the top floor, (but) (this is) not so here; the prescribed duties performed up to the end of even a thousands years are not the means of inducing that act (i.e., *Brahman-jijñāsā*) in one who is desirous of inquiring into the nature of *Brahman* because of the absence of valid proof"[106]. Hence, says he, the real cause of the eradication of all desires is on the one hand, the knowledge of the erroneous nature of worldly objectives and *Brahman-realization,* on the other. This is supported by the Scriptures where it is declared that "objects turn away from the man who practices abstinence, but not the subtle attachment to them, but even that attachment vanishes when he sees the Supreme Reality"[107]. Padmapāda warns us also of the fact that there is no proof whatsoever, not even in the Scriptures, to the effect that there is an end to the craving for worldly pleasures even on the achievement of all objects one may desire here[108]. Prakāśātman says in this context that the observance of the purificatory acts such as *nitya* and *naimittika* does help in *Brahman*-realization through purging the self of its illusory impurities if only this (purging) leads to the achievement of the means to Knowledge such as *śravaṇa, manana, dhyāna,* etc. But if these means are not achieved, then the said observance results in the attainment of *abhyudaya* (i.e., non-eternal bliss)[109]. The *Saṁskāra-s* also are instrumental in the rise of the Knowledge (discriminating the Self from the non-Self), says he, only if they lead to the achievement of *śravaṇa,* etc., as referred to above, failing which they too result in the attainment of *abhyudaya.* But as far as the desire to know *Brahman* is concerned, that arises only out of the said (discriminating) knowledge, says finally the Vivaraṇa[110]. And so long as this discrimination between the lasting and the evanescent, does not arise, there cannot be detachment from worldliness and so long as there is no detachment, there can be no desire to know *Brahman,* and without this desire how can there be *Mokṣa,* says the Pañcapādikā. The antecedent conditions, therefore, to *Brahman*-realization are, "discrimination between what is Eternal and what is not eternal; renunciation of the desire for the enjoyment of the fruit of one's deeds here as well as hereafter; the acquisition of such aids as tranquility and self-restraint; and the desire for eternal freedom[111]. So long as there is no cessation of the hankering after worldly pleasures, despite their being experienced as ephemeral in character, and despite the experience of all types of miseries and sorrow resulting from their acquisition and their consumption, and despite also the failure to derive happiness, however, shortlived, from the same, there can be no desire for Liberation, much less Liberation itself. And so long as there is no desire for Release by the practice of tranquility, control of the mind and of the senses, and endurance, etc., there can be no inquiry into the nature of *Brahman*. But even if somehow, though not equipped with the above-mentioned means, one were to undertake the inquiry into the nature of *Brahman* impelled by *merits* of past-actions, or by sheer curiosity or still, by a mere desire to learn, he will fail, due to incompetence, to comprehend the actual meaning of Vedānta, as his mind, unpurged as it is, would always tend towards the external world when it should have turned inward[112].

Prakāśātman says that all the qualifications enumerated above as prerequisites for the inquiry into *Brahman* are the subject of separate injunctions and are therefore mandatory for the inquiry in question. The injunction "*so'nveṣṭavyaḥ*", for example, enjoins upon the *seeker* the investigation into *Brahman* after making him realize the distinctness of the Eternal from the non-eternal, through discourses such as, "just as the fruits obtained of our actions here are exhaustible, in the same way are the fruits of "merits", etc"[113]. In like manner are enjoined respectively, detachment, self-control, etc. through discourses such as, "Everything here is dear for the sake of the self", "He is in a state of equipoise, self-control" etc.[114]. According to Prakāśātman, the injunction "*Vijijñāsitavyaḥ*" and "*Vijijñāsasva*" enjoin "*internal vicāra* (meditation) there being no possibility of injunction for True Knowledge or for its desire. The injunction "*śrotavyaḥ*" enjoins upon the *seeker* to investigate into *Brahman* after obtaining the *prima facie* knowledge about *Brahman* from his Guru. This first exposition to the knowledge about *Brahman* is indeed something "attainable", as is evident from the text, "To know That One he should go to a Guru". Here, says Prakāśātman, there is an injunction of *śravaṇa*. There being no possibility of any injunction for knowledge as such, as is shown by the text. "One should see the Self in oneself by one's own self", the two injunctions of *manana* and *nididhyāsana* are enjoined as auxiliaries to the injunction of *śravaṇa*—all three of which are to be regarded as enjoined means to *Brahman*-realization[115].

Throwing light on the exact meaning of "*avagati*" and its difference from knowledge, Padmapāda says that "the object of the desire as denoted by the "*san*" affix is knowledge up to, and inclusive of, the complete comprehension of *Brahman* since all desires have *phala* as their objects (as claimed by Śaṅkara). By the word "*avagati*" is meant direct experience; the word "*jñāna*" however may signify even what is mediate (*parokṣa*) and has not yet been verified by one's own experience. It arises in an undetermined form even in that which though immediately present appears improbable. Thus the Bhāṣyakāra (Śaṅkara) says—"It is indeed knowledge which is the means (*Pramāṇa*) by which the full comprehension ("*avagati*") of *Brahman* is sought to be obtained; the comprehension of *Brahman* is the *puruṣārtha* or the human end, which means the direct intuition of the Self, as identical with *Brahman*"[116].

The realization of the *Jīva-Brahman*-identity takes place by the realization of the unified meaning of the three words in the Vedānta-sentence (*Tat-tvam-asi*) illustrated by the sentence *So' yam Devadattaḥ'*. "There is first in the recognition of "*saḥ*" (i.e., he) (here) the recollection of "*Devadatta*" as existing elsewhere. Hence, at first, due to the cognition of difference, there is no cognition of unity between the recognition of "*saḥ*" as present here, and *"Devadattaḥ"* as present there. It is thus that the identity of *"Saḥ"* and "*Devadattaḥ*" is not cognized by the recognition of two entities characterized respectively by "here" and "there". Hence the cognition of duality. It is the recognition "*so'yam*" which through dropping part of its content brings about the cognition of identity with Devadatta through *lakṣaṇā*"[117]. Hence is it that in the *mahāvākya* "*Tat tvam asi*" also, there is the cognition of identity between "*Tat*" and "*tvam*" through the dropping of part of the content of "*tvam*" and identifying it with *Brahman* indicated by "*Tat*", through *lakṣaṇā*[118]. The parts of the content being dropped as discussed here, refer to the adjuncts of the *Jīva* due to which there had been the cognition of difference and the non-cognition of identity between *Jīva* and *Brahman*.

The Vivaraṇa school believes that there is no return to the world once the identity of the individual soul with *Brahman* has been realized. But due to the residual *Karma,* empirical life may persist till total extinction of *Karma*[119].

Prakāśātman says in conclusion that on the realization of *Brahman-Jīva*-identity there is absolute cessation of all illusory differences such as cognizer, cognition and cognized; doer, action and act (to be performed), and enjoyer, enjoyment and object of enjoyment, etc. since there is no more any contact of the internal organ with the objects due to the former's character of being cognizer having been sublated[120].

IV. Summary

As discussed in this chapter, *Brahman*-knowledge is of the nature of Absolute Happiness or Bliss. It signifies the cessation of all sorrow as well as the end to bondage and transmigration[121]. "A man of illumination has no wants and is impelled by no desire. He has nothing to accomplish in this world or in the next. Nor is there anything left for him to be attained here or hereafter[122]". Indeed, so long as redemption of all *prārabdha-karma* is not complete even the Self-realized cannot achieve Liberation. "*Prārabdha-karma* perishes by enjoyment. Both the released and the bound have alike to reap the consequences of their *prārabdha.* Both have to walk on a path strewn with thorns"[123], but while the enlightened acts without attachment, the ignorant acts with attachment and is therefore apt to be bound.

Both the Bhāmatī and the Vivaraṇa are of the view that Self-realization need not result in the death of the body. They both argue that due to residual impressions there is the persistence of the body until complete exhaustion of *prārabdha-karma*[124]. The *jīvan-mukta,* as such an individual is called, is verily the *sthita-prajña* the Bhagavad-gītā talks about[125]. The desire of the *mukta* is unproductive because he knows the worthlessness of the desired object. Just as fried grains are useful for eating and not for sprouting, similarly, the desires of the knower of Truth give him slight enjoyment; but do not entail in their train any more of their kind. The *karma* which has begun to take effect perishes when it has borne its fruit. Since *prārabdha-karma* is the cause only of enjoyment, it dies with the destruction of its product..... The *jīvan-mukta* lives *in* the world, but he is not *of* it. He awaits only the fruition of the residue of his *prārabdha.* Even in reaping the fruits of his *karma* he is unattached and does not lose his balanced deportment[126].

That *Mokṣa* is to be achieved through the instrumentality of *śravaṇa, manana,* and *nididhyāsana* is agreeable to both Vācaspati Miśra and Prakāśātman, but while the former believes that *śravaṇa* (or *adhyayana)* and *manana* are significant not in incantation or sheer ritualistic observance, but rather in leading to the generation of the desire to know *Brahman*[127], the latter believes that they are all enjoined upon the seeker of true Knowledge and are therefore objects of injunctions either as principal or auxiliaries. In this context, the Vivaraṇa believes that both *manana* and *nididhyāsana* are auxiliaries to the principal *Śravaṇa*[128]. It is worthy of note that where the Bhāmatī touches but slightly on the usefulness of *śravaṇa* and *manana* in the generation of the desire to know *Brahman,* the Vivaraṇa engages in a long discussion to establish the precedence of *śravaṇa, manana* and *nididhyāsana* to the apprehension of the actual meaning and purport of the Scriptures, as well as to the indubitable Knowledge of the unity of the Self and the development of the capacity to concentrate with a view to attaining *Brahman*[129].

As for the purificatory acts, such as *nitya, naimittika,* etc., while the Bhāmatī is of the view that these, together with the observance of acts of austerity, charity, etc. are necessary pre-qualifications for the seeker of the knowledge of *Brahman,* the Vivaraṇa holds on its part that no such act is mandatory in the realization of *Brahman.* According to Vācaspati Miśra, there can be no contemplation without the mind having been purged through the purificatory acts and through the attrition of sins by means of the observance of the acts mentioned above[130]. He thus falls in line with Śaṅkara who enumerates these among the pre-requisites for any deliberation on *Brahman.* or even for the generation of the desire to know the nature of the Self[131]. As for Prakāśātman, he is of the view that no rites whatsoever are required prior to any deliberation on *Brahman* or even as an aid to Self-realization. But he does concede that if these acts lead the *seeker* to the successful undertaking of *śravaṇa, manana* and *nididhyāsana,* then they are indeed instrumental in the rise of true Knowledge indirectly. But if *śravaṇa,* etc. do not follow their performance, then they are the cause of empirical bliss[132].

The line adopted by the Vivaraṇa as noticed above is in pursuance of its claim that *Brahman*-knowledge can be obtained directly from Verbal-testimony, i.e. through the hearing of the *Mahāvākya-s.* However, Prakāśātman makes here a difference between knowledge of *Brahman,* the immediate knowledge dawning as a result of Verbal Testimony, and *Brahmāvagati,* which he says is caused by the first cognition of *Brahman* referred to above, in the same way as the sense-object-contact produces cognition of the object at the empirical level. But different indeed is the line taken by Vācaspati Miśra, who believes that Verbal Testimony is instrumental in simply generating a knowledge about *Brahman,* but there is no ascertainment of this Knowledge. He says that contemplation on *Brahman* is to be undertaken only after knowing about *Brahman* through Verbal Testimony and after strengthening it through reasoning[133].

The Bhāmatī declares that the *Brahman*-knowledge or *Mokṣa* sought for is nothing but the manifestation of the true nature of *Brahman* through the removal of Nescience. *Mokṣa,* says Vācaspati, is not the generation of something new, unattained. It is simply the lifting of the veil of *avidyā* by which It is apparently shrouded. Vācaspati believes that even the manifestation alluded to above cannot be said to be the effect of knowledge or *Vidyā,* for *Brahman*-realization is not "caused" by anything and hence, it cannot be an effect, It being always 'attained'. Knowledge is capable of eradicating Nescience only [134]. In full agreement with its opponent, the Vivaraṇa too, propounds the doctrine that *Mokṣa* is of the nature of a unique knowledge which arises from the realization of the truth contained in the *mahāvākya-s,* such as, "*Tat Tvam asi*" and in the sentence "*So'yam Devadattaḥ*". This knowledge, claims Prakāśātman, unveils the true nature of *Brahman* by dispelling the root-cause of all evils, i.e., Nescience, which is responsible for the non-manifestation of *Brahman* in Its true nature. The Vivaraṇa says also that the mere discrimination of the Self from the non-self does not constitute nor leads to *Mokṣa* since it is not capable of sublating Nescience[135]. Nescience, say both the Bhāmatī and the Vivaraṇa, can be eradicated only by Knowledge[136]. Both the Schools share the view that *Mokṣa* is not something external to be attained through certain set of actions or rituals. It consists simply in the realization of the identity of the Self and the individual soul, which has for authority only the Scriptures. But while Vācaspati believes that the knowledge of the true nature of *Brahman*[137] is not dependent on man's will, Prakāśātman believes on his side, that *Brahman*-knowledge cannot be achieved without the eradication of Nescience, which in turn, is not attained through the study of Scriptures, since Nescience or its eradication is not the subject-matter of the Scriptures. The Vivaraṇa is of the view that the eradication of Nescience is brought about by the potency of the knowledge of *Jīva-Brahman*-identity. But the main cause thereof is man's desire for *Mokṣa* awakened by the study of Scriptures, followed by the observance of purificatory acts that has for effect the generation of an aversion towards the world, etc.[138].

It would not be out of place to cite Kalidas Bhattacharya here to conclude this discussion on *Mokṣa* : "The main point of the Advaitin is that whatever of subjectivity is realized as essence, there is no need for going back to the object got over. If *one likes* one *may* forgo this intrinsic joy of realization and turn again to objects which, along with this very temporal fact of recovering that freedom-in-itself, stand in their true colour as having been constructed or de-constructed symbolically or created or de-created through transcendental will. They may also appear as being *in the* process of construction, de-construction, creation or de-creation. The *jīvanmukta* can even go further: he may *utilize* that realized metaphysical freedom *to do good to the world*—and that, of course, in a total way *unthinkable* for good people who have not realized this freedom : whatever good which the *jīvanmukta* performs is a *total* good. Anyway, none of these forms of turning again to object is *necessary* for one who has realized ablsolute freedom. Realization of Consciousness-by-itself is at least a full alternative to construction, creation and moral life, if these latter are taken to be of intrinsic worth. The Advaitin just prefers this alternative. It is because he prefers it that he preaches *no-action too.* Not indeed complete no-action before full realization of Pure Consciousness, but either partial no-action before that or complete no-action after that. Partial no-action means that as a particular stage of subjectivity is attained we need not repeat the good actions that were needed for coming up to that stage, though other good actions are necessary for further progress along the line. Complete no-action means that with final realization of Pure Consciousness there need not be a turn-back to objects and, therefore, to will. It may be noted in passing that actions necessary for coming up to particular stages of subjectivity are necessary as only extrinsic means. Realization at whatever stage is *sui generis*—it is subjectivity (at the ultimate stage, consciousness) discovering Itself"[139].

NOTES

1. "ब्रह्मभावश्च मोक्षः।" —SB on BS-I.1.4, Loc. Cit., p.128.
2. "तदेतदशरीरत्वं मोक्षाख्यम्।" —Ibid, p.121
3. "तस्माद्यथोक्तसाधन-संपत्त्यनन्तरं ब्रह्मजिज्ञासा कर्तव्या।" ".....अवगतिपर्यन्तं ज्ञानं सन्वाच्याया इच्छायाः कर्म, फलविषयत्वादिच्छायाः। ज्ञानेन हि प्रमाणेनावगन्तुमिष्टं ब्रह्म।" - Ibid, p.75, p.77.
4. "अस्यानर्थहेतोः प्रहाणाय आत्मैकत्वविद्याप्रतिपत्तये सर्वे वेदान्ता आरभ्यन्ते।" —SB on BS-I.1.1, Loc. Cit., p.45.
5. Kanshi Ram, Loc. Cit., p.127
6. R. Balasubramanian, Loc. Cit., pp.102-103, Vide, "अज्ञानविरोधि ज्ञानं हि न चैतन्यमात्रं किंतु वृत्तिप्रतिबिम्बितं तच्च न अविद्याश्रयः, यच्च अविद्याश्रयः तच्च न अज्ञानविरोधि।" —Ibid, Quoting AS.
7. Ibid, p.103.
8. Ibid, Vide, "सत्-असत्-सदसत्-अनिर्वचनीय-प्रकारेभ्यःहि अन्यप्रकारैव अज्ञानस्य निवृत्तिरित्युक्ता।" IS and Saṁkṣepa-sārīraka-IV.13-14.
9. Ibid, p.104; Vide. "वस्तुतस्तु अभावस्य चैतन्यानात्मकत्वात् स्वप्रकाशचैतन्यसम्बन्धेनैव भानमभ्युपेयम्। कूटस्थासंगस्वभावस्य वास्तवसंबन्धायोगात् काल्पनिकत्वे अवश्यं वाच्ये सर्वस्यापि कल्पनायाः अविद्यामूलत्वात् अभावकल्पनाप्यविद्यामूला इति न अनिर्वचनीय-वैलक्षण्यम्।" —Vedānta-kalpalatikā.
10. "तं संसारध्वान्तविनाशं हरिमीडे।" —Haristuti quoted by R. Balasubramanian, Loc. Cit.
11. "ज्ञानाभावे अज्ञानानुवृत्तिः ज्ञानदशायां तु न तदनुवृत्तिः इत्येतावतैव अविद्यानिवृत्तेः ज्ञानसाध्यतोपचारात्, तदुक्तमाचार्यैः। तत्कैवल्यम् अतः साध्यम् उपचारात् प्रचक्षते।" —Tattvabodhinī, quoted by R. Balasubramanian, Loc. Cit.
12. Vide, Saṅkṣepa-śārīraka, IV. 9, quoted by R. Balasubramanian, Loc. Cit.
13. R. Balasubramanian, Loc.Cit; p.105.

14. ''तस्मात्किमपि वक्तव्यं यदनन्तरं ब्रह्मजिज्ञासोपदिष्यत इति। उच्यते-नित्यानित्यवस्तुविवेकः इहामुत्रार्थभोगविरागः शमदमादिसाधनसंपत् मुमुक्षुत्वं च।'' —SB on BS-I.1.1, Loc.Cit. p.71.
15. Vide, Lights on Vedānta, Op.Cit; pp.188-189.
16. ''नित्यनैमित्तिककर्मानुष्ठान''।
17. ''चित्तसंशुद्धि''।
18. ''संसारासारताज्ञान''।
19. ''संसारपरिजिहीर्षा''।
20. ''एषणात्रयत्याग''।
21. ''विविदिषा''।
22. ''विविदिषासंन्यास''।
23. ''श्रवण, मनन, निदिध्यासन''॥
24. ''ब्रह्मसाक्षात्कार''।
25. ''विद्वत्संन्यास''।
26. ''मोक्ष''।
27. M. Sircar, Loc.Cit, p.238.
28. Ibid, p.239.
29. Vide, Lights on Vedānta, Op.Cit, pp.210-211.
30. Ibid, p.211.
31. Ibid, p.212.
32. Ibid, p.214.
33. Ibid, p.234-236.
34. Ibid, p.236-238.
35. —SB on BS-IV. 1.15 Loc. Cit., pp.958-959. Vide,
''न तावदनाश्रित्यारब्धकार्यं कर्माशयं ज्ञानोत्पत्तिरुपपद्यते। आश्रिते च तस्मिन्कुलालचक्रवत्प्रवृत्तवेगस्यान्तराले प्रतिबन्धासंभवाद्भवति वेगक्षयप्रतिपालनम्। अकर्त्रात्मबोधोऽपि हि मिथ्याज्ञान-बाधनेन कर्माण्युच्छिनत्ति। बाधितमपि तु मिथ्याज्ञानं द्विचन्द्रज्ञानवत्संस्कारवशात् कंचित्कालमनुवर्तत एव। अपि च नैवात्र विवदितव्यं ब्रह्मविदा कंचित्कालं शरीरं ध्रियते न वा ध्रियत इति। कथं ह्येकस्य स्वहृदयप्रत्ययं ब्रह्मवेदनं देहधारणं चापरेण प्रतिक्षेप्तुं शक्येत? श्रुतिस्मृतिषु च स्थितप्रज्ञलक्षणनिर्देशे नैतदेव निरुच्यते। तस्मादनारब्धकार्ययोरेव सुकृतदुष्कृतयोर्विद्यासामर्थ्यात्क्षय इति निर्णयः।''
36. ''वस्तुस्वरूपावधारणं विद्यामाहुः।'' —Adhyāsabhāṣya, Loc.Cit.,p.40.
37. Bhāmatī on Adhyāsabhāṣya, Loc.Cit., p.40.
''निर्विचिकित्सं ज्ञानं विद्यामाहुः पण्डिताः।'' —Bhāmatī, Ibid.
38. ''तत्र श्रवणमननादिभिर्यद्विवेकविज्ञानं तेन विवेकाग्रहे निवर्तिते अध्यासापबाधात्मकं वस्तुस्वरूपावधारणं विद्या चिदात्मरूपं स्वरूपे व्यवतिष्ठत इत्यर्थः।'' —Bhāmatī, Ibid.
39. ''अस्यानर्थहेतोः प्रहाणाय.... आत्मैकत्वविद्याप्रतिपत्तये (सर्वे वेदान्ता आरभ्यन्ते) (इति)। प्रतिपत्तिः प्राप्तिः, तस्यै, न तु जपमात्राय, नापि कर्मसु प्रवृत्तये।'' —Bhāmatī, Ibid, p.45.

40. "आत्मैकत्वं विगलितनिखिलप्रपञ्चत्वम् आनन्दरूपस्य सतः। तत्प्रतिपत्तिं निर्विचिकित्सां भावयन्तो वेदान्ताः समूलघातमध्यासमुपघ्नन्ति।" —Bhāmatī, Ibid.
41. "ब्रह्मज्ञानमेव समस्तदुःखोपशमरूपमानन्दैकरसम्।" —Ibid, p.46.
42. "स्वाध्यायानन्तर्यं तु समानम्।" —SB on BS-1. 1.1, Loc. Cit., p.51.
43. "अत्र च "स्वाध्यायेन" विषयेण तद्विषयाध्ययनं लक्षयति। तथा च "अथातो धर्मजिज्ञासा" इत्यनेनैव गतमिति...। धर्मशब्दस्य वेदार्थमात्रोपलक्षणतया धर्मवद् ब्रह्मणोऽपि वेदार्थत्वाविशेषेण वेदाध्ययनानन्तर्योपदेशसाम्यादित्यर्थः।" —Bhāmatī on SB-I. 1.1; Loc.Cit., p.51
44. The Bhāmatī of Vācaspati, Op. Cit., p.71; Vide, "विविदिषन्ति यज्ञेन इति तृतीयाश्रुत्या यज्ञादीनामङ्गत्वेन ब्रह्मज्ञाने विनियोगात्, ज्ञानस्य कर्मतया इच्छां प्रति प्राधान्यात्, प्रधानसंबन्धाच्चाप्रधानानां पदार्थान्तराणाम्। तत्रापि च न वाक्यार्थज्ञानोत्पत्तावंगभावो यज्ञादीनाम्, वाक्यार्थज्ञानस्य वाक्यादेवोत्पत्तेः।" —Bhāmatī, Loc.Cit., pp.51-52.
45. "न च वाक्यं सहकारितया कर्माण्यपेक्षत इति युक्तम्; अकृतकर्मणापि विदितपदपदार्थसंबन्धानां समधिगतशाब्दन्यायतत्त्वानां गुणप्रधानभूतपूर्वापरपदार्थाकाङ्क्षासंनिधियोग्यतानुसंधानवतामप्रत्यूहं वाक्यार्थप्रत्ययोत्पत्तेः।" —Bhāmatī, Ibid.
46. The Bhāmatī of Vācaspati, Op. Cit., p.72; Vide, "ननु "तत्त्वमसि" इति वाक्यात् त्वंपदार्थस्य कर्तृभोक्तृरूपस्य जीवात्मनो नित्यशुद्धबुद्धोदासीनस्व-भावेन तत्पदार्थेन परमात्मनैक्यमशक्यं द्रागित्येव प्रतिपत्तुं आपाततोऽशुद्धसत्त्वैः, योग्यताविरहविनिश्चयात्।" —Bhāmatī, Ibid, p.52.
47. "यज्ञदानतपोऽनाशकतनूकृतान्तर्मलास्तु विशुद्धसत्त्वाः श्रद्दधाना योग्यतावगमपुरःसरं तादात्म्यमवगमिष्यन्तीति चेत्, तत्किमिदानीं प्रमाणकारणं योग्यतावधारणमप्रमाणात्कर्मणो वक्तुमध्यवसितोऽसि, प्रत्यक्षाद्यतिरिक्तं वा कर्मापि प्रमाणम्। वेदान्तविरुद्धतन्मूलन्यायबलेन तु योग्यतावधारणे कृतं कर्मभिः। तस्मात् "तत्त्वमसि" इत्यादेः श्रुतमयेन ज्ञानेन जीवात्मनः परमात्मभावं गृहीत्वा तन्मूलया चोपपत्त्या व्यवस्थाप्य तदुपासनायां भावनापराभिधानायां दीर्घकालनैरन्तर्यवत्यां ब्रह्मसाक्षात्कारफलायां यज्ञादीनामुपयोगः। यथाहुः "स तु दीर्घकालनैरन्तर्यसत्कारासेवितो दृढभूमिः।" इति। ब्रह्मचर्यतपःश्रद्धायज्ञादयश्च सत्काराः। अत एव श्रुतिः "तमेव धीरो विज्ञाय प्रज्ञां कुर्वीत ब्राह्मणः।" इति। "विज्ञाय तर्कोपकरणेन शब्देन प्रज्ञां भावनां कुर्वीतेत्यर्थः।" —Bhāmatī, Ibid.
48. "न खलु घटादिसाक्षात्कार इव जडस्वभावेभ्यो घटादिभ्यो भिन्न इन्द्रियाद्याधेयो ब्रह्मसाक्षात्कारो भावनाधेयः संभवति, ब्रह्मणोऽपराधीनप्रकाशतया तत्साक्षात्कारस्य तत्स्वाभाव्येन नित्यतयोत्पाद्यत्वानुपपत्तेः। ततो भिन्नस्य वा भावनाधेयस्य साक्षात्कारस्य प्रतिभाप्रत्ययवत् संशयाक्रान्ततया प्रामाण्यायोगात्, तद्विधस्य तत्सामग्रीकरस्यैव बहुलं व्यभिचारोपलब्धेः। ....तस्मात् प्रामाणिकसाक्षात्कारलक्षणकार्याभावान्नोपासनाया उत्पाद्ये कर्मापेक्षा। न च कूटस्थनित्यस्य सर्वव्यापिनो ब्रह्मण उपासनातो विकारसंस्कारप्राप्तयः संभवन्ति।" —Bhāmatī, Ibid, p.54.
49. "का पुनरियं ब्रह्मोपासना? किं शाब्दज्ञानमात्रसंततिः, आहो निर्विचिकित्सशाब्दज्ञानसंततिः? यदि शाब्दज्ञानमात्रसंततिः, न तर्हीयमभ्यस्यमानाप्यविद्यां समुच्छेत्तुमर्हति। तत्त्वविनिश्चयस्तदभ्यासो वा सवासनं विपर्यासमुन्मूलयेत्, न संशयाभ्यासः, सामान्यमात्रदर्शनाभ्यासो वा। न हि स्थाणुर्वा पुरुषो वेति वा, आरोहपरिणाहवत् द्रव्यमिति वा शतशोऽपि ज्ञानमभ्यस्यमानं पुरुष

एवेति निश्चयाय पर्याप्तम् ऋते विशेषदर्शनात्।" —Bhāmatī, Ibid, pp.54-55.

50. "निषेधशास्त्रं तु न श्रद्धामपेक्षते। अपितु निषिध्यमानक्रियोन्मुखो नर इत्येव प्रवर्तते। तथा च संसारिक इव श्रद्धावगतब्रह्मतत्त्वोऽपि निषेधमतिक्रम्य प्रवर्तमानः प्रत्यवैतीति न भिन्नकर्मदर्शनाभ्यामुपगमः। तस्मान्नोपासनायाः कार्ये कर्मापेक्षा।" —Bhāmatī, Ibid, p.60.

51. The Bhāmatī of Vācaspati, Op. Cit., pp.82-83. See also, "अत एव नोपासनोत्पत्तावपि (कर्मापेक्षा); निर्विचिकित्सशाब्दज्ञानोत्पत्त्युत्तरकालमनधिकारः कर्मणीत्युक्तम्।" तथा च श्रुतिः - "न कर्मणा न प्रजया धनेन; त्यागेनैके अमृतत्वमानशुः।" —Bhāmatī, Ibid, p.61

52. Ibid, p.83, Vide, "तत्किमिदानीमनुपयोग एव सर्वथेह कर्मणाम्? ...न, आरादुपकारकत्वात्कर्मणां यज्ञादीनाम्। ....एतानि च नित्यानि उपात्तदुरितनिबर्हणेन पुरुषं संस्कुर्वन्ति। तथा च श्रुतिः- 'स ह वा आत्मयाजी यो वेद इदं मेऽनेनाङ्ग संस्क्रियत इदं मेऽनेनाङ्गमुपधीयते' इति। अनेनेति प्रकृतं यज्ञादि परामृशति।" —Bhāmatī, Ibid, p.61.

53. The Bhāmatī of Vācaspati, Op. Cit., p.84, Vide, "यस्यैतेऽष्टाचत्वारिंशत्संस्काराः।" —Bhamatī, Ibid.

54. Ibid, Vide, "नित्यनैमित्तिकानुष्ठानप्रक्षीणकल्मषस्य च विशुद्धसत्त्वस्याविदुष एव उत्पन्नविविदिषस्य ज्ञानोत्पत्तिं दर्शयत्याथर्वणी श्रुतिः - 'विशुद्धसत्त्वस्ततस्तु तं पश्यति निष्कलं ध्यायमानः' इति। स्मृतिश्च 'ज्ञानमुत्पद्यते पुंसां क्षयात्पापस्य कर्मणः' इत्यादिका।" —Bhāmatī, Ibid, p.61.

55. "क्लृप्तेनैव च नित्यानां कर्मणां नित्येहितेनोपात्तदुरितनिबर्हणेन पुरुषसंस्कारः।" —Bhāmatī, Ibid, p.62.

56. Supra, fn.14.

57. The Bhāmatī of Vācaspati, Op. Cit., p.95; Vide, "इदं तदनृतमनित्यमिति धर्मिविशेषयोर्विवेकः; धर्मिमात्रयोर्नित्यानित्ययोस्तद्धर्मयोश्च विवेकं निश्चिनोत्येव। नित्यत्वं सत्यत्वं तद्यस्यास्ति तन्नित्यं सत्यम्; तथा चास्थागोचरः। अनित्यत्वम् सत्यत्वं तद्यस्यास्ति तदनित्यमनृतम्; तथा चानास्थागोचरः। तदेतेष्वनुभूयमानेषु युष्मदस्मत्प्रत्यगोचरेषु विषयविषयिषु यदृतं नित्यं सुखं व्यवस्थास्यते तदास्थागोचरो भविष्यति। यत्त्वनित्यमनृतं भविष्यति तापत्रयपरीतं तत्त्यक्ष्यत इति सोऽयं नित्यानित्यवस्तुविवेकः प्रागभवीयादैहिकाद्वा कर्मणो विशुद्धसत्त्वस्य भवत्यनुभवोपपत्तिभ्याम्।" —Bhāmatī, Ibid, pp.71-72.

58. "अथास्य पुरुषधौरेयस्यानुभवोपपत्तिभ्यामेवं सुनिपुणं निरूपयतः आ च सत्यलोकात् आ च आवीचेः जायस्व म्रियस्व इति विपरिवर्तमानं ...संसारसागरोर्मिभिरनिशमुह्यमानं ताप— त्रयपरीतमात्मानं जीवलोकं चावलोक्य अस्मिन्संसारमण्डलेअनित्याशुचिदुःखात्मकं प्रसंख्यानमुपावर्तते। ततोऽस्येदृशान्नित्यानित्यवस्तुविवेकलक्षणात्प्रसंख्यानात् इहामुत्रार्थभोगविरागः भवति।....ततः शमदमादिसाधनसंपत्।" —Bhāmatī, Ibid, pp.72-73.

59. "रागादिकषायमदिरामत्तं हि मनः तेषु तेषु विषयेषूच्चावचमिन्द्रियाणि प्रवर्तयत् विविधाश्च प्रवृत्तीः पुण्यापुण्यफला भावयत्पुरुषमतिघोरे विविधदुःखज्वालाजटिले संसारहुतभुजि जुहोति। प्रसंख्यानाभ्यासलब्धवैराग्य-परिपाकभग्नरागादिकषायमदिरामदं तु मनः पुरुषेणावजीयते वशीक्रियते। सोऽयमस्य वैराग्यहेतुको मनोविजयः शम इति वशीकारसंज्ञ इति चाख्यायते। विजितं च

मनस्तत्त्वविषयविनियोग योग्यतां नीयते; सेयमस्य योग्यता दम: ।.... तदेतस्य शमदमादिरूपस्य साधनस्य संपत्....ततोऽस्य संसारबन्धनान्मुमुक्षा भवतीति ।....तस्य च नित्यशुद्धबुद्धमुक्तस्वभावब्रह्मज्ञानं मोक्षस्य कारणमित्युपश्रुत्य तज्जिज्ञासा भवति।'' —Bhāmatī, Ibid, p.73.

60. ''तथा ब्रह्मविज्ञानादपि परं पुरुषार्थं दर्शयति 'ब्रह्मविदाप्नोति परम्' इत्यादि:।'' —SB on BS-I.1.1; Loc. Cit., p.75.

61. ''ब्रह्मावगतिर्हि पुरुषार्थ:, नि:शेषसंसारबीजाविद्याद्यनर्थनिबर्हणात्। तस्माद्ब्रह्म जिज्ञासितव्यम्।'' —SB, Ibid; p.78.

62. ''न केवलं ज्ञानमिष्यते किंत्ववगतिं साक्षात्कारं कुर्वदवगतिपर्यन्तं सन्वाच्याया इच्छाया: कर्म। कस्मात्? फलविषयत्वादिच्छाया: तदुपायं फलपर्यन्तं गोचरयतीच्छेति शेष:।'' —Bhāmatī, Ibid, p.77.

63. ''सत्यम्, ब्रह्मावगतौ ब्रह्मस्वभावे नोत्पत्त्यादय: संभवन्ति; तथाप्यविवेचनीयानाद्यविद्यावशाद्ब्रह्म स्वभावोऽपराधीनप्रकाशोऽपि प्रतिभानपि न प्रतिभातीव पराधीनप्रकाश इव देहेन्द्रियादिभ्यो भिन्नोऽप्यभिन्न इव भासत इति संसारबीजाविद्याद्यनर्थनिबर्हणात्प्रागप्राप्त इव तस्मिन्सति प्राप्त इव भवतीति पुरुषेणार्थ्यमानत्वात्पुरुषार्थ इति युक्तम्।'' —Bhāmatī, Ibid, p.78.

64. ''अविद्यादिनिवृत्तिस्तूपासनाकार्यादन्त:करणवृत्तिभेदात् साक्षात्कारादिति द्रष्टव्यम्।.... नखलु तज्ज्ञानं विना सवासनविविधदु:खनिदानमविद्योच्छिद्यते। न च तदुच्छेदमन्तरेण विगलित-निखिलदु:खानुषङ्गानन्दघन ब्रह्मात्मतासाक्षात्काराविर्भावो जीवस्य। तस्मादानन्दघनब्रह्मात्मतामिच्छता तदुपायो ज्ञानमेषितव्यम्। तच्च न केवलेभ्यो वेदान्तेभ्य: अपितु ब्रह्ममीमांसोपकरणेभ्य इति इच्छामुखेन ब्रह्ममीमांसायां प्रवर्त्यते।'' —Bhāmatī, Ibid, p.78.

65. The Bhāmatī of Vācaspati, Op. Cit., p.156; Vide, ''समारोपितमात्रजीविते हि ते; समारोपितं च तत्त्वसाक्षात्कार: समूलघातमुपहन्तीति। तथेहाप्यविद्यासमारोपितजीवभावे ब्रह्मण्यानन्दे वस्तुत: शोकदु:खादिरहिते समारोपितनिबन्धनस्तद्भाव: 'तत्त्वमसि' इति वाक्यार्थतत्त्वज्ञानादवगतिपर्यन्तान्निवर्तते। तन्निवृत्तौ प्राप्तमप्यानन्दरूपमप्राप्तमिव प्राप्तं भवति; त्यक्तमपि शोकदु:खाद्यत्यक्तमिव त्यक्तं भवति।'' —Bhāmatī on SB-I.1.4, Loc. Cit., p.107.

66. ''अपि च ब्रह्म वेद ब्रह्मैव भवति;'' ''क्षीयन्ते चास्य कर्माणि तस्मिन्दृष्टे परावरे।'' ''आनन्दं ब्रह्मणो विद्वान्। न बिभेति कुतश्चन।'' ''अभयं वै जनक प्राप्तोऽसि'', ''तदात्मानमेवावेदाहं ब्रह्मास्मीति'' ''तस्मात्तत्सर्वमभवत्'', ''तत्र को मोह: क: शोक एकत्वमनुपश्यत:'' इत्येवमाद्या: श्रुतयो ब्रह्मविद्यानन्तरमेव मोक्षं दर्शयन्त्यो मध्ये कार्यान्तरं वारयन्ति। —SB on BS-I.1.4, Loc. Cit., p.121.

67. ''तथा तद्धैतत्पश्यन्नृषिर्वामदेव: प्रतिपेदेऽहं मनुरभवं सूर्यश्च इति ब्रह्मदर्शनसर्वात्मभावयोर्मध्ये कर्तव्यान्तरवारणायोदाहार्यम्, तथा तिष्ठन्गायति इति तिष्ठतिगायत्योर्मध्ये तत्कर्तृकं कार्यान्तरं नास्तीति गम्यते।'' ''त्वं हि न पिता योऽस्माकमविद्याया: परं पारं तारयसि'', ''....तस्मै मृदितकषायाय तमस: पारं दर्शयति भगवान्सनत्कुमार:'' इति चैवमाद्या: श्रुतयो मोक्षप्रतिबन्धनिवृत्तिमात्रमेवात्मज्ञानस्य फलं दर्शयन्ति। —Ibid, p.121.

68. ''मिथ्याज्ञानापायश्च ब्रह्मात्मैकत्वविज्ञानाद्भवति।'' —Ibid.

69. ''तथा च आचार्यप्रणीतं न्यायोपबृंहितं सूत्रम् —दु:खजन्मप्रवृत्तिदोषमिथ्याज्ञानानामुत्तरोत्तरापाये तदनन्तरापायादपवर्ग:'' इति। —Ibid.

70. ''पाठापेक्षया कारणमुत्तरम्, कार्यं च पूर्वम्; कारणापाये कार्यापायः, कफापाये इव कफोद्भवस्य ज्वरस्यापायः। जन्मापाये दुःखापायः; प्रवृत्त्यपाये जन्मापाय; दोषापाये प्रवृत्त्यपायः; मिथ्याज्ञानापाये दोषापायः। मिथ्याज्ञानं चाविद्या रागाद्युपजननक्रमेण दृष्टेनैव संसारस्य परमं निदानम्। सा च तत्त्वज्ञानेन ब्रह्मात्मैकत्वविज्ञानेनैवावगतिपर्यन्तेन विरोधिना निवर्त्यते। ततोऽविद्यानिवृत्त्या ब्रह्मस्वरूपाविर्भावो मोक्षः; न तु विद्याकार्यस्तज्जनितापूर्वकार्यो वा-इति सूत्रार्थः।'' —Bhāmatī on SB-I.1.4, Loc.Cit., p.121.

71. ''न चेदं ब्रह्मात्मैकत्वविज्ञानं संपद्रूपम्। ...संपदादिरूपे हि ब्रह्मात्मैकत्वविज्ञानेऽभ्युपगम्यमाने, 'तत्त्वमसि', 'अहं ब्रह्मास्मि', 'अयमात्मा ब्रह्म' इत्येवमादीनां वाक्यानां ब्रह्मात्मैकत्ववस्तु प्रतिपादनपरः पदसमन्वयः पीड्येत; 'भिद्यते हृदयग्रन्थिश्छिद्यन्ते सर्वसंशयाः' इति चैवमादीन्यविद्यानिवृत्तिफलश्रवणान्युपरुध्येरन्; 'ब्रह्म वेद ब्रह्मैव भवति' इति चैवमादीनि तद्भावापत्तिवचनानि संपदादिरूपत्वे न सामञ्जस्येन नोपपद्येरन्। तस्मान्न संपदादिरूपं ब्रह्मात्मैकत्वविज्ञानम्।'' —SB on BS-I.1.4, Loc. Cit., p.123.

72. ''तदस्य अविषयीभूतोदासीनतत्पदार्थप्रत्यगात्मसामानाधिकरण्येन प्रमातृत्वाभावात् तन्निवृत्तौ प्रमाणादयस्तिस्रो विद्या निवर्तन्ते।'' —Bhāmatī on SB-I.1.4, Loc. Cit., p.125.

73. ''नापि संस्कार्यो मोक्षः, येन व्यापारमपेक्षेत। संस्कारो हि नाम संस्कार्यस्य गुणाधानेन वा स्यात्, दोषापनयनेन वा। न तावद्गुणाधानेन संभवति, अनाधेयातिशयब्रह्मस्वरूपत्वान्मोक्षस्य; नापि दोषापनयनेन, नित्यशुद्धब्रह्मस्वरूपत्वान्मोक्षस्य।'' —SB on BS-I.1.4, Loc.Cit., p.126.

74. ''अशुद्धिः सती दर्पणे निवर्तते; न तु ब्रह्मणि असती निवर्तनीया, नित्यनिवृत्तत्वादित्यर्थः'' —Bhāmatī on SB-I.1.4, Loc. Cit., p.126.

75. ''ननु देहाश्रयया स्नानाचमनयज्ञोपवीतधारणादिकया क्रियया देही संस्क्रियमाणो दृष्टः। न; देहादिसंहतस्यैवाविद्यागृहीतस्यात्मनः संस्क्रियमाणत्वात्। प्रत्यक्षं हि स्नानाचमनादेर्देहसमवायित्वम्। तया देहाश्रयया तत्संहत एव कश्चिदविद्ययात्मत्वेन परिगृहीतः संस्क्रियत इति युक्तम्। तथा देहाश्रयचिकित्सानिमित्तेन धातुसाम्येन तत्संहतस्य तदभिमानिन आरोग्यफलम्, 'अहमरोगः' इति यत्र बुद्धिरुत्पद्यते, एवं स्नानाचमनयज्ञोपवीतधारणादिकया 'अहं शुद्धः संस्कृतः' इति यत्र बुद्धिरुत्पद्यते, स संस्क्रियते। स च देहेन संहत एव। तेनैव अहंकर्त्रा अहंप्रत्ययविषयेण प्रत्ययिना सर्वाः क्रिया निर्वर्त्यन्ते। तत्फलं च स एवाश्नाति, 'तयोरन्यः पिप्पलं स्वाद्वत्ति अनश्नन्नन्योऽभिचाकशीति' इति मन्त्रवर्णात्; 'आत्मेन्द्रियमनोयुक्तं भोक्तेत्याहुर्मनीषिणः' इति च। ....ब्रह्मभावश्च मोक्षः। तस्मान्न संस्कार्योपि मोक्षः।'' —SB on BS-I.1.4, Loc. Cit., pp.127-128.

76. ''संहतस्तत्संघातमध्यपतितस्तदभेदेनाहमितिप्रत्ययविषयीभूतः; अतः शरीरादिसंस्कारः शरीरादिधर्मोऽप्यात्मनो भवति, तदभेदाध्यवसायात्...। चतसृणां विधानां मध्येऽन्यतमतया क्रियाफलत्वं व्याप्तम्; सा च मोक्षाद्व्यावर्तमाना व्यापकानुपलब्ध्या मोक्षस्य क्रियाफलत्वं व्यावर्तयतीति।'' —Bhāmatī on SB-I.1.4, Loc.Cit., pp.127-128.

77. ''ननु ज्ञानं नाम मानसी क्रिया। न; वैलक्षण्यात्। क्रिया हि नाम सा, यत्र वस्तुस्वरूपनिरपेक्षैव चोद्यते, पुरुषचित्तव्यापाराधीना च। ध्यानं चिन्तनं यद्यपि मानसं तथापि पुरुषेण कर्तुमकर्तुमन्यथा वा कर्तुं शक्यं, पुरुषतन्त्रत्वात्। ज्ञानं तु प्रमाणजन्यम्। प्रमाणं च यथाभूतवस्तु विषयम्।

अतो ज्ञानं कर्तुमकर्तुमन्यथा वा कर्तुं शक्यम्; केवलं वस्तुतन्त्रमेव तत्; न चोदनातन्त्रम्, नापि पुरुषतन्त्रम्।" —SB on BS-I.1.4, Loc.Cit., pp.128-129.

78. "सत्यं, ज्ञानं मानसी क्रिया, नत्वियं ब्रह्मणि फलं जनयितुमर्हति; तस्य स्वयंप्रकाशतया विदिक्रियाकर्मभावानुपपत्तेरित्युक्तम्। नहि 'यस्यै देवतायै हविर्गृहीतं स्यात्तां ध्यायेद्वषट्करिष्यन्' इत्यस्माद्विधेः प्राग्देवताध्यानं प्राप्तं, प्राप्तं त्वधीतवेदान्तस्य विदितपदतदर्थसंबन्धस्याधिगत-शब्दन्यायतत्त्वस्य सदेव सोम्येदम् इत्यादेः 'तत्वमसि' इत्यन्तात्संदर्भात् ब्रह्मात्मभावज्ञानं शब्दप्रमाणसामर्थ्यात्।....तस्माद् ब्रह्मज्ञानं मानसी क्रियापि न विधिगोचरः।" —Bhāmatī on SB-I.1.4, Loc.Cit., pp.128-129.

79. "तत्त्वमसीत्यादिवाक्याद्ब्रह्मस्वरूपावगाहिज्ञानान्तरोत्पत्तेरिष्टत्वात्। तद्धि ब्रह्मणोऽवच्छिद्यैव चैतन्यस्य ब्रह्मस्वरूपत्वप्रच्छादनेन जीवरूपत्वापादिकामनादिसिद्धामविद्यामहंकारादिविक्षेपहेतुं निराकुर्वदेवोत्पद्यते। ततः कारणनिवृत्तौ तत्कार्यं अहमिति जीवे भोक्तृरूपता सपरिकरा निवर्तते इति युज्यते।" —Pañcapādikā, Loc.Cit., pp.162-163.

80. "अहंप्रत्ययः पुनरनादिसिद्धोऽनादिसिद्धेनैव कार्यकारणमात्रेण सहभावादविरोधात् न स्वरूपविवेकमात्रेण निवर्तते। नापि ज्ञानान्तरमुत्पन्नमिति विशेषः।" —Ibid.

81. "ननु निरतिशयानन्दं ब्रह्म श्रूयते, ब्रह्मावाप्तिसाधनं च ब्रह्मविद्या 'स यो ह वै तत् परमं ब्रह्म वेद ब्रह्मैव भवती' त्यादिश्रुतिभ्यः, तस्मान्निरतिशयसुखावाप्तये इति वक्तव्यम्....। ननु चानर्थस्यापि समूलस्य प्रहाणं श्रूयते ब्रह्मविद्याफलम् 'तरति शोकमात्मवित्' 'जुष्टं, यदा पश्यत्यन्यमीशमस्य महिमानमिति वीतशोकः' इति च।" —Ibid, pp.163-164.

82. "आत्मैकत्वविद्याप्रतिपत्तये इत्यात्मनो जीवस्य ब्रह्मात्मकता शास्त्रस्य विषयः, तेनानन्दात्मकब्रह्मस्वरूपताप्राप्तिः जीवस्य विषयतयैव संवृत्ता। न च सा विषयाद् बहिः, येन पृथङ् निर्देशार्हा स्यात्, समूलानर्थहानिस्तु बहिः शास्त्रविषयाद्ब्रह्मात्मरूपात्।" —Ibid. p.164.

83. "नित्येनैव अध्ययनविधिना अधीतस्वाध्यायः वेदान्तवाक्येषु आपातदर्शनेन इदमवगच्छति- 'आत्मनस्तु कामाय सर्वं प्रियम्' इत्युपक्रमात् सर्वतो विरक्तस्य आत्मप्रेप्सोः 'आत्मनि विज्ञाते सर्वमिदं विज्ञातम्' 'एतावदरे खल्वमृतत्वम्' इत्युपसंहारात् अमृतत्वसाधनम् आत्मदर्शनं 'द्रष्टव्यः' इत्यनूद्य तादर्थ्येन मननिदिध्यासनाभ्यां फलोपकार्यङ्गाभ्यां सह श्रवणं नाम अङ्गि विधीयते इति।" —Vivaraṇa, Loc.Cit., pp.29-30.

84. "तदेवमशाब्दमविद्याविलयं मन्वानः श्रुतिन्यायकोविदो भगवान् भाष्यकारो विषयात् पृथक् निर्दिशति- 'अस्यानर्थहेतोः प्रहाणायेति। चतुर्थीप्रयोगोऽपि विद्यासामर्थ्यसिद्धिमभिप्रेत्य, न तदर्थमुपादानम्। प्रयोजनत्वं च पुरुषाकांक्षाया एवास्तु।" —Pañcapādikā, Loc.Cit., pp.169-170.

85. "तर्हि ब्रह्मविद्याफलत्वात् शास्त्रस्य न अनर्थनिरासः प्रयोजनम्; न- परम्परयापि पुरुषाकाङ्क्षितप्रयोजनत्वोपपत्तेरित्याह—प्रयोजनत्वं चेति।" —Vivaraṇa, Loc.Cit., p.392.

86. "ज्ञानं हि वस्तुतः प्रतीतितश्च ज्ञातुरुत्पत्त्यैव आप्तमेवेत्यर्थः।" —Vivaraṇa, Ibid.

87. "तत्र प्रत्यक्षान्तरेषु स्वविषयेण सह अपरोक्षावभासा विद्या भवति, आप्तिशब्देन च विषयेण सहापरोक्ष्यनिश्चयो विवक्ष्यते, तदिह न संभवति...।" —Vivaraṇa, Ibid.

88. "प्रकृते पुनर्विषये विद्या उदिताऽपि न प्रतिष्ठां लभते। असम्भावनाविपरीतभावनाभिभूतविषयत्वात्। तथा च लोके अस्मिन् देशे काले चेदं वस्तु स्वरूपत एव न सम्भवतीति दृढभावितं, यदि

तत् कथंचित् देववशादुपलभ्येत, तदा स्वयमीक्षमाणोऽपि तावन्नाध्यवस्यति यावत् तर्केण तत्सम्भवं नानुसरति। तेन सम्यग्ज्ञानमपि स्वविषयेऽप्रतिष्ठितमनवाप्तमिव भवति। तेन तत्स्वरूपप्रतिष्ठायै तर्कं सहायीकरोति। अत एव 'प्रमाणानामनुग्राहकस्तर्कः' इति तर्कविदः।" —Pañcapādikā, Loc.Cit., pp.170-171.

89. "यथादूरदेशवर्तिनि आर्द्रमरीचफलादौ तथाविधवस्तुदर्शनसंस्कारशून्यतया विपरीतसंस्कारवत्तया च प्रत्यक्षदृष्टेऽपि न निश्चिनोति, असम्भावितविशेषांशापरोक्षनिश्चयो नोत्पद्यते इत्यर्थः।" —Vivaraṇa, Loc. Cit., P.394.

90. "ननु प्रमाणादनिश्चीयमानः कथं तर्कप्रत्ययान्निश्चीयते इति। ......प्रसिद्धैव सहकारिसंपत्तौ फलसिद्धिरित्यर्थः।" —Vivaraṇa, Ibid.

91. "ननु तर्कस्यापि प्रमाणत्वे कथं प्रमाणद्वयादर्थनिश्चयो भवति? अप्रमाणत्वे नतराम् इति मन्वान आह-अथ कोऽयमिति। अप्रमाणमपि तर्कः सहकार्येव, प्रत्ययविशेषत्वाद्...।" —Vivaraṇa, Ibid.

92. "प्रमाणशक्तिविषयतत्सम्भवासम्भवपरिच्छेदात्मा प्रत्ययः।" —Pañcapādikā, Loc.Cit., p.171.

93. The Pañcapādikā of Padmapāda, Op. Cit., pp.134-135; Vide, "विषयासम्भवाशङ्कया तथानुभवफलानुत्पत्तौ तत्सम्भवप्रदर्शनमुखेन फलप्रतिबन्धविगमे। तथा च तत्त्वमसिवाक्ये त्वंपदार्थो जीवः तत्पदार्थब्रह्मस्वरूपतामात्मनोऽसम्भावयन् विपरीतं च रूपं मन्वानः समुत्पन्नेऽपि ज्ञाने तावत् नाध्यवस्यति यावत्तर्केण विरोधमपनीय तद्रूपतामात्मनो न सम्भावयति। ततः प्राक् विद्या उदितापि वाक्यात् अनवाप्तेव भवति। अवाप्तिप्रकारश्च वेदान्तेष्वेव निर्दिष्टः साक्षादनुभवफलोद्देशेन।" —Pañcapādikā, Loc.Cit., p.172.

94. Vide, Tātparyadīpikā on Vivaraṇa, Loc.Cit., p.403.

95. "लोके तावद् विषयस्यापरोक्षता संविदभेदाद्वा विषयस्याव्यवधानतया स्वसंविज्जनकत्वाद्वा प्रमाणकारणेन्द्रियसम्प्रयुक्तत्वाद्वा भवति; उक्तकारणत्रयहीने अनुमेयादौ परोक्षतादर्शनात्। तत्र ब्रह्मण एव सर्वसंविदुपादानत्वात् ब्रह्माकारशब्दप्रमाणजन्यसंवेदनेऽपि तदभिन्नतया वा तज्जनकतया वा ब्रह्मापि प्रथममेवापरोक्षतया अवभासते।" —Vivaraṇa, Loc. Cit., pp.403 & 407.

96. "तच्च चित्तस्यातिसूक्ष्मे अनेकाग्रतादोषाद्विपर्ययसंस्कारदोषाच्च प्रतिबद्धं भ्रान्त्या परोक्षवदवभासते। तत्रापरोक्षज्ञानमुद्दिश्य यज्ञादीनां शमादीनां निदिध्यासनादीनां च विधानसामर्थ्यात् यज्ञादिनिवर्हितकल्मषप्रतिबन्धं शमादिनिरुद्धविपरीतप्रवृत्तिदोषं मननसंदर्शितप्रमेयादि-संभावनागुणप्रदीपोज्ज्वलितम् अतिसूक्ष्मतरब्रह्मात्मविषय-निदिध्यासन-प्रचयपरिनिर्मित-तदेकाग्रवृत्तिगुणं चित्तेन्द्रियं पारोक्ष्यविभ्रमनिमित्तप्रतिबन्धनिरासेन शब्दादेवापरोक्षनिश्नयनिमित्तं भवतीति गम्यते।" —Vivaraṇa, Loc.Cit., p.407.

97. "न प्रथमोत्पन्नं शब्दज्ञानमेव प्रतिबन्धविगमापेक्षया अपरोक्षावभासं भवति; किं तु शब्द एव प्रथमं ब्रह्मणि परोक्षज्ञानमुत्पाद्य पुनः वर्णितचित्तदर्पणसहकारिकारणापेक्षया द्वितीयमपरोक्ष-ज्ञानमुत्पादयति। शब्दादीनां तद्धितप्रत्ययादिना अपरोक्षज्ञाने विनियोगसामर्थ्यात्। यथा संप्रयोगोऽभिज्ञामुत्पाद्य पुनः पूर्वानुभवसंस्कारापेक्षया प्रत्यभिज्ञामुत्पादयति तद्वत्। न च स्वयंप्रकाशे ब्रह्मणि परोक्षज्ञानं विभ्रमः। स्वयंप्रकाशेऽपि पुरुषान्तरसंवेदने परोक्षानुमानदर्शनादिति।" —Vivaraṇa, Ibid. pp.409-410.

98. "ननु ब्रह्मज्ञानं प्रयोजनम्, तदर्थः शास्त्रारम्भः। न ब्रह्मज्ञाने अर्थित्वानुपपत्तेः। ब्रह्मज्ञानाद्धि मनसोऽपि वियोगात् निखिलविषयानुषङ्गनिवृत्तिः श्रूयते। सा च सार्वभौमोपक्रमं ब्रह्मलोकावसानमुत्कृष्टोत्कृष्टसुखं श्रूयमाणं सोपायं निवर्तयति। अतो ब्रह्मज्ञानादुद्विजते लोकः, कुतस्तत्र प्रवृत्तिः। ....न हि ब्रह्मानन्दोऽननुभूतपूर्वोऽनुभूतभोग्यसुखाभिलाषं मन्दीकर्तुमुत्सहते, येन तदुज्झित्वा ब्रह्मज्ञाने प्रवर्तेत।" —Pañcapādikā, Loc.Cit., pp.220-221.

99. "नहि जीवस्य ब्रह्मात्मतावगमः तद्विषयानवगममबाधमानः उदेति।.... संस्कारादप्यग्रहणानुवृत्तेः सम्भवात् भयानुवृत्तिवत्। तथाहि-सम्यग्ज्ञानात् निवृत्तमपि भयं स्वसंस्कारादनुवर्तते कम्पना कम्पादिनिमित्तं च भवति, तथा अग्रहणमपि स्वसंस्कारादनुवर्तते अहंकारग्रन्थेश्च निमित्तं भवतीति न किञ्चिदनुपपन्नमस्ति।" —Pañcapādikā, Loc. Cit., pp. 173-174.

100. "तत्त्वज्ञानानुसन्धानादेव च क्रमेण संस्कारनिवृत्तेः कंचित् कालमवस्थायैव विदेहमुक्तिः न विरुध्यते, अविद्यालेशो वा तमोलेशवत् संस्कारशब्देनाभिधीयते इति निरवद्यम्।" —Vivaraṇa, Loc. Cit., p.415.

101. "भवेदध्ययनविधेरर्थावबोधः प्रयोजनम्। नाधिकारहेतुता, अध्ययनात् प्रागसिद्धत्वात्। प्राक् चाधिकारज्ञानेन प्रयोजनम्। अतो न विधेः दृष्टाधिकारत्वेनार्थावबोधसिद्धिः।" —Pañcapādikā, Loc.Cit., p.224.

102. "भवतु नाम 'अध्ययनेन अर्थावबोधं भावयेदर्थावबोधकामः' इति विधिः, तथापि 'विचारेण अर्थावबोधं भावयेत्' इति विचारे प्रवृत्तिरध्ययनविधिना न विधीयत इति।" —Vivaraṇa, Loc.Cit., p.491.

103. "अध्ययनात् प्राक् अर्थावबोधस्य अप्रतिपन्नस्य कामनाऽयोगात् नार्थावबोधकाममुद्दिश्य विधानमित्यर्थः।" —Vivaraṇa, Ibid.

104. "वेदान्ताध्ययनं यद्यपि केवलं न पुष्कलं कारणम्, तथापि न तेन विना उत्पद्यते ब्रह्मजिज्ञासा। उत्पद्यते तु धर्मावबोधनं विनापीत्यभिप्रायः।" —Pañcapādikā, Loc. Cit., p.240.

105. "अतो ज्ञानद्वयाभावात् एकस्य ज्ञानस्य उभयार्थताऽयोगात् न ब्रह्मज्ञानं विधेयमिति भावः।" —Vivaraṇa, Loc. Cit., p.453.

106. Pañcapādikā of Padmapāda, Op. Cit., pp.207-208; Vide, "यथा तावत् प्रसादमारुरुक्षोः सोपानपरम्परा क्रमशः प्राप्यमाणा प्रासादारोहणहेतुः न तथेह ब्रह्मजिज्ञासां चिकीर्षोः कर्माणि सहस्रसंवत्सरपर्यन्तानि तत्क्रियाहेतुतया स्थितानि। प्रमाणाभावात्।" —Pañcapadikā, Loc.Cit., p.242.

107. Pañcapadikā of Padmapāda, Op. Cit., p.209.

108. "तस्मात् सर्वत्र कामस्य विषयदोषदर्शनमेवोच्छेदकारणं नित्यवस्तुदर्शनं च 'रसवर्जं रसोऽप्यस्य परं दृष्ट्वा निवर्तते' इति स्मृतेः। न चैवंलक्षण आगमोऽस्ति हिरण्यगर्भोपभोगात् निखिलविषयावाप्तौ कामोच्छेदो भवतीति।" —Pañcapādikā, Loc.Cit., p.244.

109. "नित्यनैमित्तिककर्मानुष्ठानैः संस्कृतस्य आत्मनो यदि श्रवणमननध्यानाभ्यासादीनि ज्ञानसाधनानि सम्पद्यन्ते तदा संस्कारकर्माणि सहकारिविशेषात् आत्मज्ञानमवतारयन्ति यदा तु सहकारिकारणविरहः तदा अभ्युदयफलम् इति व्यवस्थोपपत्तेः न श्रुतिस्मृत्योः परस्परविरोधः।" —Vivaraṇa, Loc.Cit., p.540.

110. "श्रवणमननध्यानाभ्यासादिसहकारिकारणसम्पत्तावेव संस्कारो विज्ञानं साधयति, तदभावे सत्यभ्युदयमेव। विविदिषायां तु विज्ञानस्य कर्मफलत्वात् फलपर्यन्तं साधनानि सम्पाद्यापि

विज्ञानं जनयन्तीति विशेषः।'' —Vivaraṇa, Ibid, p.546.

111. Pañcapādikā of Padmapāda, Op.Cit., p.215.

112. ''तस्मात् यावदस्य हिरण्यगर्भावाप्तिपर्यन्तस्य भोगस्योत्पादपरिच्छेदाभ्यां विनाशित्वादनित्यत्वं नावैति, विनश्यदपीदं कूटस्थनित्यवस्तुपर्यन्तमेव विनश्यति अन्यथा निरुपादानस्य पुनरुत्पत्त्यसम्भव इति वर्तमानस्याप्यसम्भवादभावोऽभविष्यदिति निरूपणात् नित्यानित्यवस्तुविवेको यावन् न जायते, यावच्चाभिमुखं विनाशदर्शनात् भुञ्जानस्यापि भोगान् स्रक्चन्दनवस्त्रालंकारभोगानिवाग्निप्रवेशार्थ-भोगार्थव्यापारजनितदुःखानुभवाच्च तन्निमित्तां निवृत्तिमप्यलभमानो भोगादि्वरक्तस्ततो मुमुक्षुत्वं तत्साधनशमदमोपरमतितिक्षासमाधानसम्पन्नो भूत्वा यावन्नालम्बते, तावत् ब्रह्मजिज्ञासां कः प्रतिपद्येत कथंचित् वा दैववशात् कुतूहलाद्वा बहुश्रुतत्वबुद्ध्या वा प्रवृत्तोऽपि न निर्विचिकित्सं ब्रह्म आत्मत्वेनावगन्तुं शक्नोति यथोक्तसाधनसम्पत्तिविरहात् अनन्तर्मुखचेता बहिरेवाभिनिविशमानः।'' —Pañcapādikā, Loc.Cit., pp.251-253.

113. '''सोऽन्वेष्टव्यः' इति विधिप्रकरणे 'तद्यथेह कर्मजितो लोकः क्षीयते एवमेवामुत्र पुण्यजितो लोकः क्षीयते' इति नित्यानित्यवस्तुविवेको दर्शितः।'' —Vivaraṇa, Loc.Cit., p.558.

114. ''परीक्ष्य लोकान् कर्मचितान्'', ''आत्मनस्तु कामाय सर्वं प्रियं भवति' इति च ज्ञानश्रवणविधिप्रकरणे इहामुत्रार्थभोगविरागो दर्शितः। 'शान्तो दान्तः' इति च दर्शनविधिप्रकरणे शमादयो दर्शिताः।'' —Vivaraṇa, Ibid.

115. ''विजिज्ञासितव्यः'' 'विजिज्ञासस्व' इति च अन्तर्णीतो विचारो विधीयते, इष्यमाणज्ञानस्येच्छायाश्च विधेयत्वायोगात्। 'श्रोतव्यः' इति च स्वयमेव विचारो विहितः, 'तद्विज्ञानार्थं स गुरुमेव अभिगच्छेदिति ज्ञानस्य साध्यतावगमात् गुरूपसदनविधानाच्च तत्साधनश्रवणादिविधिः कल्प्यते। 'आत्मन्येवात्मानं पश्येत्' इति ज्ञानविधानायोगात् तत्साधने विधिरुपादीयते इति सर्वत्र मनननिदिध्यासनाभ्यां सह श्रवणं नाम अङ्गि विधीयत इति सिद्धम्।'' —Vivaraṇa, Ibid, p.559.

116. Pañcapādikā of Padmapāda, Op. Cit., P.225; Vide, ''अवगतिरिति साक्षादनुभव उच्यते। ज्ञानं तु परोक्षेऽनुभवानारूढेऽपि सम्भवति संनिहितेऽप्यसम्भावितविषये अनवसितरूपमित्युक्तं पुरस्तात्। ...ब्रह्मावगतिर्हि पुरुषार्थः। ब्रह्मरूपतासाक्षात्करणमित्यर्थः।'' —Pañcapādikā, Loc.Cit., pp.260-261.

117. ''तत्र 'सोऽयं देवदत्तः' पदत्रयस्य एकस्मिन् देवदत्ते पर्यवसानं दृश्यते। तथा हि-प्रत्यभिज्ञायामधिगतमेकत्वं परस्मै प्रतिपादयति- ''सोऽयं देवदत्तः' इति। तत्र न तद्देशकालयोः एतद्देशकालयोश्च परस्परैक्यं प्रत्यभिजानाति; भेदप्रत्ययात्। अत एव विशिष्टयोरप्यैक्यं न प्रत्यभिज्ञायते। किंतु 'सोऽयम्' इति विशिष्टद्वयोपलक्षितः प्रत्यभिज्ञागोचरः। प्रत्यभिज्ञातं चार्थं परस्मै 'सोऽयम्' इति विशिष्टाभिधायिभ्यां पदाभ्यां स्वार्थैकदेशपरित्यागेन एकादेशलक्षणया देवदत्तस्वरूपैक्यमेव प्रतिपादयति।'' —Vivaraṇa, Loc.Cit., p.714.

118. ''अतः कालद्वयपरामर्शेन तत्सम्बन्धिपदार्थैक्यमेव अवलम्बमाना पदार्थभेदप्रतिभासविरोधितया प्रामाण्यमश्नुते प्रत्यभिज्ञा। एवं तर्हि 'सोऽयम्' इति वाक्यस्यापि एवमेव प्रामाण्यं भविष्यति। तथा तत्त्वमसिवाक्यस्यापि त्वंपदेन एकदेशपरित्यागेन लक्ष्यमाणद्रष्टृस्वरूपस्य पारोक्ष्यपरित्यागेन तत्पदाभिधेयब्रह्मस्वरूपैक्ये वाक्यजन्यज्ञानगोचरेऽपि जीवब्रह्मपदार्थप्रतीतिसमये प्रतिपन्नैक्यविषयतया अनुवादप्राप्तावपि भेदप्रतिभासविरोधितया प्रामाण्यमुपपद्यत इति।'' —Vivaraṇa, Loc.Cit., p.716.

119. "तस्मान्न ब्रह्मात्माभिमानितः पूर्ववत् संसारित्वम्, तदभिमानविरोधात्। वैषयिकस्तु साक्षादनुभवाभिमानः संसारविषय आरब्धकर्मशेषनिमित्तः तिमिरनिमित्तद्विचन्द्रवत्।" —Pañcapādikā, Loc.Cit., pp.370-371.
120. "ब्रह्मात्मापरोक्षदर्शनादुत्तरकालमन्तःकरणसम्पिण्डितप्रमातृबाधात् प्रमेयसम्बन्धासिद्धेर्निवर्तत एव प्रमातृप्रमाणप्रमेयकर्तृकर्मकार्यभोक्तृभोग्यभोगलक्षणो व्यवहार इति।" —Vivaraṇa, Loc.Cit., p.788.
121. Supra, fn.41.
122. T.M.P. Mahadevan, Loc. Cit., p.275.
123. Ibid.
124. Supra, p.272.
125. Bh.G. - II. 54-61.
126. T.M.P. Mahadevan, Loc. Cit., pp.284-285.
127. Supra, p.280.
128. Supra, p.290.
129. Supra, p.292.
130. Supra, p.278-279.
131. Supra, Ibid.
132. Supra, p.300.
133. Supra, p.276.
134. Supra, p.278.
135. Supra, p.289.
136. Supra, Ibid.
137. Supra, p.288.
138. Supra, p.290.
139. Kalidas Bhattacharya, A Modern Understanding of Advaita Vedānta, L.D. Institute of Indology, Ahmedabad, 1975, pp.51-52.

CHAPTER VIII

CONCLUSION

From the discussion just concluded, it is clear that Advaita Vedānta has had a very hoary past, having within its fold a long tradition of Philosophers and teachers[1]. The basic doctrines of Śāṅkara Vedānta, such as *Māyā, Brahman, Vivarta,* etc. are found to have existed in seminal form in the Ṛg Veda and allied Scriptures[2] from where they developed into full-fledged philosophical doctrines after receiving a masterly treatment at the hands of spiritual Masters such as Yājñavalkya, Bādarāyaṇa, Gauḍapāda[3], etc. Thereafter they were carved into a rigorous and comprehensive system by Śaṅkara in his *Brahma-sūtra-bhāṣya*[4]. Śaṅkara's arguments marked with precision were so concise that they became the basis for the post-Śaṅkara philosophical speculations of a very high order that led to the bifurcation of the Advaita Tradition into two streams, namely, the Bhāmatī-Prasthāna and the Vivaraṇa-Prasthāna[5].

First and foremost among the points of dispute between the Bhāmatī and the Vivaraṇa, is the concept of *Avidyā* or *Māyā,* which in turn is the very foundation of Śaṅkara's philosophy. Not satisfied with the explanation given for the phenomenon of Error (*Adhyāsa*) by the non-Advaita schools[6], the Advaita Philosophers came up with the Theory of *Anirvacanīya-khyāti* as a rebuff to the other theories of Error, viz., *Anyathākhyāti, Sadasatkhyāti, Viparītakhyāti, Vivekākhyāti, Asatkhyāti, Ātmakhyāti* and *Satkhyāti.* Though both Vācaspati Miśra and Prakāśātman believe that *Adhyāsa* is beginningless and indeterminable[7], yet they differ from each other as to the nature of *Adhyāsa* or superimposition. While the Bhāmatī defines *Avabhāsa* or *Adhyāsa* as non-apprehension[8] of the difference between the Real and the unreal which is sublatable by Knowledge, the Vivaraṇa on the other hand holds the view that *Adhyāsa* is the manifestation of something as that which it is not, i.e., as something else[9]. This *Adhyāsa,* in its essence, is born of an uninterrupted succession of *Adhyāsa-s*. Having a dual potency of *Āvaraṇa* and *Vikṣepa, Ajñāna,* which is the material cause of superimposition, cannot be said to be merely the absence of *Jñāna*. It is something positive, says Prakāśātman, since its potency persists in residual form even in *deep sleep,* which accounts for the non-manifestation of the true nature of the self even then. Hence, superimposition cannot be said to be the non-apprehension of difference or even false-cognition. The Bhāmatī clarifies, saying that Illusion has a previous cognition as its cause and is sublatable by the Right Knowledge. To Vācaspati, though the object of superimposition is itself indeterminable, yet its locus is something '*real*', indicated by the term "*elsewhere*" in the definition of *Adhyāsa*. Stretching still further this argument, the Vivaraṇa says in addition that the substrate of illusory cognition cannot be concealed by Nescience as such because Nescience does not reside in the object of an illusory cognition, but rather in the inner-Self[10]. This leads to the postulation by this School of two *Ajñāna-s—Mūlājñāna* with reference to the Self, and *Avasthājñāna* with reference to the external objects. The position taken by the Vivaraṇa as regards the locus of *Avidyā* or *Ajñāna* is in opposition to that taken by the Bhāmatī which, though postulating the unitary nature of *Avidyā* in principle, also postulates the plurality of *Avidyā* as a matter of practice, with each *Avidyā* having one *Jīva* as its locus[11].

As to the *Jīva* and *Brahman* relation also, there are seen to be divergent views separating the Bhāmatī and the Vivaraṇa. As per the theory of *Avacchedavāda*[12] upheld by the Bhāmatī, *Brahman* though One and Impartite appears as many in the form of the *Jīva-s* due to the intervening adjuncts of the body-sense-mind complex, in much the same way as space, though one and undivided, appears as many due to the intervening adjuncts of pots, jars, etc. But to the Vivaraṇa, *Brahman,* One and Impartite, appears as many individual selves when It is reflected in the numerous adjuncts (i.e. *Upādhi-s*) such as the intellect, etc. just as the *prototype* appears as many in the form of reflections[13]. This theory of *Bimba-Pratibimbavāda* bears resemblance to that of the *Ābhāsavāda* of Sureśvara[14]. It is clear from the account given of these theories in this thesis that according to the Vivaraṇa, the *Jīva-s* are as real as *Brahman,* just as the reflections are identical with the *prototype,* and that according to the Bhāmatī also what appears to be limited in the form of the *Jīva* is essentially unlimited and real as *Brahman* Itself and hence identical with It. The root-cause of the apparent individuality of the self is *Avidyā,* due to which there is the superimposition on the *Jīva* of the notions of enjoyership, agency, etc. as a consequence of the non-apprehension of the difference between the Self and the non-Self[15]. As a result of the superimposition of the attributes of the intellect etc., the Intelligent Self appears as though finite, says the Bhāmatī, which holds that every subsequent superimposition has for its object that which has the content of each earlier superimposition and its impressions (i.e., *vāsanā-s*). Jīva is not a real transformation (*pariṇāma*) of *Brahman,* but rather Its *vivarta*[16], claims Vācaspati, and hence there is no relation of cause and effect between the *Self* and *Jīva,* but rather that of identity. This *Jīva-Brahman*-identity being absolutely real, the apparent difference, which has beginningless Nescience for its cause, is eradicable through True Knowledge. And True Knowledge, according to the Bhāmatī, is "attainable" through the realization of the purport of the *mahāvākya* "*Tat tvam asi*". With this in view, all other relations such as that of part and whole, identity-in-difference, etc., between *Jīva* and *Brahman* postulated by other schools stand rejected.

Making use of the illustration of the double-moon theory[17], the Vivaraṇa, on the other hand, declares that the difference between *Jīva* and *Brahman, Jīva* and *Īśvara,* and *Jīva* and *Jīva* is false. The material cause of the non-apprehension of difference is verily the concealing potency of Nescience, claims Prakāśātman. The Vivaraṇa postulates *Avidyā* as the efficient cause of the appearance of *Jīva-Brahman*-difference wherein *Brahman* Itself serves as the basis for its functioning. As for the *Jīva-Brahman*-identity, the Vivaraṇa uses the mirror-reflection theory to establish the reality of the individual self just as the reflection in the mirror is real and identical with the prototype, as is proved by its non-sublatability[18]. The appearance of difference is not sublatable by the mere dawning of Knowledge, because, according to the Vivaraṇa, the appearance of difference is not caused by the reflection of *Brahman* in the intellect etc., but rather by the adjuncts, which are not sublatable by Knowledge.

Omniscience and Omnipotence being the essential nature

of *Brahman*, It cannot be said to be subjected to transformation, as is claimed by the Pariṇāmavādin-s. Rejecting also the theory of *Avacchedavāda*, the Vivaraṇa holds that if this theory were accepted, then *Brahman* would have to be conceived as characterized by universal and particular adjuncts, which would be violative of the principle of Omniscience and Omnipotence of *Brahman* referred to above. The Vivaraṇa says that the individuality of the self gets dissolved merely by removing the adjuncts which are responsible for it. Like the Bhāmatī, the Vivaraṇa also rejects the theory of identity-cum-difference since this is against the teaching of the Scriptures and since *Brahman* is proclaimed to be Impartite[19].

The Bhāmatī as well as the Vivaraṇa propound the view that *Brahman* is known only through the authority of the Veda-s[20]. And since the Veda-s themselves have *Brahman* as their origin,[21] they are also eternal as *Brahman* Itself. For the same reason, the Veda-s are admitted to be also self-revealed. Hence, declares the Vivaraṇa, *Brahman* is Self-luminous, since it is not dependent on anything else for Its manifestation. The meaning of the term "*Brahman*" also is known only through Scriptures, It being beyond the range of the empirical means of knowledge. Both the schools agree as to the nature of *Brahman* which is of the essence of *Sat, Cit, Ānanda* and as such these cannot be regarded as Its attributes. *Brahman* is thus Immortal, Eternal, Intelligent and Free. It is of the nature of immeasurable Bliss and Knowledge, aver both the Bhāmatī and the Vivaraṇa[22]. While the Vivaraṇa is of the view that the study of the Scriptures is capable in itself of leading to the realization of the true nature of *Brahman*[23], the Bhāmatī holds that the study of the Scriptures leads only to the intellectual comprehension of *Brahman*, and not to the realization of Its true nature. According to the Bhāmatī, there is no injunction for the realization of *Brahman*[24]. Contrarily, the Vivaraṇa views that *Śravaṇa* has been enjoined along with *manana* and *nididhyāsana* for the intuition of *Brahman*.

Both the Schools agree that *Brahman* is both the efficient and the material cause of the universe[25] and that It is the Internal Ruler of everything[26]. The Bhāmatī says that while *Brahman* is absolutely Real, the world is not so, it being an evolute of the beginningless Nescience. According to both the

Schools, the self is the only Truth in this world, which cannot be said to have *Pradhāna* as its cause. Both the Schools agree also to the fact that *Brahman*-knowledge is not "to be" attained as a matter of fact, because *Brahman* is understood as always attained. Non-attainment is but an illusion. The Vivaraṇa holds the view that in *deep sleep* "*aham*" is revealed in its true form as Pure Consciousness divested of all adjuncts[27]. Hence, it also makes use of the illustration of the red-crystal to clarify the concept of illusoriness of agentship, etc. superimposed on the self, which, in reality, is always detached and free from the superimposition of all the adjuncts[28].

To the Bhāmatī as well as the Vivaraṇa, the apprehension of the difference between the Self and the non-Self on the one hand, and the realization of the *Jīva-Brahman*-identity on the other, constitutes the realization of Truth, with the former leading to the latter. The Bhāmatī defines *Vidyā* as the knowledge about the true nature of *Brahman* without any trace of doubt or contradiction. This ascertainment of the true nature of *Brahman* is itself *Mokṣa*[29]. The Vivaraṇa sees *Mokṣa* as *unique* Knowledge which, while revealing the true nature of *Brahman,* arises from the realization of Truth contained in the *Mahāvākya*—"*Tat tvam asi*". According to the Vivaraṇa, that *unique* Knowledge dispels, as it arises, the very root of all evils[30], viz., Nescience, which is responsible for the non-apprehension of *Brahman* in Its true nature. But the mere discrimination of the Self from the non-Self does not constitute Release, for it does not on its own bring about the eradication of superimposition. But as for the Bhāmatī, it insists on the fact that the eradication of Nescience is a must for Self-realization through the rise of intuitive knowledge in the form of a mode of the internal organ. It says that the true nature of *Brahman* becomes manifest with the very removal of Nescience. But here too, the Bhāmatī says that the manifestation of the true nature of *Brahman* is not the result of *Vidyā* or contemplation, etc. or even of any act whatsoever, for *Brahman* as such is always manifest. As a matter of fact, the Bhāmatī dismisses the contribution of any act whatsoever to the realization of *Brahman*[31]. But it does recognize the acquisition of the *sampat-catuṣṭaya,* i.e., *śama, dama, titikṣā, uparati,* etc., as a pre-requisite for the rise of the desire to know *Brahman*[32]. So does the Vivaraṇa also, which however, does not preclude the performance of acts and rituals from contributing to the rise of true Knowledge. *Idem* with the purificatory acts, which it believes, lead to *Brahman*-knowledge through the purification of the mind, through the instrumentality of which *Brahman*-knowledge is attained. Though, however, both the Schools proclaim that, "attainment of the knowledge of *Brahman*" is a misnomer, for in reality there is nothing to be "attained" as concerns *Brahman*, since It is given as "attained" at all times. Hence, what is meant by *Mokṣa* in real terms is the eradication of Nescience[33], which according to the Bhāmatī is achieved through the practice of *śravaṇa, manana* and *nididhyāsana,* resulting in the rise of the desire to know the Truth. The Bhāmatī touches upon the process through which there arises first through normal experience an aversion towards worldly pleasures followed by detachment, and eventually by a longing for release through the desire to *know* the true nature of the Self[34]. Though fundamentally this is what the Vivaraṇa also propounds, yet it believes that this is attained as a result of the performance of the acts enjoined upon the seeker of Truth. It is in this context that it claims that *śravaṇa, manana,* and *nididhyāsana* are enjoined with reference to the "*adhyayanavidhi*"[35]. But interestingly so, taking an extreme position, the Vivaraṇa believes as well that *Brahmāvagati* is possible directly through Verbal Testimony, whereas the Bhāmatī rules out any such possibility, saying that study of the Scriptures can lead at most to knowledge in general about the true nature of *Brahman,* but not to *Brahmāvagati per se.* But even the Vivaraṇa cautiously observes in this context that there is no direct cognition of *Brahman* in the very first instance[36]. But rather after the production of the cognition of *Brahman* as an *external object,* the Verbal Testimony gives rise to direct cognition of *Brahman* in the second instance through the instrumentality of the mind that has been purged of its impurities through the performance of the purificatory acts, etc. Final release, or *Brahmāvagati,* is obtained on the realization of the unified meaning of the three components of the *Mahāvākya*- "*Tat tvam asi*" as is illustrated by the unified meaning of the three components of the sentence, "*So'yam Devadattaḥ*"[37]. After this, there is no return, aver both the Bhāmatī and the Vivaraṇa. Making allowance for the possibility of *Brahmāvagati* in one's life time itself, the Vivaraṇa says that the cognition of "I"-ness may persist for sometime even after *Brahman*-realization, due to the traces of mental impressions left. It is due to this that *Avidyā* continues to influence for sometime the individual even after the realization of *Brahman*. These traces of Nescience are comparable to the traces of darkness left even on the coming of light, or to the fear that remains even on the removal of the snake-illusion. Total Release is, therefore, possible only on the casting off of the body after total consummation of the *prārabdha-karma*[38].

NOTES

1. Supra, pp.10-11.
2. Supra, pp.13-14.
3. Supra, pp.18-29.
4. Supra, pp.35-41.
5. Supra, p.51.
6. Supra, pp.64-99.
7. Supra, p.127; p.152.
8. Supra, p.125.
9. Supra, p.133.
10. Supra, p.138.
11. Supra, p.179.
12. Supra, p.177.
13. Supra, p.176.
14. Supra, p.173.
15. Supra, p.180.
16. Supra, p.187.
17. Supra, p.197.
18. Supra, p.202.
19. Supra, p.205.
20. Supra, p.255.
21. Supra, p.229.
22. Supra, p.223; p.247.
23. Supra, p.250.
24. Supra, p.233.
25. Supra, p.253.
26. Supra, p.245.
27. Supra, p.251.
28. Supra, p.253.
29. Supra, p.273.
30. Supra, p.289.

31. Supra, p.277.
32. Supra, p.280.
33. Supra, p.289.
34. Supra, p.280.
35. Supra, p.290.
36. Supra, p.292.
37. Supra, p.304.
38. Supra, p.306.

APPENDIX

ŚŪNYAVĀDA : BUDDHIST-ABSOLUTISM

The Mādhyamika philosophy of *Śūnyatā* foreshadows to a great extent the Advaita philosophy of *Śaṅkara.* The similarities of the philosophical concepts of the two schools are so vivid that one is easily led to conclude that both Buddha and Śaṅkara underwent the same kind of spiritual cum intuitional experience and vouchsafed the same Truth in different languages. Some of the concepts common to both the schools are, interalia, *Advaitavāda* or *Advayavāda,* illusoriness of the world, concept of *Avidyā* as the root cause of the world, *Anirvacanīyatā,* sublation of illusion through Right Knowledge, concept of *Mokṣa* or *Nirvāṇa,* etc.

Though the word "*Śūnya*" means "void" generally, yet in Mādhyamika philosophy it has a specific connotation : here the meaning is "devoid of" rather than simply "void". This is to be understood from two angles : from the angle of the Absolute and from the angle of the empirical world. From the point of view of the Absolute, what is meant by *Śūnyatā* is that the Absolute or the Real is devoid of *prapañca,* i.e., plurality and thought determination. It transcends the *Catuṣkoṭi;* i.e., the four categories of thought, as the Mādhyamika-s put it.

> "*astīti nāstīti ubhe'pi anta; tasmād ubhe anta vivarjayitvā madhyepi sthānaṁ na karoti paṇḍitaḥ.*"[1]

From the point of view of the world, *Śūnyatā* refers to the unreality of all empirical phenomena, in the sense that they have no essence of their own, no existence as such—they being mere appearances of the non-dual Real, as is pointed out by Nāgārjuna in the Mādhyamika-kārikā thus:

> "*na sannāsan na sadasan dharmo nivartate yadā;*
> *kathaṁ nivartako hetur evaṁ sati hi yujyate.*"

—MK-I-9.

According to the Mādhyamika School no worldly phenomenon can be conceived either as one (*eka*) or as other (*anya*), because all such notions are but ideas or mental constructs; they exist only in thought-forms and are thus not real. They are all the result of ideation and are thus devoid of reality whatsoever. Hence, all empirical activities consisting of comparison, differentiation, identification, analysis and synthesis, etc., are but *Vikalpa-s* and as such are but *śūnya,* i.e., devoid of reality. All phenomena are thus superimposed on Reality, and this itself constitutes *Avidyā.*

All phenomena (*prapañca*) have the Real as their substrate and the Real is immanent in all phenomena. *Prapañca* itself is unreal, *śūnya.* The Real or the Absolute on the other hand, is devoid of *prapañca,* i.e., plurality and determinations. It is *Prapañca-śūnya.* It is inexpressible in empirical language for it is beyond thought and cannot be objectified. Fundamentally therefore, all phenomena are void of substance, and are only illusions. Buddha says that everything here has a dependent origination. What is meant is that every object emanates from some cause and is therefore dependent on it for its existence. Hence it is *svabhāva-śūnya* or *nis-svabhāva,* not having any independent existence or essence. It is *pratītya-samutpanna.* And that which is *pratītya-samutpanna* cannot be real. Its very existence (*svabhāva*) stands negated. This negation of *svabhāva* of the empirical objects "may be regarded as *prasajya-pratiṣedha* rather than *paryudāsa-pratiṣedha,* because no affirmative proposition is intended here, the world phenomena being but appearances and mere illusions.[1(a)] "The true meaning of *Pratītyasamutpāda* is this, that there is no truth, no essence in all phenomena that appear. As the phenomena have no essence they are neither produced nor destroyed. They really neither come nor go. They are merely the appearance of *Māyā* or illusion.

The void (*śūnya*) does not mean pure negation for that is relative to some kind of position; it simply means that none of the appearances has any intrinsic nature of its own. *Śūnyavāda* does not hold that anything has any essence or nature (*svabhāva*) of its own; even heat cannot be said to be the essence of fire: for both the heat and the fire are the result of the combination of many conditions; what depends on many conditions cannot be said to be the nature or essence of that thing. That alone may be said to be the true essence or nature of anything which does not depend on anything else. If a thing has no essence or existence of its own, we cannot affirm the essence of other things to it. If we cannot affirm anything of anything as positive, we cannot consequently assert anything of anything as negative either. The phenomena of the appearances are said to be in a state of change and process coming one after another: but beyond that no essence, no existence or no truth can be affirmed of them. Phenomena sometimes appear to be produced and to be destroyed but they cannot be determined as existent or non-existent."[2]

Nagarjuna attributes to phenomena eight negatives in his doctrine of No-origination (*ajātivāda*) proclaiming them to be thus *śūnya* or *pratītyasamutpanna:* these are as follows:[3]

1. no origination
2. no cessation
3. no permanence
4 no momentariness
5. no identity
6. no difference
7. no bondage
8. no liberation

This means that these eight characteristics belong only to phenomena and not to the Absolute. *Pratītyasamutpāda* is viewed from two angles in Mādhyamika Philosophy : negatively and positively. Negatively it means *Prapañcopaśama,* i.e., cessation of *prapañca. Prapañca* here means the empirical plurality, thought categories and suffering. It is the beginningless cycle of *saṁsāra,* i.e., the wheel of birth and death which is symbolically expressed by the word *duḥkha* (suffering) and which is due to beginningless *avidyā,* the transcendental illusion. *Pratītyasamutpāda* is therefore the wheel of causation or suffering. But as this causation is relative and ultimately unreal, *Pratītyasamutpāda* itself, viewed without causation and attachment, is also the cessation of suffering or *prapañca.* "Positively therefore, *Pratītyasamutpāda* is the Absolute or *Nirvāṇa* itself. From this point of view it is *Śivam,* i.e., Pure Bliss."[4]

The Absolute or *Nirvāṇa* is thus not only the cessation of all suffering, but is also limitless Bliss.[5] The Absolute, according to the Mādhyamika School, transcends the concepts of unity and plurality, permanence and impermanence, and of relativity of any sort. In brief, it is beyond all thought-constructs and categories, for indeed, all objects of thought without exception are but illusions.[6] The Real on the other hand is immanent in the phenomenal world. There is not a single object which is not pervaded by the Real. No *Dharma* exists without the Real.[7] *Dharma*-s are neither eternal nor momentary, neither existent nor non-existent. They are mere names and forms and are therefore *Māyā*. And *Māyā* has no nature of its own; it is neither real nor unreal.[8] The world-phenomena exist only as thought-constructions. They function in subject-object duality (*dvaita*) and therefore, they cannot reveal on their own the Non-dual (*advaya*) Real. They all depend on the four categories of thought.[9] "As there are four categories of thought, four and only four views are possible on any subject. The first category (*Sat*) gives us the view of Being, affirmation, permanence, substance, identity. The second category (*Asat)* gives us the view of Non-being, negation, change, modes, difference. The third category (*Sadasat* or *Ubhaya*) affirms both *Sat* and *Asat* and gives us the view either of syncretism or synthesis of both identity and difference. The fourth category (*Anubhaya*) denies both *Sat* and *Asat* and gives us the view of neither identity nor difference which is the view of scepticism and agnosticism, of doubt and despair, of extreme non-committal. But this view is different from *Anirvacanīyatā* which gives us the view of inexpressibility."[9(a)]

But the transcendent Real cannot be bound within the thought categories. "All attempts of thought to categorise the Supreme, to describe the Indescribable, to determine the Indeterminate, to bind the Boundless, to catch the Transcendent within the network of its concepts and categories are doomed to fail. The Real is transcendent to thought and can be realised by non-dual spiritual experience alone."[10] Thought works within subject-object duality and is necessarily relational and is therefore beset with inherent contradictions. Yet, thought points to the Real, and ultimately merges in immediate experience, and it is the language itself which tries to express the Inexpressible through its imposed or symbolic use."[11]

That which is symbolic or superimposed is but illusory. That itself is *Māyā, Avidyā* or *Saṁvṛti*. Referring to *Saṁvṛti* as empirical truth, Nāgārjuna warns that those who do not understand the distinction between the empirical truth (*Saṁvṛti-Satya*) and Absolute Truth (*Paramārtha-Satya*) cannot understand the reality of the deep teachings of Buddha.[12] *Saṁvṛti* is so called because it "covers" or "veils" the real on the one hand, and on the other makes it appear as something else.[13] Appearance is *Saṁvṛti* and *Saṁvṛti* itself is *Ajñāna* or *Avidyā* with its dual potency of concealing and projecting the Truth as false or unreal.[14] Hiding the real nature of things it makes the false also appear as true.[15] "*Saṁvṛti* or transcendental Ignorance (*Avidyā*) throws a twofold veil on both the subject and the object. The first veil, which covers the real nature of the subject and makes it appear as the individual self is called the "veil of suffering" (*kleśāvaraṇa*), because it gives rise to all kinds of suffering. The second veil, which covers the real nature of the object and makes it appear as a real physical or mental object is called "the veil on object" (*jñeyāvaraṇa*) because it gives rise to false knowledge of the object. "The intuitive realisation that the individual self which is the source of the false notions of the "*I*" and the "*mine*" and the root cause of suffering, is ultimately unreal (*pudgala-nairātmya*) and is in fact the Absolute, removes "the veil on the subject" which constitutes suffering (*kleśāvaraṇa*). The intuitive realisation that the object which appears as the "thing-in-itself", is in fact but a thought-construct, which is ultimately unreal (*dharma-nairātmya*) and is not different from the Absolute which is its immanent reality, removes "the veil on the object" (*jñeyāvaraṇa*) and cancels the distorting function of thought-categories, leaving the Non-dual Real to 'shine in its pristine purity'.[15(a)]

Saṁvṛti is therefore the cause of erroneous cognition being itself Ignorance, superimposition, illusion. It is not only the non-apprehension of Truth but also the misapprehension of Truth as the false, the unreal, the phenomenon[16]. The significance of *Saṁvṛti* lies in its being the medium through which the Real, the Truth, i.e., *Nirvāṇa* or *Paramārtha* is to be realised[17]. *Saṁvṛti* serves as the means to reach the Real just as a vessel serves as the means to fetch water.[18] The Absolute, says Nāgārjuna, cannot be preached without having recourse to empirical means such as thought and language, and without realising the Absolute, *Nirvāṇa* cannot be attained.[19] Having served its purpose, *Saṁvṛti* itself gets dissolved ultimately in the Absolute, without residue.[20] *Saṁvṛti* contributes to the realisation of the Absolute by pointing to it negatively as the "undeniable ground-reality of all phenomena.[21] *Saṁvṛti* or thought-forms cover the real and distort it by misrepresenting it as this world of plurality of subjects and objects, but *Saṁvṛti* or thought itself can use words as symbols (*Saṁvṛti*) or as ascribed marks and these can serve to indicate the Real indirectly as the ground on which phenomena are superimposed.[22] This is known as the method of removal of superimposition (*Adhyāropāpavādanyāya*). There can be no other method of experiencing the Inexpressible."[23]

It has been said above that *Saṁvṛti* consists in superimposing on the object a false appearance which gives rise to a false knowledge of the object. The precise nature of superimposition of *Avidyā* consists in the tendency to indulge in conceptual construction (i.e., *saṁkalpa*). The Real is Indeterminate and is therefore *Śūnya,* hence, the viewing of It through thought-forms is *Avidyā* or *Saṁvṛti.* "To consider the Real as substance (*Ātman*), or as mode (*Dharma*), as One or Many, as Unchanging (*Śāśvata*) or Ceasing (*Uccheda*), as Existence (*Astitva*) or as Non-existent (*Nāstitva*) etc., are forms of falsification (*Viparyāsa*).[24] Not only difference, but identity too is *Avidyā;* the Real is neither One nor Many; neither Permanent nor Momentary; neither Subject (*Vijñāna*) nor object (*prapañca*). These are relative concepts and are therefore unreal. The Real is purely indeterminate, and all attempts to indentify it with Being, Becoming, Consciousness, etc. are *vikalpa,* i.e., subjective devices."[25] Nāgārjuna says in this context that" if the apprehension of the impermanent as permanent is illusion, why the apprehension of the indeterminate as impermanent is not illusion as well?"[26] *Avidyā* itself is beginningless for there is no assignable limit, prior or posterior, to the existence of phenomenal world (*saṁsāra*), and *saṁsāra* cannot be without *Avidyā* and its *Kleśa-s.* Though beginningless, it has an end. This is evident from the fact that *Avidyā* and other *Kleśa-s* (passions) which are at the root of all phenomena can be reduced to nullity on the attainment of insight (*Prajñā*).[27]

What is the scope of *Śūnya* in the Mādhyamika School of

thought can be gauged from the fact that 20 modes of *Śūnyatā* have been enumerated in this system as follows:[28]

1. The Unreality of Internal elements of existence;[29]
2. The Unreality of the external objects;[30]
3. The Unreality of Both together (as in the sense organs or the body);[31]
4. The Unreality of the knowledge of Unreality;[32]
5. The Unreality of the Great Infinite Space;[33]
6. The Unreality of the Ultimate reality of Nirvāṇa;[34]
7. The Unreality of the Conditioned;[35]
8. The Unreality of the Unconditioned;[36]
9. The Unreality of the Limitless;[37]
10. The Unreality of that which is Beginningless and Endless.[38]
11. The Unreality of the Undeniable;[39]
12. The Unreality of the Ultimate Essences;[40]
13. The Unreality of All Elements of Existence;[41]
14. The Unreality of all Determination or Definition;[42]
15. The Unreality of the Past, the Present and the Future;[43]
16. The Unreality of Relation or Combination conceived as a Non-*ens*;[44]
17. The Unreality of the Positive constituents of Empirical Existence;[45]
18. The Unreality of Non-*ens*;[46]
19. The Unreality of Self-Being;[47]
20. The Unreality of Dependent Being.[48]

The Absolute in *Śūnyavāda* is not "contentless void", for what is negated is the superimposed character and not the essential nature of the Absolute. In the stock example of illusion, snake in rope, the Mādhyamika-s not only negate the "*snake*", but the "*this*" as well. The sublating cognition, "*this*" *is not* "*snake*" points to the illusoriness of both the "*snake*" and the "*this*". The superimposed as well as the substrate are negated. The "*this*", contends the *Śūnyavādin*, cannot be had apart from the "*snake*", for the "*this*" is known only as identified with the "*snake*", and not in isolation. The "*snake*" too cannot be had but as identified with the "*this*". The emphasis is on the fact that both the "*snake*" (i.e., the predicate) and the "*this*" (i.e., the substrate or subject) are relative to each other, and this itself constitutes their falsity.[19] All relations are forms of

Saṁvṛti and *Saṁvṛti* is *Avidyā, Māyā*; this has been said already. No illusion is possible without relation, and all relations are false. "The denial" of the self (the subject) by Buddha is not the denial of the empirical validity of the ego, but only the denial of the false notion which mistakes the empirical ego as an eternal spiritual substance and objectifies it. To take the self as an eternal substance is to cling to it eternally and this is *Avidyā par excellence* which is the root-cause of all attachments, desire, misery and bondage. It gives rise to the four kinds of suffering (*Kleśa*) which are, Self-notion (*ātma-dṛṣṭi*), Self-delusion (*ātma-moha*), Self-pride (*ātma-māna*) and Self-love (*ātma-sneha*). *Ātma-dṛṣṭi* is *satkāya-dṛṣṭi,* which means taking the empirical ego as an eternal substance.[50]

The Real on the other hand, is the self-existent Absolute which is realised through immediate experience (*aparapratyayam*) which is blissfully calm (*śāntam*), which transcends the plurality and suffering of phenomenal life (*prapañcairaprapañcitam*), which is beyond all determinations of thought (*nirvikalpam*) and which is supra-rational and non-dual (*anānārtham*).[51] It is identifiable with *Prajñāpāramitā, Bodhi,* or *Advayajñāna* which is the highest intuitional knowledge, the non-dual realisation, the immediate spiritual experience,. The trinity of empirical knowledge, knower, known and knowledge, or subject-object and their relation, is transcended here.[52] *Paramārtha-Satya* or Absolute Truth is the knowledge of the Real as it is without any distortion and is devoid of all *dharma-s*[53]. It is in fact the unutterable, the unthinkable, the unteachable.[54] It is indeed the object of the innermost intuitional experience—beyond the realm of language and cognition.[55] Being of one uniform, undifferentiated nature, It is variously known as *Śūnyatā, Tathatā, Bhūta-koṭi, Dharmatā, Dharmadhātu,* etc.[56]

The *summum bonum* of one's life is therefore the attainment of *Paramārtha,* the Absolute, also called *Nirvāṇa.* For this one has to submit oneself to a series of mental and physical discipline known as the *Ṣaṭ-Pāramitā-Naya,* the sixfold path of Highest-Perfection. The Mādhyamika-s believe that "freedom cannot be attained without the realisation of the unreality (*śūnyatā*) of things," and the sooner this is done the better, for "the opportunities for the cultivation of the spiritual life are rare and the obstacles many."[57] Thus, *Nirvāṇa* constitutes the cancellation of all categorisations, of all thought-constructions of transcendental Ignorance by non-dual spiritual experience".[57(a)] Having taken the resolve, "the bodhisattva should direct all his efforts towards the attainment of *Bodhi* and Buddhahood".[58] The *bodhisattva* (i.e., the seeker of Buddhahood) has first to create a *bodhicitta* by setting his mind on enlightenment. This he arrives at after his exposure to the Four Noble Truths preached by the Buddha, namely that (i) 'the life of an individual is in essence sheer *duḥkha*; (ii) its origin (*samudaya*) is *tṛṣṇā*, the will to live; (iii) the purpose of human life is *duḥkha-nirodha*, i.e., *Nirvāṇa*; (iv) and that *Nirvāṇa* is attainable through the eightfold path, the *aṣṭāṅga mārga*.'[59] "The conviction that the worldly means are no remedies, but make for tightening the grip of *Saṁsāra* on us and that *Prajñā* alone can remove the root of suffering is the commencement of the spiritual discipline"[60]. The Mādhyamika spiritual discipline centres around the *Ṣaṭ-Pāramitā-Naya*, i.e., the sixfold path of Highest Perfection, consisting of *dāna* (liberality), *śīla* (good morals), *kṣānti* (Patience), *vīrya* (energy), *dhyāna* (trance) and *prajñā* (insight). *Prajñā* itself is referred to as *Prajñāpāramitā*. *Dāna* means surrendering one's own goods; *śīla* are actions undertaken for the good of others; *kṣānti* means renouncing anger; *vīrya* means striving for merit; *dhyāna* is unalloyed concentration; and *prajñā* is the ascertainment of the true meaning (of the teachings of Buddha). "A *bodhisattva* must ascend through ten spiritual stages (*bhūmi*) before he finally achieves *buddhatva*. The first is *Pramuditā* wherein the *bodhisattva* rejoices as he abandons the three *saṁyojana*-s and is born in the *Tathāgatagotra*. By ripening this his *dānāpāramitā* becomes eminent. The second is called *Vimalā* wherein he naturally abides by ten kinds of physical, vocal and mental stainless *karma*. This makes him an expert in making living beings avoid bad morals. The third *Bhūmi* is *Prabhākarī* wherein the peaceful light of *Jñāna* arises as *dhyāna* and *adhijñā* arise and *rāga* and *dveṣa* are completely extinguished. The fourth is *Arciṣmatī* wherein the light of *saṁyagjñāna* arises as he cultivates all the *bodhipakṣya-s* eminently. This enables him to subdue the attacks of *satkāyadṛṣṭi*. The fifth is *Sudurjayā* wherein, as he becomes skilled in understanding the profound meaning of the *āryasaṭya-s*, etc., it becomes very difficult for the *Māra-s* to gain power on him. The sixth is *Abhimukhī* where he faces the *buddha-dharma-s* as he advances to obtain *nirodha* through the cultivation of *śamatha* and *vipaśyanā*. The seventh is *Duraṁgamā* wherein he enters *nirodhasamāpatti* moment after moment.[61] The eighth is *Acalā* where the *gocara* of body, speech and mind is *acintya*. The ninth is *Sādhumatī* where he is endowed with a fine intellect by obtaining the *Pratisaṁvid-s*. The tenth is *Dharmamegha* where the rain of *Saddharma* falls on him as he is consecrated with the light of the *Buddha*. As a lord of infinite *jñāna* be becomes a supreme *maheśvara*. Subsequently he becomes *Buddha*."[62]

Prajñā is taken to exhibit three degrees, viz., *Śruti, Cintā* and *Bhāvanā*. The first constitutes the correct understanding of the Scriptures. The second constitutes a "well-reasoned" appraisal of what has been learnt from the Scriptures. The third consists in "meditating upon the results of one s learning and understanding (of the Scriptures) so as to realise them for oneself and integrate them in one's personality"[63] According to Nāgārjuna, *Prajñā* is not merely the analytical faculty which allows the *bodhisattva* to determine the *lakṣaṇa-s* and the *svabhāva* of *dharma*-s at the empirical level with certainty but it is the mediator which conveys him from a world of appearance (*saṁvṛti*) to one of Absolute Reality (*Paramārtha*). *Prajñā*, therefore, is at the outset a critical faculty constantly engaged in analysing the more or less commonsense notions presented to it by tradition or experience. The more it penetrates them and "loosens them up" the more their apparent nature vanishes and in the final analysis their true nature turns out to be "empty", i.e., devoid of substance, or simply illusory. At this stage *Prajñā* brings also its *raison d'ētre* to an end: by analysing its objects away it also deprives itself of an "objective support". "At this level the analytical understanding suddenly shifts into an intuitive *Jñāna* which has *śūnyatā*, as its 'object', i.e., which has no object. The culmination of *Prajñā*, then, is *Jñāna*, or intuitive insight into Reality (*tattva*) beyond the duality of *asti* and *nāsti*. This *Jñāna* is also the suspension of *Avidyā* which, in the final analysis is seen to be based on the wrong assumption of existence and non-existence, etc."[64].

NOTES

1. Candrapradīpa Śūrtas- IX.27 quoted by TRV Murti in "The Central Philosophy of Buddhism", Allen & Unwin, 1970, p.85
1. (a). CHR. Lintner - Nagarjuniana, MLBD, 1990, p.275
2. Ibid.
3. C.D. Sharma, The Advaita Tradition in Indian Philosophy, p.51
4. Ibid [MK - XXVI.24]
5. Ibid, Vide-
"अनिरोधम् अनुत्पादम् अनुच्छेदम् अशाश्वतम्। अनेकार्थम् अज्ञानार्थम् अनागतम् अनिर्गमम्॥
यः प्रतीत्य समुत्पादं प्रपंचोपशमं शिवम्। देशयामास सम्बुद्धस्तं वन्दे वदतां वरम्॥"
—Mādhyamika Kārikā (Invocation).
6. बुद्ध्या विविच्यमानानां स्वभावो नावधार्यते।" —Laṅkāvatāra Sūtra, p.41
7. Vide, "न तथताविनिर्मुक्तोऽन्यः कश्चिद् धर्म उपलभ्यते।" —Aṣṭasāhasrikā Prajñāpāramitā, quoted by C.D. Sharma, Loc. Cit., p.40.
8. Vide, "नामरूपमेव माया, मायैव नामरूपम्।" "मायायाः पदं न विद्यते।"—Ibid.
9. Vide, "चातुष्कोटिकं च.... लोकव्यवहारः।" —Laṅkāvatāra Sūtra, Ibid, p.41
9. (a). C.D. Sharama, Loc Cit., p.50.
10. Ibid, p.46
11. Ibid
12. Vide, "द्वे सत्ये समुपाश्रित्य बुद्धानां धर्मदेशना। लोकसंवृतिसत्यं च सत्यं च परमार्थतः॥
येऽनयोर्न विजानन्ति विभागं सत्ययोर्द्वयोः। ते तत्त्वं न विजानन्ति गम्भीरं बुद्ध-शासने॥
—MK, XXIV-8/9
13. Vide, "अभूतं ख्यापयत्यर्थं भूतमावृत्य वर्तते।" Bodhicaryāvatāra-Pañjikā, quoted by C.D. Sharma, Loc. Cit. p.48
14. Vide, "समन्तादावरणं संवृतिरज्ञानम्"। —Mādhyamika-Kārikā-Vṛtti, Ibid
15. Vide, "मोहः स्वभावावरणाद्धि संवृतिः सत्यं तया ख्याति यदेव कृत्रिमम्।"
—Mādhyamikāvatāra - VI. 29 - Ibid
15. (a). C.D. Sharma, Loc. Cit., p.64.
16. "तत्त्वाप्रतिपत्तिः मिथ्याप्रतिपत्तिरज्ञानमविद्येति।" —Bodhicaryāvatāra-Pañjikā, quoted by C.D. Sharma, Op. Cit.
17. Vide, "उपायभूतं व्यवहारसत्यम्। उपेयभूतं परमार्थसत्यम्॥" Mādhyamikavatāra-VI-80, Ibid
18. Vide, "निर्वाणाधिगमोपायत्वाद् अवश्यमेव संवृतिरभ्युपेया भाजनमिव सलिलार्थिनेति।"
—M K Vṛtti, quoted by C.D. Sharma, Ibid-p.48.
19. Vide, "व्यवहारमनादृत्य परमार्थो न देश्यते। परमार्थमनागम्य निर्वाणं नाधिगम्यते॥"
—MK - XXIV.10
20 C.D. Sharma, Loc. Cit., p.69
21. Ibid, p.68
22. Ibid, Vide, "बुद्धेरगोचरस्तत्त्वं बुद्धिः संवृतिरुच्यते।" —Bodhicaryāvatāra, IX.2, Ibid.

23. Vide, "अनक्षरस्य धर्मस्य श्रुतिः का, देशना च का? श्रूयते देश्यते चापि समारोपादनक्षरः।" MK Vṛtti, quoted by C.D. Sharma, Loc. Cit.
24. T.R.V. Murti—The Central Philosophy of Buddhism (CPB), p.238
25. Ibid.
26. Vide, "अनित्ये नित्यमिति एवं यदि ग्राहो विपर्ययः। अनित्यमित्यपि ग्राहः शून्ये किं न विपर्ययः॥ —MK, XXII.14
27. T.R.V. Murti, Op. Cit., p.240
28. Ibid, pp. 351-352, quoting from the Pañcaviñśati-Sāhasrikā-Prajñāpāramitā.
29. अध्यात्मशून्यता।
30. बहिर्धाशून्यता।
31. अध्यात्मबहिर्धाशून्यता।
32. शून्यताशून्यता।
33. महाशून्यता।
34. परमार्थशून्यता।
35. संस्कृतशून्यता।
36. असंस्कृतशून्यता।
37. अत्यन्तशून्यता।
38. अनवराग्रशून्यता।
39. अनवकारशून्यता।
40. प्रकृतिशून्यता।
41. सर्वधर्मशून्यता।
42. लक्षणशून्यता।
43. अनुपलम्भशून्यता।
44. अभावस्वभावशून्यता।
45. भावशून्यता।
46. अभावशून्यता।
47. स्वभावशून्यता।
48. परभावशून्यता।
49. Vide, TRV Murti, Loc. Cit., pp.325-326.
50. ATIP, Op. Cit, p.64
51. Vide, अपरप्रत्ययम् शान्तम् प्रपञ्चैरप्रपञ्चितम्। निर्विकल्पम् अनानार्थम् एतत् तत्त्वस्य लक्षणम्॥ —MK, XVII.9
52. ATIP, Op. Cit., p.67
53. Vide, परम उत्तमोऽर्थः परमार्थः। अकृत्रिमं वस्तुरूपं सर्वधर्माणां निःस्वभावता।" —BCAP, quoted by TRV Murti, Loc. Cit, p.244
54. Vide, "यः पुनः परमार्थः सोऽनभिलाप्यः अनाज्ञेयः अपरिज्ञेयः अविज्ञेयः अदेशितः अप्रकाशितः....।" —Ibid
55. Vide, "कुतस्तत्र परमार्थे वाचां प्रवृत्तिः कुतो वा ज्ञानस्य। स हि परमार्थोऽपरप्रत्ययः शान्तः प्रत्यात्मवेद्य आर्याणां सर्वप्रपञ्चातीतः॥" —MK Vṛtti, quoted by

TRV Murti, Loc. Cit., p.244

56. Vide, "शून्यतातथता भूतकोटि धर्मधातुरित्यादि पर्यायाः।" —Ibid, quoting from BCAP
57. TRV Murti, Loc. Cit., p.262
57. (a). Vide, "निरवशेषकल्पनाक्षयरूपमेव निर्वाणम्" —MK Vṛtti, Ibid.
58. Ibid.
59. Vide, "चत्वारीमानि.... आर्यसत्यानि। कतमानि चत्वारि ?—दुःखम् आर्यसत्यं, दुःखसमुदयो, दुःखनिरोधो, दुःखनिरोधगामिनी प्रतिपद् आर्यसत्यम्। दुःखम् आर्यसत्यं कतमत्—जातिदुःखं, जरा दुःखं, व्याधिर्दुःखं, मरणं दुःखं, प्रियविप्रयोगो दुःखम्, अप्रियसंप्रयोगो दुःखं, यदपि इच्छन् पर्यमाणो न लभते तदपि दुःखम्। संक्षेपतः पञ्च इमे उपादानस्कन्धा-दुःखम्। तस्य परिज्ञायै आर्याष्टांगो मार्गो भावयितव्यः। दुःखसमुदयम् आर्यसत्यं कतमत् ?—तृष्णा पौनर्भविकी नन्दीरागसहगता तत्र तत्राभिनन्दिनी। तस्याः प्रहाणाय आर्याष्टांगो मार्गो भावयितव्यः। दुःखनिरोधम् आर्यसत्यं कतमत् ?—यदस्या एवं तृष्णायाः पौनर्भविक्या नन्दीरागसहगतायास्ता तत्राभिनन्दिन्या अशेषप्रहाणं प्रतिनिसर्गो वान्तीभावः क्षयो विरागो निरोधो व्युपशमः अस्तंगमः। तस्य साक्षात्क्रियायै आर्याष्टांगो मार्गो भावयितव्यः। दुःखनिरोधगामिनी प्रतिपद् आर्यसत्यं कतमत् ?—आर्याष्टांगो मार्गः। तद् यथा—सम्यग्दृष्टिः, सम्यक्संकल्पः, सम्यग्वाक्, सम्यक् कर्मान्तः, सम्यगाजीवः, सम्यग्व्यायामः, सम्यक्स्मृतिः, सम्यक्समाधिः। सोऽपि भावयितव्यः।" —Lindtner, Loc. Cit, pp.233-234, quoting from Tripiṭaka
60. TRV Murti, Loc. Cit., p.262, Vide, "अविद्यायां निरुद्धायां संस्काराणाम् असम्भवः। अविद्याया निरोधस्तु ज्ञानेनास्यैव भावनात्॥" —MK -XXVI.11
61. Vide, Suhṛllekha, quoted in Nagarjuniana, Op. Cit., p.220.
62. Vide, Nagarjuniana, Op. Cit., pp 267-268
63. Ibid, p. 269
64. Ibid, pp. 269-270

BIBLIOGRAPHY

A. Primary Sources (Basic Sanskrit Texts)

1. Chandrashekharan, T. (Ed.)—Pañcapādikā (with Pañcapādikā-*Vivaraṇa*), Govt. Oriental Manuscripts Library, Madras, 1958.
2. Joshi, K.L. (Ed.)—Brahma-Sūtra-Śāṅkara-Bhāṣya (with *Bhāmatī*, Kalpataru and Parimala), Parimal Publications, 2 Vols., Delhi, 1982.
3. Śāstrī, Ananta Krishna (Ed.)—Brahma-Sūtra-Śāṅkara-Bhāṣya (with *Bhāmatī*, Kalpataru and Parimala), Chawkhamba Sanskrit-Series Office, Varanasi, 1982.
4. Śāstrī, Subramanya (Ed.)—Pañcapādikā (with *Vivaraṇa*), Maheśa Research Institute, Varaṇasi, 1992.
5. Shastri, Prof. J.L.—Brahmasūtra-Śāṇkarabhāṣyam (with Bhāṣyaratnaprabhā, *Bhāmatī* and Nyāyanirṇaya), MLBD, 1988.
6. Tailanga, Ramaśāstrī, (Ed.), Vivaraṇa-Prameya-Saṅgraha, Kishore Vidya Niketan, Varanasi, 1990.
7. Tatacharya, Dr. N.S. Ramanuja (Ed.) Pañcapādikā and Pañcapādikā-*Vivaraṇa*, Vol. I, Kendrīya Sanskrit Vidyapeeṭha Tirupati, 1985.

B. Other Sanskrit Texts

8. Āhitāgni, Śivanātha—Ṛg Veda-Sāra-Saṁgraha, Vaidika Jīvan Āśrama, Dehradun, 1976.
9. Anubhavananda, Swami—Pañcadaśī, Central Chinmaya Mission Trust, Bombay, 1994.
10. Bṛhadāraṇyaka Upaniṣad (in Īśādidaśopaniṣadaḥ), MLBD, 1964.
11. Chāndogya Upaniṣad (in Īśādidaśopaniṣadaḥ), MLBD, 1964.
12. Citsukha, Ācārya, Tattvapradīpikā, Ṣaḍdarsana Prakashana Prātiṣṭhāna, Varanasi, 1974.

13. Gopinatha Kavirāja, MM and Śāstrī, Ḍhuṇḍhirāja—Praśastapāda-bhāṣ yam of Praśasta Devācārya, Chawkhmba Amarbhārati Prakāshan, Varanasi, 1983.
14. Hiriyanna, M.A. (Ed.)—Iṣṭa Siddhi, Oriental Institute, Baroda, 1933.
15. Iyer, Subramania, (Ed.)—Vākyapadīya, Deccan College Postgraduate and Research Institute Poona, 1963.
16. Jacob, G.A., (Ed.)—Naiṣkarmya Siddhi (of Sureśvara), Chawkhamba Vidya Bhawan, Varanasi, 1992
17. Jhalkīkar, M.M. Bhīmācārya—Nyāyakośa, The Bhandarkar Oriental Research Institute, Poona, 1978.
18. Kaṭha Upaniṣad (in Īśādidaśopaniṣadaḥ), MLBD-1964.
19. Mīmāṁsaka, Yudhiṣthira, Jaiminīya-Mīmāṁsā-Bhāṣya, Yudhiṣthira Mīmāṁsaka, Balagarh, 1977.
20. Muṇḍaka Upaniṣad (in Īśādidaśopaniṣadaḥ), MLBD-1964.
21. Murty, Prof. K. Satchidananda—Ṣaḍ-darśana-Samuccaya, Eastern Book Linkers, Delhi, 1986.
22. Pandey, R.C. (Ed.), Yuktidīpikā, MLBD, 1967.
23. Pansikar, Shri Vasudev Lakshman—Īśādi-Aṣṭottara-śatopaniṣada, Chawkhamba Vidyabhawan, Varanasi, 1990.
24. Rai, Gangasagar (Ed.), Ślokavārttika of Śrīkumārila Bhaṭṭa, Ratna Publications, Varanasi, 1993.
25. Ramanuja, Ācārya—Śrībhāṣyam-Vol. I., The Academy of Sanskrit Research, Melkota, 1987.
26. Śāstrī, Ananta Krishna (Ed.)—Advaita Siddhi, Parimal Publications, Delhi, 1982.
27. Śāstrī, Pandit Chinnaswami—Mīmāṁsā Nyāya Prakāśa, Chawkhamba Sanskrit Sansthana, Varanasī, 1981.
28. Śāstrī, Pandit Dhuṇḍhiraj—Yogasūtram, Chawkhamba Sanskrit Sansthan, Varanasi, 1982.
29. Śāstrī, Ramanath (Ed.)—Bṛhatī of Prabhākara Miśra, (Tarkapāda), University of Madras, 1934.
30. Śāstrī, Subrahmania—Prakaraṇa Pañcika (of Śālikanātha Miśra), BHU, 1961.
31. Śukla, Śrī Sūryanārāyaṇa—Nyāyamañjarī, Chawkhamba Sanskrit Series Office, Varanasi, 1971.
32. Sadhale, Shri Gajanan Shambhu—Upaniṣad-Vākya-Mahā-Koṣa (An Upanishadic Concordance), Chawkhamba Vidyā Bhawan, Varanasi, 1990.

33. Satchidanandendra, Saraswatī—Vedānta-Prakriyā-Pratyabhijñā, Adhyātma Prakāśa Kāryālaya, Holenarsipur, 1964.
34. Seru, S.L.—Śrīmadbhagavad - Gītā, Nag Publishers, Delhi-1983.
35. Shastri, Śrī Candiprasad Shukla and Shastri, Śrīkrishnapanta —Vivaraṇa-prameya-sangraha, Acyutagranthamala karyalaya, Kashi, 1939.
36. Sharma, Śrī Vasudeva—(Ed.)—Īśādyaṣṭottara-śatopaniṣadaḥ, Chawkhamba Vidya Bhawan, Varanasi, 1990.
37. Sharma, Umā Śaṅkar—Mīmāṁsā Darśanam, Chawkhamba Surbharatī Prakashan, Varanasi, 1980.
38. Swami, Dr. Kiśoradāsa—Śāstra-dīpikā, Śri Sādhubelā Saṅskrita Mahavidyālaya, Varaṇasi, 1977.
39. Swami Dvarika Das Shastri—Madhyamaka Śāstra of Nagarjuna, Buddha Bharati, Varanasi, 1989.
40. Thangaswami, R.—Advaita Vedānta Sāhitya Itihāsa Kosha, [also called, Advaita Vedānta Literature—A Bibliographical Survey (AVLBS)], University of Madras, 1980.
41. Taittirīya Upaniṣad, (in Īśādidaśopaniṣadaḥ), MLBD, 1964.
42. Udāseen, Shrī Balram—Sāṅkhya-karīkā, Bharatiya Vidya Sansthan, Varanasi, 1991.
43. Upaniṣad-vākya-mahākosha, Chawkhamba Vidyabhawan, Varanasi, 1990.
44. Vedantatirtha, Narendra Chandra, (Ed.)—Vedānta-Siddhānta-Sūktimañjarī, Metropolitan Printing and Publishing House Ltd., Calcutta, 1935.
45. Vidyabhushana, Śrī Ashutosh Vidyaratna, Śrī-Nityabodh—Nyāyadarśanam (with Vāt. Bh.), Chawkhamba Sanskrit-Pratishthan, Delhi, 1987.
46. Wilson, H.H.—Ṛg-Veda Saṁhitā, Nag Publishers, Delhi, 1977.

C. Others (Translation)

47. Apte, VM, (Tr.)—Brahma-Sūtra-Śāṅkara-Bhāṣya, Popular Book Depot, Bombay, 1960.
48. Gambhirananda, Swami, (Tr.)—Brahma-Sūtra-Bhāṣya of Śaṅkarācārya, Advaita, Ashrama, Calcutta, 1972.
49. Jhā, Gaṅgānātha (Tr.)—Ślokavārttika, The Asiatic Society, Calcutta, 1985.

50. Jhā, Gangānātha (Tr.)—The Nyāya Sūtra of Gautama (with Vātsyāyana-bhaṣya), MLBD, 1984.
51. Kumar, Avanindra (Ed.)—Vedāntasāra (with Eng. Tr. by G.A. Jacob), Parimal Publications, Delhi, 1995.
52. Radhakrishnan, S.—The Brahma Sūtra : The Philosophy of Spiritual Life, George Allen & Unwin Ltd., London, 1960.
53. Śāstrī, Subrahmanya, (Ed.)—Vedānta Kaumudī of Rāmādvayāchārya, University of Madras, 1955.
54. Śāstrī, SS Suryanarayana & Raja, C. Kunhan, (Eds.)—Bhāmatī of Vācaspati, Adyar Library and Research Centre, Madras, 1992.
55. Śāstrī, SS Sūryanarayana & Sen, Saileśwar—The Vivaraṇa-Prameya-Saṅgraha of Bharatitīrtha, Andhra University, 1941.
56. Śastri, SS Sūryanarayaṇa (Tr.)—Vedānta-Paribhāṣā, The Adyar Library and Research Centre, Madras, 1971.
57. Śukla, Sūrya Narayana (Ed.), Nyāya Mañjarī of Jayanta-Bhaṭṭa, Chawkhamba Sanskrit Series Office, Varanasi, 1971.
58. Thibaut, George—The Vedanta-Sūtras, MLBD, 1962.
59. Venkataramiah, D.—The Pañcapādikā of Padmapāda, Oriental Institute, Baroda, 1948.

D. Secondary Sources

60. Agrawal, M.M.—The Philosophy of Non-Attachment, MLBD, 1982.
61. Alston, A.J. (Tr.)—The Method of the Vedanta, MLBD, 1997.
62. Arapura, J.G.—Hermeneutical Essays on Vedāntic Topics, MLBD, 1986.
63. Balasubramanian, R.—Advaita Vedanta, University of Madras, 1976.
64. Balasubramanian, R.—The Tradition of Advaita, Munshiram Manoharlal Publisher Pvt. Ltd., Delhi, 1994.
65. Ballantyne, J.R. (Tr.)—The Sāṁkhya Aphorisms of Kapila, Chawkhamba Sanskrit Series, Varanasi, 1963.
66. Beidler, William—The Vision of Self in Early Vedanta, MLBD, 1975.
67. Belvalkar, S.K. & Ranade, R.D.—History of Indian Philosophy: The Creative Period, Munshiram Manoharlal, 1997.

68. Belvalkar, S.K.—Vedanta Philosophy, Bilvakunja Publishing House, 1929.
69. Bhaṭṭ, G.P.—Epistemology of the Bhāṭṭa School of Pūrva Mīmāṁsā, Chawkhamba Sanskrit Series, Varanasi, 1962.
70. Bhaṭṭ, G.P.—The Basic Ways of Knowing, MLBD, 1989.
71. Bhattacharya, Gopinath—K.C. Bhattacharya-Studies in Philosophy, MLBD, 1983.
72. Bhattacharya, J.V. (Tr.)—Nyāya Mañjarī-Vol. I, MLBD, 1978.
73. Bhattacharya, Kalidas—A Modern Understanding of Advaita Vedānta, L.D. Institute of Indology, Ahmedabad, 1975.
74. Bhattacharya, Vidhushekhara—The Āgamaśāstra of Gauḍapāda, University of Calcutta, 1943.
75. Brahma, Nalini Kanta—Philosophy of Hindu Sādhanā, MLBD, 1993.
76. Buch, Maganlal—The Philosophy of Śaṅkara, Good Companions, Baroda, 1988.
77. Chatterjee, S.C.—The Nyāya Theory of Knowledge, Akshaymohan Ray, Calcutta, 1950.
78. Dasgupta, S.N.—A History of Indian Philosophy, Vols. I & II, MLBD, 1991.
79. Datta, D.M.—The Six Ways of Knowing, University of Calcutta, 1972.
80. Devaraja, N. K.—An Introduction To Śaṅkara's Theory of Knowledge, MLBD, 1962.
81. Dubey, Rajendra Prasad—Vācaspati Darśanam, Classical Publishing Company, New Delhi, 1983.
82. Eliade, Mircea—The Encyclopedia of Religion, Vol.15, Macmillan Publishing Company, New York, 1987.
83. Gupta, Dr. Sanjukta—Studies In The Philosophy of Madhusūdana Saraswatī, Sanskrit Pustaka Bhandar, Calcutta, 1966.
84. Gupta, Som Raj—The Word Speaks To The Faustian Man, MLBD, 1991.
85. Jhā, Ganganath—The Prābhākara School of Pūrva-Mīmāṁsā, MLBD, 1978.
86. Kar, Bijananda—Indian Theories of Error, Sophia Indological Series No.3, Ajanta Books International, Delhi, 1990.
87. Lintner, CHR—Nagarjuniana, MLBD, 1990.

88. Madhavananda, Swami (Tr.)—Viveka-Cūḍāmaṇi, Advaita Ashrama, Mayavati, 1982.
89. Mahadevan, TMP—The Philosophy of Advaita, Arnold Heinemann, New Delhi, 1976.
90. Mainkar, T.G.—The Making of the Vedanta, Ajanta Publications, Delhi, 1980.
91. Mehendale, K.C.—Tarka Sangraha, Bharat-Bharati, Varanasi, 1980.
92. Mudgal, S.G.—Advaita of Śaṅkara : A Re-appraisal, MLBD, 1975.
93. Murti, TRV—The Central Philosophy of Buddhism, Allen & Unwin, 1970.
94. Nakamura, Hajime—A History of Early Vedanta Philosophy (Part I), MLBD, 1990.
95. O'Neil, Thomas—Māyā In Śaṅkara, MLBD, 1980.
96. Pandey, G.C.—Life and Thought of Śaṅkarācārya, MLBD, 1994.
97. Pandey, Sangam Lal—Pre-Śaṅkara Advaita Philosophy, Darshan Peeth, Allahabad, 1974.
98. Potter, Karl (Ed.)—The Encyclopedia of Indian Philosophies-Vols. I-IV, MLBD, 1995.
99. Prajnanananda, Swami—The Schools of Indian Philosophical Thought, Firma K.L. Mukkhopadhyay, Calcutta, 1973.
100. Prasada, Rama, (Tr.)—Patanjali's Yoga-Sūtra-Munshiram Manoharlal, Delhi, 1982.
101. Radhakrishnan, S. & Moore, C.A., (Eds.)—A Source Book In Indian Philosophy, Princeton, New Jersey, 1957.
102. Rajgopal, L.V.—A Critique of Vedānta, Munshiram Manoharlal, Delhi, 1993.
103. Ram, Kanshi—Integral Non-Dualism, MLBD, 1995.
104. Ramachandran, TP—The Concept of The Vyāvahārika In Advaita Vedanta, University of Madras, 1980.
105. Ramamurti, A.—Advaitic Mysticism of Śaṅkara, Centre of Advanced Study In Philosophy, Viśva-Bhāratī, Śantiniketan, 1974.
106. Rao, Veluri Subha—Theories of knowledge, Sri Satguru Publications, Indian Books Centre, Delhi, 1998.
107. Rukmini, T.S.—Yogavārttika of Vijñānabhikṣu (Vols. I-III), (with Yoga-sūtra and Vyāsa-bhāṣya), Munshiram Manoharlal, Delhi, 1981.

108. Śāstrī, Dr. Śrīnivāsa—Praśastapāda-bhāṣya, Indo-Vision Pvt. Ltd., Ghaziabad, 1984.
109. Śāstri, Kokileśvara—An Introduction to Advaita Philosophy, Bharatīya Publishing House, Delhi, 1979.
110. Śāstrī, Pandit SS Sūryanarayaṇa and Ayyangar, T.R. Srinivasa (Tr.)—Jīvanmuktiviveka, The Adyar Library and Research Centre, Madras, 1978.
111. Śāstrī, SS Sūryanarayana—The Siddhāntaleśa-Saṅgraha of Appaya Dīkshita, Vol. I, University of Madras, 1935.
112. Saha, Sukharanjan—Advaita Theory of Illusion, Progressive Publishers, Calcutta, 1982.
113. Sengupta, Anima—Classical Sāṅkhya-A Critical Study, Manoranjan Sen-Gaur Ashram, Lucknow, 1969.
114. Sharma, Baldev Raj—The Concept of Ātman in the Principal Upaniṣads, Dinesh Publications, New Delhi, 1972.
115. Sharma, C.D.—The Advaita Tradition In Indian Philosophy, MLBD, 1996.
116. Sharma, V.A.—Citsukha's Contribution To Advaita Vedanta, Kaivalya Publications, Mysore, 1974.
117. Shrivastava, Surendra Kumar—The Essential Advaitism, Kishore Vidya Niketan, Varanasi, 1980.
118. Singh, Dr. Īshwar—Bhāmatī-Eka Adhyayana, Manthan Publication, Rohtak, 1983.
119. Sinha, Debabrata—Metaphysic of Experience In Advaita Vedanta, MLBD, 1995.
120. Sinha, Jadunath—Indian Psychology, Vol. I, Cognition, MLBD, 1986.
121. Sinha, Jadunath—Indian Psychology, Vol. III, Epistemology of Perception, MLBD, 1986.
122. Sinha, Nandlal (Tr.)—The Vaiśeṣika Sūtras of Kaṇāda, The Sacred Books of the Hindus Series—Paṇini Office, Allahabad, 1911.
123. Sircar, Mahendranath—The System of Vedāntic Thought and Culture, Oriental Books Reprint Corporation, Delhi, 1975.
124. Solomon, E.—Avidyā-A Problem of Truth and Reality, Gujrat University, 1969.
125. Subramanian, V.K. (Tr.)—Saundaryalaharī of Śaṅkarācārya, MLBD, 1993.

126. Upādhyāya, Veermani Prasad—Lights on Vedānta, The Chawkhamba Sanskrit Series Office, Varanasi, 1959.
127. Witz. G. Klaus—The Supreme Wisdom of the Upaniṣads, MLBD, 1998.
128. Woods, James Haughton—The Yoga System of Patañjali, The Harvard University Press, USA, 1927.

E. Journals

129. Indian Philosophical Quarterly, Vol. XXIV, No.3, July, 1997—Dasgupta, Sanghamitra—Some Reflections on the Status of the World (*Jagat*) in Śaṁkarite Advaita Vedānta, pp.359-371.
130. Indological Studies—Journal of The Department of Sanskrit, University of Delhi, Vol. III, Nos. 1-2, Dec., 1974—Śarmā, Rām Mūrti—Vedānte Vṛttinirūpaṇam, pp.214-217.
131. Journal of the Department of Sanskrit, University of Delhi, Vol.1, No.2, July, 1972—Sharma, Dr. Ram Murti—The Doctrine of Māyā of Śaṅkara, pp.59-64.
132. Journal of Indian Council of Philosophical Research, Vol. XIV, No.2, Jan.-April, 1997—Rao, Prabhakara M.—A Critique on Brahman-Realization, pp.71-82.
133. Studies in Humanities and Social Sciences, Vol.III, No.2, Winter 1996—Sharma, Ramesh Kumar—The Structure of a Theory of Error : A Three-Cornered Debate, pp.201-257.

INDEX

A

J

Q

T